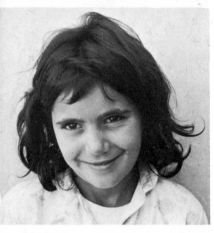

PORTRAIT OF
Israel

I Portrait of SRAEL

by MOSHE BRILLIANT

Photographs by Micha Bar-Am

Special Interest Guide by Sylvia R. Brilliant

A NEW YORK TIMES BOOK

American Heritage Press

NEW YORK

IN MEMORY OF
MAX (MORDECAI) AND
IDA BRILLIANT

———————

BOOK DESIGN *by Jos. Trautwein*

MAPS BY CAL SACKS

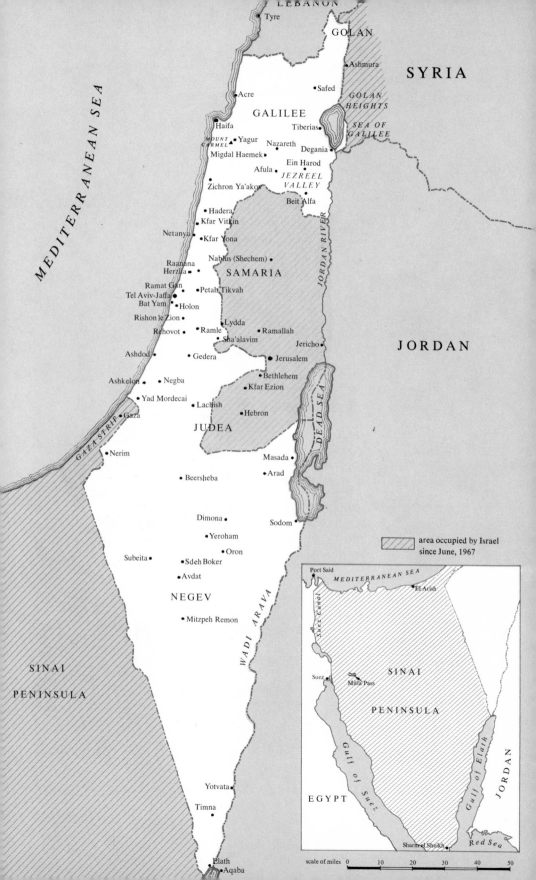

LEBANON
• Tyre

GOLAN

• Ashmura

SYRIA

• Safed

GALILEE

• Acre

GOLAN
HEIGHTS

SEA OF
GALILEE

• Haifa

• Tiberias

MOUNT
CARMEL ▲ • Yagur

Nazareth

MEDITERRANEAN SEA

Migdal Haemek •

• Degania

Afula •

• Ein Harod

JEZREEL
VALLEY

Zichron Ya'akov •

• Hadera

• Beit Alfa

• Kfar Vitkin

Netanya •

• Kfar Yona

• Nablus (Shechem)

Raanana
Herzlia •

SAMARIA

Ramat Gan
Tel Aviv-Jaffa •
Bat Yam • • Holon

• Petah Tikvah

JORDAN RIVER

Rishon le Zion •

Rehovot • • Ramle

• Lydda

JORDAN

• Ramallah

• Sha'alavim

• Jericho

Ashdod •

• Gedera

• Jerusalem

Ashkelon •

• Negba

• Bethlehem

• Yad Mordecai

• Kfar Ezion

Gaza •

• Lachish

DEAD SEA

• Hebron

JUDEA

• Nerim

• Masada

• Beersheba

• Arad

Dimona •

• Sodom

area occupied by Israel
since June, 1967

• Yeroham

• Oron

Subeita •

• Sdeh Boker

Port Said

MEDITERRANEAN SEA

• El Arish

• Avdat

NEGEV

Suez Canal

SINAI

• Mitzpeh Remon

WADI ARAVA

Suez •

Mitla Pass

PENINSULA

SINAI
PENINSULA

Gulf of Suez

Gulf of Elath

JORDAN

• Yotvata

EGYPT

• Timna

Sharm el Sheikh

Red Sea

• Elath
• Aqaba

scale of miles   0   10   20   30   40   50

Three Israeli girls, serving in the army, learn the art of camouflage.

Contents

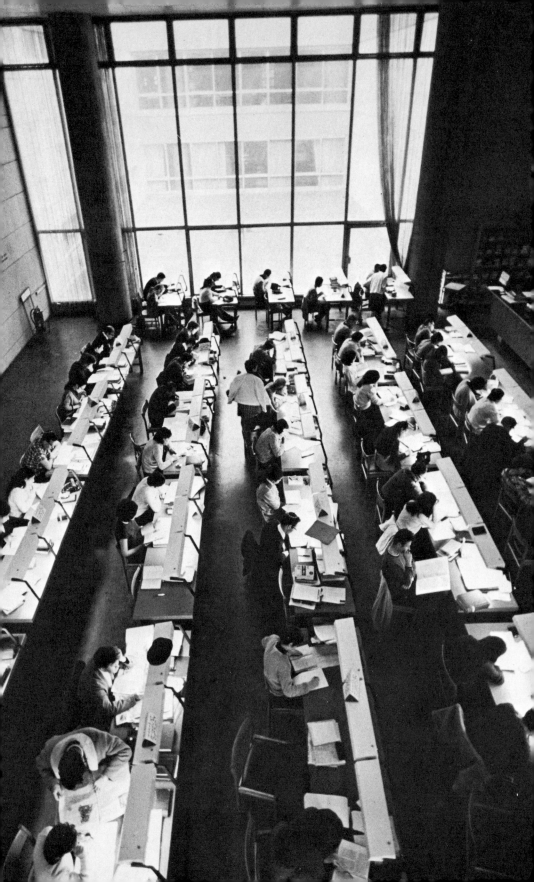

1

The Fossils Come Alive

"That's him. That's Edward Gimel Robinson."

The modern library at Jerusalem's Hebrew University (left) contrasts with the old-style religious school shown above.

New immigrants are taught Hebrew at a workshop in Carmiel.

An American tourist driving a rented car on the outskirts of Jerusalem darted ahead of a slow-moving truck. Immediately he heard the whine of a siren. A Lambretta motor scooter putt-putted up to him and a policeman in a white crash helmet motioned him to the side of the road.

The driver was in trouble. He had crossed one of those solid white lines that run along the middle of the highway where overtaking is dangerous.

There is a notion in Israel that the country's hospitable traffic cops will let tourists get away with such violations and that the trick is to display utter ignorance of Hebrew. It works, sometimes.

But this particular cop was not impressed. He was an immigrant from Aden and his English was flawless. After examining the driver's papers, he moved to the front of the car and used the hood to write out a traffic ticket.

Watching through the windshield, the driver sighed, but his resignation quickly turned to fascination. He saw the policeman's pen move across the pad from right to left in a scrawl that looked like shorthand.

"Thank you," he said elatedly as he accepted the ticket. "Can I have another one, please?"

The policeman frowned and the offender hastened to explain that he wasn't being a wise guy. "You don't understand," he said. "You don't realize how exciting it is to get a traffic ticket in Hebrew. I'd like to keep one as a souvenir."

Today, in the third decade of Israel's restored sovereignty, the resurrection of the tongue of the ancient prophets in a modern republic is no longer regarded as a miracle. But perceptive visitors, with their fresh eyes and ears, often sense the drama and the historical significance that are lost on Israelis.

It is the nonchalance with which Hebrew characters and biblical phrases are used in the most mundane circumstances that sends chills up the spines of tourists. Hebrew lettering on a manhole cover can thrill them. On the other hand, alphabetic characters previously seen only on synagogue portals can be shocking when seen on garbage trucks or public rest rooms.

Edward G. Robinson, the actor, was filled with joy when he heard a child in Tel Aviv exclaim: "That's him. That's Edward *Gimel* Robinson."

Another tourist said he had been prepared for the experience of hearing babies bantering in the words of Isaiah. But when he heard a lunatic rave at length in the tongue of the prophets, he was tremendously impressed.

The resurrection of Hebrew really is remarkable. There is no other instance in history of a fossilized language being successfully revived.

It was accomplished quickly, too. Some of the earliest Hebrew revivalists are still living in Jerusalem. They recall being reviled and ostracized by their neighbors. They remember being refused service by Yiddish-speaking shopkeepers, outraged at their use of *lashon kodesh*—the sacred tongue—to buy potatoes, clothing, or writing paper.

Lashon kodesh, according to rabbinical legend recorded in the Talmud, is a celestial language. The vocabulary and alphabet are said to have been fashioned by the Almighty and His angels at the dawn of Creation. Fundamentalists haven't the slightest doubt that when the

Lord commanded, "Let there be light!" he used the precise Hebrew phrase inscribed in the Torah scrolls.

Secular scholars are less certain of the origin of Hebrew. They generally assume it evolved from a West Semitic dialect spoken in Palestine four thousand years ago when Abraham, the progenitor of the Hebrew race, turned from paganism in Mesopotamia to worship one, invisible god in the Land of Canaan.

But Abraham's descendants spent a few centuries in Egypt. The Bible relates that Jacob and his sons communicated through an interpreter when, escaping the famine in Canaan, they first arrived in Egypt. Did later generations cling to their own language until Moses liberated them from bondage and led them to the gates of Palestine? Or did they acquire the language of their taskmasters? Scholars don't agree.

After the conquest and settlement of Palestine under Joshua, Hebrew was the vernacular. There is no argument about that. It was the language of Deborah, the poetic prophetess, and of the muscular Samson, as well as the prophets from Amos to Malachi. King David commanded his forces in Hebrew when he extended his empire to the Euphrates, and Solomon conferred in the biblical tongue with his architects when they discussed plans for the Jerusalem Temple.

When the kingdom split in two after Solomon's death, the ten tribes of Israel retained Hebrew until they were erased by an Assyrian conquest in the eighth century B.C. In the Kingdom of Judea, the biblical tongue was spoken until Nebuchadnezzar captured Jerusalem in 586 B.C. and led the Jews in captivity to Babylon.

In exile, the Aramaic tongue took over. Aramaic was the international language of the region—spoken by the Assyrians, the Babylonians, and the Persians. It wasn't a difficult adjustment for the Jews; Hebrew and Aramaic are both Semitic languages.

The Babylonian exile lasted only half a century. When the repatriates returned to Jerusalem, they continued to use the foreign tongue. Hebrew was the language of the synagogue, but even there passages of the Bible readings at Sabbath services were translated into Aramaic.

Aramaic died out elsewhere, but it remained the vernacular of the Jews for six tumultuous centuries until the Romans finally demolished the Second Jewish Commonwealth and scattered the Jews throughout Europe and Asia. It was the mother tongue of Jesus and his disciples. Greek made inroads among cosmopolitans after the conquest of Alexander the Great, but the Jewish countryside held to Aramaic. It was also the language of most of the great rabbis, whose commentaries on the law were compiled in the Talmud.

There was a patriotic fringe that used Hebrew to the bitter end. Not long ago, archaeologists ferreting through the dust and bat dung in caves hanging over the Dead Sea found documents belonging to followers of Bar Kochba, the last resistance fighter against Rome. The documents included contracts for land and military orders in Hebrew.

However, there were also orders in Aramaic and Greek in the cave. That showed that even among the extreme nationalists Hebrew was not universal. After the Bar Kochba revolt was crushed in A.D. 135 and the last Jews were forced into the dispersion, Hebrew ceased to be a living language altogether.

It then fossilized but it never quite died.

In the dispersion, Jews kept the embers aglow in study and prayer. Through the centuries fathers taught sons the ancient script as soon as the boys were old enough to distinguish the shapes of the letters, so that they could meditate on the Bible and read prayer books. The thrice-daily prayers, the grace after meals, and the benedictions they repeated day after day familiarized them with the rhythm and spirit of the language. They were also able to rattle off thousands of archaic words and expressions, although they didn't necessarily know their exact meaning, since they prayed by rote.

In their dispersion and wanderings, the Jews developed new vernaculars but they preserved the ancient alphabet. Jews who settled in the countries bordering the Mediterranean after their expulsion from Spain in 1492 continued to speak medieval Spanish interspersed with some biblical phrases. They wrote the mixture in Hebrew script and thus developed Ladino.

Eastern Europeans did the same with medieval German to create Yiddish. Jews from Arab countries who reached Morocco and Tunisia did the same with Arabic.

In the Middle Ages some communities kept their public records in classical Hebrew. Scholars translated literary works from Arabic and European languages and wrote original Hebrew prose and poetry.

Some of the works became part of the synagogue liturgy.

Those writers had a large choice of expressions to convey spiritual ideas, but when it came to practical secular matters they were cramped. Some overcame the paucity of words by borrowing foreign terms.

But the more romantic strove to use pure biblical Hebrew. They even rejected rabbinical terms from the Talmud that stemmed from Aramaic, Greek, or Latin. This required circumlocutions and contortions that resulted in prose that was cumbersome, often comically so.

A nineteenth-century writer in Russia, Kalman Shulman, needed to describe a microscope. There was no use looking for a term for it in the Scriptures. So he gathered a word from Job, some phrases from I Kings and Psalms, and gave the device the following designation: "A glass through which the hyssop that is on the wall towers like a cedar in the Lebanon."

Obviously, Hebrew was seldom used in conversation. On the Sabbath, a father might address a few Hebrew phrases to his son. When Jews who had no common language met, they used Hebrew. It could hardly be said that they conversed. They uttered quotations from prayer books or the Scriptures, usually high-flown poetic allusions rather than precise terms for things and ideas. Each probably had only the vaguest idea of what the other was trying to convey.

The movement to modernize the ancient tongue and restore it as a living national language preceded by seventeen years the political drive for the revival of the nation. The Zionist movement, which culminated in the establishment of the State of Israel, was founded in 1897 by Dr. Theodor Herzl, a disillusioned assimilationist from Vienna, at a congress in Basel, Switzerland. The movement for the revival of Hebrew was launched by Eliezer Ben Yehuda, a twenty-three-year-old medical student shrunken by tuberculosis, on board a ship from Marseilles to Jaffa in 1880.

Palestine was then a province of Turkey. The Jewish population of Jerusalem when Mr. Ben Yehuda arrived consisted mostly of paupers sustained by doles from their coreligionists, or dying men and women who had come to be buried in the Holy Land. Mr. Ben Yehuda had been told he was a dying man, but he hadn't come to be buried. He came to dedicate his last strength to the revival of Hebrew as a living tongue.

Browsers at the Hebrew Book Fair, a popular annual event

The Jews of Jerusalem at the time divided themselves into Yiddish-, Ladino-, and Arabic-speaking communities that rarely had anything to do with one another. The Oriental and Occidental Jews walked on opposite sides of the street. Mr. Ben Yehuda, a young intellectual from Lithuania, arrived in their midst wearing a crimson tarboosh.

His neighbors regarded him as an eccentric. He was. On board the ship from Marseilles, he had startled his Russian-born bride by informing her that in Palestine he would talk to her only in Hebrew, and he impatiently began fulfilling that pledge right there on deck. When they set up house in Jerusalem, he stood from dawn to midnight at a lectern, ferreting forgotten words out of ancient sources and coining new ones for a Hebrew dictionary that nobody seemed to want.

When the couple had their first child in 1882, they isolated the infant so that no foreign words could contaminate his ears. He was the first baby since the days of Bar Kochba to be reared with Hebrew as his mother tongue. Unfortunately, his mother had not yet mastered the language herself, but Mr. Ben Yehuda wrote some Hebrew lullabies and taught her to sing them. The baby, Benzion, had no playmates other than a small black snake that came through a crack in the wall. The snake never bit Benzion, but it helped itself to some of the baby's milk.

It took Benzion three years to utter his first word. It was baby talk for "snake." Eventually, however, he grew up to be a loquacious Hebrew orator and writer under the pen name Ittamar Ben Avi.

Ehud Ben Yehuda, a younger son, later recalled that his father had sent the children into the street to hurl biblical curses at other Jewish children and pick bloody fist fights in Hebrew. He told his offspring he had begotten them for one purpose only—to disseminate Hebrew— and that he had no other use for them. The shriveled consumptive, who married two sisters consecutively, set himself a goal of a dozen offspring, one for each of the twelve tribes of Israel. He missed by one.

Apart from finding him personally obnoxious, Mr. Ben Yehuda's ultrareligious neighbors regarded him as a heretic. They felt with deep conviction that the wrath of the Almighty would be brought down on Jerusalem if a small boy was taught arithmetic in His hallowed language.

However, Mr. Ben Yehuda did attract supporters and their number slowly grew. Some of them were clandestine in that they spoke Hebrew with him in the privacy of his home but Russian or Yiddish outdoors. A number of Oriental Jews befriended him.

Jewish nationalists who began trickling into Palestine from Europe after the Russian pogroms of the 1880's also went along with the movement. At the turn of the century, after the founding of the Zionist movement, they were joined by more and more Hebrew nationalists.

Curiously, the deified first president of the World Zionist Organization was among the scoffers. Having had an assimilationist upbringing, Dr. Herzl couldn't share the feelings of his followers for the old language. He assumed German would be the vernacular of the Jewish State. How, he once asked, could the ancient and sacred tongue ever be made to express a thought like, "Please, mister, give me a railway ticket to Jerusalem"?

His followers managed. When they couldn't find a word or expression in a prayer book or the Bible to fit a given situation, they turned to Mr. Ben Yehuda. If a child contracted measles or a parent bought a bicycle or some other toy that had been unknown to their biblical ancestors, Mr. Ben Yehuda supplied the missing nomenclature.

Thus Hebrew was enriched daily. Perusing Mr. Ben Yehuda's creations today affords some insights into the Holy Land of his time. He coined a word for ice cream, and a word for coquette. Life couldn't have been so austere after all.

In Jerusalem and the new agricultural villages, societies for Hebrew speech sprung up. In 1904 they merged into the Hebrew Language Council. Naturally, Mr. Ben Yehuda was the first chairman and the council became the unofficial authority on usage. However, not all the creations they endorsed have gained popular acceptance. They devised pure appellations based on Hebrew etymons for telephone, university, radio, and other things that fluent Hebraists continue to call by their foreign names.

In addition, some Hebrew terms are today not used as intended by the men who hatched them. When the colonists in Rishon le Zion organized Palestine's first orchestra, they sought a Hebrew word for orchestra. Someone reported that Mr. Ben Yehuda had coined a beautiful word, *tizmoret*. It was taken.

When news of this reached Jerusalem, Mr. Ben Yehuda raged. He had intended the word to mean tune or melody. He had already used it thus in translations.

Moreover, he argued, the word stemmed from a root relating to vocal music and was not at all suitable for an instrumental ensemble. But the musicians pleaded that they had already invested money in posters, tickets, and programs. Mr. Ben Yehuda yielded and *tizmoret* it has remained. Another word was coined for tune.

Rishon le Zion's village school was the first to adopt Hebrew as the language of instruction in all secular subjects. That was in 1888. Four years later teachers from all over the country decided on the exclusive use of Hebrew in elementary schools. The first Hebrew-language high school opened in Jaffa in 1906. Ironically, it was named Herzlia Gymnasium after the late Dr. Herzl, the Zionist leader who had believed it would never be possible to buy a railway ticket in the ancient tongue.

By the second decade of this century the rising generation of Palestinian Jews was carrying on its entire life in Hebrew, although adult social and business life were still conducted largely in Yiddish, Ladino, Russian, Arabic, and other languages. Some European supporters of Jewish national revival in Palestine continued to find it hard to conceive of a modern society functioning in the archaic tongue.

When German-Jewish benefactors planned a technical high school in Haifa in 1913, they conceded that general subjects should be taught in Hebrew, but they felt that in view of the undeveloped state of the language, technical subjects should be taught in German.

The reaction was violent. Throughout the country, teachers and children went on strike. In protest, they refused to pass the portals of their schools. They held classes outdoors.

In Jerusalem, Eliezer Ben Yehuda organized a bonfire of German-language textbooks outside the German consulate. A weeping consul on the balcony watched the book-burning.

The German-Jewish benefactors yielded. Committees of teachers, scientists, and philologists got together and busily coined Hebrew terms for the necessary mathematical, technical, and scientific conceptions.

Once the uphill struggle to implant Hebrew had been won, a rearguard action against its bastardization began. As large waves of Euro-

A girl soldier helps an immigrant child with his homework.

pean immigrants entered the country, the languages they brought with them threatened to corrupt Hebrew. Gaps in vocabulary were filled by foreign words or worse.

Oatmeal, for example, was called *kvocker*. The first cereal reaching Palestine came in boxes labeled Quaker Oats. Yiddish-speaking grocers pronounced it *kvocker*. There is now an approved appellation for oatmeal. Israel produces her own brand. But old-timers still call it *kvocker*.

Garage talk between Hebrew-speaking motorists and mechanics is studded with terms like *brreks* and *beckex* for brakes and back axle. Most horrifying of all is the term for front axle, which is *beckex kidmi, kidmi* being good Hebrew for forward.

Hebrew was internationally recognized as an official language on September 23, 1922, when the League of Nations granted a mandate to Great Britain to establish a national home for the Jewish people in Palestine. English, Arabic, and Hebrew were designated as the languages of the country. That meant Hebrew would appear on postage stamps. For the first time since Bar Kochba's revolt, it would be struck on coins. Three months after his triumphant day, on December 22, Eliezer Ben Yehuda died.

International recognition by no means ended the struggle. It was carried on by others. The problem was no longer the opposition of religious fanatics. They indeed continued to be outraged by the secular use of *lashon kodesh,* but they became a minority under the wave of emancipated immigrants. The major enemy was Yiddish, the vernacular from Eastern Europe. Immigrants found it easier to speak their mother tongue.

A society called Defenders of the Language took up the fight. One of the militants was Yisrael Galili, a Polish-born youth who later attained national leadership. He was already a Cabinet minister when he confided to me that he used to go with a friend to meeting halls where Yiddish functions were held. They approached the fuse boxes. The future minister climbed on his friend's shoulders and removed the fuses, plunging the hall in darkness. No Yiddish theater, newspaper, or lecture was tolerated. Immigrants talking Yiddish in the street were gruffly scolded.

The militants were no more tolerant of other foreign languages. I recall attending an English lecture in Tel Aviv that was broken up by a shower of stones. When I reported the stoning in my newspaper, I innocently caused a minor scandal. It transpired that the Jewish policemen who were summoned had sympathized with the stone-throwers. They covered up their traces and did not even report the attack. Their British superiors learned about it from my press report and there was hell to pay.

The scientific side of Mr. Ben Yehuda's activities was carried on by hundreds of professionals and enthusiastic amateurs. They coined thousands of Hebrew terms to replace foreign ones. The most cogent role was played by the press and radio. Journalists racing against deadlines invented or disseminated those new words that have achieved the

22

widest popular usage. Poets, authors, and playwrights created words that may have been more beautiful, but unfortunately they have not received equal circulation. To gain popular acceptance, a new word required promotion by journalists, politicians, or others with ready platforms.

After Israel's independence in 1948, the army contributed thousands of terms to the burgeoning vocabulary. A special branch was set up by GHQ to devise Hebrew nomenclature for weapons and equipment and their component parts.

With civilian word-coiners it is a matter of "cast thy bread upon the waters," but in the army it is different. When the army decided, for example, that radar was *makam,* that was that. If the next batch of recruits hears the word "radar," it will not know what it means.

In 1953, the Knesset (parliament) granted the Hebrew Language Council official status by changing it to the Academy of Hebrew Language. It thus became the supreme authority in matters of grammar, spelling, terminology, and transcription. The Academy wasn't quite empowered to prevent grocers from selling *kvocker,* music critics from using fancy foreign terms, or rabbis from preaching in the Ashkenazi accent. But it acquired legal authority to keep objectionable terms out of official documents or school textbooks and off the air. A representative keeps an ear cocked regularly to the language, pronunciation, and accents of announcers on the state radio.

There was an embarrassing hitch to the Knesset's recognition of the Academy of Hebrew Language. As the bill was about to be put up for a vote, a deputy suggested that its passage be delayed and that the august body of scholars, poets, and writers be asked to coin a good Hebrew word for "academy." They tried and failed; to this day the body is called by the Greek term *akademia.*

The Academy has been active. With new words being hatched almost daily, Hebrew dictionaries have become deficient before they leave the presses. The latest now in preparation will list some 50,000 words. The vocabulary of the Old Testament contains 7,704.

The revivalists have given priority to biblical sources in their search for new terms. They expanded old roots, built new words on old foundations, combined words, and salvaged terms unused because of their ambiguity by giving them new meanings. The term for electricity, *hashmal*, for example, was taken from Ezekiel, who used the word three times in similes or metaphors describing fire. No one can be sure what the word alluded to, but the King James Version translated it as "brightness the color of amber."

To modern Israelis *hashmal* means nothing but electricity. A child coming across Ezekiel's passages would be struck by the visionary powers of the old prophet, who used the metaphor so long before electricity was invented!

When the search for a biblical word failed, the Academy turned to rabbinical literature and other Semitic languages like Aramaic or Arabic. As a last resort, they borrowed from European languages, provided the word could be made to sound Hebrew, as in the case of *akademia*.

For pronunciation, they followed the policy of Mr. Ben Yehuda, who rejected his own Ashkenazi form—still used in most synagogues in the United States—and favored the more vibrant Sephardic pronunciation of the Oriental communities.

The new and the old have blended so smoothly that the ordinary Israeli is not at all conscious of which ingredients derived from the prophets or from the period of the Maccabees, and which were originated by the newspaperman living around the corner. Indeed, the Maccabees of two millennia ago would find a more familiar ring in Mr. Ben-Gurion's speech than Chaucer, who lived six hundred years ago, would have found in Winston Churchill's.

With Hebrew today firmly entrenched as the language of a sovereign nation of nearly three million people, the militancy of its defenders has mellowed. It is no longer considered necessary to brainwash kindergarten children into thinking it unpatriotic to speak anything but Hebrew. True, most Jews over the age of sixty still prefer foreign languages. But now they are tolerated. With 95 per cent of Israeli Jews in the eighteen to twenty-eight age group reading Hebrew newspapers only, the future of the language is assured. Among Israeli-born—who now comprise 45 per cent of the population—99.6 per cent of the newspaper readers take the Hebrew press.

The Israeli minorities—some four hundred thousand Arabs and Druses—speak Arabic among themselves, but Hebrew is their second language. It has been a compulsory subject in their elementary schools from the third grade, so the younger generation is quite fluent. Older Arabs have also acquired it. Many hundreds of Arabs and Druses attend Israeli universities. Some of their young actors have appeared in Hebrew plays and films.

But the Israelis have not encouraged the minorities to integrate culturally. They provide them with separate Arabic schools and radio and television programs. Local administrations in their own localities function in their own language. Although Arab and Druse deputies in the Knesset are fluent in Hebrew, they frequently address the House in their own language. Interpreters are provided to translate their speeches into Hebrew and to give them simultaneous translations of the Hebrew speeches. Just as the Jews retain cultural and emotional links with the Jewish world, they appreciate the demand of the minorities to preserve their affinity with their own worlds abroad.

The second language of the country is now English. It is taught in elementary schools from the fifth grade. Most of the required reading in the universities is in English. Street and traffic signs are in English for the convenience of visitors who can't decipher Hebrew script. American paperbacks and magazines outnumber Hebrew publications in bookstores.

But the zealots no longer mind. With students from countries from Japan to Nigeria attending lectures at the Hebrew University and foreign diplomats straining to learn the language, they have become as complacent about the future of their tongue as Americans are about English. And with Moscow, Damascus, Cairo, and Baghdad radio stations daily defaming the State of Israel in the tongue of the ancient prophets, the struggle for the revival of Hebrew has certainly been won.

2

The Cowhand and
the Colonel

"There will always be Arabs."

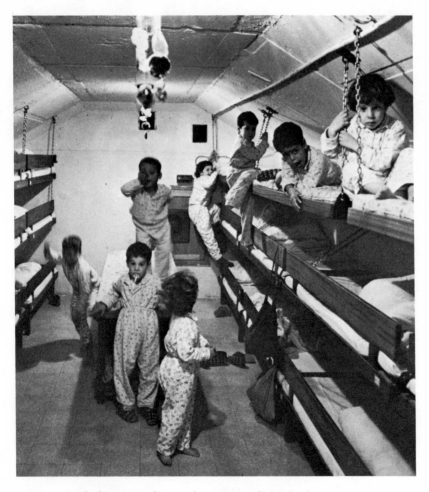

Suppertime at Nahal Yam in the northern Sinai (left); bed-time in the children's shelter in a Jordan Valley kibbutz.

A member of a border kibbutz *picks up his Sabbath meal before going on guard duty.*

The Israeli empire was at its height during the kingdoms of David and Solomon. Only during this period in history did the nation's borders extend from "the river of Egypt" to the Euphrates, as pledged to the Hebrews in the Bible.

Precisely how big the kingdom was is unclear, partly because the river of Egypt has run dry, and scholars don't agree on where it was. Some identify it as the Pelusiac branch of the Nile, which is said to have emptied into the Mediterranean some twenty miles east of what is now the Suez Canal. Others say it was Wadi El-Arish, near the date-growing oasis farther east on the coast of Sinai. Either way, the Israeli kingdom was roughly the size of Oklahoma.

Modern Israel as it emerged from the 1948 War of Independence occupied 7,992 square miles, about one-eighth of the area ruled by Solomon. Its borders were approximately where the Israeli and Arab armies stood when the fighting halted. They meandered crazily.

The country was 260 miles long. Its width varied from six and a half miles to 66. From a security point of view, the frontiers seemed hopeless.

Villages on the northeast frontier lay in the Jordan Valley, at the mercy of Arab guns in the rugged Syrian heights of Golan. A Jordanian bulge in Samaria left the Jewish State with a waistline of only nine miles between Tel Aviv and Haifa—an inviting target for an armored thrust. The armistice lines partitioned Jerusalem, making the historic capital a potential deathtrap for Israelis. And Egypt controlled a finger of land pointing up the Mediterranean coast to within thirty-four miles of Tel Aviv.

Between June 5 and June 11, 1967, the Israeli army altered the situation. Israel emerged from the Six Day War in possession of some 34,000 square miles. The pugnacious Syrians were pushed beyond artillery range of the Jordan Valley to within thirty miles of Damascus. The Jordanians were chased to the Jordan River and the Egyptians to the Suez Canal.

But notwithstanding her unaccustomed breathing space, a basic element of Israel's existence remained unchanged: the Jewish State was still an island in a vast Arab sea. In the most fervid dreams of the most wild-eyed Israeli expansionist, she would never be more than that.

And no matter how assiduously the Jews apply themselves to the fulfillment of the biblical injunction to "be fruitful and multiply and replenish the earth," they will always be outreplenished by the descendants of Ishmael.

Israel can go on whipping her neighbors in battle every ten years or so—as soundly as in the last three wars—but there will always be Arabs.

But let Israel be caught off guard just once, let her lose only one round, and it could mean the end of the Jewish State.

One doesn't visualize a Jewish town or village in Israel changing hands in a war with the Arabs and surviving, like a Minsk or a Pinsk that lived through alternate occupations by Germans and Russians.

Any Jewish locality that was ever taken by Arabs ceased to exist. This occurred during the 1948 War of Independence. When Kfar Etzion, near Jerusalem, fell to the Jordanians, the inhabitants were disarmed and massacred; only three men and one woman escaped. Elsewhere, survivors in most cases were evacuated before the fall; the others were marched off to captivity. Homes and properties were devastated. So were the synagogues and houses of Talmudic study in the fallen Jewish quarter of the walled Old City of Jerusalem.

When the Arabs set up regimes in the parts of Palestine they controlled, the only Jews living there were a handful of women married to Arabs. No Jewish civilization remained.

Jordanian documents captured during the Six Day War indicated that a similar fate was planned for Israeli localities falling into Arab hands. Reams of secret papers were found by the Israelis because the collapse of the Jordanian forces was so swift that there was apparently no time to remove or destroy files.

Documents discovered in brigade headquarters all over the west bank of the Jordan included operational orders for massacres in Israeli border villages. The battalions that were to carry out the butchery never received the orders because they were to be kept "Top Secret" at the brigade level until the time for their execution. Accordingly, they were locked in safes, where Israeli intelligence found them.

Some of the orders were made public by the Israelis. Operation Ra'ad was a plan—signed on June 7, 1966, by Brigadier General Ahmad Shehada al-Huartha—for an attack on Motza, an agricultural settlement two and a half miles west of Jerusalem. The order was found in the headquarters of the Imam Ali Ben Abi Taleb Brigade near Ramallah.

"The intention of HQ Western Front," the order said, "is to carry out a raid on Motza colony, to destroy it and to kill all its inhabitants."

The order noted that Motza was surrounded by slit trenches and that the settlers needed five to seven minutes to man the positions from the moment of surprise. The population was about eight hundred. General Huartha assigned one infantry company plus one platoon to break through the colony's defenses and "destroy it and . . . kill all its inhabitants."

A platoon of engineers would "completely destroy the colony with explosives" after the breakthrough forces had finished mopping up the houses. The houses, the order noted, were of concrete; some had red-tile roofs.

At the headquarters of the Hashemite Brigade near Ramallah, the Israelis found an order for an attack on Sha'alabim, a collective settlement of ultrareligious farmers. The village is on a height overlooking the Valley of Ayalon where, the Bible relates, the moon stood still at Joshua's bidding while the Hebrews smote the Canaanites.

The Hashemite Brigade's order said: "The intention of West Bank HQ is to attack Sha'alabim settlement, to destroy and kill all persons in it including the unit stationed there."

Similar orders found in five other brigade headquarters on the west bank indicated that massacres across the armistice lines all along the front had been planned at the top echelons of the Jordanian army.

In the actual war, Israeli farmers were never at the mercy of the Hashemite Brigade or General Huartha's men. Both were quickly routed in the battle for Jerusalem. When the Jordanian operational orders were later made public, they seemed to horrify foreigners more than the intended victims. Israelis had never expected otherwise. They had assumed all along that the alternative to victory was genocide. A paratroop colonel briefing his men on the eve of the Six Day War expressed the sense of the nation when he said: "Auschwitz will have been a health resort compared to Israel under Arab occupation."

Maybe the specter of snarling Arabs ferreting through the rubble of Tel Aviv and Jerusalem to make sure no Jews survived was exaggerated. Some Israeli pilots downed in enemy territory and some frogmen captured by the Egyptians at Alexandria reported they had been well treated as prisoners of war. Other pilots who parachuted into enemy territory were lynched and butchered, however, when they fell into Arab hands.

Exaggerated or not, the belief that an Arab breakthrough would mean the rape and slaughter of defenseless civilians was genuine and deep-felt. It has permeated Israeli thinking since the country became independent in 1948. The victory-or-genocide mood has profoundly influenced the character of the Jewish State, inspiring much of the self-sacrifice and heroism that has captured the world's imagination. It has also been responsible for things that some have found distasteful.

Security consciousness seems overdone. It is the grounds for an army press censorship that not only suppresses genuine security leaks but tries to manage the news in Israel and abroad. The involvement of the security establishment in the lives of the citizens is intimate. The adulation of the military is unabashed.

At bus stops and theater box offices all over the country, elderly people unquestioningly stand aside for young men and women in uniform. And the youngsters, even the impeccably well-mannered, go to the head of the queue. The practice started as a courtesy to soldiers on leave during the War of Independence in 1948 and it became a custom. It is now regarded as a natural privilege that comes with military service, like getting paid and buying in the Shekem, the Israeli equivalent of the PX. Young soldiers do not know the origin of the tradition and old-timers have forgotten it. So when a balding, middle-aged civilian, who may have carried explosives on his back to enemy positions before the military acquired weapons with which to shoot them across, defers in a queue to a nineteen-year-old army clerk who holds an 8 A.M. to 4 P.M. job in Tel Aviv, it may look peculiar. But to the veteran and the soldier it seems right.

At a dinner party not long ago in Tel Aviv for visiting American Congressmen, an Israeli asked a United States embassy official the name of the current chairman of the U.S. Joint Chiefs of Staff. There was an awkward silence. Nobody could think of it.

That sort of thing couldn't happen at a Girl Scouts' picnic in Israel. The Israeli Chief of Staff has always been among the best known and most highly respected personalities in the country, whether a colorful and dashing war hero like General Moshe Dayan or a reserved type like General Haim Bar-Lev. On national holidays three portraits are widely displayed in windows of shops and homes: the President's, the Prime Minister's, and the Chief of Staff's.

Perhaps the fact that practically every Israeli household is represented in the armed forces has something to do with the adulation of those in uniform. The dividing line between civilian society and the military establishment is fuzzy. Providing he is under forty-five, the taxi driver cruising for a fare, the hairdresser fussing over a matron, the storekeeper intent on selling a bauble is a soldier, a sailor, or an airman. A code word flashed over the radio or a terse telephone message may send him racing to take his place at the controls of a tank or the sight of a cannon.

In frontier areas, fields and orchards cover subterranean arsenals of machine guns, antitank weapons, mortars, and other equipment for static defense as well as shelters deep enough to withstand direct hits. In the shelters there are dormitories, electricity, running water, air conditioning, clinics, nurseries and food, supplies and toys for long spells of underground living.

The farms are crisscrossed with trenches and dotted with fortified

Nahal Tsofar, a new settlement in the Araba Depression

N

34

The map above shows the Middle East on the eve of the 1967 war.
Shaded diagonally are the fourteen independent Arab states; all but
Mauritania are members of the Arab League, a loose alliance held
together by language, religion, culture, and a common enemy: Israel.
Israel's six closest neighbors—Egypt, Jordan, Syria, Lebanon, Iraq,
and Saudi Arabia—were able to mobilize twice as many men as Israel
in 1967 and possessed three times as many airplanes. Nevertheless,
Israel won an incredibly swift victory in six days, occupying parts of
Egypt, Syria, and Jordan. (See the map on page 7.)

positions. In emergencies the women and children go down to the shelters and the husbands and fathers man the trenches to guard their homesteads and their sector of the frontier. Each fortified border village is a link in a regional system of first-line defense.

The requirements of regional defense have affected the map of Israel. When Palestine was governed by the Turks and later by the British, Jewish farms were mostly low-lying. Arab landowners preferred to sell swampy tracts to Jewish colonists and keep for themselves the hills, which were good for olive growing. The Jews drained the swamps and created fertile soil. But ever since Israel became sovereign, the military has been consulted about the location of every new town and farming community. They prefer the heights, naturally. Representatives of the armed forces on various commissions and boards have their say about details of planning, while all building plans have to be cleared with civil defense authorities.

In most nations, civil defense is only a matter of air raid precautions. But not in Israel. For the nineteen years that the armistice line between Jordan and Israel wound through the middle of Jerusalem, civilians in the Jewish sector had to be protected against sniping from the Arab part of the city. Tel Aviv, Tiberias, Ramla, Lydda, Netanya, Petah Tikvah, and other municipalities, not to mention Jerusalem itself, were within range of enemy artillery.

The population of the coastal plain, which is the most densely inhabited section of the country, had to take precautions against shelling from the sea.

All those civil defense problems are reflected in the appearance of Israel. In Jerusalem many walls facing what used to be the armistice line are of thick concrete. Windows, if any, are small and protected. Buildings near the former line were laid out in a checkerboard pattern to provide an unbroken shield for children going to school or women to market. The Knesset building a little more than a mile away was turned around 180 degrees in the planning stage so that its portals would face north instead of toward the Jordanian guns.

Throughout the country a builder's professional eye might discern the extraordinary thickness of the ceiling or concrete walls of a basement synagogue, a movie theater, garage, or discotheque. These facilities double as shelters. Every new building is required by law to have a subterranean section meeting the specifications set by the civil defense corps of the armed forces. The very newest must contain hermetically sealed shelters for protection against bacteriological, chemical, and radiological warfare.

Israel's defense doctrine has been an original one, tailored to her geographic and demographic situation. The Israeli defense forces have had officers trained in the Soviet army as well as the armed forces of the United States, Britain, France, Italy, Canada, and other countries. Quite a few attended the finest staff colleges in the West. Suitable ideas from all those armies have been borrowed. But the greatest mentor of all seems to have been the Haganah.

The Haganah was an underground militia that guarded the Jewish community in Palestine against recurrent attempted Arab pogroms during the period of British rule. The illegal organization was the alma mater of every chief of staff and nearly every officer to reach the rank of colonel in the defense forces in the first two decades of Israeli sovereignty.

However, it wasn't for sentimental reasons that Israel's officers clung to so much of the Haganah's heritage. The Haganah spirit and system simply dovetailed neatly with the needs of a country that before the Six Day War was the size of New Jersey, yet had to defend meandering borders equivalent to the length of the Atlantic coastline from Maine to Virginia. Few countries in the world had so many miles of frontier per square mile of territory and per inhabitant. There is Chile, of course, but Chile has the Andes, and her neighbors have not pledged to drive her into the Pacific.

The twin answers to Israel's problems are regional defense and the reserve system. Both evolved from the Haganah, but if they hadn't been inherited, they would have had to be invented.

As an organization of outlaws, the Haganah had to consist mainly of men and women living seemingly normal family lives—holding jobs, running businesses, or attending school. When needed, they quietly slipped away. After doing their jobs, they melted back into the population.

The Haganah bases had to be in rural areas, for though the main reservoirs of manpower were the cities, there were too many British police there. The closed societies of the *kibbutzim* (collective settle-

ments) were ideal for clandestine training and arms storage. The arsenals were underground—at least four feet deep because the British metal detectors worked to a depth of three feet—and such objects as laundry poles or the metal posts of seesaws and slides were hollow, doubling as air vents for the secret arms dumps.

These armed outpost farms saved the Jews in 1948 when the British withdrew from Palestine and three Arab kings and a president sent their regular armies across the borders to join the irregular Arab bands already trying to crush the newborn republic. The farmers of Degania, reinforced by Haganah fighters, prevented Syrian armor from crossing the Jordan River and invading Galilee. In the Negev, small contingents entrenched in *kibbutzim* like Negba, Yad Mordecai, Beerot Yitzhak, Nirim, Beit Eshel, and Kfar Darom pinned down battalions of Egyptian infantry, armor, and artillery. They prevented King Farouk's forces from advancing on Tel Aviv and Jerusalem and gave the government in Tel Aviv precious time to bring in arms, organize a regular army, and carry the fight to the enemy.

In Degania they still preserve a burned-out tank that is now partly sunk into the soil at the end of an avenue of trees and roses. It was stopped on the sixth day of the 1948 war by a member of the *kibbutz* who had learned to make Molotov cocktails in Leningrad during the Second World War. When he saw the Syrian tank plowing through the communal garden, knocking down trees and making straight for the defenders in the trenches, he raced toward the monster hurling the explosive-filled flasks at its steel sides. The tank burst into flames. So did the trees around it.

That halted the Syrian advance. The enemy was routed later that day when a pair of 65-mm. mountain guns were brought to the front directly from the Tel Aviv port in response to a tearful plea to Premier David Ben-Gurion by a delegation of *kibbutz* elders. The fieldpieces, called Napoleonchiks by the soldiers because they seemed to date from the time of Bonaparte, came without gun sights. The crews fired a few shells into the Sea of Galilee while they figured out how to use the antiques; when they mastered the technique they chased the Syrians back to their borders.

The pattern of the war was similar in the Negev, but the dimensions were bigger and bloodier. Some villages had narrow escapes. On July

A civil defense warden and his wife window-shop after duty in Jerusalem.

15 the defenders of Beerot Yitzhak, southeast of Gaza, were fighting off the Egyptians with hand grenades in the last corner of their settlement after the communal reservoir had been blasted, flooding the shelters and trenches and soaking the ammunition and communications equipment. Units of the Negev Brigade then arrived and saved what was left of the settlement.

Since 1948 the regional defense system has been vastly improved. New settlements were strategically planned and sited for static defense. They were established opposite Arab highways where the borders faced desertlike terrain and opposite gaps where the borders faced mountains. They thus covered the only routes along which mechanized enemy forces could approach Israeli territory. Settlements that were undermanned had army reservists assigned to them in emergencies. The farmers could also call upon regular artillery units in the rear for support.

The weapons in the village arsenals are capable of halting armor. But if enemy tanks should get through, the settlers are expected to remain in their positions and prevent fuel trucks and supply and reinforcement columns from following through the breach. Each border village is equipped and supplied to hold out independently for a substantial period. As in 1948, an invader will not be able to bypass those harmless-looking settlements. To keep a breach open and fan out in Israel, the enemy would have to subdue the frontiersmen of each and every village within mortar, antitank, and machine-gun range of the approach route. That should allow plenty of time for the regular forces to reach any trouble spot and for the reserves to be mobilized.

There were some sensitive border areas that were too rocky, arid, or remote for profitable agriculture. These were populated by the Nahal Corps.

The Nahal Corps consists of teen-aged boys and girls belonging to idealistic youth movements in the cities. The army encourages them to combine their military service with grooming for possible settlement on the land after their discharge. After basic training, they are assigned to vulnerable border areas where the girls mix shooting practice with housework and light farming chores while the boys clear rocks and reclaim soil between paratrooper training and other rigorous courses.

Young settlers at Nahal Argaman, in the Jordan Valley

Once the rocky slopes are terraced, the farms are linked to water sources and road networks, and the enterprises become viable, the land is offered to the pioneers for civilian settlement. Thus a most dependable element has been inhabiting vulnerable border areas.

The contributions of the frontier farmers to the military victories in 1956 and 1967 were less bloody than in 1948, but still quite vital. The knowledge that the frontiersmen were in their slit trenches and would contain Arab attacks in the north and east enabled General Dayan, the Chief of Staff in 1956, to concentrate the bulk of his forces on the southern front and sweep Egypt out of Sinai in less than a week. The possibility of fronts with Syria and Jordan as well had to be taken seriously because Damascus and Amman had just concluded a mutual defense pact with Egypt. It turned out that Egypt's allies didn't budge, but the victory in Sinai would hardly have been so overwhelming if General Dayan had not been able to count on the frontiersmen and had had to spread his forces over all fronts.

In 1967 there was multifront action, and the function of regional defense was to hold the line on some fronts while Israel's mobile forces took the offensive on others. Only on the Syrian front did the border settlements have to cope with enemy advances. Arab armor tried to sweep down on Tel Dan, Shear Yashuv, and Ashmura, but they were repulsed by the defenders and routed by Israeli armor. The defenders were not really extended, for the attacks had hardly been unexpected.

41

In fact, they had been expected in brigade strength and hardly amounted to a battalion. Apparently they were probing actions and the Syrians never got around to launching their main offensive.

However, border villages on all fronts were pounded by artillery. Those in the Jordan Valley at the foot of the Syrian heights of Golan took the most severe punishment. They were blasted for four days around the clock, before the main Israeli forces came north and drove the Syrians to the gates of Damascus.

After the Six Day War, the frontiers moved away from all the settlements facing Egypt and Syria and from most of those on the Jordanian front. Only settlements on the Lebanese border or opposite Jordan in the Beisan Valley or south of the Dead Sea were still within range of Arab guns.

Nahal settlements that overnight found themselves deep inside Israeli territory turned civilian. New paramilitary farms were established in the occupied areas on the formerly Syrian heights of Golan, in the Jordan Valley, and on the Mediterranean coast of Sinai. The traditional system of territorial defense was retained, although regular troops assumed a greater part of the burden.

The only sector in which defense was left exclusively to regular forces was the Suez Canal front, where the hostilities after the 1967 cease-fire escalated into sustained slugfests between deeply entrenched fortified positions, tanks, and heavy guns. Obviously it was no place to farm, fish, or raise families.

As to the enemy soldiers who failed to break into the border villages, many eventually reached them—as tourists.

The Israelis took thousands of prisoners in 1956 and 1967, and GHQ in Tel Aviv decided to show them something of the country before repatriating them. It wasn't just altruistic hospitality. The thinking was that some might carry the message through the curtain to the Arab world that Israel could not be pushed into the Mediterranean and that her people wanted to be friendly and neighborly.

One of those who got to see the country was Lieutenant Colonel Hanna Naguib, an Egyptian battalion commander. He was paroled in the custody of Yitzhak Oron, a Hebrew University student. In a barn three miles from what used to the the Jordanian border, he got the shock of the war.

The unusual day had begun when Mr. Oron appeared at the prisoners-of-war camp at Atlit, spread a map before the colonel, and invited him to choose the places he wished to visit. The Egyptian was rather nervous and suspicious and he stabbed a stubby finger almost blindly at Ein Harod, a *kibbutz* in the Jezreel Valley.

Two hours later they were walking through the tree-lined paths of the *kibbutz*. When they reached the barn they were greeted cheerfully by a man in rumpled clothes and black-rubber boots caked with dry dung and hay. When Mr. Oron introduced himself, the man nodded affably and said he was Uzi Zisling, the communal cowhand. When the young student was about to present Colonel Naguib, Mr. Zisling held up a hand.

"There's no need for introductions," he smiled. "We know each other."

Colonel Naguib bristled as though an intoxicated soldier had taken a liberty. To the Egyptian officer class there is no species of humanity lower than the *fellah,* the peasant. He glared at the man from his dung-crusted boots to his uncombed hair. "Impossible," he snapped. "How can you know me? How can I know you?"

"Take a good look," the cowhand prodded. "You know me."

The colonel shook his head vigorously from side to side.

"Do you recall," the cowhand asked, "sailing in a boat from Sharm el Sheikh to an island? . . ."

Colonel Naguib had indeed commanded a battalion at Sharm el Sheikh, at the southern tip of the Sinai Peninsula. That was where he had been taken prisoner. He remembered a boat journey with an Israeli battalion commander to arrange the surrender of a small force on a nearby island. Suddenly the cowman's face came into focus.

"You're, . . ." he stammered. "You're the battalion commander!"

The Israeli laughed and nodded confirmation.

"What are you doing here?" the Egyptian gasped. "Why are you dressed this way?"

"The war's over," the farmer shrugged. "I'm home."

One can imagine the Egyptian's trauma. Having been defeated in battle was humiliating enough. But he had now discovered that his conqueror had been a smelly *fellah* on a short leave from his cows!

General Haim Barlev visits Is-raeli troops near the Suez Canal.

3 Where

Chutzpah Is a Virtue
Nasser's waiting for Rabin, ai, ai, ai."

Israeli soldiers in an underground fortification on the Suez front

OF COURSE, not every Israeli cowhand is capable of leading a battalion of mechanized infantry across a desert to capture an Egyptian stronghold. But every male aged eighteen to forty-five and a good proportion of the females aged eighteen to thirty-four are cogs in the military machine, skilled in some specific branch of soldiering.

In the Six Day War, Avraham Yaffe, director of the Society for the Protection of Nature, commanded one of the three divisions that blasted their way to the Suez Canal. Issahar Shadmi, who manages the Shalom Tower in Tel Aviv, the tallest building in the Middle East, led the armored brigade that cut off the Eyptian retreat at the Mitla Pass in one of the war's crucial engagements.

Nathaniel Horowitz was called away from an insulation materials factory in Petah Tikvah, where he is a foreman, to join his armored battalion, of which he is a lieutenant. He became one of the heroes of the Six Day War when he took command of the battalion during the battle for the Syrian heights after his colonel was injured and his major killed. With only two of his battalion's Sherman tanks left, he reached the plateau and linked up with his brigade commander after fighting his way through three heavily fortified lines of defense. Toward the end he was without communications because the wires of his ear set were soaked with blood from his head wound.

Ben Zion Zohar, who made air-war history by shooting down an Iraqi Hunter interceptor in a dogfight while piloting a heavier and slower Vatour fighter-bomber, normally supports his family by flying a crop duster. Yehuda Peri, who was cited for continuing to search for a pilot downed in Jordanian territory even after his own low-flying helicopter had been riddled by seven Jordanian shells, ordinarily flies tourists between Tel Aviv and Elath for Arkia Airlines. The object of his search was Shabbetai Ben Aharon, an El Al pilot who had bailed out of a Fouga Magister but, it was later learned, was killed on the ground by Arabs near Jericho.

Four out of five soldiers who fought the Six Day War had been called away from businesses, jobs, or school books. They rushed to regional rendezvous to collect their uniforms, kits, and weapons and then moved to the fronts, sometimes at the wheels of their own cars, taxis, buses, trucks, wreckers, tractors, or bulldozers. Since means of transport are subject to mobilization, reservists may, if they wish, serve as drivers of their own vehicles. That privilege was invoked during the Six Day War even by some civilians who were not eligible for reserve duty but insisted upon serving. One of them was a former Soviet army nurse, Mrs. Olga Klein, a fifty-seven-year-old grandmother of seven from Tiberias, who served with a medical unit on the northern front as driver of her husband's grocery van.

Apart from "ineligibles" like Mrs. Klein and some other wartime ringers, the reservists are veterans of the regular army. The men serve from two to three years in the regular army and the women from eighteen months to two years, depending upon political and other conditions prevailing at the time they are of military age. After their discharge they are called up for reserve duty—sixty days a year for officers and noncoms and forty-five days a year for the rest—to hone their military skills and familiarize themselves with new equipment. Some specialists such as engineers are called up for additional service, but that requires special approval from the Minister of Defense.

Notwithstanding impressions created by the Six Day War, Israeli soldiers are no supermen. On the contrary, the armed forces draft men at whom other armies would turn up their noses. Men with physical limitations are used for administrative functions. School dropouts are taken and sent to classes. One must be a veritable physical or mental "case" to escape the draft.

Exemption is thus a stigma. Even assignment to noncombat units embarrasses young men, since administrative functions generally are performed by women. Army doctors have had to be on the lookout for male conscripts trying to hide physical handicaps from their examiners.

Deferments are rare. Entering the armed forces after graduation from high school is practically as inevitable as going from kindergarten to the first grade. The only young men allowed to go from high school directly to college are the gifted ones who wish to train for professions particularly needed in the armed forces. But they are by no means deferred.

They are inducted at eighteen, put through recruit training, and then given leave passes to go to college. During their vacations they are called up for squad commanders' and officers' training courses. Thus, when they get their degrees, they are able to begin their regular service as commissioned officers. These men provide the armed forces with its cadres of engineers, doctors, scientists, electronic and aeronautical specialists, and other experts.

Arab citizens are exempted from the draft in consideration of the fact that the only enemies Israel is likely to fight are Arabs. However, some have volunteered. Bedouins have served with particular distinction as trackers. Leaders of the Druses, a community which broke away from Islam in the eleventh century, and the Circassians, a Moslem sect that came from Russia in the nineteenth century, have asked that their young men be drafted just like the Jews. They are.

In the Jewish community, the only young men receiving special consideration are a few thousand deeply religious youths who believe with sincere conviction that their poring over Talmud tomes to please the Almighty is as essential for the well-being of Israel as a strong army. They get deferments.

Girls are also drafted at eighteen; Israel is the only country in the world with compulsory military service for women in peacetime. The girls don't fight as they did in the Haganah, but they are taught to handle weapons and are then assigned to auxiliary functions, sometimes in combat units as far down as the battalion level.

Actually, the army can't use all of Israel's womanpower. Married women are exempt by law from the regular forces and mothers from reserve duty as well. Recruiting offices have also been lenient in exempting girls for social and economic reasons. Religious girls may claim exemption from service under the law but many prefer to serve. Despite everything, an eighteen-year-old girl in civilian clothes causes some eyebrow raising.

Thousands of girl soldiers from well-to-do homes have been assigned to render their national service in remote villages inhabited by emigrants from backward Asian and African countries, to help narrow the social and cultural gap. They serve there in uniform—mainly as teachers—after their basic military training.

Training and maneuvers, both for regulars and reservists, are tough. The emphasis is on close combat and night fighting, the kinds of warfare the Arabs dislike most. The conditioning doesn't simulate what soldiers are likely to experience in actual battle. It is rougher. The thinking at GHQ is that a soldier will not do in war what he has not done in training and that it is necessary to compensate in training for the mines, the psychological factors, and the other imponderables the soldier will encounter when he faces the real thing.

Twenty-five-mile night marches with full kits up steep, craggy slopes or through water and mud are normal for combat units, partly to toughen the men and partly to show them that they are capable of enduring more than they imagined.

When Israeli forces were posted on the Egyptian border during the crisis preceding the 1967 war, Major General Ariel Sharon removed them from their positions, battalion by battalion, and sent them on daily sixteen-mile marches with fifty-five-pound packs through the sands of the Negev at a quick pace. When his men finally received orders to attack, they reached their objective ahead of schedule.

The men and women who hand down orders in the Israeli defense forces are professional soldiers, but not in the usual sense. There is no officer class. There is no equivalent of West Point or Annapolis. Every officer comes up through the ranks.

The three years of compulsory service barely provide time for a conscript to reach the rank of lieutenant. To rise higher, he must volunteer for additional service. An air force recruit must sign up for at least five years before he is sent to flying school. A pilot is trained to fly a more advanced plane only if he is under contract for several years' service. In that sense they are career officers. Contracts are renewable only for two or three years at a time. Only the up-and-coming are retained. There are no old colonels in the Israeli forces. No one past his middle forties has been appointed Chief of Staff since General Yaakov Dory, who was chief of the Haganah general staff at the time of its transformation into a regular army.

The relationship between officers and men is remarkably relaxed, especially in the reserves. I had an opportunity to observe it shortly after the Six Day War when I flew to the Suez Canal with some top brass, including Lieutenant General Yitzhak Rabin, the Chief of Staff.

Our helicopter landed in a cloud of dust outside a camp and the visiting officers were met by its commander, who escorted them toward it on foot. About fifty soldiers stood in the gateway. The only one to raise his arm in a casual salute was a man in a white crash helmet, the sentry. The others said *"shalom."* The Chief of Staff nodded and answered *"shalom."*

A company of tankmen who had fought their way to the Suez Canal marched toward the party singing the latest war song, "Nasser's waiting for Rabin, ai, ai, ai." The general chuckled.

The men halted near the Chief of Staff and swung around to face him. The general addressed them tersely in his warm, deep-bass voice. "I don't have to tell you that you've done a good job," he said.

Then he asked which of the men had taken part in a certain night engagement. Several raised their hands and General Rabin spoke to a soldier in the front row.

Beaming elatedly, the man said he was from Beit Alpha, a *kibbutz* in the Jezreel Valley. He had been a reservist in the tank company for more than ten years. He answered questions about the battle and then, suddenly, in the middle of a sentence, he seemed to have decided that the Chief of Staff merited some military courtesy.

Casually, without breaking his flow of words, he brought his feet together and stood at attention. General Rabin flicked his wrist and

An off-duty soldier tends to her hairdo and adjusts her uniform.

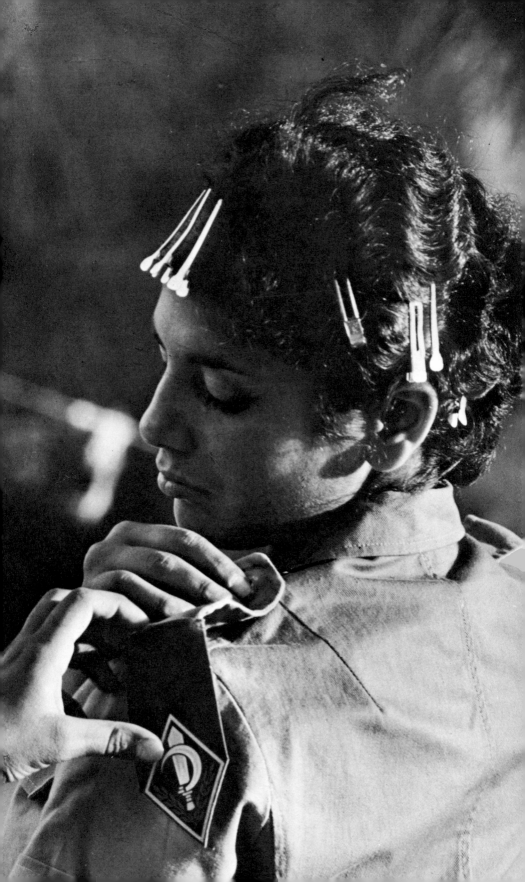

said, "No need." The soldier slouched back into his previous posture.

General Rabin talked to several of the men. None manifested any self-consciousness except one who kept shifting his weight from leg to leg.

Nobody called General Rabin "sir." In fact, there is no Hebrew word for it. There is a Hebrew term, *hamefaked,* which means the commander and is used as a form of address to superiors. Nobody called General Rabin *"hamefaked"* either.

Yet the men showed reverence. Those loafers in the gateway who said *"shalom"* when General Rabin passed had assembled there just to get a glimpse of him. Israeli soldiers dislike parades, but the tank-men had themselves requested the company commander to arrange one, and some officers who didn't belong to the company infiltrated just for the chance to see General Rabin. Certainly the soldiers who asked friends to snap pictures of them with the Chief of Staff in the background were manifesting esteem. The manner in which they showed it was simply rather unmilitary.

As for the men's attitude toward the others in the retinue, the crossed olive branches and swords on the shoulders of the generals and the three fig leaves on the shoulders of the colonels didn't arouse the least attention or curiosity.

I asked a sad-faced colonel: "Doesn't your rank impress them?"

"No," he shrugged.

"Well," I pressed, "does that attitude affect discipline?"

"Yes," he replied, "of course."

"But," he added quickly, "in battle they're disciplined.

Considering where we were and how the men had gotten there, the statement hardly seemed arguable.

The informality in the armed forces reflects the "all Jews are brethren" conception, a feeling of basic equality between one Jew and another that became deeply ingrained during the nearly two thousand years of dispersion, when Jews were for the most part in a status of inferiority compared to the world around them. It is also part of the Haganah heritage. In the underground it was undesirable for security reasons for members to know one another's family names. They addressed each other by first name or nickname. That's still common in the armed forces.

During the Six Day War I interviewed Lieutenant Colonel Yaakov Yoffe in Tel Aviv and we arranged that I should return later to pick up some material he would prepare.

He wasn't at his desk when I returned. When I asked for Colonel Yoffe, a pug-nosed female second lieutenant said I must have come to the wrong place.

"Ridiculous," I replied, "I talked to him an hour ago. He was sitting right there at that desk. He's a short fellow. . . ."

"Oh," she exclaimed, " 'Djook.' You want 'Djook.' " (The nickname means cockroach in English.)

In the Haganah, where the authority of superiors was more charismatic than legal, officers led by example and inspiration more than by command. They still do. A commander of a tank unit is expected to be the best gunner and best driver in his outfit, apart from possessing imagination and other qualities of leadership. To maintain that kind of officer superiority, a lieutenant in an infantry, engineer, artillery, or armored unit is trained as a paratrooper. Captains are trained as commandos. If they aren't good enough to be paratroopers or commandos, they don't qualify to lead ordinary troops.

The leadership-rather-than-command tradition was formulated as a doctrine in the mid-1950's when the army was engaged in a series of reprisal raids across the borders. Officers, the doctrine said, must expunge the term "forward" from their military vocabularies. It must be replaced by the term "follow me."

What that meant was quickly illustrated in the case of a driver charged with refusal to obey an order to recover a truck abandoned during a border engagement near the Gaza Strip. The case against the driver was dropped and the officer who had filed the complaint was demoted. If it was dangerous, he was told, he should have salvaged the truck himself.

Some time later an infantry corporal was pinned down near the Syrian border by enemy fire. He had volunteered to plow a field in the Jordan Valley that was exposed to Syrian emplacements in the hills of Golan. The Arabs had driven away a civilian tractor driver. When the corporal appeared they reopened fire and succeeded in disabling the tractor.

Crouching behind the stranded vehicle for cover, the corporal saw an Israeli half-track churning toward him. A soldier next to the driver was blazing away with a machine gun, drawing the Syrian fire from the tractor. When the half-track drew near, the corporal recognized the machine gunner. It was his battalion commander.

The corporal received a citation for bravery. The lieutenant colonel's action was regarded as nothing more than his duty. No one cited him.

The casualty lists reflect that kind of leadership. There is one officer to every ten men in the army and navy and one to eight or nine in the air force. In the Sinai campaign of 1956, one out of every five Israelis killed was an officer. In the Six Day War in 1967, officers accounted for one out of every four casualties.

The losses of officers in the Six Day War were heaviest in the fiercest battles. The Golani Infantry Brigade lost fifty men fighting its way up the steep Golan heights, where the Syrians were entrenched in bunkers and pillboxes rooted deep in the rocky soil with heavy slabs of concrete and sandbags overhead and barbed wire and mines all around. Thirty-four of the fifty Israeli dead were officers.

On the Egyptian front, Major General Yisrael Tal's division, consisting of Patton, Centurion, and Sherman tank columns and paratroopers in armored half-tracks, lost seventy men in the first day of the war when it broke through Rafah and fought its way to the outskirts of El Arish. Thirty-five of the seventy were officers, hardly surprising since the tank commanders fought standing in open turrets.

Apart from the American-made Pattons, the tanks and armored vehicles used by the Israelis in the Six Day War were old types dating back as far as the Second World War. The larger naval units were even older. But the aircraft, artillery, and light weapons were up-to-date.

The guns were for the most part manufactured in Israel. So was the ammunition, apart from some odds and ends. But the planes, tanks, half-tracks, and larger naval units had been purchased abroad, as were tens of thousands of spare-part items. That was a mistake Israel hoped not to repeat.

President Charles de Gaulle's sudden embargo at the height of the crisis stunned Israel's military leaders. France had been the country's principal supplier of plane and aircraft parts. True, in 1967 the war ended too quickly for the embargo to affect the outcome, but the warning was agonizingly clear.

Accordingly, there was a reappraisal. Israel's tank and aircraft requirements had not been large enough to warrant tooling up for domestic production, but future needs were reaching dimensions that might justify this. The spare parts had been purchased abroad because Israeli industry was not geared to meet the precise specifications or because domestic production was more expensive. Those factors had to give way to security considerations.

By chance, the Six Day War coincided with a period of economic recession and large-scale unemployment. The security establishment pointed out that domestic arms and industries could contribute to economic stability.

Israel certainly had the technical abilities. In the electronics field her scientists had invented some remarkable and still top-secret devices that could not be purchased abroad at any price. Israelis had designed improvements for their French-made warplanes and many of these were incorporated by the French manufacturers in the new Mirage V interceptors. World War II model tanks and half-tracks had been rebuilt in Israeli plants. Shermans with new engines and new guns, Centurions with new cannon, and half-tracks with new weapons systems, including mortars, had held their own in the 1967 war against the modern Soviet armor employed by Egypt and Syria. The rebuilt tanks were, of course, not as good as new weapons, but they cost half as much.

But would rebuilt tanks be effective enough for a war of the future? If not, should Israel manufacture her own tanks and half-tracks or continue to buy them abroad? Whom would she have to fight in the next war apart from her immediate neighbors? Iraq? Algeria? Saudi Arabia? What would the Russians do?

These questions were explored by the General Staff in the post-victory reappraisals. Conclusions, if any, have not been announced. The decisions will come to light gradually over the years.

But the consensus was that in the near future there was no danger of direct Soviet intervention on a major scale. The generals foresaw that Soviet instructors might man antiaircraft guns and other weapons on Egyptian soil, but it seemed unlikely that they would cross the frontiers.

General Bar-Lev was asked about this shortly after he became Chief of Staff in 1968. He replied in his typically deliberate manner: "I believe that for the near future the danger is small. Active intervention by the Soviet army or navy is not to be assumed so long as the balance of power and the balance of terror in the global context remain what they are today."

"And what of Russian 'volunteers'?" someone asked.

"I don't think it's worthwhile for Russia to risk it," he replied. "We are an army that in one generation was compelled to fight three times in three wars against armies equipped with superior weapons and some of the most modern armaments in the world. Consequently, our boys— our pilots, our tankmen, our paratroopers, and the men of the other corps—are not inferior in any way to soldiers of any other country. On the contrary, I believe the battle experience of our boys fighting on their own soil gives us a great advantage and superiority over any foreign volunteer who has no battle experience and after all does not fight on his own soil or for his own soil.

"So," he concluded, "I believe they'll not find it worthwhile sending volunteers. True, we've heard of Russian pilots flying planes in the Yemen but there, at least theoretically, their risks were very small. But I don't believe a Great Power will consider it worthwhile risking having a pilot shot down over 'enemy' territory or losing a 'volunteer' in some other way. I can't imagine a Great Power taking such a risk, particularly when her contribution in any case could be only marginal."

Cocky? Perhaps. Cockiness is considered a virtue in the Israeli defense forces. If each Israeli soldier didn't believe he could lick ten Arabs, the Israelis would feel hopelessly outnumbered.

The brazenness, improvisation, ingenuity, and cockiness that personify the Israeli soldier were displayed by Lieutenant Colonel Uri Yarom in an encounter with American brass some time ago when he was a helicopter pilot.

Colonel Yarom flew his Sikorsky 58 to the eastern Mediterranean to remove a sailor from the *Negba*, an Israeli freighter, and fly him to a hospital in Tel Aviv. But the colonel had difficulty finding the vessel. His fuel supply was running low and he had to discontinue the search and head back to Israel.

On his way he saw units of the U.S. Sixth Fleet, including an air-

A brigade commander awards campaign ribbons to the kin of Israeli soldiers killed during the 1967 fighting at the Syrian heights of Golan.

craft carrier. Sikorsky 58's, like his own, were landing. The American helicopters were white and his was camouflaged. Nevertheless he flew over the carrier until a signalman waved a green flag for him to come down.

He was summoned to the bridge, where an angry captain bawled: "Who are you?"

"An Israeli pilot," Colonel Yarom answered.

"How dare you land on an American ship!"

"Excuse me," the Israeli answered. "From above it looked like one of ours."

It was the height of *chutzpah,* from a representative of a country whose biggest warship was a clunky pre-World War II destroyer. But it got results. The pilot got his fuel. The Americans helped him find the *Negba.* He delivered the sailor to an Israeli hospital, where he recovered.

The Haganah veterans who molded the Israeli defense forces will fade out of the army and navy during the 1970's, and the generation that reads about the underground in history books will take over the top echelons of command. By the time of the Six Day War the successor generation had reached the rank of lieutenant colonel.

Over the decades the armed forces have gradually become more sophisticated, not only in their advancement from Napoleonchiks to guided missiles but also, albeit less perceptibly, in character. I recall visiting an air base during the 1948 war and being in a control tower when an alert was received. I heard the commanding officer say to a subordinate in Hebrew, but with a Yiddish intonation: "Yosef, would you mind sounding the alarm?"

Today orders are no longer delivered in an interrogatory tone of voice; they are crisp and authoritative. Their transmission may be accompanied by an inordinate amount of chit-chat and shoulder-shrugging, but authoritative sources say that orders are not really questioned; sometimes subordinates only want to know the reasons why.

In the early days one could see a brigade commander queuing up at a field kitchen behind a buck private with neither showing any self-consciousness. Today officers and sergeants have messes apart from the lower ranks, although the food comes from the same kitchens.

Uniforms are identical except for insignia. A seamstress sewing a pair of army trousers doesn't know whether they will be worn by a general or a private. But officers and enlisted men who sign up for the regular army are now permitted to buy summer uniforms of dacron to supplement their general issue.

Soldiers today are somewhat tidier. In some units, notably the armored corps, there is more saluting and addressing of officers as *"hamefaked."*

Some generals believe a little more formal discipline would be a good thing, but they consider the intimate relationship between officers and men a prime asset. A former Chief of Intelligence noted after the Six Day War that when captured Egyptian company commanders were asked the names of the soldiers in their units, they could name the platoon commanders but were offended by the suggestion that they should know their privates by name. That difference between the Egyptian and Israeli armies is considered one of the explanations for the quick rout of the Egyptians in battle.

So despite the separate messes and the dress uniforms and the saluting in the armored corps, the Israeli defense forces remain informal, relaxed, and egalitarian.

How Jewish?
How Peculiar?

"A walkie-talkie is less sinful than a telephone."

eft, the marriage of a Beni Israel couple from India;
bove, reservists mobilized in 1967 pause for services.

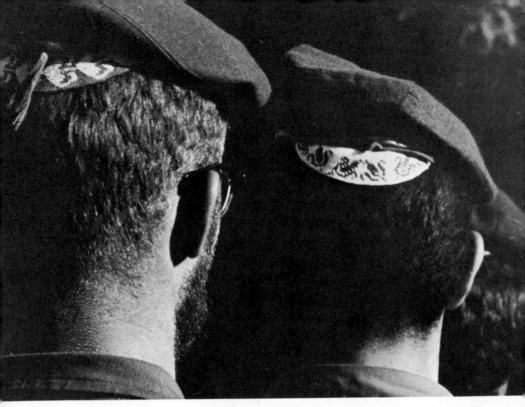

The skullcaps of Orthodox soldiers are visible under their army hats.

T HE ARMED FORCES of Israel have problems that no other fighting machine in the world faces.

There are complex Sabbath prohibitions, dietary regulations, and rituals deeply embedded in the Jewish way of life. Can a modern army respect them without impairing its efficiency?

Take Yom Kippur, the Day of Atonement. It may seem incredible that the army of the Jewish State dispenses meals to its soldiers while Jews the world over are fasting and praying. But wouldn't the withholding of food from nonobservant soldiers constitute unseemly religious coercion?

In the Haganah and other underground forces there had been separate units for Orthodox Jews, who were scrupulous about dietary rituals and who would not ride in a truck or clean a rifle on the Sabbath unless there was an obvious emergency. The other units largely ignored the religious injunctions.

When the State of Israel began conscripting citizens for military service, the Chief Rabbinate and the Orthodox political parties wanted the old divisions continued. They suggested that Orthodox conscripts be posted to separate battalions where the religious way of life would be followed. They petitioned Premier Ben-Gurion, who formed a ministerial subcommittee headed by himself.

In the subcommittee's deliberations, the representative of the agnostic far left delightedly supported the idea of keeping the devout soldiers apart. Mr. Ben-Gurion would have nothing of the kind. He shrank from the thought of religious and nonreligious tank columns, religious and nonreligious fighter squadrons, or religious and nonreligious warships. He strongly opposed political or social concentrations of any kind in the armed forces. In fact, he later broke up formations that from Haganah days had been associated with the *kibbutz* movement. Accordingly, he ruled that Orthodox soldiers should serve in regular units and that the entire army should be run in a way that would enable the most stringently observant to serve without violating any religious principle.

Religious laws require the scrupulous to worship three times a day in male groups of at least ten, apart from uttering a string of solo benedictions from the moment they get out of bed in the morning until they retire at night.

These laws can be observed in the armed forces. Every camp, warship, and air base has a fully equipped synagogue. Prayer shawls with their ritual fringes, phylacteries that are worn on the head and arm during weekday morning devotions, and prayer books are issued to soldiers who ask for them. Standing orders provide that time for worship be sacrosanct, but participation is optional.

Dietary laws forbid religious Jews to eat the flesh of animals that the Bible says are unclean or that have not been slaughtered in accordance with rabbinical ritual. All traces of blood must be removed. Mixing meat and dairy food is forbidden, and the devout keep separate sets of kitchen utensils and dishes.

So standing orders in the armed forces call for at least two inspectors, designated by the military rabbinate, in every army, navy, and air force kitchen. They see to it that the ingredients coming in are kosher and that the cooks don't do anything with them that is contrary to the dietary laws. Every pot is marked "Meat" in red paint or "Milk" in blue. Plates for meat dishes are white and for dairy dishes blue, while cutlery also have distinguishing marks to guard against their being mixed.

Double sets of personal utensils are optional for individual soldiers. Whether the soldier adheres to rabbinical regulations after the state gives him the kosher food is his own business.

The Yom Kippur dilemma was solved through a similar approach. All army kitchens are closed, but soldiers who do not wish to fast get field rations a day earlier.

There was also a problem with submarines. There was no room on the crews for rabbinical inspectors. That difficulty was overcome by authorizing the chaplaincy to pick the cooks themselves. All submarine cooks are accordingly devout Jews thoroughly acquainted with the dietary laws and trusted to comply with them.

The submarine cooks in effect double as chaplains. On Friday evenings they recite the Kiddush, the Sabbath eve benediction, over the intercom. Before frogmen aboard the submarine *Tanin* entered the escape hatch for their daring mission to mine enemy warships in Alexandria harbor during the 1967 war, they stood solemnly with bowed heads before the cook, who recited prayers for the success of their venture.

On the Sabbath and during festivals when the Bible forbids any manner of work, standing orders in the defense forces forbid training, parades, and exercises. Essential and immediate security functions are performed, which the rabbinate sanctions. No one questions that borders have to be guarded on holy days.

But some Orthodox soldiers had qualms about duties that were seemingly not of an emergency nature, like manning a telephone switchboard or writing messages. They obtained guidance from Major General Shlomo Goren, the Chief Chaplain.

General Goren, a widely respected authority on the interpretation of Torah law, was a Haganah sniper and later a machine gunner in the 1948 battle for Jerusalem. He wears the paratroopers' wings on his breast, having taken the rigorous course voluntarily when the high command made it compulsory for combat officers. Repeatedly he has gone to the front with combat troops, hugging a little Torah scroll to his bemedaled bosom and flourishing a *shofar,* a ritual ram's horn.

With those accouterments he was with the first soldiers to reach the Wailing Wall during the battle for the Old City of Jerusalem in 1967, and during the capture of Hebron he personally battered down the gates of the Cave of the Machpela, the burial place of the Hebrew patriarchs. In rabbinical matters General Goren has been similarly bold, deviating sharply from the Establishment with his liberal interpretations. But as a strictly Orthodox rabbi, he has granted no dispensations that he could not base on a Torah source.

He believes that God-fearing Jewish warriors of old like Bar Kochba and the Maccabees ran their armies effectively on the basis of the Torah, and that the laws on which they founded their conduct must have been forgotten or misunderstood during the centuries upon centuries of Jewish dispersion. He has been ferreting through ancient sources for those forgotten edicts.

General Goren has established that Torah law recognizes that the continuity of services essential to guard against enemy threats transcends Sabbath restrictions. Therefore, communications equipment must be operated on the Sabbath even when there is no immediate emergency.

However, he said that messages not stamped "Urgent" should be transmitted after the Sabbath. The Chief Chaplain further declared, various instruments of communication involve different degrees of Sabbath violation, and those involving lesser transgressions should be given preference. A walkie-talkie, for instance, is less sinful to use than a telephone, and a telephone is preferable to a teletype.

The chaplain's directives were duly promulgated, and he assured Orthodox soldiers that functioning in accordance with them would be consistent with Torah law. On the other hand, changing places with a willing nonobservant Jew to evade Sabbath duties would be a grave offense, since it would cause another Jew to work on the Sabbath when he didn't have to.

But, the chaplain was then asked, what should a soldier do if he receives an order requiring an outright violation of the Sabbath? He replied that the soldier should inquire of his superior whether the matter really could not be deferred until after the Sabbath. If the officer is evasive, the soldier should regard the order as illegal and not execute it. If the assurance is given but the soldier believes it is insincere, he should execute it and then file a complaint against his superior for issuing an illegal order.

In addition to his law research, General Goren has been revising and updating liturgies. A new prayer for the safety of submarine crews includes such passages as "the deep compassed me about" and "all Thy billows and Thy waves have passed over me."

If they have a familiar ring to those well acquainted with the Bible, it's because Rabbi Goren lifted the verses from Jonah's prayer in the belly of the whale.

The Chief Chaplain composed the prayer in 1958 when Israel acquired her first two submarines from Great Britain. The original text included a verse based on Psalms: "He calmed the waves into a whisper and stilled were the waves of the sea."

When the chaplain met the commander of one of the submarines at its launching at Portsmouth, the officer objected to that passage, saying that the waves helped submarines elude detection and so their crews preferred rough seas.

An Israeli newspaper columnist heard the story and quipped that if the submarine had been faulty and the prayer all right, there would have been something to worry about; but since the submarine was all right and the prayer was faulty, it didn't matter.

Rabbi Goren deleted the objectionable verse from later editions of the armed forces prayer book. Ten years later, when the *Dakar,* a newly acquired submarine, went down with a crew of sixty-nine in rough seas off Cyprus, he wondered with a heavy heart whether he had been right in yielding to the commander's objections.

He related the incident in his office at GHQ in Tel Aviv. Lying open on his desk were no fewer than twelve huge Talmud tomes. I had intruded while he was working on a report establishing that the missing sailors could be considered dead under Torah law.

The *Dakar* had been hunted fruitlessly for five days by ships and planes of five nations covering 100,000 square miles of sea. After the search was abandoned, the Israeli navy conducted further investigations for more than a month before proclaiming the vessel and crew lost. But for Rabbi Goren's purposes, that proclamation was not sufficient.

Unless he could find a basis in the Torah for a ruling, the wives of the lost seamen could not be recognized as widows. Establishing widowhood in cases of drowning is one of the most difficult rabbinical problems. Since the rabbinate is by law the exclusive authority in matters of marriage and divorce in the Jewish community, the bereaved women would never be able to remarry until they were declared widows under rabbinical law. So without Rabbi Goren's clearance, the armed forces could not issue death certificates.

Israel is by no means a theocracy, but neither is there a separation of church and state. The country is a Jewish State in that its population is overwhelmingly Jewish, but the rabbinate has no more status than the Moslem, Christian, or Druse religious authorities. Secular law and not the Torah is the law of the land. However, the rabbinate firmly and relentlessly exercises its share of the jurisdiction vested by the state in the religious authorities, such as control over marriage and divorce. It is a power in the land.

The rabbinical establishment is Orthodox, but it is not like the Orthodox rabbinate in the United States. It is more puritan and Old Worldish. There are Israeli rabbis who go swimming or enjoy an occasional movie or stage show, but they are in business or in government service, or function as administrators and public relations officers in religious institutions. They are never the actual rabbinical authorities. I have never seen a rabbi of a community smooth-shaven —nor a judge in a rabbinical court, nor an army chaplain.

The hierarchy is a closed shop, since the Chief Rabbinate must clear every candidate for a rabbinical post. All the approved candidates are puritanical types. No rabbi of the Reform branch of Judaism (which regards the Bible as man-given and changeable) or of the Conservative (which is more strictly observant than the Reform but less than the Orthodox branch) can get a foot inside the door, not even as a public relations officer.

The Orthodox Establishment appears totally insensitive or indifferent to the deep resentment among nonobservant Jews who unwillingly come into the rabbinical orbit and sometimes suffer personal agony as a result of the rigid enforcement of ancient laws. The Establishment would much rather outrage public opinion than risk irking the Almighty, and it believes with unshakable conviction that the Torah laws are eternal and that God wants them enforced unyieldingly.

An odd feature of Israeli life is the religious courts, which operate parallel to the secular judicial system. Rabbis and their Moslem and Christian counterparts, cadis and priests respectively, adjudicate civil cases when the litigants are of the same faith and all involved want their disputes tried on the basis of the Torah, the Koran, or canon law, as the case may be. The Ministry of Religious Affairs finances and administers the Jewish, Moslem, and Druse courts, but those of the Christians are run by their world hierarchies. State law enforcement agencies execute the judgments of rabbis, cadis, and priests when called upon to do so. Once cases are voluntarily submitted to religious adjudication, the decisions are as legally binding as those of secular courts.

The religious courts have no competence at all in criminal matters, but their jurisdiction over marriage and divorce is exclusive. Abdication of competence in marriage and divorce by the state to the religious authority of each community was the practice in the country throughout the periods of Turkish and British rule. The Israelis simply kept it up.

The result is that there can be no weddings within the country between persons of different faiths. There are no facilities for civil marriage. Traditionally, since the days of the ancient Hebrew prophets, intermarriage by Jews was considered a betrayal. But many modern Israelis chafe at the ancient curbs. They consider them intrusions into personal freedoms.

The rabbinate stands bastionlike. Before issuing a marriage license, registrars check carefully into the Jewishness of the applicants. Under rabbinical law, a child takes the religion of its mother. So children of Jewish fathers and Christian mothers have to go through conversion processes before they can marry Jews.

There have been painful situations in which young men or women reared as Israeli Jews have suddenly found that the rabbinate considers them Christians. One who experienced that trauma was the granddaughter of David Ben-Gurion, Israel's first Prime Minister.

Mr. Ben-Gurion's son Amos served in the British army during the Second World War and met an English nurse, Mary Callow of Liverpool. She embraced Judaism and became his wife.

David Ben-Gurion, who is not observant, was wont to remark in the Knesset that his daughter-in-law observed more rituals than he did. But when the daughter of Amos and Mary applied to the Haifa rabbinate for a marriage license, the rabbis wanted to know the details of Mary's conversion in England. They were not satisfied that the proper Orthodox ritual had been followed. The upshot was that the granddaughter of David Ben-Gurion, the George Washington of Israel, had to be immersed in a ritual bath and go through a conversion ceremony before she could marry a Jewish boy.

Similar experiences have befallen other individuals and entire sects. There were the black Falashas of Ethiopia, who clung to a primitive form of biblical Judaism for centuries and believed they were the only remaining Jews. Christian missionaries kept telling them that all the other Jews in the world had already converted. The Falashas kept apart from the non-Jews to the extent that they plunged into the river to purify themselves after physical contact. A handful reached Israel. The rabbinate ruled that they weren't really Jews and would have to go through conversions if they wished to become part of the religious community.

And there were the Beni Israel of India, who responded en masse to the call from Jerusalem for the "ingathering of exiles." The Beni Israel look more Hindu than Semitic. According to their traditions, they are descendants of eight Jewish families who fled the persecution of Antiochus Epiphanes in Palestine in the second century B.C. and were shipwrecked near Navagon, south of Bombay. In the eighteenth century a Jewish agent of the Dutch East India Company found them practicing a primitive form of Judaism.

He took them in hand, instructed them in the Bible, about which they had been unaware, and taught them some Jewish history and customs. Their Jewish education remained incomplete, however, and when Jews from Baghdad moved to India in the nineteenth century, they noted that the Beni Israel were ignorant of many religious practices. They didn't accept them as coreligionists and refused to intermarry. In 1915 the ban on marriage with the Beni Israel was upheld by the rabbinates of Jerusalem and Baghdad "until the coming of the Messiah."

When members of the sect encountered religious obstacles in Israel to marriages with Jews, it was a shattering blow to the Beni Israel. Some returned to India brokenhearted. The country was deeply touched by their tragedy and Chief Rabbi Yitzhak Nissim came to their support. He invoked an 1870 ruling by the rabbinate of Safed recognizing the Beni Israel as full Jews. When some local rabbis stubbornly continued to balk at marrying them, regional marriage registrars were appointed and empowered to go over their heads.

A similar measure answered the problems of the Karaites, whom some local rabbis refused to marry to Jews. The Karaites are a Jewish sect that adheres to the strict letter of the Bible but rejects the laws which Orthodox Jews believe were transmitted orally by Moses and later compiled in the Mishnah. Communities of Karaites survived in Russia and Egypt. There are some ten thousand of this sect in Israel.

Hundreds of Israelis who were prevented by religious complications from marrying at home went abroad for the purpose. The rabbinate, the competent authority in the matter, did not recognize the validity of the weddings, so the government refused to look upon such couples as man and wife.

In 1963, however, a Christian woman of Belgian nationality won a test case in the secular Supreme Court. She had sued to be registered by the Minister of Interior as Mrs. Israel Schlesinger by virtue of her marriage to an Israeli Jew in a civil wedding in Cyprus. By a 3–2 majority, the court ruled that it wasn't the Israeli government's business to investigate how the couple was married. As long as the wedding was legal in the country where it took place, the government had to register it.

Since then the Ministry of Interior has been registering all couples who produce official documents attesting to their marriage abroad. Registration does not certify validity. That is still the competence of the religious authorities, but government departments recognize the registration for such purposes as income tax deductions and the issuance of passports.

Among those who faced legal obstructions to his marriage and evaded them by going abroad was Justice Haim Cohn of the Supreme Court. (He had not been on the bench that decided the 1963 test case.) Like others named Cohn, Cohen, Kohn, Kagan, and Katz, he traces his ancestry to Aaron, the brother of Moses. That makes him a *kohen* or priest. The Bible accords him privileges and also imposes restrictions..

An injunction in Leviticus that deals with regulations concerning priests says: "Neither shall he take a woman put away from her husband for he is holy unto God."

There is no provision in rabbinical law enabling a *kohen* to renounce his holiness. The rabbinate accordingly refuses to solemnize any wedding between a *kohen* and a divorcée.

Judge Cohn's fiancée, the daughter of a former Chief Justice, was a widow, but an earlier marriage had ended in divorce. She joined the judge in New York, where he was representing Israel in the United Nations Commission on Human Rights. They obtained a marriage license from the State of New York and were wed by a Conservative rabbi.

The wedding caused an outcry in the Knesset, the press, and among the public. It was a dichotomous outcry. Some said with burning indignation that Justice Cohn's action disqualified him from the bench. Others said with equal fire that the scandal demonstrated how unworkable the ancient laws were.

Liberals like Justice Cohn advocate an option of civil marriage in Israel as the obvious solution to many problems. But Orthodox leaders have warned that the proposed solution would be worse than the problems. It would, they say, cleave the Jewish community for eternity, with one sector of the population questioning the legitimacy of the other's children.

Orthodox Jews would keep a special register of who was properly married and who was not. They would oppose their children's fraternization with those in the other sector of the community for fear that friendship might lead to marriage, just as many Jewish parents outside Israel try to hold the reins on their children's social life to guard against marriage out of the faith.

The problem is actually not so much civil marriage as divorce. According to Torah law, children born out of wedlock are not necessarily illegitimate. The only bastards are children born in adultery. The complication is that a woman who is divorced not in accordance with rabbinical law is considered an adulteress if she remarries, and offspring from her second marriage are branded illegitimate.

For ten generations they may marry only other bastards, since it is written: "One born from prohibited connections shall not enter the congregation of the Lord: even the tenth generation of him shall not enter into the congregation of the Lord."

That's that.

In dietary matters, the rabbinate's authority is charismatic. There is no secular law against consuming non-kosher edibles, but Jews who observe dietary laws, apart from a small group of extremists, recognize the rabbinate's competence to rule on where and what one may eat without violating religious principles.

Accordingly, for business reasons, nearly all butchers, bakers, and manufacturers of processed foods voluntarily apply for rabbinical supervision. They then display framed certificates testifying to the fact. The only enterprises arbitrarily required to submit to rabbinical inspection are those operated by the government. Otherwise the state would have to open separate hospitals, jails, and railway dining cars for its citizens who observe the dietary laws.

Most first-class restaurants do not submit to rabbinical inspection and their cuisine is not kosher. Operating kosher kitchens is complicated and costly. It involves large areas to allow for separate cold-storage facilities and dishwashers, double sets of utensils, crockery, and cutlery for meat and dairy meals. Meat prepared according to dietary laws is 20 per cent more expensive than meat not so prepared. Desserts after meat meals are usually more costly too because chefs cannot use milk products. The restaurateurs also have to pay inspectors appointed by the rabbinate to keep an eye on them.

The leading hotels, however, observe the dietary laws. For Orthodox proprietors it is a matter of conscience, but for most entrepreneurs the considerations are commercial. Many Jewish tourists who are not particular about what they eat at home regard themselves as pilgrims in Israel and feel they should be more religious.

One observant Jew, on the other hand, ate non-kosher food for the first time in his life during a visit to Israel. He had been so scrupulous about the dietary laws that he lost fourteen pounds during his service in the United States forces because he had eaten only fruits, vegetables, and dairy products except when kosher food parcels from his family reached him. In Tel Aviv, the Hebrew lettering on a restaurant window tripped him up. It never entered his mind to ask if the food was kosher. Only when coffee with milk was served after a meat dish did he realize his unhappy error.

Another Jewish visitor said the most rewarding experience of his stay had been overhearing a waiter in the Tel Aviv Hilton tell an internationally famous statesman that he could not have strawberries and cream for dessert because he had just eaten meat. Non-Jewish guests are generally acquiescent but puzzled, particularly when informed that if they want cream in their coffee after a meat dinner they must move from the dining room to the lounge. The requirement is a precaution lest the hotel mix its meat and dairy utensils.

Another consideration for hotel owners is that state banquets and public functions have to be kosher. These are an important source of revenue. So are weddings, and rabbis will not perform them in halls where the catering does not conform to the dietary laws.

The rabbinate thus has a strong hand in dealings with hotel managements—and it plays it not only in the kitchen. The supervisors insist that smoking be prohibited in the dining rooms on the Sabbath in deference to the biblical injunction: "Ye shall not kindle any fire throughout your habitations upon the Sabbath day." They also check that hotel barbers and gift shops shut down on Fridays before the Sabbath starts.

Under threat of withdrawing its inspectors, the rabbinate has compelled hotels in Jerusalem and Haifa to shut nightclubs on the Sabbath. In cosmopolitan Tel Aviv they are open, but no instrumental music is permitted. Hotels that scheduled Christmas and New Year's balls have been forced to cancel them. Supervision of the cuisine in one Jerusalem hotel was canceled because the management allowed men and women to swim together in the hotel pool.

Clashes over girls in bikinis and civil marriage and smoking on the Sabbath and kosher meals are symptoms of a deeply emotional and philosophical conflict over the image of Israel. There is substantial agreement that the State representing the answer to two thousand years of Jewish prayers should be peculiarly Jewish. The argument is: How Jewish? How peculiar?

90%
מהאזרחים
מתנגדים
לנתוחי
המתים

*Orthodox Jews in the Mea Sherim quarter
of Jerusalem demonstrate against autopsies.*

5 What Is a Jew?

"Are Jewish nationality and religion identical?"

Religious extremists turn their backs on girl soldiers marching through a Jerusalem street.

T HERE ARE THOSE who equate Jewishness with the Torah. To their way of thinking, a Jewish State not governed by rabbinical law is an incongruity.

That outlook may bring to the mind's eye a zealot with an untrimmed beard and flowing sidecurls, dressed in an austere black caftan and a broad-rimmed hat, stoning Sabbath traffic. The image would be out of focus.

The average Orthodox Jew is modern and fully integrated in Israeli life. He is identifiable only by the fact that his head is never uncovered. He wears a hat or a *yarmulke,* a skullcap. He probably doesn't use a razor blade in obedience to the biblical injunction "neither shalt thou mar the corners of thy beard," but his cheeks are smooth. He uses an electric shaver.

76

Orthodox Jews are businessmen, scientists, manufacturers, and farmers. They are policemen, bus drivers, plumbers, university professors, doctors—everything. Young men wearing knitted *yarmulkes* that resemble doilies live in the most vulnerable outpost *kibbutzim* and serve in the paratroopers, the naval commandos, and the most elite volunteer corps in the defense forces.

They fight for the character they want for their country mainly through Orthodox political parties. There are three religious parties represented in the Knesset. In the seven elections since independence, they have aggregated between 12 and 15 per cent of the national vote.

Orthodoxy is stronger than the polls would seem to indicate. But it is hardly disputed that the Orthodox are a minority. The Old World types who cling to the garb and mode of life of ghettos abroad are a minority of that minority. To some extent, they tend to separate from the mainstream of Israeli society and concentrate in quarters of their own. A small part of that element, in turn, are the militant zealots.

Their principal stronghold is the nearly century-old Mea Shearim quarter of Jerusalem, a hive of narrow streets crowded with little synagogues, ritual baths, houses of Torah study, stalls, and children. The inhabitants cling to the mode of life of the East European ghettos. On the Sabbath, come rain or baking sun, they don silken robes and fur hats like those their forefathers wore on the steppes of Eastern Europe in the Middle Ages.

Their womenfolk's blouses are buttoned to the neck. The sleeves extend to the wrists and the skirts well below the knees. Woe betide the female who passes through the archways of Mea Shearim in a sleeveless dress. She risks being spit at and called prostitute.

Modern Israelis shun the ghettolike atmosphere which they associate with the persecutions and humiliations of an era of Jewish history they would rather forget. But the inhabitants of Mea Shearim are convinced that their attire and mode of life pleases God and that the movie theaters and bars in modern Jerusalem are repugnant to Him.

From time to time zealots living in Mea Shearim have burst through its archways to register their fury against the Jews of modern Jerusalem, whose sins they believe have been delaying the coming of the Messiah. They have thrown stones, sticks, and bottles at Sabbath motorists. Vigilantes have snatched bodies from hospital morgues to

prevent autopsies. Hotheads have fought the Israeli police in demon-
strations against post-mortems and other sovereign transgressions
against religious law.

The fanatical fringe in Mea Shearim is the Neturei Karta, a sect of
a few hundred that does not recognize the legitimacy of the Jewish
State at all. The members of the sect say the *Kodesh Borech Hoo*
(Holy One, Blessed be He) has clearly ordained that the Jewish people
must suffer under foreign rule until the Messiah comes. So to their
minds the mortals who restored Jewish sovereignty insolently tried to
set the pace for messianic redemption. They have no doubt whatsoever that the heresy will bring Divine wrath and disaster to the people.

Israeli Independence Day is for them a day of mourning. They fast.
They will have nothing whatsoever to do with a Jewish government. So
intense is their hatred that they have refused to pray at the Wailing
Wall since its liberation. They pay no taxes. They refuse to register
for military service. They do not vote. There have been complaints
that they have prevented other pious Jews from voting by taking their
identity cards from their pockets while they were immersed in ritual
baths purifying themselves on Sabbath eve. They have vilified the
Chief Rabbis for giving their stamp of legitimacy to the "blasphemous
state." Their associates in the United States have daubed swastikas
on the doors of the Israeli consulate in New York. The Israeli government has tended to turn a blind eye to the Neturei Karta sect's infringements of the law except when they have created overt disturbances.

On the other extreme, there is a fringe element among Jewish atheists
that manifests more affinity for Arabs than for the Mea Shearim Jews
or Jews abroad. Their denigrators call them Kna'anim after the
Canaanites, the pagans who inhabited Palestine at the time of the
Hebrew conquest.

But they aren't offended. They say they rather like it. They maintain
that the Israelis have created a new Hebrew nation that is part of the
Jewish people but not identical with the Jewish people. They think the
new nation should be oriented toward integration with the people of
the region and should dissociate itself from Jews abroad. They believe
that the Hebrew nation will gradually grow apart from the Jewish
people and evolve a relationship with them similar to that between
England and Australia or the United States.

While the philosophy of the Kna'anim is repugnant to the great majority of Israelis, there has indeed been a pronounced withdrawal from some traditional forms of Jewish consciousness. Visitors have often expressed surprise at the empty synagogue pews at Sabbath services. Many persons who had been regular synagogue-goers in their countries of origin began spending Sabbaths on the beaches after they became Israelis. As Jews seeking Jewish identification in a Christian world, they had felt a compulsion to attend services. In Israel there is Jewish identification on the beaches. Synagogues are exclusively houses of worship. They offer no social programs.

Only during the high holidays and festivals are synagogues crowded, especially for Yizkor, the service for deceased parents. A poll conducted by the Institute of Applied Social Research established that three out of four Israelis attended Yom Kippur services. Synagogue attendance and religious observances are greatest among immigrants from Islamic countries.

The break with religious traditions by part of the older, immigrant generation was a conscious act. Their children, however, were raised without traditions and many of them later come to rue it.

An Israeli student in London, invited by a Jewish family to a Sabbath dinner, was mortified because he had no conception of the ritual. A pianist from Tel Aviv who was studying in Vienna was asked by Austrian actors rehearsing *The Diary of Anne Frank* to take them to a synagogue so they could absorb the Jewish atmosphere. The Israeli had to confess that she herself had never been inside one.

Most pathetic of all was the experience of soccer players who went to Moscow to represent Israel in an international match. They wanted to meet Russian Jews, and the synagogue was the obvious place. When they got there they felt like strangers. They didn't know how to join in the service. The rituals that had kept the Jews together through centuries of dispersion were outlandish to the Israelis. It is hard to say whether the encounter was more painful to the soccer players or the Russians.

The situation distressed Israeli leaders and in 1957 the Ministry of Education organized courses in Jewish consciousness in all state schools. Selected prayers from the Sabbath and holiday liturgies were taught—as literature lest the school system be accused of religious coercion. Boys were taken to weekday services in synagogues and stared at what they had never seen before, praying Jews wearing phylacteries. There were classroom discussions on the traditions of the Sabbath and the festivals and on religious thought and lore. The principal object of the consciousness program was to foster the identification of the *sabra*, the emancipated Israeli Jew, with the Jewish people of the dispersion, past and present.

But consciousness or no, the *sabras* are practicing Jews. The line between religious observance and ethnic tradition is nebulous because some religious rituals are so deeply embedded in the Jewish way of life that secularists perform them naturally and subconsciously.

Torah study is a cardinal *mitzvah*, or commandment. The pious go at it assiduously to fulfill the injunction: "This book of the law shall not depart out of thy mouth; but thou shalt meditate therein day and night." Any Israeli high school kid can give Bible lessons to the average synagogue-goer in the United States. Some of the busiest Israelis, including government officials and senior commanders of the armed forces, find time to participate regularly in Bible and Talmud study circles, not because they believe it will please the Almighty, but because the ancient books are part of their national culture.

The Institute of Applied Social Research established that 24 per cent of Israeli Jews identify themselves as secularists with no attachment whatsoever to the faith. But it's a safe bet that these secularists had their sons circumcised. An announcement in the press that a Communist leader is inviting friends to attend the ritual circumcision of a newborn raises no eyebrows at all.

When the Knesset debated restrictions on pig-raising a few years ago, some of the most zealous fighters for strict curbs were secularists, even though the sponsors of the legislation were Orthodox Jews. The objection of the Orthodox to pig-raising stems from the injunction in Leviticus: "and the swine . . . of their flesh ye shall not eat and their carcasses ye shall not touch; they are unclean unto you."

Some Israelis argued that the passage of gastronomic legislation would not only infringe on personal liberties but also make the legislature a laughingstock. However, Mr. Ben-Gurion, who was Prime Minister at the time, had pledged to obtain passage of the measure. It was an act of political expediency, as he needed to assure the religious deputies' support for his government coalition.

But the ardor with which some totally secular Socialist deputies fought for the measure was amazing. One confided privately that he ate and enjoyed pork products but considered pig-raising in the Jewish State an abomination.

The motivation of the secularists was national honor, not religion. Throughout history, they reasoned, enemies of the Jewish people had used the swine as a symbol when they wanted to debase, humiliate, and insult the Jew. The Bible also forbids Jews to eat horse, rabbit, camel, and the flesh of many other animals but somehow, through the ages, their persecutors always knew that the pig would wound the Jews most deeply. When Crusaders, Inquisitionists, or pogromists wanted to establish who was a Jew, they put swine flesh before the suspects. Jews preferred exposure and death to touching it.

So, the argument went, piggeries in a Jewish State would make a mockery of Jewish martyrdom. How could children raised in a free Israel with pigsties around them regard the sacrifices of their forefathers with proper awe and reverence?

The Knesset thereupon enacted a law confining the raising of pigs to cantons in predominantly Christian areas remote from centers of Jewish population. The courts later held that the restrictions applied to the transportation of live pigs but not their meat. So pork reaches those who want it elsewhere in the country. A few local authorities outlaw its sale, but most restrict it to specific shops or neighborhoods. In theory they're to serve diplomats and other gentiles. In practice, anyone can buy.

Attempts to coerce the nonreligious, through parliamentary legislation or the hooliganism of the Neturei Karta extremists, into compliance with the rabbinical concept of Jewish traditions is the main source of friction in the culture conflict.

There is no argument about Israel's Sabbath being the traditional one that runs from sunset Friday to nightfall on Saturday. The Sabbath and eight biblical festival days are prescribed days of rest. For employing a Jew on any of those days, except in special circumstances with the approval of the Minister of Labor, one can be sent to jail for a month. Moslems may not be employed on Fridays, nor Christians on Sundays.

But the Orthodox concept of a traditional atmosphere of total physical rest with dedication to prayer and spiritual matters clashes with the secular majority's wish to go on outings, putter in the garden, and enjoy other forms of recreation typical of an American Sunday.

The sound of automobile engines and lawn mowers on the Sabbath and the sight of a Jew smoking a cigarette deeply hurt the devout. A woman beating a carpet next door or the clink of coins at a Friday night poker game on a neighbor's terrace can shatter the spirituality of their Sabbath. They don't understand why legislators who support zoning laws dictated by nuisance, health, and economic considerations should hesitate to enact measures in behalf of behavior norms that preserved the Jewish national identity for centuries.

Fighting for such legislation is the *raison d'être* of the religious political parties. Those parties have aggregated between 15 and 18 of the 120 Knesset seats, but their strength is not in their size.

Orthodox deputies have frequently constituted the margin of a coalition government's majority in parliament. One of Mr. Ben-Gurion's governments fell when the National Religious Party withdrew its support as a protest against his education policy; the regime had sent children of pious immigrants to secular schools.

The price for the Orthodox parties' allegiance has been religious concessions in legislation along with budgetary allocations for projects like synagogues, ritual bathhouses, and schools. These were conditions that Socialist government leaders generally found easier to meet than those of alternative coalition partners, who demanded revisions in economic and foreign policies.

In many municipal councils since the days of British rule in Palestine, Orthodox members have been in a position to tip the scales between one coalition administration and another. Consequently, minority views were sometimes thrust on the population through political deals.

Laws and regulations imposing Sabbath restrictions stud the statute books. Many of them date back to the period of British rule. Out of a desire to defer a showdown in the culture conflict, the ruling parties have agreed since 1948 to maintain the status quo, as far as possible, with all its inconsistencies.

Ships reaching Israeli ports on the Sabbath are piloted into the basin and moored to the quay, but they don't begin loading or unloading, except for security reasons, perishable cargoes, or in other special cases authorized by the Minister of Labor. Passenger liners avoid touching Haifa on the Sabbath. However, international airlines schedule arrivals and departures at Lod Airport, and customs, frontier control, health, and other officials are on hand to clear travelers. El Al, the national airline, refrains from takeoffs from its main terminals in Lod and New York except during peak seasons, when Sabbath flights are scheduled but discreetly unlisted. It flies overtly from other airports. Arkia, the inland service, operates on the Sabbath with similar discretion.

All trains are idle. So are interurban bus services, but chartered sightseeing buses roll along the highways.

In most towns local buses are parked from late Friday afternoon until Saturday night. Haifa is an exception. When the British ruled Palestine, Haifa was a mixed Arab-Jewish city and the buses ran seven days a week. Under the status quo agreement they still do.

When the Haifa municipality built its subway up the slope of Mount Carmel, there was a big political argument. The mayor, citing the status quo agreement, said the trains should run on the Sabbath. Orthodox Jews said the status quo certainly didn't apply to a city-owned train service. There was a near-crisis in the government. The Orthodox position prevailed.

During the period of British rule Jerusalem was also a mixed metropolis, generally with an Arab mayor, but it never seemed right for Jewish buses to ply the Holy City on the Sabbath. So only Arab bus companies operated. After the city was divided between Israel and Jordan in the 1948 war, there were no Sabbath buses at all in the Israeli sector. In the reunited city, Arab buses continue to operate in the Arab portion of town but not in the Jewish sector.

The routes of the idle buses in Jerusalem and other cities are plied by taxis operating a jitney service called *sherut*. (*Sherut* means "service" and it's only a coincidence that it's pronounced "share-route.") Passengers shell out two-and-a-half times the regular fare for a Sabbath journey. The rates are fixed by the Ministry of Transport.

In addition, the ministry has authorized ordinary taxis to set their meters at night rates, 25 per cent above the regular fare. Car-rental

agencies also prosper on the Sabbath. They are required to close their offices, but they rent out their fleets on Friday for the weekends.

Businesses in all Jewish localities are closed on the Sabbath under municipal bylaws. There is no national law mandating this. Knesset law prohibits only the employment of hired labor. It does not prevent a merchant from opening his shop or a self-employed artisan or cooperative factory from producing goods.

Most cities allow hotels, restaurants, cafés, and a few pharmacies to do business. Nearly all prohibit Sabbath movie or theater performances but allow soccer matches at which admission is charged. Some cities permit Friday night shows when organizations or societies buy all the tickets in advance and call them "private showings." A few don't bother with that fiction and permit box offices to open. Museums, zoos, and the like are open on the Sabbath but tickets usually have to be purchased in advance.

The administrative division of the Israeli population into national and religious groups has given a new twist to an old question: Are Jewish nationality and religion identical?

The question was raised in the nineteenth century by Reform Jews in Germany who said they belonged to the Jewish faith but were German by nationality. They argued that there was no such thing as Jewish nationality.

In the Jewish State the question cropped up in reverse when survivors of the Second World War came to the country from Eastern Europe with Christian wives and their children.

They were mostly Polish Jews and they were not Zionists. On the contrary, they were assimilationists. They had hoped to bury their Jewish origins and start new lives in an enlightened, postwar Communist Europe as full-fledged Poles. But the Christians wouldn't let them. They remained outsiders. They might have acquiesced in their destiny, but when Polish children derided their children as "Jews" it was too much. To enable their unhappy offspring to grow up free from oppression, the frustrated assimilationists went to Israeli consulates and applied for immigrants' visas.

When they got to Israel they had a surprise in store. Their children were not recognized as Jews, since under rabbinical law a child takes the religion of its mother. They were outsiders again.

An aged rabbi at his prayers in Safed's old synagogue

The parents wanted their children raised as Jews, but some opposed having them converted. They said they didn't believe in any religion at all. They contended that their children could become part of the Jewish nation in Israel without belonging to the Jewish faith.

There was no difficulty about their becoming Israelis. The government is competent to accord Israeli nationality to Moslem, Christian, Druse, Jew, agnostic, and atheist. But could the State recognize a person as a Jew by nationality if the rabbinate did not recognize him as belonging to the Jewish faith?

For a decade there were no standard regulations governing the matter, but in 1958 the government decided that in cases where both parents agreed that children should be raised as Jews, those children would be registered as Jews by nationality. The Minister of Interior issued commensurate directives. This touched off a bitter controversy. The Chief Rabbinate denounced the directives and the two Orthodox members of the Cabinet resigned.

Mr. Ben-Gurion then shelved the directives while he solicited the views of fifty Jewish scholars in various lands. Overwhelmingly they replied that a child born of a non-Jewish mother is not a Jew unless converted. The government then quietly issued new directives for the registration of children as Jews by nationality. They corresponded with the rabbinical definition of "Jew." Many of those boys and girls converted when they reached maturity and joined the armed forces.

Judaism is not a missionary religion. Since the dispersion from Palestine after the destruction of the Second Temple by the Romans in A.D. 70, the rabbinical rule has been to accept converts only if they acted of their own free will. Compulsion, such as a desire to marry a Jew, disqualified a candidate. Reform and Conservative rabbis are more liberal about accepting converts, but they have no status in Israel and their conversions are not recognized by the Chief Rabbinate, which is exclusively Orthodox.

Orthodox rabbis were required to discourage candidates by pointing out the disadvantages of Jewishness—the discriminations they might expect to experience and the hardships involved in observing the Sabbath and dietary laws. They accept proselytes only if they are convinced the applicants sincerely wish to be strictly observant Jews.

When Chief Rabbi Isser Yehuda Unterman of Israel was a young rabbi in Liverpool, a workingman was puzzled by that approach.

"I don't understand," he protested. "I have many Jewish friends in the factory. They work Saturdays. They eat whatever they want. Why can't I be a Jew like them?"

The rabbi answered: "There are many Englishmen in British jails. They're criminals but they remain Englishmen. If an alien wants to become British, he isn't accepted unless his record is unblemished."

In the Israeli defense forces the Chief Chaplain has been more liberal. General Goren reasons that factors which influenced the rabbinical attitude in the dispersion do not apply in the Jewish State. He recognizes that proselytes living in Israel will undoubtedly remain loyal Jews with their children completely integrated into Jewish society.

Accordingly, he has eliminated various formalities in the conversion procedures, particularly with regard to children of mixed marriages. He has completed conversions in less than a month. The civilian rabbinate generally requires applicants to wait a year.

There have been some curious cases arising out of the "Who Is a Jew?" dispute. The most bizarre involved Brother Daniel, a Catholic monk.

He sued the Minister of Interior for the right to become an Israeli under the Law of the Return, which accords every Jew the intrinsic right to live in Israel and acquire citizenship automatically on arrival.

The monk was born Oswald Rufeisen, a Polish Jew, but was baptized during the war while he was hiding in a convent from the Nazis. He argued that in changing his religion he had not changed his nationality.

The way had been open to him to become a citizen of Israel by naturalization after completing requirements of residence, but Brother Daniel, with proverbial Jewish stiff-neckedness, stubbornly demanded recognition of his birthright.

Jews have always regarded apostates with revulsion. The Hebrew term for apostate is *meshumad,* which means "destroyed." The family of a *meshumad* traditionally tears its garments and sits on the ground in mourning, as though he had actually died. But this *meshumad* was different. His motive in being baptized apparently had been sincere conviction, certainly not the usual social and materialistic aim of facilitating assimilation in a Christian world. He had been a lifelong Zionist and remained one after embracing Catholicism. In his petition to the court, Brother Daniel wrote that he had been "born a Jew, grew up as a Jew, suffered as a Jew, and feels a Jew in the national sense."

Moreover, he was a hero of the anti-Nazi underground in Poland and saved the lives of numerous Jews who were now living happily in the State of Israel.

At the outbreak of the war in 1939 he had been in a Zionist training farm in Vilno, preparing for immigration to Palestine. The Gestapo caught him in 1941 but he soon escaped. He then obtained a certificate attesting that he was a German Christian.

The Nazis then hired him as a secretary and interpreter at the German police station in Mir, a district capital in Poland.

According to survivors, he utilized his position to help Jews in the region. He smuggled arms to the partisans and tipped off Jews when the Nazis decided to liquidate the ghetto. He was credited with saving the lives of 150 Jews, who then joined the partisans.

He was betrayed to the Nazis, apparently by a Jew, and again arrested. He broke out of jail a second time and found refuge in a convent. There he was converted to Catholicism.

Later he left the convent and joined up with Russian partisans. They didn't believe his tale and were about to execute him as a German spy. At the last minute a Jew whose life he had saved in Mir turned up and testified to his true identity. Eventually the Russians decorated him for his service with the partisans.

His story sounds incredible but he has witnesses.

He became a monk after the war and chose the Carmelite order because it had a chapter in Israel and he wanted to go there. During the Israeli War of Independence in 1948 and thereafter he kept asking his superiors for permission to go to the Israeli chapter. He received it in 1958.

In his application to the Polish government for permission to leave he wrote: "I base this application on the ground of my belonging to the Jewish people, to which I have continued to belong although I embraced the Catholic faith in 1942 and joined a monastic order."

He referred to Israel as "the land for which I have yearned since my childhood when I was a member of a Zionist Youth Organization."

The Poles allowed him to go after he agreed to waive his Polish nationality. He entered Israel on a temporary visa and then applied to the Ministry of Interior to have his status changed to that of a resident under the Law of the Return.

When his application was rejected and he sued, five justices were appointed to hear the case because of the unusual principle involved.

Curiously, the court held unanimously that under rabbinical law the monk was a Jew. The justices reasoned that Torah law regards apostates as sinners—but as Jewish sinners. Under Torah law a Jew forever remains a Jew.

But to the man in the street and to secular scholars "Jew" and "Christian" are contradictory terms, the court decided. By a 4–1 decision it held that the monk could not invoke the Law of the Return.

The lone dissenter was Justice Haim Cohn, the same Justice Cohn who later had trouble with religious law concerning his marriage. He argued that an independent Israel should look ahead and apply values other than those to which Jews had been educated as a persecuted minority in exile.

The other justices held that Israel could not sever herself from Jewish history.

"We do not deny our heritage," Justice Moshe Silberg said in a majority opinion. "We shall drink from the waters of our past."

"The channels have changed but we have not sealed the well," he continued. "Without our past we would be as the 'poor that are cast out.'"

The consensus was that a Jew who is antireligious and lives in Israel does not sever the umbilical cord to historic Judaism, for his language, his idiom, his festivities, and his thoughts derive from it; but a Jew who switched to another religion cut himself off from the national past of his people.

"I have not the least doubt that Brother Daniel will love Israel," Justice Silberg said. "This he has proved. But this brother's love will be from without—the love of a brother far away. He will not be a true part of this Jewish world."

The monk bowed to the verdict. He returned to his monastery on Mount Carmel and became an Israeli by naturalization.

6

Shove and Pull

*"No fewer than 113,000 Jews were
actually in the country illegally."*

*...housands of Jews were smuggled into Israel prior to
...dependence (left). Above, a newcomer from Kurdistan.*

Today every fifth or sixth Jew in the world is a citizen of the Jewish State. There are nearly 2.5 million Jews in Israel, roughly the same number as in New York City and its suburbs. Israelis now constitute the third largest Jewish community in the world. They hope shortly to edge out the Soviet Union for second place. Overtaking the United States with its 6 million Jews is still a dream.

The whole thing developed practically from scratch, well within the space of a human lifetime. There are citizens of Israel who remember when 99.5 per cent of the Jewish people were still scattered around the world. Just before the turn of the century, when David Ben-Gurion was preparing for his *bar mitzvah* in Plonsk, Poland, there were only 50,000 Jews in Palestine. The Holy Land was then a province of the Turkish Empire.

Those 50,000 Jews were by no means the embryo of the Jewish national renaissance. They weren't even an integrated society. They lived in self-segregated communities according to their ethnic origins. They spoke the languages and wore the garb of their pilgrim ancestors who had trickled into the Holy Land over the centuries from Europe, North Africa, and the Middle East. One group had little intercourse with another.

Mostly they dedicated themselves to the service of God. The men spent days and nights in houses of worship and Torah study. They worshiped in a variety of traditions and accents. But they all prayed for the same thing—the coming of the Messiah, a scion of King David,

Ein Harod, an early kibbutz, *was founded in 1921.*

to lead the dispersed Jews proudly back to their redeemed ancestral homeland.

Jews in the dispersion who yearned for the same miracle piously dropped pennies, kopecks, piasters, and drachmas into collection boxes to support their brethren in Palestine. They regarded the Palestinians as a religious elite who maintained a foothold on the holy soil pending the coming of the Messiah.

In Palestine there were also small pockets of worldly Jews. They were mainly recent arrivals from Russia who were regarded by the pious and the mystics as heretics. They preached that national emancipation need not wait for a signal from Heaven. They had immigrated after the pogroms of the 1880's, which marked the end of relative religious tolerance in czarist Russia. They were Israel's "Mayflower Pilgrims."

They laid the foundations for much of modern Israel. City-bred for the most part, they became farmers in Palestine for idealistic reasons. Their goal was to rejuvenate the land and the people. They started the first Jewish agricultural villages, including Petah Tikvah, Rishon le Zion, Zichron Yaakov, and Gedera. They planted vineyards and instituted the wine cellars whose products now grace tables in Europe and America. They pioneered the citrus production, which is to this day Israel's staple industry.

There was no United Jewish Appeal in those days to help finance them, but Baron Edmond de Rothschild of Paris took some of the colonies under his wing. Despite the baron's generosity, many former ghetto Jews couldn't quite make a go of it on the farms. Some moved to Jaffa, then the principal harbor city, and went into business. Others returned to Europe or moved on to the United States.

A major turning point in the destiny of the country came in 1897 when Dr. Herzl created the World Zionist Organization. It transformed Jewish redemption into a dynamic movement that mobilized international diplomatic, political, financial, and other resources. When Dr. Herzl said at the first World Zionist Congress in Basel, Switzerland, that the Jewish State would rise in fifty years, most Jews thought he was crazy.

He erred, it turned out, by nine months.

In those fifty years the number of Jewish settlers in Palestine increased thirteenfold, reaching 650,000. It was not the pull of Zion alone that brought them. They were also shoved. The shove was supplied by a succession of anti-Semites in Eastern and Central Europe. Had they not cracked the whip, there would be no State of Israel today.

In 1903 Russians raided Jewish homes in Kishinev to the tolling of church bells, ferreted terrified inhabitants from hiding places in garrets and cellars, gouged out eyes, drove nails through skulls, dropped babies from windows of upper stories, raped, plundered, and burned.

So the tide to Palestine swelled.

There were further orgies of bloodshed after the failure of the Russian Revolution of 1905. This time the principal targets were Jewish workers who had been involved in the abortive emancipation movement.

So a new element—Socialist-oriented Jews—joined the flow to Palestine. The 35,000 to 40,000 refugees who immigrated from Russia in the years from 1905 to the outbreak of World War I were devoted Zionists. Otherwise they would have gone with the mainstream of Russian refugees to the United States. Most of them were single; some were young couples. They included many teen-agers who interrupted their studies in Europe to build a new society in Palestine, where Jews would be masters of their own fate.

In that stream were adolescents who were to go on to become Israel's first three Prime Ministers. Typically, their lives in Russia had been tinged by persecution.

David Gruen, who later Hebraized his name to Ben-Gurion, came in 1906 from Plonsk at a time when Poland was part of Russia. He had hidden arms in his father's house for defense in case the pogroms should reach his community.

Moshe Shertok, later Sharett, arrived from Kherson the same year, not long after an infamous massacre in a synagogue during a Yom Kippur service.

Levi Shkolnik, later Eshkol, came in 1914 from Kiev. He recalled discussions in the darkness of his home behind boarded-up windows in which his family weighed whether they should flee to Palestine or the United States. Three years after Levi left for Palestine his father, who remained in Russia, was killed in the infamous Petlura pogroms.

The wave of young immigrants from 1905 to 1914 brought not only the figures who led the country well into the first stages of statehood, but also many of the characteristics, mental attitudes, and values that have made it unique. This influx is retrospectively called the Second Aliyah to distinguish it from the first wave of nationally conscious immigration that followed the pogroms in the 1880's.

The farms of the First Aliyah were worked mainly by Arab labor. Jews were employed only in the wine cellars of Rishon le Zion and Zichron Yaakov, and then only because there was no alternative. Wine produced by non-Jews isn't kosher.

With the pioneers of the Second Aliyah, however, manual labor was an ideology. The heroes and heroines of that era were the callus-handed, dry-haired, prematurely wizened former students who contracted malaria draining infested marshes or broke their backs clearing away rocks to reclaim long-neglected soil for Jewish farming.

They were poor and underfed but they scarcely complained. They made a credo out of their hardships. They held that one didn't work for material advantages, only for spiritual aims, to prepare the ground for future generations and future shiploads of Jewish immigrants. Actually only a small minority measured up to the altruistic ideal, but they were recognized as the elite. Their standards set the tone of values for decades.

The pioneers' contempt for money dovetailed with their desire to break away from the traditions of ghetto life in Europe, where Jews had been a nation of shopkeepers.

In the atmosphere created by the pioneers, businessmen in Palestinian cities were a despised group. Jewish entrepreneurs accordingly maintained, perhaps even convinced themselves, that they were really in business for patriotic reasons—to develop the country and increase its capacity to absorb Jewish immigrants. They pretended that their profits were a side matter for which they really couldn't be held responsible.

That is a clue to a puzzle that has mystified many. Jews throughout the world are renowned for their business acumen. One would have expected that business would be a field in which the Jewish State would excel. The opposite has been true. Israel has excelled in the most unexpected areas, but not in business.

Today the climate for entrepreneurs has improved. Now that Israel is striving to achieve economic independence and rid herself of the need for foreign aid and charity, industrialists and bankers are regarded with more respect. But the early discouragement, during the period when it was considered unpatriotic to make money, handicapped the business world. Overcoming that handicap is taking time.

Another deficiency traceable to the pioneering days is gastronomic. The Second Aliyah settlers couldn't afford good food and dismissed it as a material matter unimportant in a spiritual society. Here, too, the credo coincided with the wish to break from the European past. It was part of a revolt against the important place of food in a typical East European Jewish household.

The void was partly filled by North African and Middle Eastern dishes. The children of European immigrants found such dishes cheap and tasty in restaurants run by Arabs or by Jews from Islamic countries. Grilled meats and highly seasoned pastes of sesame seeds or chickpeas became popular. *Felafel,* ground chickpea balls deeply fried and served in pancake-shaped flat bread with finely sliced raw vegetables and highly spiced sauces, became a national dish. Lately, however, the European kitchen has been making a comeback, largely under the impact of tourists' criticism of unimaginative cooking.

The impact of the Second Aliyah has thus gradually blurred as Israel has developed, but it has certainly left its imprint. Its spirit and traditions, but happily not its poverty, have been most faithfully preserved in the *kibbutzim,* the collective farms where there is no money-making. Members work to the best of their ability and receive housing, food, clothing, entertainment, education, medical care, and all other services according to their needs, regardless of what they contribute.

Moshavim, villages where settlers have separate farmsteads but develop them cooperatively, were also a creation of the Second Aliyah. This system has become a model for a good number of developing countries in Asia and Africa.

Many important institutions, including the trade unions, were founded by the Second Aliyah. In a way the Second Aliyah even laid the foundations for the Israeli defense forces.

Jewish property in the first decade of the century was guarded by Arab watchmen. Some Second Aliyah settlers pressed for a change. One of them was David Ben-Gurion, then a wavy-haired young plowman in Sejera, in Galilee.

When he proposed that the settlers dismiss the Arab watchmen and guard their flocks and corn fields themselves, old-timers said he must be out of his mind. They wanted to remain on friendly terms with their neighbors, who were capable of riding into Sejera and massacring all its inhabitants in a day. Why risk whipping up resentment and recrimination, they asked with undeniable logic.

Young Ben-Gurion was already a persuasive speaker. He said he wanted friendly relations with the Arabs no less than anyone else. But if Palestine was to become a center of Jewish national rebirth, he went on, the Jews would have to stop relying on hired bayonets.

He won the argument. The Arab watchmen were fired and replaced by Jews. Then the old-timers' warnings proved right. The dismissed watchmen murdered some replacements. A blood feud ensued.

But in the perspective of history, of course, Mr. Ben-Gurion was right. The Jewish watchmen in time formed a national association called Hashomer. Hashomer evolved into the Haganah. In 1948 the Haganah was transformed into the Israeli defense forces. Without that evolution the history of the country might have been quite different.

Many Second Aliyah immigrants who remained Russian subjects found themselves enemy aliens when World War I broke out. The Turkish rulers of Palestine confronted them with the choice of expulsion or accepting Ottoman citizenship. Some, including Moshe

Sharett, became Turks and joined the sultan's army. Others, such as David Ben-Gurion, chose expulsion, joined units of the British army under Lord Allenby, and fought their way back to Palestine. Meanwhile, the Jewish population of the Holy Land receded to what it had been at the time of Ben-Gurion's *bar mitzvah*.

During the war, hopes for a Jewish State received a tremendous boost when the British government issued the Balfour Declaration of 1917, in which Britain's Foreign Secretary pledged his government's readiness to facilitate the establishment in Palestine of a national home for the Jewish people.

Considering the excitement the declaration generated and the fact that the British took over Palestine from the Turks, the rate of Jewish immigration after the war was highly disappointing. Fewer than 8,000 came a year. This human material was the finest, however. The settlers were mostly young proletarians who had been prepared in Zionist training camps in Europe for pioneering in Palestine. They joined *kibbutzim* and *moshavim* and were ready to do any kind of work. They drained marshes and built roads. But they were too few.

Then the anti-Semitic whip cracked in Europe again. Immigration nearly doubled in 1925. The following year it reached a record 35,000.

This time the lash was swung by Poland, newly emancipated after the collapse of the Russian Empire. The Warsaw government enacted measures excluding Jews from many trades. Consequently, the flow of young Zionists was reinforced by older people with families, businessmen and artisans with modest means to invest. They settled mostly in Tel Aviv. They entered commerce and started small factories, producing soap, textiles, jams, and cement. The pressure for housing created a real estate boom, but the artificial prosperity quickly burst and was followed by a severe depression. Jews began to leave. During the three years starting in 1926, emigration exceeded immigration.

Altogether, about 120,000 Jews settled in Palestine in the half century from 1880 to 1930. They were part of a mass migration of 3 million refugees from Eastern Europe. The West was wide open to immigrants in those years and offered great opportunities for the Jews' talents in commerce, industry, and the sciences.

The 96 per cent of the fugitives who decided to go west included the grandparents and great-grandparents of most American Jews. The 4 per cent who spurned the glitter, detached themselves from the mainstream, and went south to Palestine, were committed to an ideal. Whether they went to drain swamps or open soda fountains in Tel Aviv, they shared a passionate consciousness of their mission—to create a society where being a Jew would be no problem.

From the 1930's onward, immigrants who didn't necessarily share this sense of mission came in growing numbers. They included Jews who would have preferred to assimilate in Germany and other European lands if Hitler had let them.

Prosperous Western countries were by then severely limiting the entry of immigrants. There was no place else for them to go. So they went to Palestine.

But the gates of the Jewish national home were by no means wide open either. Under pressure from the Arabs, who were becoming restive at the growing strength of the Jewish minority, the British government set quotas restricting Jewish immigration. The Jewish community never accepted the restrictions, so the Haganah and the Irgun Zvai Leumi, a rival Jewish underground group, infiltrated refugees into Palestine by stealth.

After Israel became independent in 1948, it was revealed that no fewer than 113,000 Jews were actually in the country illegally. That's not a misprint! Of the 650,000 Jewish citizens at the time, 113,000 were illegal.

Most of the illegal refugees were transported from Europe in leaky old vessels that included at least one former Hudson River Dayliner. They were transferred to rowboats near Jewish coastal settlements and husky young Palestinians waded into the water in the darkness to meet them and carry them ashore. Buses and trucks whisked them inland, where they were quickly dispersed. Some of the vessels were intercepted by the British navy after fierce, bloody, and sometimes fatal resistance. The passengers were deported or imprisoned.

Thousands of other refugees were smuggled into Palestine across the borders of neighboring Arab states.

Subtler devices were also employed. The Maccabee Sports Organization promoted World Jewish Olympic Games in Tel Aviv. The sports-minded British issued visitors' visas for thousands of entrants.

Some entrants didn't know a pole vault from a safe-deposit box. They melted into the population as soon as they arrived.

Bona fide Palestinian Jews went to Europe, got married, returned with spouses, and promptly divorced. Similar weddings were arranged in Palestine between citizens and tourists wishing to settle in the country. The divorce rate among Palestinian Jews in the 1930's was five or six times greater than normal.

At the close of World War II, Palestinian Jewish units of the British forces in Europe effectively serviced the refugees' underground railway. They liberally provided British supplies, British transport, British uniforms, and false British movement orders for young displaced Jews. Every home-leave party led by a Palestinian Jew included refugees traveling with false papers.

One sergeant major almost had a conniption.

His home-leave party was lined up before him. At his command the men snapped to attention. He then commanded: "At ease."

Half the men joined their hands behind their backs properly and slid their right feet to the side. To the sergeant major's horror, the other half slid their right feet forward, as they did in the Polish army.

Luckily there were no British officers in sight. Signals were promptly flashed through the underground warning Haganah agents that they had better put the displaced persons through some basic British drills before they were dressed in British uniforms.

The refugees who received precious immigration certificates from the Zionist Organization out of the legal quota or who were smuggled into Palestine by the Zionist underground didn't necessarily share the ideals of their rescuers. Their contribution to the development of the country was nevertheless substantial.

Gifted men thrown out of universities and hospitals by the Nazis gave a tremendous boost to science, medicine, and hygiene. Musicians expelled from the finest ensembles in Europe formed an orchestra of international repute. The first violins of four eminent European orchestras were in the string ensemble of the Palestine Symphony Orchestra, which made its debut in Tel Aviv in 1936.

So many professionals and intellectuals poured in that they couldn't all be absorbed in their specialized fields. Some became farmers. They introduced new standards of efficiency. Bankers, industrialists, and businessmen modernized economic life. Under the impact of the immigrants from Germany, occupation and education began to assume some importance in terms of social status.

But the pioneering ideals remained supreme and the old Eastern European leadership retained authority.

The Germans scarcely sought leadership. The Zionist idea of creating a new Jewish identity didn't appeal to them at all. They clung to their German culture and values and remained insulated. They read German books and magazines, flocked to see German-language movies, and talked German with one another. Many never took the trouble to learn Hebrew.

Even in tropical summers they continued having their big meals of schnitzel and potatoes at midday as they had done in Central Europe. They packed cafés at 5 P.M. for their coffee with *schlagsahne* and strudel.

Emigrants from Germany who became fully integrated in political life were exceptions. They were mostly men and women who had been active Zionists in prewar Germany. The majority were too rigid to fit into the regular parties. Some formed an ethnic political party called Aliyah Hadasha (New Immigration), which functioned until the establishment of Israel, when it merged with other groups to form the Progressive party.

Another sidestream in the community during the period of British rule consisted of Orientals—Jews from the Islamic countries of North Africa and the Middle East. Unlike the German refugees, they were intensely conscious Jews, deeply traditional and with a strong mystic attachment to the ancestral homeland. But they were self-segregated. Political Zionism and the movement to develop a new Jewish identity were European. The Orientals were not part of it.

The picture changed kaleidoscopically after independence in 1948. Minutes after the Provisional State Council proclaimed on May 14 that Israel was a sovereign nation, all British legislation restricting Jewish immigration was erased from the statute books.

On the state's fourth birthday, the 650,000 founding citizens were already a minority in their country. By the end of the first decade of independence, they accounted for only one-third of the citizenry. The Oriental Jews, who made up 11 per cent of the Jewish population of

Israel in 1948, became a majority.

Shiploads of immigrants were already at sea on the Friday afternoon that the state was being proclaimed. The following morning the first ship reached the port of Tel Aviv in the midst of an Egyptian aerial bombardment.

The Jewish Agency, the executive arm of the Zionist Organization, had prepared eight hostels to accommodate the arrivals until they found places to live in towns, villages, or collective settlements. It was a joke. The hostels overflowed in a few days.

The Agency then took over barracks abandoned by the British army. It hurriedly cleaned them up and pressed them into service as clearance camps.

The refugees were settled mainly in houses abandoned during the war by Arabs who fled to enemy territory. More than 100,000 Jewish immigrants filled the Arab ghost cities of Jaffa, Ramla, and Lydda, and the former Arab quarters of mixed cities like Jerusalem, Haifa, Safed, and Tiberias. The supply of housing then dried up. At the end of Israel's first year there wasn't a hovel or dank cellar unoccupied. And there were still 112,000 immigrants in the clearance camps.

Large-scale housing projects were under construction but they couldn't keep up with the feverish pace of immigration. The clearance camps burst at the seams. As barracks overflowed, tents were pitched around them. There were races between trucks bringing immigrants and others bringing tents. Sometimes the immigrants reached the camps first and the tents were pitched over their heads.

Slowing down immigration was out of the question. The early arrivals were women, children, and elderly men from camps in Cyprus, where the British had detained illegal entrants intercepted at sea. The British wouldn't let the men of military age leave Cyprus during the Arab-Israeli war, lest they strengthen the Israeli army. They were permitted to leave only after the truce. By early 1949 the last camp in Cyprus was empty. How could those people have been asked to wait?

Immigrants during Israel's first year also included 75,000 people from displaced-persons camps in Germany, Austria, and Italy. Could they have been asked to remain patiently in those graveyards until houses were built for them in the homeland?

Immigrants were also coming from Bulgaria, Rumania, Poland,

A frightened and bewildered new immigrant, photographed just after her arrival at Haifa

103

Czechoslovakia, Yemen, Libya, Turkey, and Iran. There was no way of knowing how long those Communist or Moslem countries would keep their gates open. The Jews had to be evacuated while the going was good.

So tent cities kept mushrooming on the Israeli landscape. I shall never forget a visit to a typical camp late in 1949.

I accompanied some ladies from Tel Aviv who brought toys for Chanukah, the Feast of Lights, to the kindergarten of Kfar Yona in the Sharon Plain. It was a dreary day. Rows of tents stretched up a gentle slope and over the crest. Each was surrounded by a low earthen embankment to keep out the floodwaters that streamed through the plain from the hills of Ephraim to the Mediterranean. Neatly dressed children with their hair carefully parted stood on the fragile dikes watching us.

A middle-aged woman invited the party into her tent. Incongruously it contained heavy carved pieces of furniture that had obviously come from a fine European household. An older woman lay in a massive bed under a pile of blankets. She apologized in German for not getting up. She was ill.

The top of the tent was patched. Vessels were laid out on the ground to catch the rainwater that leaked through the weak spots in the canvas before it turned the earthen floor to mud.

Later we met the Jewish Agency official in charge of the camp. The ladies from Tel Aviv assailed him in fury. Why should human beings be kept in such conditions? Why weren't the women moved to a better tent?

The official threw out his hands.

"There are many such cases," he replied. "We have no more tents."

He said the women had been asked to move in with other families. They had refused, preferring to remain in a leaky tent. After all the regimentation they had experienced in European camps during and after the war, they wanted to retain some privacy.

We returned to our taxis dejectedly and headed toward the camp gate feeling that we had seen human beings debased to the limit.

At the gate we passed a truck. A man in a peaked cap stood beside it. He was arguing agitatedly with a camp official.

The official was explaining that there was no room in the camp. He was pointing down the road to the next one.

The new arrival was on the verge of hysteria. He didn't want to move anymore. As we drove off to Tel Aviv, we left the wretched man fighting bitterly to get into one of those miserable tents.

It may sound incredible but conditions got worse—much worse—before they got better. The winter of 1949–50 was the most severe that old-time Israelis can recall. It was the winter that Knesset sessions had to be canceled because snowdrifts marooned Jerusalem. The whole country was blanketed with snow.

Emigrants from tropical countries had never seen snow before. Primitive Yemenites believed it was another of God's mysterious blessings.

Flown from the Dark Ages to modern times in the space of a few hours, they had thought they were experiencing the fulfillment of the biblical prophecy of redemption "on eagles' wings." When they awoke one morning and found the ground covered with a strange white substance, the Bible again came to mind.

"Manna!" they exclaimed ecstatically. "Manna!"

Children rushed into the snow in their frozen bare feet. "Warm! Warm!" they called out to their friends.

But they soon learned that the fall from heaven was no godsend. It was a terrifying winter. Hundreds didn't survive it.

With refugees continuing to stream into the camps faster than they could be moved out, the situation was becoming desperate. No light was visible at the end of the tunnel.

There was a severe food shortage. Practically everything was rationed. People got less than one pound of meat a month and two eggs a week. Poultry was issued only several times a year, on the eve of festivals. Some city dwellers took their rations live and kept chickens on the balconies of their apartments to get an occasional extra egg.

At the same time, paradoxically, good cultivable land that could ease the shortage was lying fallow and more than 10 per cent of the country's manpower was idle, living on charity in encampments that were in effect no longer clearance centers. The inhabitants were settling down for indefinite stays.

The authorities reappraised the situation. They decided that for reasons of finance and morale, family heads in the camps must be required to work to feed and clothe their dependents.

In the spring of 1950 drastic reforms were introduced. Until then immigrants had been kept in concentrated areas. Camps had been located wherever accommodations were available, usually in former British army bases. When the camps filled up, the authorities considered it more expedient to enlarge them than to start new ones, because they could thus make fuller use of existing schools, clinics, and other facilities.

Under the new policy the main criterion for locating camps was the availability of jobs. In 1950 a big immigration from Iraq started. The arrivals were dispersed in areas where there was land to be cultivated, houses to be built, and work to be done in factories. They were accommodated in tents, but instead of food and clothing they were offered loans to start businesses or learn trades.

Pressure was put on the inmates of the old camps to move. They were required to pay for their families' food. The sick and the aged were concentrated in special camps where they continued to be cared for. The kitchens in the other clearance camps were closed down. There were protests. There were fights. But the difficult mission was accomplished. The old camps were gradually depopulated to the extent that their remaining inhabitants could earn livelihoods in the vicinities.

The new policy, moreover, tended to promote the absorption of immigrants among old settlers. Instead of living in segregation as wards of the Jewish Agency, supported by contributions raised by United Jewish Appeals abroad, the immigrants began getting services from government departments and municipalities like other citizens. They thus began to blend into the mainstream of economic, social, and political life.

In due course living conditions in the camps improved. Tents were gradually replaced by corrugated-metal shacks, abodes of asbestos or wood, and canvas-walled huts with plank floors. But as the stream of immigrants continued unabated, the housing gap kept widening. By the spring of 1952 there were 250,000 citizens—more than one-sixth of the population—still living in camps.

One had to be either stouthearted or apathetic to stick it out under such conditions. Many were neither. Thousands lined up at Canadian or Latin American consulates for visas. Thousands returned to their countries of origin.

By the end of 1952 the European concentration-camp survivors had already been totally ingathered. The immigration from Yemen and Iraq was complete. The gates of the Communist countries were closed so that Jews in those countries couldn't leave. Jews in the West weren't interested in leaving. A tin shack on a Galilee hilltop or a canvas-walled hut in the Mediterranean Plain was hardly a magnet for a Jew who wasn't desperate. Accordingly, immigration fell off in 1953 to 10,000. That same year 20,000 emigrated.

The slump in immigration continued until late 1954 and gave the authorities a breathing spell in which to narrow the absorption gap.

Preference was given to absorption in agriculture. That was consistent with the traditional Zionist aspiration of tying ingathered Jews to the soil. It was, moreover, advocated by defense forces GHQ, which wanted the open spaces between the Hebron bulge and the Gaza Strip populated. The economists wanted the outlying areas cultivated to ease the food shortage.

Immigrants were consequently offered land, livestock, equipment, and homesteads at giveaway terms. They were guaranteed employment in public works or afforestation until their farms yielded a livelihood.

The response was disappointing. Fewer than 10,000 took up the offer. The majority insisted upon living within easier reach of movies and neon lights. Some moved to houses in urban areas, but the bulk remained in the camps.

When the big wave of Moroccan and Tunisian immigration began late in 1954, there were still 170,000 immigrants in the encampments.

The push that propelled North African Jews toward Israel was the Moroccan and Tunisian struggle against the French for independence. The Jews didn't relish the thought of becoming subjects of the bey of Tunis or the king of Morocco after the French withdrew.

There were exceedingly wealthy Jews in North Africa, but they, the intellectuals, and the middle-class Jews with means of their own for the most part crossed the Mediterranean to start new lives in France. Others loath to part from businesses or property chose to stick it out and hoped for a fair deal from the new rulers.

Left for the Jewish Agency to mobilize for Israel were the poor, the semiliterate, the unskilled, the peddlers, and the lower middle class.

In Jerusalem the authorities were determined not to allow the new influx to flood the camps again. So they undertook a reappraisal of the whole situation, a really agonizing one.

They decided for the first time since the establishment of Israel to exercise selectivity in immigration. The Law of the Return indeed provided that every Jew could make his home in Israel unless he was liable to endanger public health, security, or peace. Every Jew turning up at the border had to be admitted. However, the Law of the Return didn't require the government to buy a steamship ticket for every Jewish pauper.

To the extent that entire North African villages were brought over, they were taken together with the cripples, the blind, the chronically ill, the aged, and the large families without breadwinners. Otherwise such cases were left behind.

The immigrants were no longer installed in camps. Jewish Agency officials met them aboard ship and offered them a choice of places to live. When they landed, their baggage was already labeled with their Israeli addresses. Buses picked them up and took them directly to their farmsteads or apartments in outlying areas.

When they crossed their thresholds the immigrants found beds and bedding, tables loaded with a week's groceries, and kitchens equipped with essential utensils. Often a welcoming cake baked by a neighbor added a human touch. From their first night in Israel the immigrants ate meals cooked in their own pots. They slept in their own beds. They were home.

But despite the government's selectivity in admitting the immigrants, many former peddlers and small tradesmen from the casbahs weren't cut out to be frontiersmen. Together with their families and belongings they abandoned their far-flung homesteads for city lights. Many moved into condemned houses in slums near the big cities.

However, a good number stuck it out and in due course did well for themselves. They changed the map of Israel, adding scores of new place names in the northern Negev and Lachish.

The North African immigration tapered off after Morocco and Tunisia gained independence and it got harder for Jews to leave. At about the same time Poland and Hungary suddenly unlocked their gates.

Immigrants from the Soviet Union seem well adjusted in a new Israeli housing project.

These two Communist countries had a disproportionate number of Jews in high positions in government, light industry, science, and medicine, for after World War II it hadn't been easy to find untainted intellectuals. Jews obviously couldn't be suspected of Nazi affiliations, so they could safely be given appointments.

Meanwhile, a new generation of Polish and Hungarian intellectuals, too young to have collaborated with the Nazis, matured. They wanted advancement. Jews were in their way.

Both the Polish government (after the rise to power of Wladyslaw Gomulka) and the Hungarian leaders (after the brutal suppression of the 1956 revolt) were insecure. They felt that resentment by anti-Semites of the large number of Jews in high positions was undermining their regimes. Accordingly, they lifted the restrictions on emigration. In 1957 about 30,000 Polish and 8,000 Hungarian Jews entered the State of Israel.

Obviously the Jewish Agency's ship-to-farm policy couldn't be applied to them. The Eastern Europeans possessed professional and technical skills that would be welcomed in many countries. In fact, scouts representing big Western European and American corporations had tried to intercept some of them en route to Israel with offers of contracts.

The brainpower was precious. It was clear that if it was to be kept in Israel and if more was to be encouraged to come, the immigrants would have to be absorbed in developed parts of the country near the sophisticated industries, universities, scientific institutions, libraries, and conservatories of music. Sending them to bleak and dreary development towns or villages would have been carrying egalitarianism to a ridiculous extreme.

So they were accommodated on arrival in hotels. They were given intensive courses in Hebrew, civics, Jewish history, and other subjects that would help them integrate. Then they were provided with apartments in special housing projects in the Mediterranean Plain.

The preferential accommodations of the Europeans aggravated another problem. Oriental immigrants had grumbled all along that the Israeli Establishment, which was predominantly of European stock, was discriminating against them. They felt that immigrants who could kibitz in Yiddish with a Jewish Agency official got all the breaks.

Now they saw their suspicions blatantly confirmed.

Officials explained that the preferences were accorded on the basis of professional criteria, not ethnic ones. Intellectuals and professionals from North Africa would be entitled to the same treatment. The rub was that the North Africans who would qualify weren't in Israel. They had gone to France or remained in Morocco and Tunisia.

The Orientals wouldn't buy it. Their fury simmered. As men sulking in camps and slums watched later arrivals from Europe move into the new housing projects, their wrath grew. In the summer of 1959 it erupted.

The first ethnic riot occurred in the Wadi Salib quarter, near the Haifa harbor, a former Arab slum packed with North African Jews who had quit homesteads in development areas. It was touched off by a false rumor that a resident of the quarter, who had been shot by a policeman while resisting arrest, had died of his wounds.

Hundreds marched out of the slum to protest the shooting. They were led by men carrying Israeli flags smeared with blood. They soon got out of hand. They overturned cars, tossed rocks through windows of shops and banks, wrecked a café and a restaurant, and smashed clubrooms of the Haifa Labor Council and Mapai, the ruling party.

A few days later North Africans in Migdal Haemek, in Galilee, smashed furniture and windows of the Labor Council offices, demanding higher pay for relief work in afforestation.

In Beersheba, North Africans for no apparent reason broke windows of shops and cafés and tried to set fire to the city tax office.

Whatever the direct cause of each local disorder, it was apparent that the eruptions reflected the bitterness of the Orientals against social and economic inequality. Fair-minded Western Jews acknowledged that the bitterness was legitimate.

The storm soon blew over. Only a few hundred persons had actually been involved in the violence, and they were repudiated by most Orientals.

But the disorders served a purpose. They shook Western Jews out of their complacency and made them realize how dangerous the social and economic stratification of the citizenry along easily identifiable ethnic lines could become.

7

The Twain *Shall* Meet

"They couldn't conceive of Jews who were polygamous and wore burnooses."

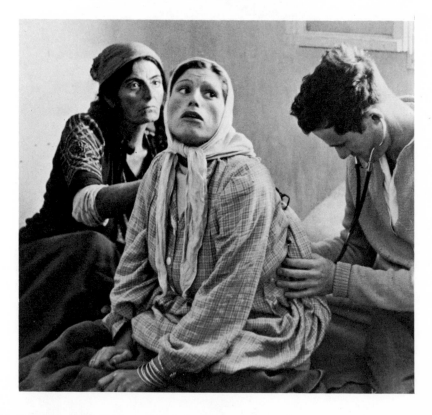

At left is a modern Tower of Babel. Above, a new immigrant to Israel undergoes her first medical examination.

*Immigrants from Hadhramaut arrive in Israel as part of
a project called Operation Magic Carpet.*

Aʟʟ ɪɴ ᴀʟʟ, the reception of the Orientals has been ambivalent. They're wanted, badly. What the Jewish State needs above everything else is Jewish people. Arab citizens of Israel have been begetting babies more than twice as fast as Jews. If Jewish reinforcements don't come from abroad and the birthrates remain unchanged, the Arabs will achieve in due course via the delivery room what they failed to accomplish in three attempts on the battlefield. They'll submerge the Jewish State.

So Oriental Jews who streamed to Israel, usually with substantial broods, have been eagerly raked in. Demography aside, assembling scattered Jews in the homeland is the heart of Israel's mission. It fulfills biblical prophecies of "the ingathering of exiles." And nothing dramatizes the fulfillment of the prophecies so vividly as outlandish types from obscure places like the Hadhramaut, Cochin, or Kurdistan shuffling down the gangway to the homeland.

Ideologically, therefore, the Oriental Jews have been embraced like long-lost brothers. In their hearts, however, many Western Jews have found it hard to accept them. They couldn't quite conceive of Jews who were polygamous and wore burnooses, who spoke Arabic or Ladino but didn't know a word of Yiddish, who drank araq but never touched borscht, blintzes, or gefilte fish.

Straight-backed dusky women in bangles, ornamented robes, and heavily embroidered leggings didn't fit their image of *Yiddishe Mamas* at all, although they no doubt looked more like the original Hebrew matriarchs than do the Jewish matrons of Europe and the United States.

It took time for some Western Jews to accept the idea that what is regarded in Europe and the United States as typically Jewish isn't necessarily so; that their own culture and heritage has in fact been only a variant of Jewishness developed in a particular atmosphere.

In addition, there is the belief that the Jewish State will be doomed unless it enjoys substantial moral and intellectual superiority over its Arab neighbors to compensate for their advantages in manpower, arms, and wealth. So there was some forehead wrinkling over the integration into Israel of Jews raised in Arab societies. Would they dilute technical, moral, and educational standards? Would they Levantinize the country? Would they jeopardize its survival?

In the light of the six-day victory over Egypt, Jordan, and Syria in June, 1967, those doubts seem to have been groundless. Half of General Rabin's army consisted of immigrants or the sons of immigrants from Moslem countries. Many of them were decorated for heroism in the armored corps, the infantry, and the paratroopers.

But when the primitive types first came as immigrants, they certainly hadn't inspired confidence. They came with a mystic enthusiasm that was touching but utterly unrealistic. They believed they were experiencing the messianic redemption for which they and their ancestors had prayed. They believed in miracles.

Little wonder. Strange men had appeared in their midst. They had ferreted them out of slums and caves and shepherded them to airfields. They were then transported to the Promised Land "on the wings of an eagle," as the ancient Hebrew prophets had foretold.

They had assumed that the wonders would surely continue after they reached the sacred soil. They had expected that in some inscrutable manner their poverty, backwardness, and trachoma would automatically disappear and that they would be transformed into well-to-do and respected citizens. It had never entered their minds that advancement in their new world would depend on work—harder work than they had ever done before.

It was pathetic. In the Jewish State, instead of finding themselves part of the prestige class akin to the Moslem elite in the old countries, their status was lower than ever. In the Moslem countries there had always been some Arabs more backward and primitive than they were. In Israel there was nobody lower. They were at the very bottom of the social and economic ladder.

In the old countries they had been called Jews, never anything else. Oriental Jews had never held philosophical discussions about what being Jewish meant. They took it for granted like a male takes it for granted that he is a man and a female is a woman. The Orientals were never hyphenated Jews like Europeans or Americans. But in the Jewish State they found themselves designated for the first time in their lives as Moroccans, Yemenites, Kurds, or Iraqis. It hurt. It smacked of rejection.

Most immigrants from North Africa and the Middle East came without the skills needed for advancement in a modern society. Naturally they became the "hewers of wood and drawers of water." If you encountered a road gang in the early 1950's, you could safely wager that the men swinging the pickaxes and spreading the tar were Orientals and the man in the saddle of the steamroller was of Western stock. Executives, officials, and foremen were predominantly of European origin; their errand boys and scrubwomen were Orientals.

It could hardly have been otherwise, but the situation disturbed thoughtful Israelis. They feared that a society in which well-fed Jews of Western stock occupied the comfortable homes and positions of authority, while Orientals crowded the slums and monopolized the menial jobs, could explode from within. The rift could be as tragic as the split of the Hebrews into two nations after Solomon's death.

The Oriental Jews had never dreamed of protesting discrimination in those Moslem countries where they had been barred from owning land, excluded from certain occupations, and denied equality before the law. They had shrugged off abuses and insults fatalistically as part of the divine curse of Jewish dispersion.

But in Israel they began to react vigorously against their inferior status, and they found that the authorities were sensitive to their grievances. The authorities were there to help. There was prejudice, certainly, but when it conflicted with ideological commitments, ideology prevailed.

So the relationship that evolved between the established community and the Oriental immigrants was like that between a Jewish mother—a typically overanxious one—and her children. There were frictions, exasperations, and explosions; but the basic kinship was never forgotten.

Historically, the conspicuous absence of Orientals from the ruling element was due to their own wishes. During the periods of Turkish and British rule, the Orientals already living in Palestine hadn't wanted to collaborate with European Jews. They had little interest in the Zionist aim of creating a new type of Jew and a new society. On the contrary, their desire was to live their old-fashioned, patriarchal, and segregated way of life more fully, freely, and securely. Only a few exceptions sought to penetrate the westernized society. The leadership of the Jewish community was thus almost exclusively European.

When Israel attained sovereignty in 1948, that leadership became the backbone of the administration. It was overwhelmed by the task of providing homes, food, jobs, education, hospitals, and other facilities for a spiraling population, and it determined to be fair to Europeans and Orientals alike.

However, officials naturally thought in terms of their own backgrounds, experiences, and tastes. For example, food rations were devised according to Western eating habits. Orientals received rations of jam, hard cheeses, margarine, and other items they didn't know what to do with. The authorities, on the other hand, were totally unaware of certain spices that the Orientals felt were vital to a meal.

Houses were built with the needs of a typical Western family in mind. They were too small for Oriental broods. Schools were organized also along Western lines.

Official policy in the camps was "first in, first out." Exceptions were made only on medical grounds or for immigrants who had been active Zionist workers in their countries of origin. The principle seemed fair enough, but the practice favored Jews from Western countries, where there had been Zionist organizations. Secondly, the doctors who signed recommendations for urgent housing on grounds of health were Westerners. The Oriental Jews suspected prejudice.

So all in all, immigrants from North Africa and the Middle East unhappily experienced feelings of resentment, frustration, and inferiority in the Jewish State. Those feelings were diluted, oddly enough, by the armed forces. It was odd because the ethnic gap is as pronounced in the armed forces as anywhere else in the country, maybe even more so. The rifleman on patrol, the infantryman slogging over the landscape, or the soldier loading shells is generally an Oriental. There are few Orientals at the controls of warplanes. There has never been one on the General Staff.

When Mr. Ben-Gurion was Prime Minister, he ordered that if Oriental and Western applicants for a government job were equally competent, the Oriental should get the appointment. In practice Orientals were given breaks even when they were less than equally qualified. The discrimination-in-reverse went all the way to the top. Men who would not have been considered for Cabinet posts if they had been born in Austria or Poland were appointed ministers precisely because they were born in Syria or Yemen.

Orientals didn't and still don't get such breaks in the armed forces. The General Staff insists that ability and achievement be the sole criteria for advancement. Yet the high command is fully conscious of the army's role as a melting pot. The induction center has often been the first meeting ground between immigrants and the scions of old Israeli families. The command deliberately puts primitive recruits who have to be taught how to use toothbrushes into units with budding scientists, lawyers, musicians, and businessmen.

Getting them to work together, sweat together, march in unison, eat the same food at the same tables, sing the same Hebrew songs, and wear identical uniforms is calculated not only to mold recruits into good soldiers but also to fashion good Israelis.

When units go into the field, their commanding officers lecture the men about battles fought by their ancestors in the same hills and plains back in biblical times. Thus they dramatize to both Oriental and Western youths that their respective branches of Jewry reach back to a common trunk with roots deep in the soil of Israel.

Basic training helps to dilute an underprivileged Israeli's sense of inferiority. Lack of education doesn't handicap a recruit in the early stages of service. An illiterate person can learn to shoot as well as a bookworm, if not better. He can also match the erudite in physical ability, orientation, and courage. He can make friends as easily.

His successes are recognized and rewarded. That recognition, often the first enjoyed by the underprivileged in competition with the advantaged classes, is sweet. It does wonders for morale.

About half the Orientals, including some from the most primitive homes, earn corporals' stripes. Many become sergeants. But even those who remain buck privates to the end of their periods of service enjoy some status. They feel superior to the green recruits. They handle weapons with more confidence.

The ethnic separation begins when the better educated are siphoned out of the units for advanced technical courses or officers' training school. Most Orientals lack qualifications for advancement toward commissions. But complaints of discrimination are rare. By that time the Orientals are convinced of the fairness of the armed forces. They understand that the army must maintain the highest possible standards and that only the most capable should advance toward the top.

Getting young male immigrants from backward countries to appreciate that their own efforts and achievements determine advancement has been an important breakthrough in their psychological preparation for integration into a modern society. It has also taught them to value education as a key to success in the modern world.

Unfortunately, the underprivileged girls don't go through the military experience. Indeed, the law provides for the conscription of women, but Oriental girls tend to marry young and the army doesn't draft married women. Moreover, a large proportion of Oriental girls are Orthodox and claim exemption on religious grounds. In addition, those culturally backward girls who are not exempt are rejected.

GHQ, as mentioned earlier, believes it's better for backward girls to stay home. Illiterate boys find new vistas in military service, which affords them unmatched opportunities for distinction. But girls don't, since female soldiers are used for auxiliary services. The semiliterate therefore could be employed only in cleaning, washing, and cooking. Instead of opening new worlds for them, military service would intensify their feelings of inequality.

Men, tens of thousands of them, have acquired skills during their service that have enabled them to make better livings as civilians. Conscripts receive one-tenth the pay of regular soldiers, so rather than employing regulars for technical jobs, it paid to keep training conscripts as mechanics, storekeepers, cooks, telephone repairmen, and other specialists. Since the period of military service was limited and the training period was often long, the turnover was great.

The policy changed after the 1967 war because manpower needs were greater. Today there is more reliance on regulars and graduates of military boarding schools that train youngsters as technicians before they begin their service. Nevertheless, the armed forces' role in grooming the underprivileged for a better life is unmatched.

The new spirit, outlook, and skills that many Orientals have absorbed during their military service have permeated their families and neighbors and have been a major influence in lifting their communities out of apathy.

Gradually Orientals have become the backbone of the stable industrial force. Their agricultural settlements have prospered. Onetime dwellers in tents or corrugated-metal shacks have attained fairly comfortable middle-class standards. They now own refrigerators, washing machines, and television sets.

Orientals have become functionaries in the lower echelons of government, the trade unions, and the Jewish Agency. A few have reached fairly responsible positions. They are prominent in the police force, which has done a lot to dispel feelings of inferiority. On the day-to-day level the police uniform symbolizes official power.

Small houses originally allocated to the immigrants by the Jewish Agency have been enlarged and modernized as their inhabitants' economic conditions improved. Many Orientals have left their ethnic neighborhoods and acquired homes in Western communities.

As their children went to the same schools as Westerners and played with them, their accents, gestures, and bearing became less distinctive. Consciousness of ethnic differences has diminished in the younger generation. Intermarriages have increased. The countrywide average has reached 15 per cent; in Tel Aviv it has approached 20 per cent.

That's one extreme. At the other there are Orientals whose return to civilian life after military service intensified their bitterness. That happened particularly in times of economic difficulty, when the discharged soldiers didn't get the jobs they believed they were fitted for. Some turned to crime.

The ringleader of the North African eruption in Haifa in 1959 was a demobilized sergeant. He had served with distinction in the army but had failed to get civilian employment he considered appropriate to a former noncom in the Israeli defense forces.

Fortunately such Orientals have been the exception, but obviously the gap between Orientals and Westerners can't be closed in a single generation. It's millennia old.

The Jewish dispersion had already begun in the days of King Solomon, when individuals left Palestine for other countries of the Middle East for business reasons. The first major breakup occurred in the sixth century B.C., when Palestine was overrun by Nebuchadnezzar, who carried off nearly the entire population to exile in Babylonia.

Many exiles prospered in Babylonia. When Cyrus the Great conquered the region and permitted the Jews to return to Palestine, the prosperous ones chose to stay with the fleshpots. As during the modern return to Zion, the well-to-do Babylonian Jews prayed for Jerusalem, visited the Holy Land, and liberally financed the poorer Jews to rebuild it. But they remained Babylonians. They stayed where they were through Persian, Greek, Mongolian, Turkish, British, and Arab rules until the Arabs, smarting from their defeat in Palestine in 1948, made life unbearable for them.

The Second Jewish Commonwealth in Palestine was broken up by the Romans. That dispersion lasted nearly two thousand years. The Romans scattered the Jews all over their Empire, from the Atlantic Ocean to the Persian Gulf. The Jews maintained their identity by adhering to their religious practices, but over the generations they

gradually absorbed the traits of their host civilizations.

Jewish intellectual and cultural standards rose or fell with the fortunes of their hosts. The Golden Age of Islam was also the Golden Age of the Jewish communities living in the countries of Islam. The greatest Jewish philosophers, scientists, doctors, statesmen, and rabbis of those centuries lived in Moslem lands. As the Moslems swept from the Middle East across North Africa to Spain, Jewish merchants followed in their wake. They prospered.

And when Islam gave way to European ascendancy, so did Jewish civilization in Islamic countries. In the last five centuries the most important Jewish philosophers, scientists, doctors, statesmen, and rabbis have been Europeans or their descendants in the Western world.

The Jewish communities in North Africa and the Middle East degenerated over the centuries. There are still some small pockets of cultured and prosperous Jews in the Islamic world but, on the whole, Jewish civilization there became a backwater.

Perhaps the most primitive Jews from Moslem lands have been the cave dwellers of the Sahara Uplands of North Africa and the Yemenites of the Arabian Peninsula.

An immigrant from Yemen who had been housed with his family near Beersheba entered the office of the Jewish Agency the following day with a complaint. "The well ran dry," he said.

Officials were puzzled. There had been no well on his property. But the man was emphatic and someone went home with him to see what the trouble was.

The Yemenite led the Jewish Agency man to the lavatory and pointed to the toilet bowl. He had scooped water from it for his family's use and now there was none left.

Yet Yemenites were literate. The menfolk of the community could read the Bible. They could read it, in fact, not only right side up, but upside-down and from the sides. This peculiar accomplishment stemmed from a shortage of books in their corner of the world. Classes studied the Bible in circles, squatting around the books. So they learned to read from all angles.

Tripolitanian cave dwellers, on the other hand, were not only illiterate but were mystified by the very concept of reading. A teacher engaged in adult education recalled that at her first lesson she wrote

A girl soldier assists a new Israeli upon her arrival.

the name of a pupil, Sarah, on a small blackboard.

"This says 'Sarah,'"she explained.

Sarah scrutinized it from all angles and giggled. "It doesn't look like me at all," she remarked.

The teacher had Sarah copy the characters on a sheet of paper and then told her: "Now take this to the grocer. He can read."

The woman left and returned excitedly. "He said it's me!" she cried. "He said it's Sarah!"

In the early, heady days of the Jewish State, Israelis deluded themselves by assuming that once Sarah's children were put through the same school program as the sons and daughters of the erudite Westerners the cultural gap would gradually disappear.

The smoke from the War of Independence had hardly lifted and the armistice agreements were still unsigned when the government introduced legislation in the Knesset making a year of kindergarten and eight years of primary school free and compulsory for all boys and girls aged five to fourteen. Those who failed to get their elementary-school diplomas by the age of fourteen were required to continue their studies until they reached seventeen. If they worked, employers were bound by law to give them time off to attend classes.

The Ministry of Education prepared a standard program for the whole school system based on European-type achievement.

Expectations that the pressure-cooker approach would equally equip young Israelis to compete for advancement in life turned out to have been naive. In the very first grade 25 to 30 per cent of the children from Oriental families failed to acquire sufficient familiarity with letters and figures to warrant promotion. Over the years they fell further behind. Many dropped out despite the law.

The accomplishments of the system and its failings were mirrored in the eighteen-year-old boys conscripted for military service. A survey by the defense forces in 1961 showed that among draftees who were born in Asia or Africa about 36 per cent had had no schooling at all or were elementary-school dropouts. Only 25 per cent had gone beyond primary school. The picture among the Israeli-born children of Oriental immigrants was substantially better. Primary-school dropouts fell to 15 per cent; the proportion going beyond elementary school rose to 27 per cent. Among children of European immigrants, dropouts did not exceed 1 per cent; 86 per cent went on to high school. So the equality envisaged by the legislature was nowhere in sight.

The intellectual gap is not genetic, as has been proven scientifically. In *kibbutzim* where the children of Oriental and European parents are raised together from birth in communal nurseries, play with the same communal toys, eat identical food from communal kitchens, and attend the same classes, there is no significant difference in intellectual abilities. This has been shown in a study conducted by Dr. Moshe Smilansky of Tel Aviv University among twelve hundred children aged four to fourteen in forty different communal settlements.

Certainly the poverty in the slums, raw border towns, and bleak farming communities inhabited primarily by Orientals had much to do with their offsprings' deficiencies. Children doing their homework in cramped dwellings among pallets, crying babies, and harassed parents were obviously handicapped. Moreover, the disadvantaged communities couldn't get really competent teachers. Often they had to be content with the high school graduates posted to outlying areas by the army in lieu of their military service.

But there's more to it than that. An earlier study by Dr. Smilansky showed that even when children of European and Oriental stock came from similar economic and occupational backgrounds, the Orientals lagged.

The finger pointed to differences in child-rearing practices brought over from the countries of origin. In the old Eastern European ghettos, no matter how poor a family was, education was the focal interest of the household.

Christian neighbors may have taken pride in the physical attractiveness of their children or the way they rode horses, but Jewish parents were concerned primarily with their offsprings' intellect. Fathers who worked long hours to provide their families with bread, potatoes, herring, and mush managed to find time to engage their children in constant dialogue. They enriched their vocabularies, taught them to count, to identify colors, to understand ideas.

The way Tevye in *Fiddler on the Roof* shared his family's meager food with a young student, just to have him teach his daughters, reflects the sacrifices poor Jewish parents were willing to make for book learning.

The tradition came down to the present generation. Nothing makes the descendant of an East European Jew prouder than imagined intellectual precociousness in an offspring. The little ones know it and it stimulates them to use their brains.

In most countries of Islam, on the other hand, it was considered unbecoming for a man to spend time with children. The father's function was to provide for his family. He spent his leisure outside the home in other adult male company. Child-rearing was left to the mother, who didn't have the capacity to stimulate her children intellectually. By the time one child learned to talk, she generally had another at her breast. She had no time or patience for the inquisitive child. The one she held up as a model to all the others was the taciturn one who accepted his food and retired quietly to his corner.

So the typical Oriental child, who had heard little more than brief commands or phrases at home, entered school with an inadequate vocabulary. Some of the most common words used by the teacher were unfamiliar to him. Long sentences confused him. He wasn't as handy with a pencil as Occidental children who had been scrawling with crayons at home. He simply wasn't ready for a school program geared for Occidentals.

Furthermore, some Oriental parents resented compulsory education as an intrusion into their personal freedoms. When mothers needed older children to look after younger brothers and sisters, they kept them home. When fathers needed hands to help with the crops, they kept entire broods home.

Consequently, Oriental children fell behind from the start. Cumulative setbacks convinced many that book learning was not for them. Some dropped out and went to work. Others dropped out and became delinquents. Many who stuck it out and finally got diplomas never really learned enough to be able to read a newspaper.

At the end of Israel's first decade only two hundred Oriental children a year completed high school. They represented 7.8 per cent of the graduating classes, although Orientals by then already made up half the population. The situation cried danger.

The virtual monopoly of power, prestige, and wealth by Western Jews was hard enough for the immigrant generation of Orientals to swallow. The generation born and bred in a free Israel couldn't be expected to stomach such stratification at all.

Yet the school system was not grooming the rising generation for equitable representation in leadership, management, and the professions. During the first decade the educational authorities had their hands full just providing classrooms, teachers, supplies, and other facilities for a school body that was quadrupling.

At the start of the second decade the authorities took a hard look at the developing situation and decided on some basic reforms. First, they adapted the curricula and the pace of studies to the capacities of pupils. Secondly, they got at the roots of the difficulty by moving children from primitive environments into classrooms as early in life as possible and for as long as possible. They opened free day nurseries for three- and four-year-olds in underprivileged areas. Summer vacations in those areas were reduced to one month. School days were extended into the late afternoons and the children were helped with their homework.

Pupils who showed an aptitude for higher education were given extracurricular tutoring in Hebrew, the sciences, and current events. Norms for admission to high schools were substantially lowered for children of Oriental immigrants. They were also given free tutorial assistance to help them keep up with their classes.

This discrimination-in-reverse occasioned some curious reactions. In Beisan, an immigrants' town in the Jordan Valley, a Jew from Rumania named Leibowitz changed his name to Bar-Lev. He said his European Jewish name had handicapped his son in school.

With help from American Jewish philanthropists, the authorities opened boarding schools for particularly gifted boys and girls who were regarded as potential college material but who might not be able to attain their potential if they continued to live with their parents.

The Israeli defense forces were also called upon to help. Girl soldiers were asked to volunteer to spend their military service in out-of-the-way towns and villages among immigrants from backward countries. Their specific assignment was to canvass homes and induce the illiterate adults to learn to read and write.

The girls in corporals' and sergeants' uniforms organized small classes that usually met in private dwellings. As their pupils became accustomed to using ballpoint pens instead of thumb prints to acknowledge receipts in cooperative stores, and became able to read signs well enough to catch the right bus without asking for directions, their whole outlook changed. They stopped keeping their children home to help around the house. They prodded them to do their homework. They even began buying books.

The girl soldiers living among the Orientals, sharing their rice, couscous, and table talk as well as the discomforts of primitive life, have been an important bridge between the newcomers and the Israeli Establishment.

The defense forces also tackled school dropouts in their ranks. A regulation requires every soldier who has not completed his primary education to attend an army school for three months before returning to civilian life.

The school, on Mount Carmel in Haifa, is called Camp Marcus. The name was chosen advisedly, as both a tribute and an admonition. It memorializes Colonel David "Mickey" Marcus, a West Point officer who fought on the Israeli side during the 1948 War of Independence and whose ignorance of Hebrew cost him his life. He was shot by a sentry near Jerusalem when he answered in English to a challenge from the guard.

A few years ago an attempt was made to get the dropouts into classes at the onset of their military service. The idea was that the army would then derive some benefit, too.

The experiment proved disastrous. The dropouts were deeply insulted when they were separated from the other recruits and sent to classrooms instead of basic training. They resisted violently. They smashed furniture, sabotaged the plumbing, and sang defiant songs. One ruffian grabbed a terrified girl teacher around the waist and made an indecent proposal. Another carved swastikas in the barracks. He said later he hadn't known what the symbol represented, but he knew it was evil; that, in fact, was why he had carved it.

Dropouts coming to school at the end of their military service are disciplined and willing students as a rule. On the threshold of their demobilization, they realize that the knowledge they can gain in classrooms may help them obtain a better place in civilian society.

The new outlook they have achieved through their military experience aids in surmounting psychological barriers. Schooldays have bitter memories for dropouts, but apparently the self-confidence they acquire as soldiers contributes to breaking down their defense mechanisms, including contempt for learning. It gives them the courage to attempt to recover their youthful fumbles.

The fact that the instructors are young women freshly graduated from teachers' seminaries and of the same age as the students poses a problem. The soldiers at first tend to concentrate on the physical attributes of their mentors rather than their textbooks. The girls are conscious of the scrutiny. They can sometimes be observed during the first few lessons pressing their backs against classroom walls for support. But the problem works itself out and the students apply themselves diligently to their schoolwork.

Lessons are given not only in the three R's but in world history, Jewish history, geography, citizenship, the Bible, and basic science. Two teachers are assigned to each class of ten students. About 75 per cent of the students usually complete the courses satisfactorily and obtain diplomas from the Ministry of Education that are equivalent to elementary-school graduation certificates.

Tens of thousands of underprivileged Orientals who have gone through the school system and military service are now heads of families. They differ considerably from their parents.

The older generation had 5 children per couple; the younger averages 2.3, which is not much different from their Western brethren. The younger generation's babies are healthier and heavier at birth. Relations between husbands and wives and parents and children are more relaxed and open. Homes are less crowded and tense. Food is more wholesome. Middle-class attitudes toward education have developed. Consequently, youngsters of Oriental parentage have been doing better in school.

If high school and college are the corridors to real equality of opportunity, the ethnic gap has narrowed. The Oriental graduates from academic high schools increased during Israel's second decade from 7.8 to 20 per cent. Taking into account vocational high schools, the proportion of Oriental graduates has risen from 15 to 32 per cent. In the universities, the scale went up from 5 to 12 per cent.

The road to full equality is still long. But the Orientals seem to be on it.

8

A Society of
Contradictions

"We're not Egyptians, we're not Iraqis. We're Israelis."

*Left, a Syrian-Orthodox Easter service. Above, a statue
of Anilewitz, the hero of the Warsaw ghetto uprising.*

*A symbolic washing of feet is part of the Armenian
church's Easter week ritual.*

THE SOCIETY EMERGING from Israel's mishmash of Jewish types,
with their cultures, dreams, and aspirations, is full of contradictions
and confusions.

It's young, modern, dynamic, and forward-looking. At the same
time it is old, conservative, and very much tied to the past.

The most popular newspaper cartoon image, created by the talented
"Dosh," depicts Israel as on the brink of adolescence, both lovable
and brash.

But the Jewish State is also extremely conscious of its heritage. It
sees itself as an outgrowth of one of the world's oldest civilizations,
going back to biblical times.

The new type of Jew that the Second Aliyah pioneers aspired to
develop is not yet fully formed, but certain traits are emerging.

He is taller, straighter, more relaxed, and less complex than his parents, He is a *sabra,* the Arabic term for the fruit of the cactus plant. He has been led to believe he was so-called because the *sabra* is prickly and tough on the outside but soft and sweet inside.

Old-timers say it wasn't quite so. In the 1920's, when the country was still desolate, the *sabra* was the most popular indigenous fruit. So parents fondly called their home-grown offspring their "little *sabras.*" The business about the toughness and the softness was an afterthought by some wag. But it tickled everybody. It received such wide circulation that the witticism became the accepted explanation.

Either way, the *sabra* is full of surprises for those with conventional notions about what Jews should be like.

When Gian Carlo Menotti came to Israel to stage *The Consul,* he said Hebrew was the fifteenth language in which his opera would be performed but by rights it should have been the first.

"It's an opera that was inspired by the plight of the Jews," he explained.

I attended a performance of it with a *sabra,* a political science student at Hebrew University. We watched the hero stumble onto the stage and heard him sing to his anguished wife and mother about how the police had raided a meeting of his underground cell, killed his friend, and shot him in the leg. Three sinister-looking detectives appeared and the hero hid outside while they searched his house. When they departed, he limped back into the room, staggered over to a crib to kiss his baby good-by, and then left to escape over the border.

"Do you sympathize with that man?" my companion whispered.

"Certainly," I replied.

"I felt for him only when he kissed the baby," the *sabra* said. "He could be Fatah."

I gasped. Fatah is an organization of Arab gunmen who have raided Israeli territory to murder and sabotage.

But on second thought the *sabra*'s reaction made sense. He didn't identify himself instinctively with the persecuted. He had never been persecuted. The *sabra* was not a fighter for freedom. He had been born free.

The complexes of the classical, suffering, sensitive Jew who inspired Menotti offend *sabras.*

When the Habimah Theater presented the musical *Oliver!* in Tel Aviv, the portrayal of Fagin the Jew was sugar-coated as it had been in the Broadway and London productions. *Sabra* critics turned up their noses. They pointed out that Dickens' cast of characters in *Oliver Twist,* on which the musical is based, was full of rogues, thieves, scoundrels, even a murderer. All apart from Fagin were standard English types.

No scriptwriter had ever found it necessary to sugar-coat the wicked English types, the critics observed. So why the sensitivity about portraying an evil Jew? Why couldn't they present Fagin faithfully, as Dickens had created him?

Sabras now make up some 45 per cent of the Jewish population of Israel, compared to 25 per cent at the end of the period of large-scale immigration in 1951. The average native-born Jew is in his early teens; the average foreign-born Jew is past middle age. So it will not be long before Israel becomes a homogeneous country with a predominantly native-born population.

The natives are as casual about Jewish sovereignty as Americans are about their independence. They are bemused by elders who become misty-eyed on Independence Day and who still can't get over the fact that the Jewish flag flies at the United Nations and at the Olympic games. *Sabras* also tend to chuckle over the emotionalism displayed by Jewish visitors from abroad.

Some non-Jews from countries with anti-Semitic traditions, like Germany and France, have told *sabras:* "You're different. You're nothing like the Jews we know at home." Truth to tell, some *sabras* lapped up the left-handed compliments. Cocky after their own victories over seemingly hopeless odds, the children and grandchildren of emigrants from Europe like to think of themselves as descendants of the Maccabees and Bar Kochba in ancient Palestine and to forget about the intervening generations that were debased in the dispersion. As students they had despised those chapters of Jewish history about persecutions and martyrdom. Jews who had marched sheeplike to Nazi ovens offended their national pride. They tended to think of Jews abroad, but not of themselves, as the successor generation to the victims of persecution.

Their outlook underwent a sharp reappraisal at the time of the Six

Day War. Arabs from as far off as Algeria and Iraq were ganging up to snuff out the Jewish State. The United Nations, with indecent haste, pulled out their Emergency Force, which was to have been a buffer between Israel and Egypt. France, whom Israelis had regarded as their best friend in Europe, had imposed a treacherous arms embargo and banned the delivery of jet fighters Israel had paid for and desperately needed. The Western maritime powers who had guaranteed Israeli navigation between the Gulf of Aqaba and the Red Sea were reneging one by one after President Gamal Abdel Nasser mounted Egyptian guns on the Sinai coast and proclaimed a blockade. The Israelis felt abandoned and isolated.

Then in the midst of the bustle at Lod Airport, where edgy visitors were clamoring for passage home, a plane landed with a Jew from a South American country. "I'm not a soldier," the man said. "I can't shoot. But I can drive. Maybe they'll let me drive an ambulance."

The next day volunteers landed by the score. Then by the hundreds. They included doctors who had abandoned their practices, workers who had quit their jobs, and students who had left school and—it was June, remember—passed up their final exams. The volunteers reported that tens of thousands more were besieging Israeli embassies and consulates in their countries for passage to Israel.

They told of older Jews who had drawn their savings from banks, sold precious paintings off their walls, given up their vacations, or gone into debt to scrape together all the money they could raise to help Israel. *Sabras* were heartened. They found they had allies. They learned that Jewish brotherhood was not just a corny expression.

After the victory, volunteers kept coming. Some were posted to Nahal settlements. Others helped build installations in the occupied areas or worked in border villages that were harassed by enemy sniping and shelling. The foreign Jews showed more guts than many *sabras* had credited them with. Many asked specifically to be posted to trouble spots.

Older Jews from Europe and the United States also demonstrated that boldness and pride were not Israeli monopolies. True enough, some were frightened by Arab terror and canceled their planned visits to Israel, but tens of thousands defied the terrorists and came in numbers that broke all records for tourism. They visited the border areas and moved through the narrow, winding casbahs in newly taken Arab towns. By shooting at fully loaded El Al airliners in European airports, Arab gunmen had thought they would scare off tourists to Israel. They miscalculated. There were some cancellations, of course, but they were offset by stiff-necked Jews who insisted upon having their tickets from other airlines endorsed to El Al to demonstrate their solidarity with Israel. El Al planes flew as fully loaded as ever.

Sabras were impressed. One way they reacted was by taking a fresh look at their roots. They became curious about the bonds that had held the Jewish people together in the dispersion. They developed a greater interest in their heritage and in the observances and traditions that were common to Jews all over the world.

Many of their elders had discarded Jewish traditions when they first came to Palestine as part of their revolt against their Jewish ghetto background. Now there was a counterrevolution—small-scale but pronounced. Synagogue attendance increased perceptibly. A few irreligious communal settlements opened synagogues in response to members' requests. Jewish festivals were observed more in accordance with the old traditions. It wasn't so much a religious revival as a search for roots and a return to traditions and customs.

The new spirit was reflected on the stage. One of the biggest hits after the war was a show called *Once There Was a Chassid*. Three boys and three girls in jeans, sweaters, and loose blouses, looking like a well-scrubbed rock group, narrated legends of Chassidism, the eighteenth-century movement in East European ghettos that spread the message of serving God through joy. The performers strummed guitars and sang traditional Chassidic melodies.

Some Orthodox Jews found the performance offensive. Bareheaded youths singing old synagogue tunes and relating the hallowed tales of the wondrous Chassidic rabbis while they shamelessly held girls around the waist struck them as irreverent. But *sabras* flocked to the show. Here were boys and girls who looked like them and talked their language telling them about their old culture in a language they understood. They loved it. The Chassidic tunes became popular hits. The record of the show was a best seller.

Another postwar stage hit was a musical called *I Like Mike* about an American hippie who came to Israel as a volunteer in the Six Day

With Israeli flags waving above them, Druse dancers perform at a holiday feast.

136

War. The grand finale was a rousing song about how good it was that Jews were the way they were. It was chauvinistic but with a new twist. Ordinarily, chauvinism is Israeli, not Jewish.

The liberation of historic sites during the war also inspired a spate of popular songs based on biblical texts and episodes. But that wasn't a new trend. Israeli writers, composers, and choreographers, although mostly modern in style, had often reached back to the Bible for themes. It was not unusual for the Hit Parade to be headed by a song like "To the Chief Musician, a Song of Psalm," composed by Dov Selzer with lyrics from Psalms 66:1. Unlike Chassidism, which was European and alien to the average *sabra,* the Scriptures were indigenous and very much part of their lives.

The closest thing the Israelis have to a World Series is the International Bible Championships held in Jerusalem every other year.

Lights burn long past midnight in many a home on the nights of the finals. Entire families sit with copies of the Scriptures before them, following the contest on television or the radio. The first two world titles were won by Israelis. The third time Israelis were stunned when a New Zealander nosed out the local hope.

The night in 1969 when the title returned to Israel was a night to remember. Eighteen countries were represented by contestants who qualified by winning competitions in their home countries. The questions at the Jerusalem finals had to be translated for the contestants into Amharic, English, French, Spanish, Finnish, Dutch, Italian, and Swedish.

The local champion, a rubber cooker in a Netanya factory, was patently nervous and stumbled over a question in an early round. He fell behind a Protestant pastor from Holland, a Seventh-Day Adventist from Bolivia, and a New Zealand housewife active in the Salvation Army. There were boos, derisive whistles, and groans in the audience.

Later, as the questions got more difficult, the Israeli began to prove superior knowledge. He supplied perfect answers to such questions as: "Quote three verses from three prophets who linked the concepts of loving-kindness and justice in divine and human behavior." There was a deafening roar when he shot into the lead.

There wasn't a vacant place in the 3,000-seat Convention Center at 2:15 A.M. when President Shazar awarded first prize to the Israeli. The enthusiasm of the public amazed the foreign contestants. Some of them were recognized in the streets by people who had seen them on television and wished to shake their hands. "In New Zealand," a runner-up remarked, "soldiers and people in shops or on buses wouldn't be particularly interested in a Bible contest."

Sabras learn the Bible as soon as they can read—from the second grade onward. In the religious-school network, it is studied as a holy book; elsewhere the emphasis is on its historical, literary, and cultural aspects. In either case, pupils are required to know substantial parts by heart.

Matriculation from the Israeli high school system without passing Bible exams is as unthinkable as an American graduating from high school without passing United States history. Along with mathematics and Hebrew, Bible is a compulsory subject. Students can choose between English and French as a foreign language. The sciences, history, and geography are optional. But there is no avoiding the Bible.

That has led to another contradiction in the Israeli self-image. The country strives to be among the world leaders in scientific development, but a Jewish student who doesn't pass his Bible tests doesn't qualify for admission to Hebrew University, the Technion-Israel Institute of Technology, or any other institution of higher learning.

Not long ago the Technion invited Professor George Feher of the University of California to help establish a new department of solid-state physics. The professor accepted the invitation. Upon his arrival in Haifa, he revealed that twenty-five years earlier he had been refused admission by the Technion as a student. He had failed his Bible exams, mainly, he explained, because he had difficulty with Aramaic. At the time he had been a recent immigrant from Czechoslovakia. So he moved to the United States for his academic training and became a respected international authority in his field.

There's no telling how much more brainpower was lost to Israel in that manner. On the other hand, familiarity with the Scriptures has sometimes proved useful to Israelis in the most improbable situations.

Two Israeli policemen once came upon an Arab leading a donkey on a side road in the Gaza Strip. The Arab panicked and plunged among the trees of a citrus grove by the side of the road. The Israelis searched the saddlebags and found hand grenades and explosives that were obviously destined for a terrorist group.

Left holding the ass, the Israelis pondered their dilemma. Into the mind of one of them there flashed a verse from Isaiah he had learned by heart in school: "The ox knoweth his owner and the ass his master's crib."

The policeman mounted the donkey. The beast trotted off. Its journey ended at a crib. Sure enough, it was his master's. The cop made his arrest.

Israeli Arab students are not required to attain such proficiency in the Old Testament. The State acknowledges the legitimacy of the minority communities' insistence on pursuing their own cultures. A separate school network where the language of instruction is Arabic was set up for them. In those schools, Hebrew is taught as a second language and the Bible studied within that framework. Pupils learn some fifty chapters, which the authorities believe is the least any person of culture should know regardless of race or creed.

In general subjects, such as mathematics and science, the program of studies parallels that of regular schools. In history, literature, civics, and to some extent geography, the curricula is different. For religious instruction, classes in the minority schools split up. Moslems study Islam, Christians their own religious teachings according to their respective denominations, and the Druses get none at all. Theirs is a secret religion known only to their clergy. The clergy objects to its being taught in school.

The minorities are not in the Israeli melting pot. Jews don't want them there and the Arabs certainly don't want to be in it. Emotionally, ethnically, and culturally, their links are across the borders in enemy countries. So the most the Jews expect of them is that they respect law and order, not that they be ardent patriots. There are indeed some Arabs who take Hebrew names, wish to date and marry Jewish girls, and hang portraits of Zionist leaders on their walls. They are regarded with suspicion by Jews and ostracized by Arab society, especially the Moslems. Islam allows men to take Jewish wives provided the children are brought up as Moslems.

Even the Druses, whose loyalty to Israel has been demonstrated time and again on the battlefield, wish to retain their national identities

Moslem Arabs leave Hebron to go on a pilgrimage to Mecca

and their link with coreligionists in enemy countries. The elders of the community who demanded that their sons be conscripted just like Jews for military service have also insisted that the Druse soldiers comprise units of their own.

Some 30,000 Arabs live in predominantly Jewish towns. The rest, representing more than 90 per cent of the minority population, live in separate communities. The 30,000 Druses live mainly in remote villages in mountain areas, a carry-over from the period of Turkish rule when they had to protect themselves against Moslem persecutions. The 70,000 Christian Arabs tend to concentrate in towns and larger villages, while the 300,000 Moslems, as the principal minority, are everywhere: in the towns, villages of all sizes, and Bedouin encampments.

In the minority localities, the language of business and social intercourse is Arabic. They have their own local administrations. The weekly day of rest is Friday or Sunday, depending on the religion of the inhabitants.

The State broadcasting service runs Arabic television and radio stations for the minorities. The Hebrew press, particularly the afternoon papers, circulate in their towns and villages and are read by younger Arabs. However, the minorities get much of their news, opinion, and entertainment from the television and radio stations of Egypt and other Arab countries. In fact, it was to offset the seditious propaganda of the enemy stations that Israel set up her own television service.

The minority communities sing their own songs, tell their own jokes, and play their own games, notably *sheshbesh*, a kind of dominoes. *Fellaheen*, the peasants, dress in their traditional loose robes and cover their heads with the *keffiya*, a white kerchief, held down by a black cord, an *egal*. But most Arabs dress in clothes made in Israeli factories and are not different from Jews in their attire.

The veil has been disappearing, but older Moslem women still keep their faces covered in the cities and in the villages of Abu Gosh and Kalansawa, whose inhabitants consider themselves sheiks, or aristocrats. Polygamy, permitted by Moslem law, is banned by Israeli civil law.

Arabs living in predominantly Jewish towns have been variously received. In Tel Aviv they are concentrated in localities of their own in the part of the city that was formerly the separate Arab town of Jaffa. A survey in Tel Aviv after the Six Day War established that 80 per cent of the people didn't know any Arabs and didn't want to. In Haifa, there has been more fraternization. The Arabs there are more dispersed. Arabs and Jews sometimes have flats in the same apartment houses and maintain cordial neighborly relations. Some Jews live in preponderantly Arab quarters.

On the whole, the Jewish population's attitude toward the minorities has been ambivalent. It is yet another aspect of Israeli life that is full of contradictions. There is a tendency to regard the Arabs as enemy aliens whose loyalty to the Jewish State will always be dubious, no matter how they are treated. Hence their exemption from compulsory military service. At the same time the consensus is that the Arabs are citizens who are entitled to the same rights and services as Jews.

Israelis like comparing living conditions and the freedom of expression enjoyed by Arabs in the Jewish State to those of Arabs in Arab states. The Israeli Arabs acknowledge they're superior but reject the comparisons. "We're not Egyptians," they say. "We're not Iraqis. We're Israelis."

They don't consider themselves aliens in a Jewish State. Enemies, perhaps, but not aliens. Some don't even acknowledge they're a minority. They see themselves as part of the Middle East majority. They feel the privileges of citizenship in Israel are their birthright. It offends them that some Jews seem to expect them to be grateful for the schools, health services, and other amenities that have modernized their lives whereas Jewish immigrants were assumed to take them as a matter of course.

The Arabs, in 1948, had been a majority in the part of Palestine that later emerged as a Jewish State. There had been 700,000 of them to 650,000 Jews. During the fighting, all but 150,000 abandoned their homes, expecting to return after the armies of the neighboring Arab countries wiped out the Jews. But when the war ended, the fugitives became homeless refugees and the Arabs who stayed with their property found themselves in a Jewish State. They were stunned and bewildered. They saw Israel as an apparition. They hated it but felt impotent to fight it. They sulked and expected that somehow, some night the

apparition would go away as suddenly as it had appeared.

The Israelis, from the start, acknowledged that their unwilling subjects were entitled to full citizenship rights. The armistice agreement of 1949 was as yet unsigned when Arabs were permitted to vote in the first national parliamentary elections. They returned three deputies to the Knesset. Two of them were elected on progovernment slates, and one was a Communist. Facilities for simultaneous translation into Arabic were quickly installed to enable them to follow the Hebrew proceedings. The Arab deputies in turn addressed the legislature in their own language and parliamentary interpreters translated their speeches into Hebrew.

The rights of the Arabs to use their own language had been guaranteed as a fourth freedom in an eleventh-hour revision of the draft Proclamation of Independence. As the signatories of the historic document studied the draft on the morning of May 14, 1948, and raced against the clock to complete their task before the British mandate ended, they adopted only one proposed amendment. It had been submitted by Meir Grabovsky, later chairman of the parliamentary foreign affairs and security committee, who proposed that "language" be added to the freedoms of religion, conscience, and culture already accorded in the draft.

At the same time, the Arab citizens were regarded as a threat to security. Concern was heightened by the fact that they were predominant near the borders in sensitive areas: in parts of Galilee, the Samarian foothills overlooking the narrow coastal waistline, and the Negev.

Those areas were quickly put under military rule. Inhabitants needed permits from military governors to move around the country, to conduct business, and to do practically anything else. Some of their land was requisitioned. Those measures were geographic, not racial. But in practice they applied to regions where nearly 80 per cent of the Arabs lived.

Many Arabs suspected that the Israelis' real aim was to dispossess them. There were strong suspicions that they were being ghettoized not so much for security reasons, but to obviate cheap Arab labor interfering with the absorption of Jewish immigrants, who had begun to stream into the country.

A group of bearded Druse elders get together for a discussion.

145

The authorities, on their part, didn't pay much heed to the Arab mood. Hostility and distrust were no more than they had expected. They were preoccupied with integrating the newcomers and with security. As long as the Arabs refrained from violence, they were satisfied that their provisional military government was a success.

After Israel's resounding victory over Egypt in the Sinai Campaign of 1956, there was a mutual reappraisal of their relationship by Arabs and Jews. Many Arabs came to realize the Jewish State might not be as ephemeral as they had hoped, and that perhaps they should learn to make the best of it. They were not ready to commit themselves politically, but they thought they might as well take advantage of the progress and development the new society could offer, particularly in the economic field.

The Jews, on their part, having more or less absorbed their own immigrants, were able to devote more thought and resources to making the minorities happier. Moreover, with President Nasser licking his wounds, they could afford to worry less about the Israeli Arabs as a potential fifth column—for there had been no subversion by Israeli Arabs during the war with Egypt.

So the restrictions of military rule were progressively lifted. Arabs were free to move around the country. Villagers were able to go to Jewish localities, where they found jobs as unskilled construction workers, garage hands, and kitchen help. The Histadrut (General Federation of Labor) dropped "Jewish" from its title and admitted Arab workers to full membership, assuring them trade-union wages and social benefits.

Most villagers commuted to work. Some whose jobs were far away from home preferred to sleep near their places of employment, but their reception was unhappy. Few Jews were ready to sublet rooms to Arabs, and some workers were compelled to lodge in leaky shacks.

Meanwhile minority villages were transformed by government development programs. Old clusters of mudlike dwellings disappeared from the landscape and modern functional houses mushroomed. Running water and paved roads reached the remotest villages. Most of them were hooked up with the electricity grid. Farming and marketing methods were modernized. Health services improved and life expectancy among Arabs reached sixty-nine, compared with fifty-two in

146

Egypt and approximately fifty in Jordan. Jewish life expectancy in Israel is seventy-two or seventy-three.

Hundreds of schools were opened in villages and in the desert near Bedouin encampments. Attendance in primary schools reached 95 per cent for boys and 75 per cent for girls, compared with less than 50 per cent, nearly all boys, when the country was under British rule. The enrollment of Arabs in universities rose from year to year.

But progress and prosperity produced new problems. The generation of Arabs bred in Israel could not find proper niches in society. Graduates of schools where Hebrew was a second language naturally were handicapped in their competition for administrative or clerical jobs in the Jewish sector. Some areas of employment were barred to Arabs altogether, due to security considerations. The Arab sector offered few opportunities for white-collar careers. There were only so many teachers, bank clerks, and civil servants it could absorb.

In the Jewish community, it was perfectly natural for a village boy who graduated from high school to return to the family farm, diploma and all. For an Arab, it was unthinkable. The education gap between the generations was so great that even a school dropout considered himself too erudite to be a *fellah*.

Arab university students constituted a special problem. A small number who matriculated alongside Jews from regular high schools—where they had taken a full program of Bible, Talmud, and four thousand years of Jewish history—were equipped for Israeli universities; the great majority who went through the Arabic school system were obviously handicapped.

Those who obtained degrees in engineering, architecture, medicine, agronomy, or law generally had no problem establishing themselves. Most of the teachers were also absorbed. The difficulty was that Arab students tended to major in political science, sociology, or Arab literature. Those fields were problematic also for Jews seeking employment.

So frustration and bitterness ate deeply into young Arab intellectuals. Many joined the Communist party, not necessarily because they shared Marxist ideologies, but because the Communists were the only recognized party that gave them an outlet for their hostility. There were desperate young Arabs who stole across the armistice lines to Arab countries, where they felt certain they would find outlets for their talents and skills. Some were sent back to spy but never got back. They were shot by border sentries guarding against marauders.

A new situation was created by the Six Day War that restored contact between the Israeli Arabs and the million in the west bank of Jordan and the Gaza Strip. For many Israeli Arabs, the reunion was a shattering experience.

They found across the former armistice lines a patriarchal, highly class-conscious and clan-conscious society. The villas of the landowners, professionals, and other men of means were extraordinarily posh and the hovels of the poor incredibly poor. Agricultural methods appeared to lag a generation behind those of Israeli Arabs. Rich Moslems kept harems and their wives seemed to evaporate when a visitor called. The archaic atmosphere seemed dimly familiar to the Arabs from Israel. It dawned on them that that was the way they themselves had lived twenty years earlier. It shocked them to discover how much they had changed, how much of Israel had rubbed off on them, how Israeli they had unknowingly become despite their hostility to the Jewish State.

Israeli Arabs found their kin across the lines irrational and unrealistic and impossible to reason with. A visitor who remarked that the Israeli national insurance system was interesting was promptly labeled a Zionist propagandist.

It stunned them to discover that the Arabs on the other side regarded them as quislings and collaborators for their passive acceptance of Israeli rule for two decades. A Hebrew newspaper reported the following discussion between Israeli and Jordanian Arabs:

Jordanian: "Have you been to the refugee camps yet?"

Israeli: "I haven't had a chance."

Jordanian: "You've had plenty of time."

(An awkward silence.)

Jordanian: "You're well off. You've waxed rich doing business with the Israelis and you expect others to do things for you."

Israeli: "We've never asked for anything."

Jordanian: "In other words, you're satisfied with things as they are. You don't mind the degradation and the humiliation, the alien rule. The plight of the refugees doesn't concern you?"

The Druse community in western Galilee holds a funeral for one of its members, an Israeli border policeman killed in action.

Israeli: "Of course it does, but what could we do?"

Jordanian: "Plenty. First of all, you must be an Arab."

Israeli Arabs reacted in varying ways to the encounters. Some shrugged off the reproaches. They felt they no longer had a common language with the Arabs across the lines. They had grown too far apart. The confrontation made them feel more closely identified with Israel and they wished to integrate more fully.

Others were stung into stronger Arab nationalism. They felt bolder now that they belonged to a more substantial minority. Some manifested their nationalism by addressing Israeli officials in Arabic, whereas they had previously done so in Hebrew. Some protested that Israeli state schools were not sufficiently Arabic in spirit. Some joined the terrorists.

The first to cross the lines to Jordan were suspected as Israeli agents, beaten up, and sent back. Later, cells were organized in Israeli Arab villages. Arab Hebrew University students participated in bombing the cafeteria on their campus and were involved in other terrorist acts.

The terrorists and the Arabs who wished to become integrated Israelis were both fringe elements. The great majority stood somewhere in the middle. Whatever their sympathies, they were expedient. Their outlook was expressed by an intellectual who said: "The Turks were here and they've gone. The British were here and they've gone. Now the Jews are here. Who knows?"

So they refrained from committing themselves to the Israelis for fear of Arab vengeance, and they refrained from cooperating with the terrorists for fear of the Israelis. In turn, they were trusted by neither.

Arab raiders in Israel carried their explosives and food supplies on their backs considerable distances from enemy territory. They were under orders not to contact local Arabs for provisions or shelter lest they be betrayed to the authorities. The Israelis didn't count on the Arabs' loyalty either. They trusted a small element that was so committed to the Israeli Establishment that they would be the first to be executed if ever the Arabs captured Israel. For the rest, it was impossible to know who was a terrorist and who wasn't.

The security authorities cast a very wide net for terrorists and took precautions against sabotage. The measures inconvenienced everybody, Arab and Jew, but Arabs more so. Visitors to public places had to submit to searches by civil defense wardens. Anyone leaving his seat in a theater in the middle of a show to answer a call of nature had to identify himself to a warden and explain. With Jews, the checks were somewhat perfunctory and not offensive. With Arabs, they tended to be more thorough.

There were police roadblocks at the approaches to cities: Jewish motorists were waved through; Arabs were stopped. Their cars were searched and notes taken of their destination.

At bus terminals and other busy places, policemen, civil defense wardens, and girl soldiers picked people who looked like Arabs out of the crowds and asked them to show their identity cards. If they were Oriental Jews, they got their cards back with a smile and a "Thank you." Arabs were searched and questioned. Buses were stopped on the highways and policemen walked down the aisles scanning the faces of the passengers. The security forces thus tried to keep a record of every Arab moving in and out of a city. If a bomb was thrown, they were liable to be rounded up for interrogation. Sometimes the screenings took a day or two.

The vigorous measures no doubt curbed sabotage and contributed to a remarkable police record in tracking down and smashing terrorist cells. But there was a price. The humiliation and ill feeling that were created appeared to have snuffed out the spark of mutual trust which seemed to have been growing in the decade preceding the Six Day War.

In the new situation, the most tragic figures were those Arabs who wished to be loyal Israelis. In the crisis that preceded the war, they had lined up at Red Magen David stations to donate blood and had volunteered to work in Jewish farms to relieve reservists called to the armed forces. But how could the civil defense wardens know it? They picked those Arabs out of the crowds also for questioning. In Jewish coffee houses, the Arabs sensed fingers pointing at them and guarded whispers behind their backs. After terrorist outrages, they felt their employers and fellow workers glaring at them as though every Arab had a personal responsibility for the bloodshed. It got so they hated going to work or visiting Jewish localities. The unhappy people felt alienated from Arabs and unwanted by Jews. It was pathetic.

Israeli paratroopers on the liberated Temple Mount

9 The Holy City

"If I forget thee, O Jerusalem, let my right hand wither. . . ."

*The walls dividing the Jewish and Arab sectors of Jerusalem
are pulled down after the Six Day War.*

IN THE SOUTHEAST CORNER of the walled Old City of Jerusalem there
is a little hill. The Jews call it Har Habayit (the Temple Mount) because
their holy temple stood there. Moslems call it Haram esh-Sherif (Noble
Sanctuary). The Bible calls it Mount Moriah.

It was there, the Scriptures relate, that the Lord tested Abraham by
commanding him to sacrifice his beloved son Isaac, but then prevented
the patriarch from plunging the knife when He was satisfied that the
old man really meant to go through with it. The hill has remained
sacred to Abraham's feuding scions—to the Jews who descended
from the spared Isaac and to the Arabs who came down from his half
brother, Ishmael.

Fourteen generations after Abraham's, when David conquered Jerusalem and moved his royal headquarters there from Hebron, the hilltop was owned by a Jebusite farmer named Araunah. David, the Bible relates, paid Araunah the full price for the land and built an altar on the threshing floor where he made burnt offerings to the Lord. His son and heir, Solomon, erected a temple on the hallowed spot as a "house unto the Lord."

King Solomon's Temple was destroyed in 586 B.C. by Nebuchadnezzar, who deported the Jews to Babylonia. When Cyrus the Great allowed the exiles to return, those who did so promptly built a new temple over the ashes of Solomon's. The Second Temple was enlarged and beautified by Herod the Great, a contemporary of Christ. It was gutted by the Romans in A.D. 70.

The Romans, to make sure the destruction was thorough, plowed the ashes into the ground. But the ruins of the colossal retaining wall of the Temple enclosure were left standing. Those surviving stones west of the Temple became the focal point of Jewish worship and the symbol of the Jews' onetime glory. It became known as the Wailing Wall because of the tears shed over it down the ages by Jewish pilgrims lamenting the destruction of the Temple and the fall of their kingdom.

There is a rock cropping out of Mount Moriah. The Moslems believe it marks the exact spot where Abraham prepared to sacrifice Isaac. Mohammed, the Prophet of Islam, said one prayer at that spot was worth a thousand anywhere else. Moslem tradition has it that the Prophet ascended to heaven from that rock astride Buraq, the winged horse with a woman's face and a peacock's tail. There's a dent at the side of the stone that looks like a heel mark. Moslems say the heel mark is Mohammed's.

Thus, after the Moslems, led by the Caliph Omar, conquered Jerusalem in the seventh century, they built a magnificent mosque over the stone. They called it the Dome of the Rock. Its large gilded dome is to this day the most striking feature of the Holy City's skyline, and the octagonal edifice whose interior is faced with marble and ceramics is one of the most sacred and beautiful Islamic shrines in the world.

Standing as it does on the site of Solomon's Temple, the Dome of the Rock is precisely where devout Jews expect the Third Temple to rise. Throughout the world Orthodox Jews face Jerusalem three times a day and utter: "May it be Thy will, O Lord our God and the God of our fathers, that the Temple may be speedily rebuilt in our days. . . ." For nearly two millennia rabbis, Yeshiva students, and learned laymen have assiduously studied the minutiae of the Temple ritual to be prepared for the day when their prayers would be answered.

Now that the site is again in Jewish sovereign hands for the first time in nearly two thousand years, Moslems from Morocco to Indonesia are deeply concerned about the rabbis' designs on their Mosque.

They needn't be. The rabbinate holds that for man to rebuild the Temple would be impious arrogance. "We have done all that human hands can accomplish," Chief Rabbi Yitzhak Nissim stated shortly after Israeli forces took the holy site in the 1967 war. "Now there remains that which only God can accomplish. For this we have received from our sages: the Third Temple will be rebuilt by God himself."

Moreover, the rabbinate holds that it is forbidden for Jews to set foot in the Temple area altogether. The Wailing Wall is approachable. It's outside the Temple area. But Torah law says the Temple area may be approached only in a state of ritual purity.

Any Jew who has been in a cemetery or in contact with a dead body is ritually defiled until he has gone through a purification ceremony in accordance with complicated regulations set forth in the Book of Numbers. The ceremony includes sprinkling the body with water containing the ashes of a red cow free from blemish and unbroken by a yoke. Since there haven't been any red cows in these parts for some time, it's a pretty fair assumption that every Jew is levitically unclean.

The Chief Rabbinate accordingly posted signs at the entrances to the Temple area, cautioning Jews that they are forbidden to enter. Other Jews protested. They said it was tantamount to defaulting the sacred spot to Islam. The municipality took down the rabbinate's signs. The Ministry for Religious Affairs then scolded the municipality for exceeding its competence. The signs were restored. However, the police do not enforce the rabbinical prohibition and the warning signs are largely unheeded.

During the Crusader period, the Christians maintained a base on the holy site. They used the Dome of the Rock as a church, put a cross

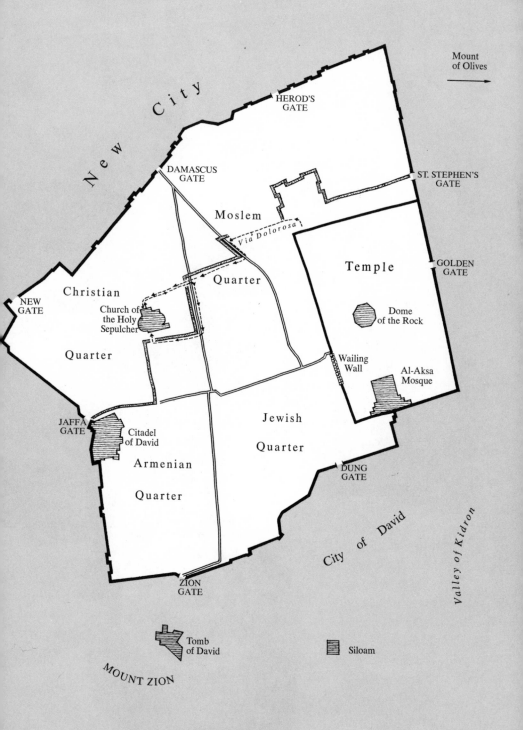

Mount
of Olives →

HEROD'S
GATE

DAMASCUS
GATE

ST. STEPHEN'S
GATE

New City

Moslem

Via Dolorosa

Quarter

Temple

Christian

GOLDEN
GATE

NEW
GATE

Church of
the Holy
Sepulcher

Dome
of the Rock

Quarter

Wailing
Wall

Al-Aksa
Mosque

JAFFA
GATE

Citadel
of David

Jewish

Armenian

Quarter

DUNG
GATE

Quarter

City of David

Valley of Kidron

ZION
GATE

Tomb
of David

Siloam

MOUNT ZION

JERUSALEM
(Old City)

on the golden dome, and placed paintings and images inside. The larger, silver-domed Mosque of el Aqsa, a rectangular structure built in the eighth century in the southeast corner of the compound, was used as Baldwin I's palace. However, Christian attachment to the Holy City doesn't center on Mount Moriah.

It focuses a little to the north and west on Via Dolorosa, a narrow, twisting street lined with small chapels and churches, Moslem dwellings and tourist gift shops. Jesus was said to have carried the Cross through that street from Pontius Pilate's judgment seat to Mount Calvary. At the end of the street stands the Church of the Holy Sepulcher, housing the presumed sites of the Crucifixion and burial.

The route was enshrined early in the fourth century by Saint Helena, mother of Constantine the Great, the Byzantine emperor who was the first major ruler to embrace the Cross. Saint Helena had come to Jerusalem to seek out the scenes of Christ's life and the Stations of the Cross as depicted in the New Testament. She located the final stations under shrines to Jupiter and Venus. The pagan shrines were demolished and chapels were built. Over the years, as Jerusalem changed religious hands, the chapels were alternately destroyed and rebuilt. The present Church of the Holy Sepulcher was constructed by the Crusaders in the twelfth century but restored almost beyond recognition in the nineteenth century after a fire in the rotunda.

Sometimes in the Holy Land, Jews, Christians, and Moslems venerate the same spots. This is in part the result of the interwoven origins of the three faiths. Due to the cycle of conquests, sackings, and reconstructions, moreover, synagogues, churches, and mosques were often built on one another's ruins, making for discord.

Christendom's attachment to the site of the Holy Sepulcher is not shared by other religions, but Christians themselves have been feuding bitterly over rights and privileges at their most sacred shrine.

For a while after the Moslems ejected the Crusaders from Palestine, at the end of the thirteenth century, the Franciscans were the guardians. The holy places were purchased from the sultan of Damascus by a French prince, Robert d'Anjou, who presented them to Pope Clement VI on condition that he appoint the Franciscans guardians for eternity. Clement, a Frenchman, complied with a papal bull in 1342.

The sultans respected the arrangement to a great extent. But they

Tisha B'Av, the anniversary of the destruction of the Temple, Jews congregate at the Wailing Wall to bemoan the fall of the Temple.

also tended to favor their own subjects in the various Eastern churches, particularly when political relations with France were not so good. The Greek Orthodox Church thus gradually gained ascendancy.

When the situation in the holy places was regulated in 1757 in a firman by Sultan Osman III, the position of the Greek Orthodox Church was the strongest. Its claim to 65 per cent of the Basilica of the Nativity in Bethlehem was recognized. Osman's firman was reaffirmed in 1852 by Sultan Abdul Mejid and has been adhered to by the British, the Jordanians, and the Israelis, who succeeded the Turks as temporal powers.

The document recognizes the titles of the various churches to their respective chapels in the Church of the Holy Sepulcher and regulates rights and privileges in the common sections, like the rotunda. It governs details from the precise hour when each denomination may wash floors to the times for masses in the rotunda.

So jealous are the churches of their privileges under the status quo that when a nail has to be hammered into a common wall, the depth of its penetration becomes a tense issue.

When the Church of the Holy Sepulcher was damaged by an earthquake in 1927, discord over who should fix what held up repairs for decades and the shrine remained in scaffolding. Finally a committee of architects and laymen representative of the Greek Orthodox, Armenian, and Roman Catholic churches was formed to supervise the repairs in a manner that would not infringe on the status quo in any way.

Jerusalem's prime importance to Christendom is unquestioned, although Christ's birthplace at Bethlehem is also deeply venerated. In addition, Catholics have Rome, their Eternal City.

To Moslems, Jerusalem is the third-ranking city after Mecca, where Mohammed was born, and Medina, where he labored after his flight. When Moslems between Mecca and Jerusalem pray, they get down on their knees and bend their bodies toward Mohammed's birthplace with their backs to Mount Moriah.

In Judaism there is Jerusalem and nothing but Jerusalem. Rabbinical law provides that when a Jew prays anywhere in the world he must face Jerusalem. Synagogues in the United States are positioned so that worshipers face east. In Japan the worshipers face west. In Jeru-

Jews stream to the Wailing Wall after its liberati
the Dome of the Rock is in the backgrou

160

salem itself they face the direction of the Wailing Wall.

In traditional Jewish households the spell of Jerusalem is cast over children from infancy. It is the theme of lullabies and bedtime stories. Judaism's equivalent of the Pledge of Allegiance is an oath that was first taken by the exiles in Babylonia. Children in Jewish parochial schools throughout the world recite it:

"If I forget thee, O Jerusalam," they chant, "let my right hand wither, let my tongue cleave to the roof of my mouth . . . if I set not Jerusalem above my chief joy."

The custom of the bridegroom crushing a glass during the wedding ceremony—thereby recalling the destruction of the Temple—is a form of compliance with that pledge.

If a husband or wife wishes to live in Jerusalem and the other partner objects, it is grounds for divorce under rabbinical law.

The liturgies of the Yom Kippur service and the Passover Seder conclude with the chant, "Next Year in Jerusalem!" Jews who observe those festivals in the Holy Land substitute for the traditional cry the slightly amended, "Next Year in a Rebuilt Jerusalem!"

The allusion obviously is not to the wide boulevards, functional houses, supermarkets, and traffic lights of the new city, but to the hive of ancient streets in the historic section.

One might have suspected that the liturgical and ritualistic expressions of yearning for Jerusalem were contrived. But during the Six Day War, Israelis themselves were amazed to find out how sincere they were.

The liberation of the walled, historic section of the city was drenched in sentiment. The Old City was liberated by Colonel Mordecai Gur and his brigade of paratrooper reservists. One company was commanded by Captain Yoram Zamosh, a deeply pious, former Yeshiva student. Obviously, the return to the Wailing Wall would be particularly meaningful for him.

Colonel Gur thought of his pious company commander when he crashed through Saint Stephen's Gate in his half-track and headed for the Temple Mount. He radioed Captain Zamosh to lead his company to the Wall.

Captain Zamosh's men had been advancing toward Saint Stephen's Gate when the order came. They raced ahead into the Old City. In his excitement, the company commander lost his way in the winding alleys. He asked an old Arab woman for directions. She fainted. Another Arab directed him.

He reached the Temple esplanade and from that the top of the Wall. He hung an Israeli flag over it. Then he descended a narrow staircase to the pavement. Somehow he had become separated from his men. For a while he stood alone, staring open-mouthed at the worn stones with moss growing out of the chinks.

Trembling with emotion, he felt an irresistible urge to share his feelings with those he loved. He thought of the men who had imbued him with the understanding to savor the great moment. Into his mind flashed the image of the venerable Rabbi Zvi Yehuda Kook, the head of the Merkaz Harav Yeshiva, where he had studied before beginning his army service. He sent a runner to the Yeshiva in western Jerusalem to fetch the Talmudic sage.

The blood on the cobblestones was still wet and snipers were still firing from the buildings when Rabbi Kook was escorted through the Old City. He and his escorts passed a file of soldiers advancing cautiously. One of the soldiers, Hannan Porat, was another student from the Merkaz Harav Yeshiva. He spied his rabbi and made no attempt to restrain his impulse. He left his column and followed the rabbi to the Wall.

Only in Jerusalem.

A carpenter who had been born in the Jewish quarter of the Old City commanded the company of reservists who retook it. As he moved among the dilapidated houses, vaguely familiar from his childhood, he recalled the day in 1948 when the Jewish quarter had fallen to the Jordanians. He had gone with his father into Jordanian captivity, although the enemy soldiers had told him to go with the women and children to freedom in the western part of the city. Now he also felt an irresistible urge. He posted his men, turned command of the company over to his deputy, and went home to fetch his father.

Another officer remembered a hermit living in the Israeli sector of Jerusalem, a Jewish refugee from the Old City who had taken an oath never to leave the four walls of his home until the Wailing Wall was liberated. A recoilless-gun carrier was sent to fetch the man.

The rapture of the pious over the liberation of the Wall was predictable. What was amazing was the ecstasy of the nonobservant, who homed in on it from all directions.

Paratroopers who had remained dry-eyed when their friends fell beside them, burst into tears on sighting the Wall. Men pressed their bodies against the ancient stones and kissed them, shaking with sobs. Others ran their fingers over the stones, ever so lightly. Some just stood and stared.

Rabbi Goren was quickly on the scene, hugging a Torah scroll and flourishing a *shofar*, which he kept blasting. When he recited a prayer for the fallen, men who had never been to a synagogue responded with fervent "Amens."

A C.B.S. reporter choked up and couldn't broadcast. An Israeli state radio reporter sobbed into a microphone: "I'm not religious. I have never been religious, but. . . ."

General Dayan arrived. He is not a praying Jew, but at the Wall he scribbled a prayer on a scrap of paper. "May peace come to the Jewish people," he wrote. Like pious pilgrims down the ages, he slipped the note into a crack in the wall.

It was unbelievable how many sophisticates and cynics solemnly crammed the chinks that day with prayerful notes on cigarette boxes and other odd scraps of writing material.

Soon civilians began coming, undeterred by warnings that Arab snipers were still operating and that minefields had not yet been cleared. The impatient were not only religious enthusiasts and Yeshiva students, but also miniskirted girls and children.

The Jewish world had waited nearly two thousand years for this moment. When it arrived, many Jews couldn't wait even a few hours more to touch the sacred stones. Some paid for their impatience with their blood. Some were crippled for life.

Today it seems incredible that before June, 1967, most Jews had appeared perfectly ready to live out their years cut off from the Wailing Wall and other holy places by the 1948 armistice lines. Certainly they didn't want to go to war to recover them.

The Wall was liberated on June 7. On June 5 Premier Eshkol had sent a message through United Nations officials to Amman, Jordan's capital, pleading with King Hussein to stay out of the fight between Egypt and Israel. Most Israelis had prayed that the Jordanian ruler would be prudent. However, the King chose to fight, blood was spilled, and the reunion with the old places intoxicated Israelis. To most of them now, a withdrawal from the Old City would be unthinkable.

The situation was somewhat similar before the 1948 war. Most Jews then wanted a peaceful settlement of the Arab-Jewish dispute even at the cost of excluding Jerusalem—all of it—from the planned Jewish State. The city then had 100,000 Jewish and 60,000 Arab inhabitants. The United Nations plan for partitioning Palestine into Arab and Jewish states envisioned Jerusalem as an international enclave within the proposed Arab state. A Jewish state without Jerusalem was hard to swallow, but Jewish leaders in Palestine felt they had better take what they could get. They feared they might regret it if they passed up the historic opportunity to restore Jewish sovereignty.

So they accepted the United Nations plan and hoped the Arabs would do so too. Mr. Ben-Gurion sent Mrs. Golda Meir, later Prime Minister but then head of the political department of the Labor Federation, to appeal to King Abdullah, the grandfather of King Hussein, to accept the partition plan. Mrs. Meir put on the black robes and veil of a typical Arab woman and slipped across the lines to a rendezvous with the King's emissaries, who whisked her to the palace.

She returned unhappily to Jerusalem to report that Abdullah wouldn't listen to reason. When the British left, the Arab Legion would invade Jewish territory. Moreover, on her way home, she saw the Iraqi army moving toward the front with heavy equipment and extensive field artillery.

The full-scale war that followed the British withdrawal went on for just over two months and ended on July 17 in a truce. In Jerusalem the truce found the forces of King Abdullah in control of the Old City, including all of the major religious shrines. The Jews occupied most of the new city outside the walls. A narrow corridor through the Judean hills linked the Jewish sector with the rest of Israel.

The provisional government that Mr. Ben-Gurion set up in Tel Aviv the day the British left did not officially regard the Jewish sector of Jerusalem as part of the Jewish State. Having embraced the United Nations partition resolution as the basis in international law for the proclamation of the Jewish State, the government was afraid to flout any part of it. The area was administered independently by an emergency committee headed by Dr. Dov Joseph, an attorney.

After the truce, however, the government felt morally entitled to incorporate the Jewish sector of Jerusalem into Israel, since the United Nations had done nothing at all to implement the internationalization plan for the city. But it proceeded gingerly.

Two weeks after the truce a trial balloon was sent up. Premier Ben-Gurion announced the appointment of Dr. Joseph as Military Governor of the Occupied Area of Jerusalem. Officials waited for the reaction from foreign powers.

It came in forty-eight hours. There were two letters in Dr. Joseph's letterbox. They came from the American and the Italian consuls general. They were addressed: "The Military Governor, Israel-Occupied Jerusalem."

So far so good.

The following month the Supreme Court was transferred from Tel Aviv to Jerusalem. There were no protests. In January Jerusalemites voted in Israel's first parliamentary elections. Who could complain?

In February the annexation was formalized. An official announcement proclaimed that Jerusalem was no longer "occupied territory." Dr. Joseph happily stepped down as Military Governor. Government departments began moving to Jerusalem.

The regime confidently expected that the internationalization plan would be officially killed in the United Nations General Assembly in 1949. To its astonishment, a coalition of Catholic, Communist, and Moslem countries pushed through a resolution on December 10 re-affirming the plan and delegating the Trusteeship Council to work out regulations for its implementation.

Israelis were stunned but Premier Ben-Gurion reacted typically, in accordance with his credo: "What the *goyim* say doesn't matter. It's what the Jews do that counts."

He promptly moved his own office from Tel Aviv to Jerusalem and initiated the transfer of the Knesset and most government ministries. The defense and political ministries were kept in Tel Aviv for reasons of security since Jerusalem, at the end of the *cul-de-sac,* was obviously too vulnerable. The foreign ministry remained in Tel Aviv in deference to friendly governments, which refused to move their diplomatic missions.

A pair of lovers ignore passersby at Jerusalem's Damascus Gate

At the same time King Abdullah integrated the Arab sector of Jerusalem into the Hashemite Kingdom of Jordan. Other Arab heads of state pushed for internationalization. But not Abdullah. He made it clear that he had no intention of relinquishing his sector.

So when the Trusteeship Council met to consider regulations for the implementation of the plan, the United States, the Soviet Union, and Britain concurred that internationalization was unworkable. The plan was thus virtually killed, although the resolution remained in the General Assembly's books.

By 1953, when Israel was a strapping five years old, the government felt sufficiently self-confident to move the foreign ministry to Jerusalem, although all the major powers made it clear they would not move their embassies. Friendly governments explained that acquiescing to Israel's action was one matter, but shifting their own embassies was another. The latter could be construed as collusion in contravening a United Nations resolution, which they felt would be most improper.

So Jerusalem has the dubious distinction of being the only capital in the world boycotted by ambassadors and ministers accredited to its government.

The setup is curious. Consulates that functioned in Jerusalem when the British governed Palestine continue to operate there independently of their country's diplomatic missions in Tel Aviv. Even Spain, which doesn't recognize Israel, has a consul in Jerusalem. The consuls are accredited not to the Israeli government but to an individual official of the Ministry of Interior, the District Representative in Jerusalem.

After the 1948 war, the consuls established separate offices in the Jewish and Arab sectors of the city and shuttled between them through the Mandelbaum Gate checkpoint. After the 1967 war, when the armistice lines were erased, they stubbornly continued to maintain their separate offices in the Arab and Jewish sectors.

For a while the United States Consul General stamped passports, anachronistically, "Jerusalem, Palestine." There were indignant protests. In 1964 it dropped the "Palestine."

During the years that Jerusalem was partitioned, the Jewish sector was a provincial, rather stuffy city. A sharp-penned American reporter once described it as "half as big as the Brooklyn cemetery and twice as dead."

The inhabitants were mainly civil servants who were underpaid and staid, and religious extremists who were austere and puritanical. The Hebrew University brought thousands of young men and women to the city, but even they didn't give Jerusalem much zest, for Israeli students are generally more serious than students elsewhere. They are older, most of them having served two or three sobering years in the armed forces, often as officers. A high proportion are married and work for a living. The young men, especially the officers, are called up repeatedly for military-reserve duties. That doesn't leave them much time to fool around.

So Jewish Jerusalem, despite the influx of students, was serene. It had the greatest libraries and museums in the country. It offered the richest choice of lectures on any given evening. As for the theater, however, it was strictly a road town. Tel Aviv companies brought shows to the capital from time to time. Jerusalem's movie theaters were mostly shabby, but they did show fairly recent pictures.

The Kol Israel Orchestra, the ensemble of the Israeli broadcasting service, held weekly symphonic concerts in the capital, and the larger Israel Philharmonic visited regularly from Tel Aviv with world-famous conductors and soloists.

There were a few discotheques and cellar-type nightclubs for young people. The leading hotels had bars and dance bands. But Jerusalemites didn't patronize them. The civil servant with his modest income and the Orthodox Jew didn't go in for that kind of night life. They preferred to socialize in one another's homes.

As for tourists, there wasn't much reason for them to spend more than a day in Jewish Jerusalem. It was sad. Practically everything that made the city famous was inaccessible.

A United Nations survey in 1948 had recognized thirty holy sites in Jerusalem and Bethlehem. Half of them were Christian, ten were Jewish, and five were Moslem. Only two were in Israeli territory. Twenty-seven were in the Arab sector and one was in no man's land.

The tourist who visited Jewish Jerusalem could hear the bells from historic churches and the muezzins' calls from famous mosques, but he couldn't get to them. Even the cries of Arab peddlers in the exotic bazaars came over the walls tantalizingly. But Jordanian sentries on the battlements stoned and sometimes fired at people who drew too near.

The best that visitors to western Jerusalem could do was to climb to the tops of hills or towers for a view of the spires, domes, minarets, ramparts, and steeples that make up the skyline of the historic portion of the city. Guides would point out the location of the Wailing Wall, but it was out of sight.

Visitors could also inspect a miniature replica of the Old City at the time of the Second Temple. It had been painstakingly put together on a hilltop near the Holyland Hotel by Israeli architects, archaeologists, and historians. It was beautiful, interesting, and instructive— but an inadequate substitute.

So when the Arab sector was taken in 1967 the Israelis set to work with alacrity, clearing the minefields, rubbish, barbed wire, wrecked buildings, and the ugly fire walls that had divided Jerusalem.

Forty-eight hours after the war, General Dayan summoned his army engineers. He told them he wanted a safe way for throngs of Jews to visit the Wailing Wall. He was told it would take a week to clear the minefields.

"I'll give you forty-eight hours," he said.

Arabs were quickly evicted from their homes in the Moors' quarter opposite the Wall, and bulldozers moved in. They flattened the condemned houses. When the debris was cleared away, there was a broad plaza opposite the Wall with space for tens of thousands of pilgrims and worshipers in place of the cobbled alley with room for only a few hundred.

Before the end of the month the reunification of Jerusalem was effected. The Arab sector couldn't be formally annexed by the State of Israel. To do so during a cease-fire situation would have contravened international law. And powers friendly to Israel warned strongly against it.

The difficulty was skirted by having the Israeli Municipality of Jerusalem incorporate the Arab sector. An enabling law empowered the municipality to extend the area under its jurisdiction. The power was invoked at once.

The Jerusalem Arabs thus did not become Israeli citizens, but they did come under the administration of the civilian instead of the military government. The transfer on June 29 was marked by a most audacious gamble in a month full of audacity and danger. General Dayan said that if Jerusalem were to be united, it should be united all the way. No more checkpoints. No passes. No searches. No curfews. No nothing. Any resident of the former Jordanian sector who wanted to enter the former Jewish sector should be able to do so freely at any hour of the day or night. It was his city, too.

The war had then been over for only three weeks. Officials were frankly scared. The mayor pleaded for time to make preparations. The police asked for time to organize security precautions. There weren't even proper traffic routes between the two sectors. General Dayan was adamant. "If you're unwilling to accept responsibility," he told a senior police officer, "I'm willing to accept your resignation."

The gamble was an incredible success. The day the barriers came down was a day to remember. There was a carnival atmosphere in the reunited city. One had to pinch oneself to make sure it was no dream.

Thousands of Jews crossed the former lines and melted into Arab crowds in the dark, musty, labyrinthian alleys of the Old City. Men brought their wives and small children with them. Nobody suffered even a scratch. The travelers all came home safely, laden with purchases.

Arabs crossed into the former Jewish sector warily, in small groups, at first. Later in the day they came confidently in a steady stream. They seemed elated, like children on a picnic.

A veteran Arab journalist, who for decades had written diatribes against Jews, observed the reunion from the window of an automobile. He saw the beaming faces of happy Arabs. He watched Jews and Arabs embrace and kiss in the streets. A tear rolled down his cheek. "It's the happiest day of my life," he exclaimed.

It would be nice to be able to report "and they lived happily ever after," but life isn't a fairy tale. Decades of animosity cannot be erased in a day.

Yet Jerusalem has never been the same since the barriers came down. The ugly scar that physically divided the two sectors is gone. Today one can't tell where the old armistice lines had run. A national park, extending from the Jewish section through the former no man's land to the battlements of the Old City, has been started and will eventually encircle the Wall. Farther north, an Israeli residential quarter extends across the former lines near Ammunition Hill, where some of the worst fighting occurred in the Battle for Jerusalem.

Roads, water and sewage mains, and telephone, electricity, and bus lines cross what was formerly not crossable. Every morning, thousands of Arabs in their *keffiyas* stream westward over Paratroopers Road, one of the newly opened thoroughfares, to jobs in the Israeli sector. Arab women with baskets on their heads and men on bicycles peddle fruits and vegetables in the Jewish section. Newsboys from the Old City hawk *Maariv* and *Yediot Ahronot*. In the afternoons, the tide reverses.

There is also a steady countertraffic of Jews into the Arab sections. Mornings and evenings, Orthodox Jews, many of them conspicuous in their austere black caftans, move through the alleys of the Old City to the Wailing Wall for religious services. Others go for shopping. The old goods in the bazaars have been gobbled up long ago and have been replaced largely by products from Israeli factories. Soap and chocolate in Hebrew wrappers, kosher toothpaste, and Hebrew newspapers seemed strange there for a while, but now they seem to belong.

Israelis found that there were still bargains in the Arab market. Meats and vegetables were substantially cheaper than in the Jewish sector. Tailored garments, shoes, rugs, scarves, straw matting, and other handicrafts were among the good buys.

Traffic to eastern Jerusalem for shopping and recreation swells on Jewish Sabbaths and festivals when restrictions button up everything in the western part of the city. Arab bars, nightclubs, hotels, restaurants, and places of entertainment bustle on Friday nights. A seamy aspect of the reunification has been the appearance of prostitutes from Haifa and Tel Aviv, mostly Arabic-speaking girls from Oriental families, who have been arrested for loitering in the Old City.

Fraternization between Arabs and Jews has been almost exclusively commercial and professional. Social intercourse has been rare. Hopes that the spirit of the day the barriers came down would be sustained evaporated quickly. East has remained east and west has remained west.

Among other things, Arab terrorism has impeded closer integration. Terrorists left a car loaded with explosives in an open market, where it blew up and killed a dozen people. A woman shopper from Ramallah left a bomb in a supermarket and killed two students. Such outrages were followed by police roundups and searches. For an Arab to be caught in the Jewish sector after a terrorist attack was obviously unpleasant. Arabs therefore tended to go there no more than they had to for business or actual employment.

Some Arabs from eastern Jerusalem joined Israeli unions. In the 1969 elections of the General Federation of Labor, a few accepted nomination as candidates of the Maarach, the Israeli Establishment list. But shortly before the elections, they withdrew, apparently under threats from the nationalists.

All in all Jerusalem has become a livelier city since its reunification. From a *cul-de-sac* and a frontier town, it has become a thriving hub and a base for excursions to Bethlehem, Hebron, Jericho, and Nablus. The tourist trade has thrived. Streets that were formerly deserted at 9 P.M. are alive late into the night. Before the June war, there had been six hundred empty apartments in the Jewish sector. After the war, a severe apartment shortage developed and rents spiraled.

Inside the walled city, some of the synagogues, yeshivas, and other religious institutions that were destroyed during the period of Jordanian rule have been restored. Arabs living in the former Jewish homes were evicted and relocated. A few thousand Jews moved in; most, but not all of them, were pious. One building was remodeled and made the official residence of the Deputy Prime Minister.

Exciting changes have taken place at the Wailing Wall, too. The weather-beaten stones and the cracks filled with scribbled prayers from General Dayan and the liberators of Jerusalem are now over the heads of the pilgrims.

The Wall is taller because archaeologists scraped away the ground below, exposing three additional rows of stone. Worshipers now face smooth, beautifully chiseled ashlars that were underground for centuries.

Around the corner from the Wailing Wall archaeologists uncovered the southern retaining wall of the Temple Mount. They dug down to the floor laid during Christ's lifetime. The pavement trod by the last Jews who brought animal sacrifices to the Second Temple has thus again been exposed to the light of the sun.

In 1908, on the sand dunes northeast of Jaffa, Jewish settlers began building Tel Aviv.

10 A Brash Metropolis

"Tel Aviv had no majesty or grandeur. But it was Jewish."

Young Israelis gather at a sidewalk café on Tel Aviv's Dizengoff Street.

JERUSALEM HAS NO equal in majesty, serenity, or grandeur. It is exotic and colorful. Its air is pure. It has inspired veneration, awe, and rhapsodic poetry. Jews have always been ready to fight for Jerusalem, to pray, fast, and die for Jerusalem.

But they have preferred to live in Tel Aviv.

Nearly one-third of the Jewish population of Israel—approximately 750,000 people—lives in the coastal city and its suburbs. More than 200,000 live in Jerusalem.

Tel Aviv is Israel's undisputed leader in business and finance, theater and music, political and union activities—and life in general.

The Oriental bazaars in Jerusalem, the medieval-type ghettos, the picturesque clerics in colorful robes, the muezzins' calls from the minarets, and the peal of famous church bells are indeed exotic. But cackling venders and braying donkeys in crowded alleyways didn't inspire Jews from Vienna or Budapest to want to live among them. The Chassidic Jews in their medieval attire and swaying ear locks personified the ghetto life that was precisely what most emigrants from Europe had sought to escape by coming to the Jewish homeland. The same went for the church bells and clerical robes, which victims of persecution in Europe associated with their persecutors.

Tel Aviv had no majesty or grandeur. It did not even have history. Built on sand, its landscape was flat and unexciting. It was never pretty. But it was Jewish.

Immigrants streamed to Tel Aviv because they wanted to live in an emancipated Jewish society, and Tel Aviv was the first all-Jewish city in the world.

Sabras who take world-renowned Israeli generals and statesmen in stride now chuckle over their parents' quaint sentimentality about the Jewish policemen of early Tel Aviv. But those policemen, with Hebrew lettering on their tunics, represented the first glimmer of Jewish self-rule for a people who had been subjugated for millennia. The Jewish mayor, judges, street cleaners, and firemen were Tel Aviv's magnet for immigrants. So were the Hebrew commercial signs, the chain across Herzl Street to exclude Sabbath traffic, and the bearded Jew who walked the thoroughfares on Friday afternoons sounding a trumpet to signal the approach of the Sabbath.

Tel Aviv's founders never dreamed they were creating a metropolis. Its godfathers were Jewish businessmen from Jaffa, the ancient port city where King Solomon landed timber from Tyre for the Jerusalem Temple.

Jaffa was part of the Turkish Empire and predominantly Arab. Some 25,000 Jews lived in the city. They were mostly shopkeepers and commercial agents, and they lived over their stores on the main shopping street or in Jewish quarters such as Neve Zedek on the northeastern outskirts.

Those quarters are now part of Tel Aviv, but they retain their original Middle Eastern character. Streets are narrow; solid blank walls face the roads. Service rooms abut the front walls and the dwelling rooms are in the rear, reachable through patios or courtyards. The homes were designed for security.

The Jaffa businessmen's intentions were modest. They wanted a quiet all-Jewish suburb. They expected to go on commuting to the port city for their livelihoods, their shopping, and their entertainment, but wished to raise their families in cleaner, more modern homes on wider streets. They wanted houses set back from the roads with gardens in front and yards in back. The garden city was then the latest thing in Europe.

They therefore bought thirty acres of sand dunes northeast of the ancient port, just beyond Jaffa's municipal boundary. One afternoon in 1908 they trudged across the windswept sands and parceled their holding into sixty half-acre plots. Construction began the following year. One- and two-story houses rose along Herzl Street, and they named four intersecting streets after a Hebrew poet, a Zionist, a philanthropist, and a philosopher.

For the five years up to the outbreak of World War I, the hamlet expanded slowly eastward and northward, away from Jaffa. In 1914 there were 180 houses with 2,000 people living in them. Then the war transformed Tel Aviv into a ghost town.

The Turks were suspicious of the Jews, many of whom were subjects of countries at war with the Ottoman Empire. The government gave the Jews a choice: either accept Turkish citizenship or get out. Some got out. Some became Turks.

Later in the war, when the British were approaching Palestine from Egypt, the Turks treated those Jews who had acquired Turkish citizenship as security risks. They didn't trust them near the coast. The government picked four Jews to stay in Tel Aviv as watchmen and evacuated the rest of the community inland. The deserted hamlet became a sad sight. Weeds began to grow in cracks in the pavement.

The city came to life again after the British conquest. Not only did the evacuees return, but immigrants from Europe joined them. The town expanded and the dream of a quiet dormitory suburb burst.

The spur to faster growth was supplied mainly by Arabs. There was some genuine alarm among the effendis over the increased rate of Jewish immigration. Some suspected that Great Britain's Balfour Declaration would involve the expropriation of land held by Arabs for the settlement of Jews. They organized massacres in various parts of the country.

Arab terror hit Jaffa on the day after Passover in 1921. Toughs with clubs and crowbars butchered forty-two Jews in two days. Jaffa's Jews fled. Artisans gathered their tools and retail merchants their stocks, and they all moved to the Jewish suburb.

Tel Aviv welcomed the fugitives but tried to confine their stores and workshops to an area across the railway tracks, south of the original garden city. The attempt to preserve the character of the quiet hamlet proved futile. The pressures were irresistible, and retail stores popped up in the midst of the residential areas.

In 1929 there was a bloodier wave of pogroms. It gave further impetus to Tel Aviv's development. This time Jewish wholesalers also abandoned Jaffa. Insurance and shipping agencies directly serving the port were virtually the only Jewish enterprises remaining.

The separation of the Jews from Jaffa became total during the 1936 riots, which were accompanied by a countrywide Arab strike. The strike paralyzed the port of Jaffa. The Jews raised funds to build their own port off Tel Aviv. The populace was invited to buy shares in a public company and the response was remarkable. I recall being swept along with the citywide wave. I was earning eight dollars a week at the time, and I invested twenty dollars in the port. The company built a jetty near the estuary of the Yarkon River. One day after a heavy rainstorm, the whole town went out to check that the port was still there.

The little harbor, as well as Jaffa's superior installations, were abandoned by the State of Israel after more modern ports were built elsewhere on the coast, but the first bag of cement landed at Tel Aviv is still on display in the Tel Aviv Museum. The sack bears the signatures of the Jewish boatmen who ecstatically brought it ashore from a Yugoslav freighter.

Technically, about 30,000 Jews remained citizens of Jaffa until the end of British rule in Palestine. They lived within the Arab city's municipal limits in areas abutting Tel Aviv. But they had nothing to do with Jaffa. They received all their services from the Jewish city. Their whole orientation was toward Tel Aviv.

So Tel Aviv grew rapidly—so rapidly that its expansion could not be planned. One thing led to another.

Theaters, newspapers, publishing houses, banks, an orchestra, an opera company, and other enterprises were organized in a community where there were people to patronize them. These amenities, in turn, attracted more people. The city thus evolved into the hub of the country. It just came about naturally.

It was the natural place to build the first all-Hebrew high school, the Herzlia Gymnasium, which had been founded in Jaffa in 1906. The classes in Jaffa were held in rented premises. When Tel Aviv was established three years later, it went without saying that the school building should rise there.

The Herzlia Gymnasium caused Tel Aviv's first transformation. It made it something of a school town. Students from all parts of Palestine and Europe enrolled. Small hotels and boarding houses mushroomed.

When the Habimah Theater, which had been founded in Moscow in the midst of the Russian Revolution, settled in Palestine, Tel Aviv was its obvious base.

Tel Aviv attracted the lion's share of the post-World War I immigration. Middle-class Jews from Poland started small factories to supply the rapidly growing population with consumer goods: ice, hosiery, underwear, silk, leather, and chocolate.

The trade unions made their headquarters where there were workers; the political parties where there were voters.

Tel Aviv's development picked up steam in the 1930's when the refugees from Hitlerism began arriving. As the most modern and Occidental city in the country, it cushioned their transition from European urban centers to the Middle East.

That wave lifted the population past the 100,000 mark. The city outgrew Jaffa and Jerusalem to become the largest in Palestine.

The German influx brought Tel Aviv such new assets as the Palestine Symphony Orchestra, created by Branislaw Huberman, the violin virtuoso, who recruited refugees ousted from the leading ensembles of Europe.

But the hectic growth in the 1930's also deprived the city of its early warmth and intimacy. Buses no longer dropped passengers at their homes, but halted only at regular stops. Old-timers scanning the crowds at the movies or on the streets were amazed to find that there wasn't a familiar face in sight. The Friday evening folk dancing in

Allenby Road was discontinued because the traffic was too heavy.

Efforts were made to preserve some of the happy traditions of Tel Aviv, such as the annual carnival on Purim. But the charm disappeared. Tel Aviv became the noisy, bustling, brash, hectic, and impersonal metropolis it is today.

The downtown area developed haphazardly. Lots purchased from Arab landowners consisted of small pockets here and there. That was a consequence of Moslem laws which fragmented properties on inheritance. Streets accordingly meandered. The city acquired a crazy-quilt pattern.

Allenby Road, the main thoroughfare, ran from south to north and then veered westward to the coast, for no logical reason except that it was where land could be acquired at the time.

In the original streets of the projected garden city three-story buildings rose side by side on plots intended for cottages. Street-level apartments were transformed into shops; the upper stories into offices. As business life became more sophisticated under the impact of the German immigration wave, impressive bank and office buildings replaced earlier structures. The transition culminated in the 1960's with the construction of a thirty-two-story skyscraper on the site of the Herzlia Gymnasium, which moved uptown to modern premises.

Prior to Israel's independence, the city was hemmed in. When its eastward growth reached what is now Ibn Gvirol Street, it hit the borders of Sarona, a village owned by German Christians. They wouldn't sell an inch to Jews.

Expansion southward was cut off by Jaffa. On the west was the Mediterranean. Arabs who owned land in the north and the southeast were under threats and political pressure not to sell to Jews. Those who could be induced to sell held out for exorbitant prices—which they got. Some were killed by Arab gunmen for their fancied betrayal of the Arab cause.

Accordingly, builders endeavored to exploit the precious sands to the maximum. Because the streets were narrow, regulations limited structures, with rare exceptions, to three stories. So builders put up houses on stilts. Roofed-over gardens led to the front entrances. The houses had three-story facades in compliance with the regulations. In the rear, however, the builders compressed five floors into them.

*Sprawling Tel Aviv, photographed from the Shalom Tower,
tallest building in the Middle East*

Still the pressure for places to live and room to open shops mounted. It grew so great that the authorities had to shut an eye when the spaces between the stilts were walled up and laundry rooms on the roofs were converted into dwellings. On the most fashionable streets of the 1930's and 1940's, Rothschild Boulevard and Chen Boulevard, entrances to the nicest homes are to this day disfigured by grocery stores, vegetable stores, laundries, and other businesses tucked into the walled-up spaces between the stilts.

In 1948 Tel Aviv became a battlefront. Under the United Nations partition plan for Palestine, Jaffa was to have been an Arab enclave in Jewish territory. The Arabs set out to torpedo the whole plan. They set up mortars in Jaffa and indiscriminately shelled the Jewish city. Snipers took up positions in minarets towering over the flat-roofed buildings of Tel Aviv and attacked motorists and pedestrians.

A few days before the British Mandate ended, the underground Irgun Zvai Leumi launched a counterattack. The Arabs fled in panic and the State of Israel took over a nearly empty Jaffa.

Tel Aviv had burst at its seams up to 1948. When Israel became independent, the seams were opened. Jaffa (Yafo in Hebrew) was incorporated into the municipal boundaries in 1950. The official name of the city became Tel Aviv-Yafo.

The Sarona lands on the east also became available. The German owners had been deported to Australia as enemy aliens during World War II by the British, who used their property as a police base. When the British left, the Israelis took over the villas, orchards, and farms.

The first five years following Israel's independence were Tel Aviv's most strenuous. The population grew from 215,000 to 350,000. Jaffa's houses were allocated to immigrants by the government's Custodian of Abandoned Property. The Sarona lands, state domain, and abandoned Arab lands were utilized for housing. More than 8,000 buildings with 62,000 rooms went up in those five years.

The boom strained the city's facilities. Hospital authorities were tormented by a shortage of beds. Wards were so jammed that patients were kept in drafty corridors. Hopeless cases were sent home to die to make room for people who could be helped.

School facilities were so inadequate that classes had to be held in three shifts. Wooden shacks were quickly assembled in some neighborhoods to cope with urgent needs. Due to power shortages, house-wives had to refrain from using electric stoves, irons, heaters, and other appliances during most hours of the day. The water supply frequently failed tenants living in upper stories.

The growing pains were not peculiarly Tel Aviv's, of course, but existed countrywide. They gradually eased as new water mains, power stations, hospitals, schools, and other projects were completed.

The older sections of the city emerged from the strenuous post-independence period more congested, shabbier, and dirtier than ever. Government rent restrictions had discouraged landlords from re-plastering and painting the peeling façades of their properties. They were left to dilapidate. Unfortunately for Tel Aviv's reputation, the neglected downtown parts of the city are the sections that visitors see.

The new quarters took advantage of the greater elbow room afforded after independence. Consequently, streets there are broader. Widely spaced apartment houses of up to fourteen floors are interspersed with one-, two-, and three-story houses to break the monotony of the old Tel Aviv skyline. There is more greenery. The newer apartment houses are nearly all condominiums and better tended.

The city has also been enriched by a handsome university campus, spacious fairgrounds, a modern concert hall, new theater buildings, museums, and scores of other amenities. A row of luxury hotels rose along the seafront. Dizengoff Street, named after Tel Aviv's first mayor, is lined with attractive shops and restaurants and has become the teeming, glittering center of night life.

But the more it teemed and glittered, the more Tel Aviv lost its early virtues. The more cosmopolitan it got, the more it was derided. It came to represent the antithesis of the old pioneering values—a city of careerists and seekers after an easy life.

The national government turned sour on Tel Aviv. An all-Jewish city was no longer distinctive once there was a whole Jewish state. The government was distressed by the preference of immigrants for the lights and crowds of the metropolis. It offered citizens incentives to move out to newly opened areas.

Tel Aviv's growth slowed down. In 1963 it reached its peak population of 395,000. Then a decline began. The net loss was several thousand inhabitants a year.

However, the loss did not affect the city's pulse. The defectors were mostly young couples who sought cheaper and better houses in the suburbs of Ramat Gan, Holon, Bat Yam, and Givatayim, but they continued to commute to Tel Aviv for business, employment, shopping, and entertainment.

The defections resulted in thinner enrollments in kindergartens and primary schools, but they didn't weaken Tel Aviv's position as the center of Israeli life. About 150,000 people enter the city daily; 43 per cent of all Israelis employed in commerce and banking work in Tel Aviv, whether or not they live there. Thus the city's leadership in business and finance remains unchallenged.

In heavy industry, however, Tel Aviv has yielded supremacy. There are about 10,000 manufacturing enterprises in the city, but most of them are tiny. In 3,800, the bosses do all the work themselves. In 3,400 more, there are fewer than five employees. Tel Aviv's factories are in the light-industry category. They produce electronic products, refrigerators, metal fittings, clothing, shoes, furniture, electrical appliances, and household goods.

Israel's more impressive installations—the shipyards, the automobile assembly plants, chemical factories, oil refineries, cement works, and foundries—are mostly sixty miles or so up the Mediterranean coast on the shore of Haifa Bay. That region offered what Tel Aviv couldn't match.

The port of Haifa, tucked into the southwest corner of the bay, was the first harbor in the country where ships could berth at deep-water quays instead of anchoring offshore and transshipping passengers and goods in launches and barges. When it was completed in 1933, it succeeded Jaffa as the major gateway to Palestine.

The British needed the port as a royal navy base and fueling station. They made Haifa the outlet for a 621-mile pipeline from the oil fields in Kirkuk, Iraq. British interests built the refineries that commenced operation in 1939. The port was thus ready on the eve of World War II for its role as the main supply base for the Allied forces in the Eastern Mediterranean.

Historically, the major city on the bay was Acre, at the northern end. It had been a port since Roman times and was the administrative center of the region before the British conquest. However, the bay at

Acre was too small for modern shipping.

The Haifa end was preferable for security reasons, too. Mount Carmel extended through the Haifa promontory right up to the sea. The height thus sheltered the harbor. In addition, the mountain obstructed observation by planes approaching from the sea. Indeed, when Haifa was bombed by the Germans and Italians during the war, the port was not hit.

The modern shipping facilities at Haifa were the main attraction for industrialists. But hardly less important was the availability of plant sites at reasonable terms on the bay shore, extending nine miles to Acre. Marshes had been drained in the 1920's and the reclaimed land was reserved for an industrial zone. Tel Aviv had nothing of the kind. Land prices there were prohibitive.

The town of Haifa itself was unimportant when the British chose the site for the harbor. It was predominantly Arab and rather primitive. Some Jews lived downtown among the Arabs. There was also a small Jewish community on the lower slope of Mount Carmel that clustered around a technical high school that a German Jewish society had built in 1912 to serve the Jews of the Turkish Empire.

The lower slope gained more inhabitants during the influx of middle-class Jews from Poland after World War I. But the scenic beauty and superior climate of Mount Carmel couldn't compete with the lure of the all-Jewish city to the south, and Haifa received only a sidestream of the Zionist immigrations.

When Haifa became Palestine's major port, the Zionist leadership felt that the Jewish foothold in the city, and particularly the harbor, had to be strengthened. The Arabs couldn't be allowed to monopolize such a vital strategic position.

The British had brought thousands of primitive Hauranis from Syria and Jordan (or Trans-Jordan, as it was called until 1949) to work as cheap, unskilled laborers in the construction of the harbor. Many remained in Haifa when the port was completed to work as porters. The pay was fifty-six cents a day. They didn't have any competitors.

The General Federation of Labor (Histadrut) sent brawny young idealists from nearby collective farms to the harbor to get jobs. The British officials and Arab contractors who controlled the port resented the intrusion. They hired the Jews and put them to work hauling three-hundred-pound sacks on their backs. The novice porters couldn't take it for long.

The problem was discussed by the top Zionist leaders in Jerusalem. Mr. Ben-Gurion and Yitzhak Ben Zvi, who later became President of Israel, had studied law in Turkey before World War I. They remembered visiting the harbor city of Salonika, where muscular Jewish workers dominated the port to such an extent that it was closed on Saturdays. Salonika had since passed from Turkey to Greece in the Balkan Wars. Abba Khoushi, secretary of the Jewish port workers, was sent to Greece to recruit the muscles for Haifa.

Mr. Khoushi visited Salonika a number of times in 1933 and 1934. He talked to its port workers in their clubs and homes, singly and in groups. He told them there was no future for Jews in Europe. He signed individual contracts with eleven hundred of them. Unhappily, others turned him down, only to be destroyed a few years later when the Nazis occupied Greece.

When the first fifty Salonikans reported for work in Haifa, a half-ton safe that had been shipped to the Anglo-Palestine Bank lay on the quayside. The new workers were assigned to handle it. The Arabs stood by to watch.

The Salonikans formed a file and walked in circles around the object.

A ritual? someone asked.

No, he was told, they were ascertaining where the object was heaviest so they could decide how best to lift it.

One man, not much more than five feet tall, stood with his back to the safe. He was the cantor of the community, but that was just a coincidence. Two others got the load onto his back. The Arabs' mouths hung open as they watched the little fellow walk off with the half ton on his back.

He walked from the quayside through the port gate to the bank on Kingsway, a distance of a quarter of a mile. A Salonikan walked on either side of him chanting psalms for moral support.

The Salonikans became the hotshots of the harbor. They outclassed the Hauranis. Shippers who had balked at hiring Jewish workers from the collective settlements for fear they would break down during a job and leave their employers to the mercies of vengeful Arabs were happy to hire the Salonikan pros. When the British had a challenging

A ship is unloaded at Haifa's busy port.

assignment they, too, called upon the Salonikans.

The Jewish foothold soon yielded political dividends. When Arab leaders proclaimed their general strike in 1936, the port of Haifa continued to function. Even the Hauranis stayed on the job. Striking Arab longshoremen from Jaffa beat up some of the Haifa Arabs for breaking the strike. The Hauranis then stayed away from the harbor for a few weeks, but when the Jews kept the port going anyway, they returned.

Apart from the Salonikans, Haifa was enriched in the 1930's by a substantial influx of German Jews. The Germans, unlike earlier im-

189

migrants, were not Zionist idealists. They were refugees seeking a haven. The solid fabric of Jewish life that had lured Eastern European Jews to Tel Aviv did not necessarily appeal to them. The mainstream of German immigration flowed to Tel Aviv because it was, after all, the most modern and Europeanized of Palestine's cities, and offered the widest opportunities for making a living. But many thousands were attracted to the prettier harbor city.

They developed the upper slope of Mount Carmel, creating new communities with a Central European atmosphere. Some coffee houses there still print their menus both in Hebrew and German.

When Haifa was hit by the Arab riots of the 1920's and 1930's, Jews abandoned mixed residential and business sections, but there wasn't the polarization that marked Jaffa. While Mount Carmel was almost exclusively Jewish, the lower town was a patchwork of Jewish and Arab quarters.

In Jaffa a Jewish manufacturer had been able to load his sewing machines or carpentry tools on a truck in troublesome times, move to Tel Aviv, and set himself up in business there. Obviously the cement works and the other heavy industries in Haifa couldn't be transferred up Mount Carmel.

Most factories in the Haifa area were Jewish-owned and employed Jewish labor exclusively. Arabs owned some small factories that employed only Arabs. Labor was mixed in the British oil companies, the refineries, the port, the railways, and government offices.

Livelihoods couldn't come up the mountain to the Jews, so the Jews had to go down the mountain to their livelihoods. They had to run the gauntlet through Arab neighborhoods in the lower town where terrorists sniped and threw hand grenades. The Jews traveled in armor-plated buses with steel shutters for windows and slanted wire mesh over the roofs to deflect the grenades.

The Jewish-owned factories had sandbagged emplacements and pillboxes at strategic points. Each plant had a few guns licensed by the British and a larger arsenal of illegal weapons in secret caches. Stocks of food and other supplies were on hand in case of siege. Haganah experts drilled workers in how to leave their machines at times of danger and man the prepared positions.

Haganah officers joined the work gangs in the harbor. They concealed guns in secret compartments of tractors and other equipment. Similar precautions were taken elsewhere when Jews and Arabs worked together. The measures were on the whole effective, but in the refineries one day in December, 1947, hundreds of Arabs suddenly turned on helpless Jewish specialists scattered over the vast plants and butchered forty-two men with knives, iron bars, and tools.

Haifa was the first big prize to fall to the Jews in the War of Independence. On April 21, 1948, three weeks before they terminated their rule, the British withdrew their forces from most of the city and retained control only of the routes to the harbor to protect their line of withdrawal. It was a signal for the Haganah and the Arab forces to fight it out for the city.

It was one of the few battle areas in the country where the Jews had tactical advantages. They were in the hills and the Arabs were down below. In twenty-four hours the entire city was won.

Most of the Arabs fled. British landing craft and trucks took the refugees to Acre, from which most of them proceeded to Lebanon. Only about 3,500 remained.

The mass flight was a lucky break for the Jews. The security gain was obvious. Moreover, the abandoned homes were later utilized to accommodate Jewish immigrants.

It is interesting to note that at the time the Jews pleaded with the defeated Arabs to stay. People refuse to believe it today, but it's true.

The Jews had not been a self-governing people for two millennia. They were conditioned to feel that their political status was in the hands of others. They were extremely sensitive to what the Christian world thought of them. Mr. Ben-Gurion's credo, "It's what the Jews do that counts," developed much later, when Israel was already firmly established.

In April, 1948, the Jews behaved largely as though some international referee would ultimately decide whether or not there was to be a Jewish State. Therefore they felt it important to impress on the world that the establishment of a Jewish State need not displace Arabs.

When local Arab leaders met with Jews on April 22 to discuss surrender terms, they were promised full equality if they turned in their arms and military equipment. Iraqis and other foreign Arabs fighting with the defeated forces would be free to go home. The only prisoners the Jews wanted were the Europeans who had trained the Arabs and fought with them. They included Germans who had escaped from Allied prisoner-of-war camps in the region, deserters from the British forces in Palestine, and Yugoslav Moslems who had fought for Hitler.

Mayor Shabbetai Levy, an Oriental Jew with excellent personal relations with Arabs of the middle and upper classes, pleaded with them to remain and promised them full protection.

The Arabs asked for time to consider their reply. They communicated with their national leadership in Jerusalem and were told to clear out for the time being. They were advised that they would be able to return when the regular Arab armies swept in from neighboring countries immediately after the British withdrawal.

The Israelis are now frankly delighted that the Arabs didn't heed Mayor Levy's pleas. But in 1948 they felt deeply that the Arab flight was a misfortune.

Haifa began an era of unprecedented progress after it became virtually an all-Jewish city. The population grew from 66,000 to 220,000 in the two decades from 1948 to 1968. Counting the suburbs in the bay area, it's an urban center of 300,000 people.

The harbor's capacity has trebled and further expansion is under way. An auxiliary port for medium-size and small vessels and a shipyard have been established at the estuary of the Kishon River, which empties into the bay.

The oil refineries that the British shut down in 1948 resumed limited production two years later under Israeli management. At first crude oil was brought from the Caribbean and used only to meet domestic needs. Later a 258-mile pipeline was laid to link the refineries with Elath, on the Gulf of Aqaba, where tankers unloaded petroleum from Persian Gulf sources. The refineries then resumed work at full capacity, exporting surpluses to Europe.

About one-third of Haifa's breadwinners earn their living from the sea as port and shipyard workers, sailors, fishermen, shipping agents, and insurance brokers. An additional one-fourth hold factory jobs in the bay area. Thus the city is largely a workers' town.

The inhabitants live mostly in modern, functional, stone-faced apartment houses on the slope of Mount Carmel. The main business section has remained down below. A cable subway with peculiar stepped cars shuttles passengers up and down the steep slope.

Haifa is the best-tended, greenest, and cleanest of Israel's major towns. The top of Mount Carmel is a resort area with fine hotels catering to tourists and vacationing Israelis. The view from the top reminds visitors of San Francisco.

The harbor city hasn't the throb and bustle of Tel Aviv, and ambitious professionals and businessmen sometimes find this confining. Only twenty miles from Israel's northern border, Haifa is too much out of the way to be a national center. Ever since the government built a new cargo harbor in the 1960's at Ashdod—closer to Tel Aviv, Jerusalem, and the Negev—Haifa has been more remote than ever. Businessmen and professionals who have opened branch offices in Tel Aviv have tended to spend more time in them than in their main offices. Some of them have moved to the larger city.

The coastal railway has brought Tel Aviv within an hour's journey of Haifa. Many of Haifa's residents commute to work in Tel Aviv and travel there frequently to shop.

Like the staid people of Jerusalem, the hard workers of Haifa don't go in much for night life. They prefer exchanging visits at home. Thus there are few night spots in the city.

Tel Aviv's theater companies and the Israel Philharmonic Orchestra visit Haifa regularly. Such cultural dependence on Tel Aviv offended the local pride of Abba Khoushi, the one-time port worker who in 1961 succeeded Shabbetai Levy as mayor. He organized a municipal theater and brought some outstanding Hebrew dramatic talent to town. He also sponsored a civic symphony orchestra and started a municipal college. That college is separate from the Technion-Israel Institute of Technology, the latter being an outgrowth of the technical high school founded on Mount Carmel in Turkish times.

Haifa still has great hopes for a more prominent place in the sun. Those hopes rest on a Middle Eastern peace. Haifa's port is a natural gateway to the Mediterranean for the Arab hinterland. In 1951, when there were prospects of an accord with King Abdullah, a section of the harbor was designated as a free port for the Hashemite Kingdom of Jordan. When the Arabs start to use its harbor, Haifa will come into its own.

Israeli workers laying a new pipeline through the Negev

11 Moses

"Mr. Ben-Gur

Knew His Mineralogy

...anted a chain of Jewish towns through the wilderness.

THE JEWISH STATE that emerged after the War of Independence was shaped like a telephone receiver. The listening end was the size of Rhode Island, the mouthpiece slightly larger than Connecticut.

Bridging the two was a coastal strip of only 875 square miles. The strip constituted 11 per cent of Israel's territory; but it contained nearly 80 per cent of the population—some 500,000 persons.

Settlement virtually ended twenty-two miles south of Tel Aviv at Gedera, beyond which there were wide open spaces. There was prairie land down to biblical Beersheba where the patriarch Abraham had grazed his cattle. But most of the terrain stretching beyond Beersheba all the way to the Gulf of Aqaba was rock desert—the stark Negev. The area south of Gedera, equal in size to Connecticut, comprised 70 per cent of Israel's territory. Yet fewer than 6,000 Jews—less than one per cent of the population—lived there. Bedouin nomads outnumbered the settlers three to one.

In the country's northern sector, 50,000 Jews lived among 90,000 Arabs. Another 80,000 Jews lived in the Jerusalem area, where there were few Arabs.

Lopsided? Of course! But Jews adored their infant state like doting mothers. Only the father of the new country sounded a sour note.

A new beehive-style building complex at Hatzeva in the Negev

"In our days," Premier Ben-Gurion warned, "Tel Aviv can be destroyed by a single bomb. If Tel Aviv, God forbid, goes, there goes the State."

Most Israelis shrugged off his Jeremiah-like scoldings. Citizens well established in modern cities or in the verdant citrus belt didn't fancy themselves frontiersmen. Only a few young idealists responded to the Premier's call to spread out.

So the main burden of populating the hinterland fell to immigrants, especially the poor and the unskilled who depended entirely on the authorities for a place to live.

For the first two years or so, the unwitting and rather unseemly pioneers were directed to areas abandoned by Arab refugees or to the peripheries of small Jewish localities in the interior. Such locations had obvious advantages. They had roads of sorts, water sources, and other facilities that provided cores for encampments where immigrants could be lodged until their homes were built. Naturally, most of the locations were in the northern 30 per cent of the country. Mr. Ben-Gurion wasn't satisfied. He wanted the main thrust of settlement directed to the southern 70 per cent, particularly to the Negev, where there were no roads, no water, no trees, and hardly any soil.

197

The tough-minded leader knew exactly what he wanted—and why. The armistice agreement gave Israel 165 miles of border with Egypt. Egypt was the most dangerous of Israel's neighbors. The best-defended territory was settled territory. So the Egyptian border had to be settled. True, the land was so poor that even Bedouins had snubbed it. So what?

Then there was the prairie land north of Beersheba. It was a wedge between Jordan's Hebron hills and Egypt's Gaza Strip. In places the wedge was only twenty miles wide. Arab smuggler caravans crossed it brazenly. Jews had to plug that gap.

The beachhead on the Gulf of Aqaba was Israel's gateway to the Indian Ocean and the Far East. It was a historical trade route. That was where King Solomon landed the sandalwood from Ophir and Tarshish for the railings of his Temple and for his singers' harps and psalteries. Gold, ivory, and silver, apes and peacocks from the fabled Orient also came ashore there. So did the Queen of Sheba on her royal visit to the amorous king.

Mr. Ben-Gurion wanted that outlet re-established. To protect the line of communications to the port, he wanted a chain of Jewish towns through the middle of the wilderness.

The idea was not as wild as it seemed. There had been towns in the Negev before. Archaeologists have been digging them up. The remains of Nabataean and Byzantine streets, towers, archways, churches, and cloisters have been dusted off and restored as tourist sites.

The Nabataeans, contemporaries of Christ, were a pagan Semitic people who were based in North Arabia and traded with Europe. They established posts in the Negev at strategic points where their camel caravans to the Mediterranean coast intersected routes between Egypt and Mesopotamia.

Mounted guards to protect the caravans were based at the desert stations. Cameleers replenished water and other supplies there. Some posts like Avdat and Subeita developed into substantial cities. They thrived as Byzantine towns after the Romans crushed the Nabataean kingdom, but faded after the Persian and Arab conquests of the seventh century. When Bartholomeu Dias discovered the Cape of Good Hope in the fifteenth century and opened a new route between the Orient and Europe, the importance of the Negev as a crossroads of international

198

trade ended.

But where did the ancients get their food and water in the desert? Israeli scientists delved into the mystery and solved it. The Nabataeans had chosen pockets of bottomland for cultivation and had built dams and canals on the surrounding hills to channel rainfall run-off to their fields, where it was trapped. For every acre they cultivated, the Nabataeans accumulated run-off from thirty to forty acres. They let the water sink into the loess sufficiently to permit the cultivation of legumes, wheat, barley, grapes, figs, and dates. The Israelis have reconstructed the Nabataean farms and irrigation systems for research purposes.

Mr. Ben-Gurion's obsession with the Negev predated the State of Israel. In June, 1935, he wrote a remarkable letter to Justice Louis D. Brandeis of the United States Supreme Court, an active supporter of the Jewish cause in Palestine.

He proposed recruiting fifty to one hundred young Jews to settle near the Gulf of Aqaba to fish, farm, and stake a foothold. He needed $100,000 for fishing equipment and aircraft for quick communications with the north.

"Until the place develops," Mr. Ben-Gurion wrote, "there will be no profits. But the investment is worthwhile so as to open the Negev and the sea route to India to Jewish labor and initiative."

He noted that the country had outlets to the Mediterranean and the Gulf of Aqaba and added: "The Suez Canal is too narrow for large modern ships and it can easily be blocked in time of war. It is sufficient to sink one ship and make the canal impassable. There is no other way to India except the Red Sea route via Haifa and Elath."

Mr. Ben-Gurion failed to raise the money. And four years later the British put up a legal obstacle to his plan. On the eve of World War II, they wanted to appease the Arabs who had been rioting in protest against the Jewish entrenchment in Palestine. The British prohibited the acquisition of land by Jews in most parts of the country, including the Negev.

The Zionists asked their legal experts to find loopholes in the restrictions. They did. In 1943 small contingents of Jews tiptoed into the Negev. They set up three "observation posts" in the plateau between Beersheba and the Egyptian border, purportedly to study soil conditions, climate, vegetation, and water resources.

In 1946 the Jews took a bolder step. On the night after Yom Kippur, they established eleven more settlements in one swoop. Britain's days in Palestine were then numbered. If the government considered legal action to evict the Jews, they weren't left with much time to take it.

The settlers extended a small water pipeline into the wilderness from Nir Am. They had barely had time to plant a few trees when their venture bore fruit—political fruit. The little Jewish colonies scored the desired impression on the majority of the United Nations considering the partition of Palestine. The Jewish dots on the map persuaded them that ceding the desert to the Arabs would doom it to indefinite desolation; granting it to the Jews would give it a chance to live. So they assigned the Arabs the inhabited and cultivable strip along the Mediterranean coast around Gaza, as well as a belt of desert adjoining the Egyptian border. The Jews got the rest of the Negev down to the Gulf of Aqaba.

So far so good. But the Jews still had to fight for the country. In the war, the role of the Negev settlements was still more cogent. Each was a fortified position in the Egyptian army's way. Thirteen of them held out against King Farouk's tanks and armor; only Kfar Darom astride the coastal road was crushed.

The Egyptian columns advancing toward Jerusalem and Tel Aviv bypassed the holdouts. They were to rue it. When the fighting stopped in July, 1948, and the truce lines were drawn, the Arab forces controlled most of the Negev, but there was a Jewish-controlled pocket in the middle.

Under the terms of the truce, the Egyptians were required to allow supply columns through the truce lines to the encircled colonies. They refused. The Israelis organized an airlift. They flew a battle-weary brigade out of the pocket and a bigger, fresher, and better equipped one in. When the encircled force was strong enough to lash out, a trap was set.

The United Nations truce supervision organization was informed that the Jews intended to send a supply column to the besieged villages at noon on October 15. The UN officers duly informed the Egyptians, who in turn swallowed the bait.

No sooner did the convoy come within range of the checkpoint than the Egyptians opened fire. One truck was set ablaze. The others turned back. That was all the pretext the Israelis needed.

The encircled brigade slammed out. The Israeli forces north of the truce lines burst forward. It took a week before the United Nations could get the sides to agree to another cease-fire. At the end of the week, the tables were turned. The Israelis had most of the Negev and the Egyptians had a pocket. In that pocket at Faluja, there was an embittered young major named Gamal Abdel Nasser.

Further engagements in the Negev eliminated the pocket and reduced the Egyptian hold to a finger extending twenty-five miles up the Mediterranean coast from the Egyptian border. King Farouk called it quits. He sent emissaries to negotiate an armistice with Israel on the Greek island of Rhodes. The pact was signed on February 24, 1949. It left Egypt with the coastal finger, which was swollen with several hundred thousand refugees from other parts of Palestine.

Then there were the Jordanians to reckon with. They came to the armistice table in March with an unexpected claim: the eastern fringe of the Negev down to the gulf. The area had been assigned to the Jewish State by the United Nations, but the Israelis had never taken possession and Jordanian troops had moved in.

When the Israeli delegates reported this development to Tel Aviv, which was then still the seat of government, Mr. Ben-Gurion promptly ordered his army to rectify the oversight. An Israeli force reached the coast on March 10 and took it without a shot. There was nobody to shoot at; the Arab Legion had prudently pulled out the night before. A soldier inked a Jewish star on a sheet. It was hoisted on a pole in front of mud shacks that had comprised a police post.

The improvised flag fluttering on the beach did more than make Israel a two-sea country. It affected the power balance of the whole region. The seven-mile Israeli coastline at the head of the gulf broke an otherwise uninterrupted stretch of Moslem-ruled territory between the Atlantic and the Indian oceans. The beachhead separated Egypt from Jordan.

That wedge was to block President Nasser's path to empire. In the 1950's there were several occasions when the Kingdom of Jordan was ripe for his taking if only he could have gotten there. Syria actually merged with Egypt—the new nation called itself the United Arab

Republic—but lack of territorial contiguity prevented President Nasser from controlling the province. The union was undone after a while by a revolt, and the United Arab Republic became just another name for Egypt.

If Egypt had had a common border with Jordan, and through Jordan, with Syria, the history of the region would have been different. Iraq, Saudi Arabia, the Persian Gulf sheikdoms, Western oil interests, and the survival of Israel herself would have been imperiled if that hand-made blue-and-white flag hadn't been raised at Elath.

Once the Negev was securely Israeli, Mr. Ben-Gurion focused the full force of his personality and prestige on its development. He ordered the country's best resources diverted southward: the principal rivers, rainfall run-off, people, scientific and research institutions, industries, money—even himself.

In 1952 the then sixty-six-year-old Premier picked Sdeh Boker in the Negev plateau as his new home. While driving through the waste-lands in an official convoy, he came across young men and women clearing boulders to get at some soil they could cultivate. They lived in a bare encampment between outcroppings of rock. "I resolved then and there to join them," Mr. Ben-Gurion recalled later.

When he returned to Jerusalem, he wrote humbly to the young pioneers, asking whether there was room for him in their settlement. The following year he stunned the country by suddenly resigning the premiership. He packed his books, took his wife, Paula, and set out for the wilderness. A wooden prefab was erected for the couple in Sdeh Boker. Mr. Ben-Gurion sheared the communal sheep and did other farm chores.

His career as a sheep-shearer was cut short a year later by a crisis in Jerusalem that necessitated his return to the government. But Sdeh Boker remained his home. When he retired from the premiership finally in 1963, he returned to his prefab. Sdeh Boker was by then an oasis with peach and apricot orchards; sheep-raising had been given up as unprofitable.

The area that supported 6,000 Jews in 1948 now supports 250,000. Most of the settlement has been north of Beersheba, not in the Negev proper. The settlers founded 14 towns and 150 agricultural villages. The number of Arabs in the region has increased to 25,000—mostly

A packing house in Hatzeva crates the fruits and vegetables produced in the torrid Araba Depression.

203

Bedouins whose tents are pitched in the valleys, where they raise sheep, goats, barley, and wheat.

The elite of the region are about 13,000 idealists living in some thirty communal farms at strategically sensitive points. Nearly all of the farms were established along the armistice lines with Egypt or Jordan. The founders were mostly young people from old Israeli families, but they also included some immigrants groomed in Zionist youth movements in Western countries. These front-line farmers planted their crops right up to the armistice lines. By day they tilled with guns ever handy and by night they took turns guarding. Some were killed and others were crippled by terrorist mines buried in the fields or while defending crops and equipment against marauders.

Veteran Israelis were also among the settlers of the new southern towns and smallholders' villages away from the front lines, but they were a small minority there. Not quite as altruistic as the founders of the border communes, they generally mixed their dedication with an eye for personal advancement. The business opportunities and responsible jobs they may not have been able to get in the developed north attracted some of them. The government also held out bait.

Entrepreneurs who built factories in the undeveloped areas received free sites and long-term loans up to the full cost of the buildings and 65 per cent of the equipment. Housing at easy terms attracted newlyweds who couldn't afford decent homes in the north. Settlers were also offered pay bonuses and income tax remissions. In torrid parts of the Negev, the government permitted settlers to buy air conditioners and refrigerators tax-free.

For the most part, however, the muscle power for the development of the south was supplied by immigrants from Yemen, Iraq, Iran, Morocco, and Tunisia. Jews from Western countries generally had skills, money, or connections that enabled them to make their way to more attractive parts of the country.

In the early 1950's the national interest required that the new immigrants raise food. They were given farmsteads, but water was scarce. Irrigation did not become available until 1956 when water from the Yarkon River was diverted southward from Tel Aviv. In 1964 the situation was eased further; the completion of the national carrier brought the waters of the Jordan River system to the south. Neverthe-

A new apartment building sprouts in the desert at Beersheba.

less, the region is still underirrigated. Its thirst will be slaked only when sea-water desalinization is introduced on a large scale.

The mid-1950's were hard years. Arabs in the Gaza Strip discovered that the sprawling immigrants' villages were softer touches than the compact settlements on the front line. So they slipped between frontier villages to rustle cattle from immigrants' barns, steal equipment from fields, dynamite outlying houses, and sometimes murder. The harassment continued until the end of 1956, when the Israeli army slashed through the Gaza Strip during the Sinai Campaign. After that, President Nasser leashed the Arab terrorists for a decade.

Few of the immigrant farmers had had agricultural experience or had ever come close to a live farm animal. That created obvious problems, but in one respect it was advantageous. The novice farmers didn't have the veterans' traditional resistance to innovations. Their willingness to experiment was particularly fortunate, since the authorities themselves didn't quite know what, how, and when to plant in the unfamiliar region. After unsuccessful experiments with sheep, olives, and apricots, suitable crops were found. The region is now an important producer of sugar beets, cotton, peanuts, and out-of-season vegetables.

Curiously, it was the least promising settlers who persevered and finally became competent husbandmen. Those with some schooling or initiative abandoned their farmsteads during the lean years and drifted to the cities.

They populated Beersheba—a ghost town abandoned by some 3,500 Arabs during the 1948 war—which became the commercial, administrative, and recreational hub of the region. It is now a metropolis of 70,000, with a major-league soccer team and a Rotary Club.

Immigrants from North Africa and the Middle East were the backbone of most of the other new cities as well. They built harbors at Ashdod, which is built near the ruins of the old Philistine city on the Mediterranean coast, and at Elath on the Gulf of Aqaba.

They also paved roads in the desert, helping the Negev resume its role as a thoroughfare for international trade. Hundred-ton trucks roll over asphalted highways to Elath with potash, phosphates, fruit juices, textiles, tires, and cement for Asia and Africa. They return north with imported seeds, hides, coffee, and beef.

Mr. Ben-Gurion also saw his 1935 vision of the Negev as a dry-land alternative to the Suez Canal materialize. After the Egyptians blocked the waterway during the 1967 war by scuttling vessels, some European exporters shipped goods to East Africa across Israeli territory. The cargoes were landed at Ashdod, trucked two hundred miles to Elath, and transshipped.

The desert also became an international oil route. Crude oil from the Persian Gulf area is brought by supertanker to Elath, fed into a forty-two-inch conduit, and pumped through the Negev to Ashkelon on the Mediterranean coast. Most of it is then loaded on smaller tankers for shipment to various Mediterranean clients. About 5,000 tons a year— the capacity of Israel's refineries at Haifa—are pumped northward through a smaller pipeline.

Israel's own oil fields at Heletz supply only a fraction of the country's needs. Oil was struck in 1955 at 1,520 feet, just 420 feet deeper than British prospectors had drilled at the spot. The British had cemented their hole in a hurry in 1948 when the war overtook them.

The Israelis who captured the Negev in 1948 had little idea that they were fighting for land with mineral resources. The only mineral wealth exploited in the country before the establishment of Israel had been potash and bromine, both extracted from the Dead Sea. That extraordinary body of water, in a deep trough 1,285 feet below the level of the Mediterranean, receives the water of the Jordan River but has no outlet. The atmosphere is so arid there that the sea would have dried up had it not been for the steady supply of fresh water from the Jordan. The mineral content is so high that no fish and only low forms of vegetation can survive in the water. It's so buoyant that a person can't sink in it. When water from it is spread in shallow pans, it evaporates quickly, leaving crystalline masses of potash salts.

A corporation headed by a Russian Jew operated the potash plant under a concession from the British. The main installations were at the northern end of the sea, which had road connections with Jerusalem. They fell to the Jordanians in the 1948 fighting and were wrecked.

Evaporation pans in the south, which had been connected by a barge service with the main plant, remained in Israeli hands. They were separated from the nearest highway, telephone pole, or electric pylon by forty miles of formidable, bare, saw-toothed mountains.

The British withdrew from Palestine in 1948 believing there was no other natural wealth in the country worth exploiting. In a survey prepared in 1946 for an Anglo-American commission studying the Arab-Israeli dispute, they wrote:

"Apart from the mineral resources of the Dead Sea, Palestine is a country exceptionally poor in minerals. . . . There are no metallic minerals of economic importance."

Some suspect the British of perfidy, since it didn't take the Israelis long to discover a wide assortment of minerals after they took over the Negev. However, the British apparently said what they believed. The Israelis have evidence of it.

They are in possession of the confidential geological files that the British had ordered destroyed. The papers were salvaged thanks to the professional conscience of S. H. Shaw, the British geological adviser to the High Commissioner in Palestine.

When the British administration began winding up its affairs in Jerusalem, Mr. Shaw was summoned to Government House on the Hill of Evil Counsel. The order he received—to destroy the geological records—went against his grain.

He returned to his office, mulled the matter over, and came to a decision. He summoned his Jewish deputy and informed him of the instructions. "I'll probably be ill for the next three days," he added.

When Mr. Shaw returned to the office on the fourth day, there wasn't a scrap of paper he could put a match to. Haganah trucks had carried off the files.

Jewish geologists studied the papers and found little in them to cheer about. There was some data about manganese outcroppings near the Gulf of Aqaba, but it wasn't very promising. The general view of Palestine as a source of mineral wealth was dim; it was consistent with the government's report to the commission.

But it contradicted an earlier assessment. When another generation of Hebrews had been about to take over the Holy Land, Moses told them, as related in Deuteronomy: "For the Lord thy God bringeth thee into a good land . . . whose stones are iron and out of whose hills thou mayest cast copper."

Mr. Ben-Gurion decided to have his own experts explore the situation. Immediately after the War of Independence, he summoned Professor Yaakov Bentor of the Hebrew University, a geologist of international repute, and ordered a quick survey.

Premier Ben-Gurion was in a hurry. It was assumed that the armistice agreements about to be negotiated would be followed immediately by peace talks. There might be some give-and-take in territory. The Premier wanted to know which desert rocks were potentially valuable and which worthless, what territory should be fought for tenaciously and what could be bartered, where Jews might conceivably support themselves and where settlement wasn't feasible.

The expedition was sponsored by the Ministry of Defense. An army officer was put in command. Ammunition carriers and jeeps were loaded with wireless equipment, tents, field rations, and guns. A mechanic, drivers, a signalman, and a cook were attached to the mission. The air force made a Piper Cub available for urgent delivery of rock samples to Jerusalem for analysis.

Professor Bentor recruited scientists. He picked colleagues and students with physical endurance and cast-iron stomachs who also were handy with rifles as well as with magnifying glasses.

They went into the uncharted wilderness for two weeks at a time. They explored, collected samples, and mapped. Then they returned to Jerusalem to recuperate physically, analyze their finds, overhaul their equipment, and write their reports.

Within two weeks of the occupation of Elath, the geologists were on the way to the region. It seemed the area with the most promise. Two decades earlier archaeologists had found traces of copper smelting in hills north of Elath. The work had been attributed to King Solomon's time, although experts now believe they are at least a century older. The British had also found the outcroppings of manganese in that region.

The explorers motored over the rocky desert in thirty-six hours, covering the distance that now takes five or six hours. They found the smelting works without difficulty. There were heaps of slag with traces of copper. The geologists also found the sources of the ore. It was black stuff, really high-grade, containing as much as 48 per cent copper. But it was embedded in huge volumes of sandstone. When miners using slave labor had been happy to extract a few pounds a day, it had no doubt been very profitable. In modern times, the mine didn't merit prospecting. There simply wasn't enough copper there to justify the investment. The disappointed explorers moved on.

The manganese deposit seemed somewhat more promising. It wasn't rich, but it appeared to have possibilities. Pits and trenches were dug to ascertain the extent of the reserves. Samples were sent to Jerusalem for analysis. After considerable study, it was regrettably decided that the deposit was too marginal to merit exploitation.

Meanwhile the team continued mapping the region. One day in April, the geologists were walking through a broad valley covered with gravel and sand. Professor Bentor stumbled over a loose stone. It contained green impregnations. He picked it up and at once recognized the rust that covered it as copper carbonate.

The men hopefully ferreted through the sand and gravel and found similar stones. They proceeded with hand-digging and found the bedrock itself impregnated. It was an entirely different deposit from the one worked by the ancient miners. This rock, Professor Bentor told his colleagues, was hundreds of millions of years older. The ore wasn't nearly as rich, but it was continuous. It went on and on and on.

The mine is today Israel's most profitable mineral deposit. It yields close to 13,000 tons a year, which is sold in the form of copper cement, mainly to Japan. It earns millions of dollars.

The peace talks the Israelis had thought were imminent in 1949 didn't materialize, and the geologists went on with their survey. They confirmed Moses' statement about the country's stones being iron, but unfortunately the ore was mixed with other minerals and was too dispersed to merit exploitation in modern times. However, they found a variety of other resources that hadn't been useful in Moses' time but which are worth tapping today.

There was marble, white cement, and various stones used for building. There was glass sand, which replaced materials that glassworks near Haifa had been importing all the way from Belgium. All sorts of clays were unearthed; they supplied raw materials for white cement, tiles, wash basins, linings for kilns, bricks, and practically all ceramics apart from the finest porcelain.

The second major discovery was made in 1951. The explorers' convoy was grinding and creaking over the lunarlike hills of the Negev plateau, miles away from nowhere. Every few hundred yards the geologists alighted and roamed the terrain for a closer look at the rock.

Professor Bentor spotted an odd light-brownish stone. He picked it up and looked at it through his magnifying glass and was able to identify it as the raw material from which an important inorganic fertilizer was manufactured. "Phosphate!" he shouted across the plateau.

Standing near the professor was the military commander. "Quick," he exclaimed, "throw it away. I don't want to come back to this wretched place again."

That's how the Oron field was discovered. It was the first of more than a score of phosphate fields found in the Negev. Israel had been importing rock phosphate for a chemicals and fertilizer plant in Petah Tikvah, which manufactured superphosphates for domestic agriculture. The Negev soon yielded many times more phosphate than Israel needed; surpluses were exported as rock phosphate, mainly through Elath to the Far East and Africa.

Unfortunately, the exports didn't make money. Hauling rock through the desert was costly and took a big bite out of the selling price. An obvious solution was to eliminate worthless bulk like calcium right there in the desert and to produce high-value fertilizers for export.

Luckily for Israel, the rock is quarried in one of the few regions in the world where the three major inorganic fertilizers—phosphate, potash, and nitrate—are available within a radius of thirty miles. Potash is extracted from the Dead Sea; nitrates come from natural gas that was discovered by prospectors drilling for oil at Rosh Zohar, only seven miles from the Dead Sea but towering three thousand feet over it. So the chemicals are to be combined at a new plant in the desert, producing highly concentrated fertilizers.

The combine and improved transportation facilities are calculated to make big earners of the Negev minerals. But moneymakers or not, the mines and quarries have already served their main purpose.

Israel's approach to Negev resources had not been the conventional one of an entrepreneur exploiting labor to tap mineral wealth. Rather it has been a case of exploiting mineral wealth to tap labor. In other words, the mines and quarries were viewed primarily as a means of attracting thousands of workers and their families to a chain of new cities that were wanted in the desert for political and security reasons.

Elath is now a fairly busy harbor town of 13,000 people. It bustles particularly in the winter, when its hotels are packed with foreign and

Israeli tourists who come to swim in the Gulf or sail in glass-bottom boats to view the fantastically colored fish and corals in the extraordinarily clear water. A lagoon has been dredged inland to create additional waterfront for more resort hotels.

But when trade with Asia and Africa had not yet begun and when skeptics couldn't imagine why any sensible tourist would ever want to spend time in the scorched region, the copper mines sixteen miles to the north brought the city its first inhabitants. Even today the Timna mine is the city's most important employer. Nearly one out of four wage earners in Elath is on the Timna payroll.

Dimona, on the plateau between Beersheba and the Dead Sea, is a city of 22,000 inhabitants with several textile factories near the larger of Israel's two atomic reactors. It got its start in 1955 as a dormitory town for employees of the potash and phosphate works and the other quarries in the region. So did Arad, which was founded in 1962.

Arad is developing as a spa. Its dry climate is comfortable for people suffering from asthma and allergies; sanatoriums and hotels were built to accommodate them. The facilities in the new town are also used by rheumatic and skin patients, who take the cure at sulfur springs at Zoar on the coast of the Dead Sea.

The Arabic name for the spring is Ein Mruha—the stinking spring. It fits. It smells like rotten eggs. But for generations Bedouin women bathed in the warm, green, slimy waters that oozed from the hillside and the beach. They have maintained unshakable faith in its ability to induce fruitfulness.

Zoar is the biblical town where Lot took refuge while Sodom and Gomorrah were devastated by fire and brimstone. As related in the Scriptures, Lot's wife turned into a pillar of salt during the flight when she disregarded an admonition from God and looked back. Bedouin legend has it that Sarah, the Hebrew matriarch who was Lot's aunt, went to Zoar to pay a condolence call on her bereaved nephew. While she was there she took a dip in Ein Mruha and subsequently—although she was ninety and had been barren all her life—bore a son.

While the efficacy of Ein Mruha in gynecological matters has never been scientifically confirmed, the waters have indeed been found to possess therapeutic qualities.

In 1951 Emanuel Rabinowitz, director of a field team making a hydrological survey of the Negev, was collecting samples of water on the shore of the Dead Sea when he stumbled into a slimy hole. He cursed his luck as he laid his clothes out to dry. But soon afterward he was amazed to discover that the itching on his feet from eczema had eased.

Mr. Rabinowitz's superiors were amused when he requested permission to camp on the beach and soak his feet in the smelly waters, but he persuaded them he was serious. Two weeks later he returned to Jerusalem and reported a marked improvement in his condition. An analysis of the spring waters established they were thermal, sulfurous, and radioactive.

The government then built installations to collect, heat, and distribute the waters. Pools were dug on the beach and surrounded with latticed walls. Bathhouses with tubs were built for those willing to pay for privacy. Tens of thousands of patients visited the beach annually. A hotel, guest houses, and other accommodations were erected, but many patients preferred lodging in Arad, high above the stinking spring, and commuting daily to the eerie shore for the cure.

Two other Negev towns, Mitzpeh Ramon and Yeruham, were founded near the sources of clay and glass sand. They are still bleak and underdeveloped. Mitzpeh Ramon in the central Negev is situated at the rim of an enormous depression that drops straight down more than a thousand feet. It would be an extraordinary setting for a Western.

The first enterprise in Mitzpeh Ramon was a roadhouse. An American tourist motoring to Elath stopped there for refreshments not long ago. The place was deathly quiet except for music from a transistor radio on a shelf behind the counter. A man stood behind the counter polishing glasses expressionlessly, as though he had been put there by a Hollywood director. The only patron was an elderly man, an intellectual type, who sat in a corner painting stones. "He must be called 'Doc,'" the American chuckled to himself.

Suddenly the portals swung open and a huge man strode through. He was covered with dust. A holster with a pistol hung from his hip. He sauntered up to the counter, leaned an elbow on it, and ordered . . . a glass of tea.

The visitor was shaken back to reality.

Tales of Two Villages

"They hadn't planned a kibbutz. It just happened."

bove, a spring festival at the kibbutz *Ramat Yohanan.*
eft, Iraqi date palms are planted on the Dead Sea coast.

A group of Jewish farmers, photographed at Rehovot in 1912

THE NEGEV'S eastern frontier is the Araba Depression. It is at the bottom of the weird geological fissure extending from Asia Minor through Palestine and the Red Sea to East Africa. The sterile trench looks like an ideal spot for a penal colony. At least that's how some Tel Aviv judges seemed to feel. In the early days of Israeli statehood, their honors banished swindlers and petty thieves to the region to work on a new potash plant on the shore of the Dead Sea or to erect the foundations of Elath on the Gulf of Aqaba.

216

There isn't a drop of surface water in the 110 miles between the sea and the gulf. Rainfall is ordinarily so scarce that run-off from the flanking hills seldom has sufficient force to reach the sea. It stagnates in the valley. Part of it is gulped down by the parched sands; part evaporates in the intense heat. The bed is thus caked with a salty crust and the rainwater seeping through to the aquifer is saline.

That's what happens ordinarily. But once in a camel's age, freak floods from the hills flash through the Depression. They are so furious that they send rocks tumbling into the valley, and gouge canyons out of the bed.

The Israelis have exploited this hellhole as a God-given hothouse. Gladioluses that fetch fifty cents each on Christmas Eve in Bonn and Rome grow there. So do winter cantaloupes that grace affluent tables in London and Paris, and tomatoes that fetch ninety cents a pound in Europe in the early spring.

The scorched ditch also yields green peppers, eggplant, squash, and other vegetables between February and April, when there is a sellers' market in Jerusalem and Tel Aviv. All year round, the desert farms supply eggs, poultry, beef, and dairy products for Elath's hotels and households. Araba dates are another popular item in Israel and abroad.

There is a tale behind every one of the Araba products, but the story of the dates is the most extraordinary. Like many bizarre accomplishments in Israel, the date venture was initiated by one stubborn man with an obsession. Benzion Yisraeli, a veteran farmer of the Kinneret communal settlement in the Jordan Valley, was obsessed with the idea of covering the Araba with date palms. Dates sustained nomads in other deserts, he reasoned. So why not grow them in the Araba?

Israel had some plantations in the Jordan Valley, but they yielded wet dates that were regarded as too messy to eat politely. The strains of dry and half-dry dates that Mr. Yisraeli coveted grew in Iraq on the shore of the Persian Gulf. In the best of circumstances, date-producing countries jealously guard their seedlings. The idea of getting some for Israel from a member of the Arab League was wild. But Mr. Yisraeli determined to acquire them.

He secured the backing of Premier Ben-Gurion, who always loved to attempt the impossible. In 1953 Mr. Yisraeli left Kinneret on his mission. A more improbable secret agent was hard to conceive, since he spoke only Hebrew and Yiddish.

He flew to Teheran and mobilized a friend, Yani Avidov, who was in Iran organizing Jewish immigration to Israel. Mr. Avidov spoke some French and had Iranian contacts. Through them the two Israelis made a deal with an Afghan contractor who had business ties in Iraq.

Unfortunately, Mr. Yisraeli did not see his mission accomplished; he went home for a visit and was killed in an air accident. But his friend Mr. Avidov took over the mission and succeeded beyond expectations, abetted unwittingly by an Iranian officer who couldn't spell and an Iraqi consul eager to sell rice to Iceland.

Getting near the Iraqi date-growing region was a problem. The Iranian territory adjacent to it was a restricted zone to visitors. It was Iran's rice-growing area. Mr. Avidov happened to have a letter from the Israeli Ministry of Commerce asking him to look into the possibility of buying rice. He took the letter to the Iranian authorities and applied for a pass to visit Khurramshahr, near the Persian Gulf, to inspect the rice fields.

An army officer took his Israeli passport and gave him a military document for the journey. The officer wasn't so confident of his spelling and he asked Mr. Avidov to help. When the Israeli collected the pass, it described him as "Islandienne" (Icelandic) instead of "Israelienne."

In Khurramshahr he went directly to the Iraqi consulate. Over tiny cups of black Turkish coffee, he told the consul he had been shopping in the region for rice, but that he would like some information about Iraqi sources before he signed any contracts. The consul was enthusiastic. He urged Mr. Avidov to visit Iraq. He assured his visitor over and over again that he would get much more satisfaction dealing with Iraqis than Iranians.

"Do you have any Jews in Ireland?" he asked suddenly.

Mr. Avidov maintained his composure. "I'm from Iceland, not Ireland," he replied. "No, we don't have Jews."

"You're lucky," the consul answered. "In any case, the Iranians are as tricky as Jews."

He filled out Mr. Avidov's visa in person and the following morning the Israeli crossed the Karun River to Iraq. As previously arranged, he met local representatives of the Afghan contractor. They went through the date plantations, selected the right strains, and got things organized. Night after night, boatloads of seedlings crossed the Karun River to Khurramshahr.

Through a Teheran Jew with connections in the shah's palace, Mr. Avidov obtained an Iranian license to export the seedlings to Italy. Nobody asked what the Italians could possibly do with subtropical date seedlings. A chartered Italian freighter, the *Simeon,* picked up the cargo. She sailed through the Suez Canal without arousing Egyptian suspicions. After the *Simeon* cleared the canal, a director of the shipping company, who was on board and had been in on the secret, instructed the captain to change course. The skipper balked and protested to company headquarters in Genoa. Headquarters confirmed the instructions and the captain sulkily sailed to Haifa, where he unloaded seventy thousand seedlings.

The only agricultural settlement in the Araba when the date seedlings arrived in Israel was Yotvata, twenty-five miles north of Elath. It was still a paramilitary outpost of the Nahal Corps, but it was to become a civilian village in two years. Five thousand seedlings were planted there. The others were taken to nurseries in the north. Each Araba settlement founded since then has received a fifty-acre orchard. The groves of towering palm trees have changed the desert skyline.

The grand Israeli design for the Araba is to stud the valley with farms so that oases of green fields, fruit orchards, or vegetable gardens will sprout every ten or fifteen miles between Sodom and Elath. Until recently, that seemed like a pipe dream. But not anymore. At the start of Israel's third decade, there were seven agricultural villages, two private farms, and a government wildlife preserve in the valley.

The frontier farmers live in modern, air-conditioned homes a short distance from their fields and orchards. Some of the homes are urban-type, two-story, four-family houses. Trap doors lead to underground shelters, while walls and roofs are of reinforced concrete to protect against Arab guns on the other side of the valley.

The settlers are mostly *sabras;* some are second-generation farmers. They're Israel's finest human material. Most of them are veterans of Nahal, the army corps combining agricultural pioneering with military service. Thus they had first begun working the unseemly Araba land in army uniforms.

The patches they were assigned to bring to life were generally in the deltas, where sand washed down from the hills by winter rains formed pockets that could be transformed into cultivable loam. Tamarisks often indicated where the sands were not entirely sterile, but these shrubs also meant trouble. They accumulated salt near their roots. So the pioneers' first job was to uproot the tamarisks and dig out the concentrations of salt.

Then the soil had to be washed. Sprinklers were set up. They whirled and whirled month after month, drenching the land and dissolving the salty crust. This was kept up incessantly until the salts drained below the root level of the plants that would eventually be cultivated there.

Then the soil had to be enriched. Rhodes grass and alfalfa were planted. They are rich in organic content and thrive under saline irrigation. For two or three years the grass was sowed, cut, and plowed back to enrich the soil, and the cycle repeated over and over again. Then the fields were fertilized with nitrogen and phosphate. Finally, vegetable and melon crops were planted experimentally.

Israel's best scientific brains pitched in. The Hebrew University and the Ministry of Agriculture set up an experimental farm at Yotvata. They worked to develop strains suited to the soil of the region and to saline irrigation.

Scientists also perfected an original drip system of irrigation that has eased the water problem. Plastic hoses with openings eighteen inches apart are stretched at the bottom of furrows. Seeds are planted in the mounds. Water is released in a thin, steady trickle that is quickly absorbed. The moisture soaked up by the earth mounds is relatively pure since the salts descend below the root level, with the water draining downward. The method also saves precious water by eliminating evaporation, which is very high when conventional water-spreading methods are used in the extraordinarily dry atmosphere.

After all that investment, how much must each tomato cost? That would seem to be a valid question, but the authorities don't think so. The way they look at it, cost accounting begins when the land is cultivable, and making the badlands cultivable is the responsibility not of the farmers but of the Jewish people.

They bear it, indeed, through the United Jewish Appeal in the

220

United States and fund-raising organizations elsewhere.

One of the U.J.A.'s beneficiaries, the Keren Kayemet L'Yisrael (Jewish National Fund), finances land reclamation. The fund was established in 1901 to buy Arab land, parcel by parcel, for Jewish colonization. But since Israel acquired large chunks of state domain with independence, the fund's resources have been directed to afforestation, the exploration for water, and other forms of land improvement. It finances the agricultural work in the Nahal settlements as long as they are under army command. When they turn civilian, the Keren Kayemet continues to cover the cost of experiments until the settlements learn the answers to what crops will grow in the area and how to go about raising them.

The way Israelis have made the Araba badlands yield food has caused some eyebrow-raising among visitors who never considered farming a Jewish occupation. Actually, it is very much a part of the Jewish heritage. Agriculture was the life of the Jewish people during the first millennia of their nationhood. They gave it up only in the dispersion. Driven as they were from country to country, they couldn't very well tie themselves to the soil. Moreover, some countries prohibited Jewish ownership of land. So the Jews concentrated on occupations they could take with them in their wanderings.

But they retained an attachment to agriculture. It was a ritualistic attachment, focused on Palestine. In cobbled ghettos and frozen steppes, Jews prayed during the Passover season for the awakening of the earth's fertility. On Pentecost they decorated synagogues with greenery to mark the ripening of the first fruits. During the Feast of Tabernacles they paraded in synagogues with palm branches, citrons, myrtle, and willow twigs as tokens of the autumn harvest.

Every morning, afternoon, and evening between October and April, they prayed for rain. The rest of the year they prayed for dew. It didn't matter whether they were living north or south of the equator, whether they were experiencing monsoons or droughts—they prayed for weather that suited the farmers of Palestine.

For eighteen centuries—if these Jewish prayers were efficacious—they benefited Byzantines, Arabs, Crusaders, Mamelukes, Turks, or whoever happened to be cultivating the Holy Land. But hardly ever Jews. Jews there were mostly concentrated in the cobbled lanes and alleys of Jerusalem, Safed, Tiberias, and Hebron.

The first practical attempt to get the Jews out of the cities and onto the soil was initiated by French Jewish philanthropists toward the end of the last century. Adolphe Crémieux, a Jewish minister of justice in France, determined to do something to help his coreligionists in the Middle East after the Jews in Damascus had been the victims of a blood libel: a French consul and Franciscan monks had charged that Jews had murdered the superior of a convent to use his blood for Passover celebrations. Crémieux founded the Alliance Israélite Universelle to promote the welfare of the Jews in the region.

One of the institutions set up, in 1870, was the Mikveh Yisrael Agricultural School near Jaffa. Teachers were sent from France to make farmers out of the boys from the cities. It was a sound idea, but Jewish parents in those days wouldn't dream of sending their sons to study farming. So the school taught French, carpentry, and other crafts. Only after seven or eight years did they begin to infiltrate agricultural courses into the curriculum.

At about the same time some Jerusalem Jews independently decided to move out into the countryside and become farmers. They bought land across sand dunes ten miles northeast of Jaffa, and in 1878 established Petah Tikvah, which retrospectively claimed the title Mother of the Colonies. The pioneers had no agricultural know-how since Mikveh Yisrael had not yet turned out its first agricultural graduates. The novice farmers copied their Arab neighbors. They cultivated grain under dry-land conditions, raising barley and wheat one year and letting the land lie fallow the next.

They couldn't make a living and their venture might have gone under but for an unexpected shot in the arm. Refugees from the East European pogroms of the 1880's began reaching Palestine. As nationalist-minded Jews, settlement on the land was part of their ideology. Not only did they reinforce Petah Tikvah, but they founded new agricultural colonies. By 1897, when the Zionist movement was launched, there were already eighteen Jewish agricultural villages in Palestine.

The emigrants from the European ghettos were no more competent as farmers than the Jerusalem Jews. But they did recruit a benefactor. Baron Edmond de Rothschild of France took their settlements under his wing. The philanthropist sent experts to Palestine; and they ad-

222

vised the Jews to stop copying the Arab farmers. Being Frenchmen, their first recommendation was a wine industry, so they introduced vineyards. They also urged a shift from grain cultivation to growing citrus, olives, and almonds for export.

The baron subsidized the farms and sent supervisors to keep an eye on them. The colonists thus made a living, but their enthusiasm was lost. With their lands managed by the baron's agents and worked by Arab peasants, they became gentlemen farmers. Some left the villages and moved to Jaffa.

The second wave of nationalist immigrants, who came after the failure of the 1905 Russian Revolution, was appalled to discover what had become of the vanguard. The new element was largely socialist-minded. The last thing they aspired to be was Jewish plantation owners in pith helmets looking down from donkey-back on Arab peasants working their fields. They wanted to reclaim the soil with their own hands, not for profits but for the Jewish people.

The distaste was mutual. The old colonists, with few exceptions, balked at employing the newcomers. They were disturbed by the revolutionary ideas of the young socialists. Religious farmers were perturbed by their agnosticism. Most colonists preferred hiring Arabs, who were more experienced workers and, moreover, acknowledged who was boss.

The Second Aliyah pioneers were indeed a phenomenon. Educated boys and girls from middle-class urban families whose mission in life was to become peasants! There was no community setup in the world that fitted such a society. So they evolved their own.

It developed out of their experiences. The youths, many of them not yet out of their teens, were lonely and hungry. Competition with cheap Arab labor was hard. Their earnings didn't suffice to fill their stomachs. Their basic diet consisted of black bread, olives, and tea. Some ate *halvah,* a sweetmeat of sesame oil and nuts, to kill their appetites. In later years, some of the pioneers confided that they hadn't been as tough as they had pretended; when they lay their aching bodies down in fields or haylofts at night, they cried quietly.

They found that by grouping together they cheered one another up and stretched their earnings further, so they formed small societies. Sometimes they worked for individual farmers and pooled their earn-

Now verdant and prosperous, the moshav *Nahalal was founded on swampland in the Jezreel Valley.*

ings. Sometimes they worked as a group in road construction or soil reclamation.

Those communes became the kernel of the *kibbutz* movement. The Second Aliyah began after there was already a World Zionist Organization. It was a small, poor movement in those days, but it was dedicated to creating conditions for immigrants without means of their own to settle on the land. In 1906 the Keren Kayemet bought land in the Jordan Valley where the Sea of Galilee flows into the Jordan River. The Zionist office in Jerusalem engaged a commune made up of emigrants from Romny, in the Ukraine, to prepare the soil for cultivation.

The Jordan Valley is also part of the great intercontinental rift, but in contrast to the Araba, it was well watered—in fact, too well. The holding bought by the Keren Kayemet was six hundred feet below the level of the Mediterranean. It was extremely hot when the workers arrived in the summer of 1908. The Jordan River flowed sluggishly past their tract on its course to the Dead Sea.

When the winter rains came, the river overflowed. In the spring the waters receded, leaving swamps that bred mosquitoes. The pioneers worked in mud that sucked off their boots as they laid out fields for cultivation and planted eucalyptus trees to drain the marshes. Nearly everybody contracted malaria or yellow fever that first year.

The Zionist office then invited the workers to take over the land as permanent settlers. The ten men and two women of the commune were offered 750 acres on the east bank of the river under an automatically renewable and hereditary lease at a nominal rental.

The offer caused some serious soul-searching. Some said the improved land should be turned over to softer immigrants and that the toughened pioneers should move on to conquer other wildernesses. Others—and they turned out to be the majority—argued that settlement in the outpost was itself an appropriate challenge for pioneers.

They took over the land in 1909 and called their village Degania, after the cornflowers that grew in the valley. It became the hearthstone of the workers' land settlement movement.

The Romny group hadn't a clear notion of the kind of society they wanted at Degania because they hadn't come intending to stay. They had some abstract theories imported from Russia about doing away with money and hired labor, and living by mutual cooperation. They translated those principles into practice as they went along.

They hadn't planned a *kibbutz*. It just happened.

The settlers decided against following the pattern of the older Jewish colonies, which raised specialized crops. That would have involved managers, middlemen, seasonal wage earners, and money.

They decided to raise food to satisfy their own needs. They sowed grain, raised cows and poultry for milk and eggs, and planted tomatoes, potatoes, carrots, cucumbers, and radishes in a small garden behind the collective kitchen. They also raised some bananas, oranges, and grapefruits. What their communal table didn't need they sold outside the village. The members lived as one family with a common purse, a common kitchen, and a common wardrobe.

Practical problems that arose were discussed by the entire membership after supper in the wooden shack that served as the first communal dining room. Decisions reached at those meetings became the fundamental principles of the *kibbutz* system.

More than two hundred collective settlements have been founded since Degania. They each have their individuality, in accordance with the personalities, backgrounds, and political and religious views of the membership. Some have prospered and some are still struggling. But they all follow the general principles devised six decades ago.

Some suggestions raised at those meetings were happily stillborn. One handsome twenty-year-old named Shmuel suggested members pledge not to marry for five years.

"How can we have children," he asked, "living as we do in this climate and in danger from nomads?"

Luckily for Israel, dark-haired Dvora Zatolovskaya came from Russia shortly afterward and joined the *kibbutz*. She was a cultured young woman, full of talk of literature, art, and poetry. The advocate of celibacy beat a hasty retreat. Shmuel and Dvora's son was the second child born in Degania.

For a time it seemed the father's earlier caution had been warranted. The baby was weak and sickly. However, his health later improved. In fact the boy, Moshe Dayan, grew up to be quite a fighter.

The arrival of the first children raised some questions the founders of Degania had not thought out in advance. Where did the babies fit into the collective society? There were discussions in the dining

An apartment house in Arad, the newest town in the Negev

shack long into the night. The conclusion, as formulated by the *kibbutz* treasurer, was: "The children belong to their parents but the responsibility for them must be shared by all."

The *kibbutz* accordingly selected a girl member to look after the babies and set aside a house for a nursery. The arrangement freed the mothers to do their *kibbutz* functions. In the evenings and on weekends, the parents took their children to their own quarters.

The basic Degania principle was adopted by the whole *kibbutz* movement, but most of the newer settlements went a little further in their collectivism. They maintained separate sleeping quarters for children. Parents had them to themselves only during their leisure hours.

Lately there has been a trend back to the Degania practice of having children sleep with their parents. Mothers wanted to tuck their babies into bed at night and see them when they got up in the morning. Moreover, some psychologists noted an inordinate amount of bed-wetting, thumb-sucking, and night fears in *kibbutz* nurseries, which they attributed to lack of parental care.

The first child born in a collective was Gideon, the son of Yosef and Miriam Baratz of Degania. Gideon showed an aptitude for mechanics. When he finished the *kibbutz* schooling, he wanted to enroll in a technical high school in Haifa. His parents favored the idea and brought the matter before the *kibbutz* general meeting. The collective view was that Haifa might subject the lad to city influences and it would be better for him to remain on the farm. There were mechanics in the *kibbutz* who could train him to work on the settlement's own machines, the members decided.

Yosef Baratz wrote in his memoirs: "Miriam and I felt no disappointment over the decision. On the contrary, we were very happy. It had been a good meeting. Everybody had felt deeply concerned over Gideon. Everybody wanted the best for him. Where else, we asked ourselves, would a question touching one family be so close to the hearts of all? . . . There was no conflict between personal and communal interests. . . ."

Not everyone in Degania was that saintly. There certainly were conflicts between personal and communal interests. With such limitations on privacy, initiative, and individuality, members were bound to get on one another's nerves now and then. There were defections. The defectors, incidentally, included Gideon Baratz. He never got to a technical school, but he moved to town anyway after he married. The elder Baratz, however, remained a happy and contented member of Degania until his death in 1968.

The dissatisfied also included Shmuel and Dvora Dayan. They went along with the *kibbutz* principles of national ownership of land, personal labor, and mutual aid. But they felt those ideologies need not necessarily conflict with freedom for members to run their own lives and make their own decisions. In 1921 the couple took Moshe, who was then six, and moved to the Jezreel Valley to found Nahalal.

Nahalal was the first *moshav* or smallholders' cooperative village. Unlike Degania, it had a blueprint. The idea had been carefully thought out by Eliezer Joffe, an American immigrant who had studied agriculture in New Jersey. In 1919 Mr. Joffe published a Hebrew pamphlet advocating a form of settlement that would combine features of the *kibbutz* with individualism.

The Jewish National Fund assigned swampland in the Jezreel Valley for Nahalal. Mr. Joffe and some followers from the United States were among the eighty founders. They left their wives and children in Nazareth, a few hours' walk away over the mountain paths, and they pitched tents on the high ground in the middle of the property.

After they had built wooden houses that they roofed over with branches, the pioneers sent for their families. Then they set to work draining the swamp, clearing the soil of rocks, building a road to their land, and surveying. They worked as employees of Keren Hayesod (Foundation Fund), which had been established a year earlier by the World Zionist Organization to finance Jewish immigration and agricultural settlement. The Fund paid for all the work, including the first deep plowing. When the land was ready, the settlers received loans to start running their farms independently.

In accordance with Mr. Joffe's plan, the land was divided into holdings that were carefully calculated to be large enough to support a family but not so large that a farmer's family couldn't work it without hired help. The village cooperative acquired farming equipment and machinery and handled the marketing and purchasing. Individual members were credited by the cooperative for the produce they delivered and debited for the supplies they drew.

The *moshav* thus maintained the *kibbutz* principles of national ownership of land, self-labor, and mutual aid—but not the egalitarianism. Equality began and ended with each member getting the same initial means of production. What he made of it depended on his own efforts, ability, and desires. He couldn't buy up his neighbor's farm to enlarge his holding or hire farm hands, but he could invest all he wanted in cows, poultry, or orchards. Whether he plowed his profits back into his farm or used them to buy a piano for a tone-deaf daughter was his

230

A celebration of the first fruits of the season at Kibbutz *Beth Hashita*

own business. As long as he worked the land, it was his to run.

There is a third type of workers' settlement called *moshav shitufi* (cooperative village) that is a compromise between the collective and the smallholders' cooperative. The economies are run as collectives, the households as family units. The *moshav shitufi* divides profits equally in monthly allocations instead of supplying food, clothing, and services to members, as in the *kibbutz*.

The *kibbutz* used to be the predominant form of agricultural settlement, but today it's the *moshav*.

Before independence, there had been cogent political reasons for the Zionist leadership to favor the collectives. They were self-contained, compact societies. Each grouped men and women who shared a particular ideological and political outlook. They ran the gamut from Marxists, who hung Lenin's pictures all over their walls, to ultra-Orthodox, whose cows were milked onto the ground on the Sabbath to relieve the animals and yet to avoid a transgression by producing goods on a holy day.

Such cohesive communities were ideal bases for training Haganah units, stocking secret arms, hiding immigrants smuggled ashore illegally, and for other clandestine activities in the struggle for statehood. Indeed, when the British pulled out of the country and let the Jews and Arabs fight it out, the *kibbutzim* were springboards for Haganah units that emerged from the underground and took on the Arabs.

After the war, the *kibbutz* movement had its last burst of expansion. Several million acres that had been barred to Jewish settlement by British land sale restrictions became available. Units of the Palmah, the Haganah commando corps made up of volunteers belonging to pioneering youth movements, established chains of new communal farms along the new borders. More than seventy *kibbutzim* were founded in two years. Some of the founders made the settlements their permanent homes, but others returned to their families after demobilization. The major part of *kibbutz* manpower potential for years to come had to be committed to keeping the undermanned new outpost settlements up to strength.

Moreover, as a volunteer movement, the *kibbutzim* were hurt by a general decline in volunteering spirit after independence. Once there was a Jewish government to tell each citizen exactly what service he had to render the nation, individuals tended to feel that was that and there was no longer a need for volunteering. Those who wished to serve the country had new avenues open to them in the foreign service, the armed forces, and government posts—avenues that seemed particularly glamorous and exciting when the trimmings and trappings of sovereignty were still new.

National interest and *kibbutz* ideology didn't dovetail as snugly in a sovereign Israel as it had under British rule. When immigrants were pouring into the country after independence, a prime national interest was creating jobs for the newcomers. *Kibbutzim* preferred to curtail their economic expansion than hire them. Some relaxed their principle under government pressure, but the left-wing settlements were adamant. Frequently they mechanized even when hand labor was more feasible because they were short of members and they didn't want to have to exploit hired labor.

The *kibbutzim* were indeed the most convenient instrument for absorbing immigrants. Obviously it was easier to integrate city-bred youths into communal farms than to give them holdings to run on their own responsibility. The flourishing collectives enabled newcomers to adjust gradually to the climate and to the unfamiliar physical work. In societies where outmoded clothes or unfashionable furniture held no stigma and there was no drive to accumulate property, the immigrants were relieved of the tensions of economic competition.

The trouble was that the post-1948 war immigrants simply weren't *kibbutz* material. The remnants of the Nazi holocaust in Europe were fed up with regimented living; they wanted corners of their own to rebuild family lives.

Fugitives from Soviet bloc countries recoiled from anything faintly resembling Communism. Immigrants from countries of Islam came with feudal traditions and messianic dreams. They expected an idyllic life in the Holy Land as prophesied by Micah, who said: "And it shall come to pass in the last days . . . they shall sit every man under his vine and fig tree." A society in which labor was an ideology, private property did not exist, decisions were reached at general meetings, and women were permitted to express views was obviously too revolutionary a change for them.

So the immigrants were sent mainly to smallholders' cooperatives. In twenty years the number of *moshavim* grew from 72 to 344, their membership from 25,000 to 120,000.

In the same period the number of *kibbutzim* rose from 142 to 232, their membership from 50,000 to 81,000. While *kibbutz* members comprised 8 per cent of the Jewish population in 1948, they are now down to 3.5 per cent.

Arab farmers learn to grow crops under plastic.

13 Slogans and Realities

"We don't have such good soil in California."

An Oriental immigrant poses proudly with one of the chickens he is raising.

THE *kibbutzim* AND *moshavim*, along with enterprises owned by the trade unions and cooperative societies, constitute the workers' sector of the Israeli economy—an extraordinary multibillion-dollar empire.

It accounts for 25 per cent of the country's national output, but it gives the impression of being even bigger. The trade unions' holdings include some of the heaviest industries, the biggest chain of department stores and supermarkets, the second-biggest insurance company, the third-largest banking chain, and the most extensive network of hospitals and clinics. Valuable real estate, including office buildings

236

in major cities, are also owned by the unions.

Bus service—the principal means of public transportation—is monopolized by driver-owned cooperatives affiliated with the Histadrut (General Federation of Labor). Truck drivers' cooperatives do most of the road haulage. Cooperative and collective farms produce 75 per cent of the food.

The Histadrut owns interests in airlines, shipping companies, and the national water grid in association with the government and the Zionist Organization. Nowhere in the Western world are workers so deeply involved in entrepreneurship.

The State is also deeply involved. The government together with the Zionist Organization and other institutions constitute the public sector, which accounts for nearly 25 per cent of the national output. The government owns factories, most of the mines, the electric power works, the railways, the ports, the telephone system, and major interests in other ventures and public services. More than 90 per cent of the land in Israel is publicly owned. In addition, billions in public funds have gone into private and Histadrut enterprises as loans.

The government has been involved in some extraordinary business ventures. One state company was formed to pirate Soviet scientific literature, which is not protected by international copyright. The project began as a kind of unemployment relief, to create work for intellectual immigrants who were not able to pioneer on the frontiers. Their knowledge of languages and science was tapped when they were put to work translating Russian books into English. The manuscripts were carefully edited and they found a good market in the United States. It turned out to be a thriving business. Exports netted one million dollars a year. The government eventually sold the business for a good price to a private investment corporation.

The case illustrates official policy. The government went into the kind of businesses that profit-seeking cost accountants would hardly be likely to approve but which were calculated to benefit the country. If perchance they turned out to be moneymakers, the government was inclined to sell them to private investors and to plow the revenue back into new high-risk ventures. Public utilities were not for sale, but quite a few factories and other enterprises were sold by the State to capitalists in the 1960's.

So despite all the economic activity in the workers' and public sectors, Israel is basically a country of free enterprise. The private sector's output exceeds that of the other two sectors combined. Capitalists are predominant in industry, commerce, and finance. Factories and merchandising houses owned by trade unions may be more impressive, but private enterprises are more numerous.

In principle the Histadrut, like the government, believed that its function was to invest in areas where private capital could not go; in practice that has not always been the case. Sometimes labor put up plants that competed with free enterprise operations. Sometimes labor, state, and private capital formed a partnership. In some cases workers' and capitalists' enterprises got together and formed cartels to keep prices up.

On the whole, however, the multimillion-dollar Histadrut projects originated as modest enterprises designed to answer modest problems confronting the old pioneer settlers.

Take Kupat Holim. In 1911 a young farm hand named Baruch Prywer lost an arm while trying to start a balky well motor in a citrus grove in Petah Tikvah. The accident stunned his fellow workers. They had been used to death and illness; they hadn't considered themselves acclimated until they had contracted their first case of malaria. But the amputation was something else.

Prywer's friends resolved to do something for the care of the sick and the injured, most of whom, like the majority of pioneer settlers, were without family. The problem was raised at a meeting of the agricultural workers union of Judea and it was decided to organize a society called Kupat Holim, which is Hebrew for "Sick Fund."

Apart from paying a small initiation fee and five cents dues per month, the society required every member to undertake "to sit by the bed of a sick coworker or send someone else in his place." A room in Jaffa was rented and the sick who couldn't be admitted to a hospital were cared for there.

Kupat Holim developed into a network of sixteen hospitals and more than a thousand dispensaries. It serves 70 per cent of the population. One of the main hospitals is in Petah Tikvah, not far from where Baruch Prywer lost his arm. The first heart transplant in Israel was performed there.

Bananas are grown in the torrid Jordan Valley

During World War I, when the Turks were fast losing control of Palestine, the Jews were hungry. There was some grain in Galilee but none in Judea. By means of a loan from the Palestine Office in Jerusalem, a society called Hamashbir (the Provider) was set up by the workers to assure an equitable distribution of the scant supplies. The Galileans sent grain southward, and the Judeans reciprocated by sending a sugar substitute—grapes boiled down to produce jam—northward through Hamashbir. These were the first transactions of a cooperative that was to grow into a complex of corporations which now supply all the needs of the workers' settlements and also run department store and supermarket chains.

Hamashbir and Kupat Holim were taken over by the Histadrut when it was organized in 1920. The labor federation was never meant to be only a trade union aimed at getting its members a fairer share of the cake. There wasn't any cake; it had to be produced.

The British, who had taken the country over from the Turks, didn't seem at all interested in producing the cake. They governed through their colonial office. They considered it their function to maintain law and order and to provide services. But their services were geared to the level of the natives; European-bred Jews found them impossible. Nor were the Jews satisfied with British law and order. So they ran their own schools, hospitals, and clinics, and maintained the Haganah which, although quite unlawful itself, was more conscientious than the British law enforcers about guarding Jewish villages and urban centers. In all those spheres, the Histadrut played a leading role.

As for economic development, the British showed little enthusiasm. They knew of no natural resources in Palestine worth their attention. Politically they were in a dilemma. Their official policy was to limit Jewish immigration to numbers they believed could be absorbed into the economy. The limitation had been imposed in a White Paper designed to appease the Arabs, who had rioted in 1921 against the opening of the country to Jewish immigration. So anything the British did that enlarged the absorptive capacity of the country enraged the Arabs. And British inactivity enraged the Jews, who attacked it as a betrayal of the Mandate the League of Nations had given Great Britain to facilitate the establishment of a national homeland for the Jews. The British contented themselves with organizing public works.

The Histadrut grasped that straw. The labor federation set up a contracting office called Solel Boneh to bid for road-building and construction contracts. To be competitive, Solel Boneh couldn't dream of profits. It didn't matter. The main thing was to create employment opportunities and to enable Jewish immigrants to make a living.

From construction, Solel Boneh gradually branched into manufacturing materials and supplies needed for its work. The company quarried for lime and stone and founded factories to make bricks, sheet metal, shovels, wash basins, toilet seats, pipes, and all sorts of fittings.

Before long, Solel Boneh became the biggest contracting office in Palestine. Then it became the biggest in the Middle East. During the Second World War, the company built installations for Allied forces all over the region. It grew and grew and got so big that after the establishment of Israel, the Histadrut decided to break up the giant. The industrial complex is now run independently by a holding company.

Solel Boneh has built entire towns, airports, defense installations, superhighways, bridges, and some of the most impressive buildings and factories in the country. An overseas department operates in more than a dozen countries in Asia, Africa, Europe, and Latin America. The contracting office's turnover exceeds 150 million dollars a year.

The industrial holding company, Koor Industries and Crafts Limited, controls twenty-four factories and owns shares in thirteen others. Products range from *objets d'art* to steel, and the annual sales total 200 million dollars. In industry, however, the Histadrut has never played a leading role.

Some extraordinary private entrepreneurs appeared on the scene early in the period of British rule. The most fascinating was Pinhas Ruttenberg, a former Russian revolutionary who had been implicated in the strangling of a notorious agent provocateur and who later became governor of Petrograd during the brief Kerensky regime. He came to Palestine in the 1920's and obtained a concession from the British to build a hydroelectric station on the Jordan River. Another Russian Jew, Moshe Novomeysky, obtained a concession to extract potash from the Dead Sea.

Jewish industrialists also started a cement plant, a foundry, glassworks, and light industries for the manufacture of underwear, socks, leather, silk, candy, oil, soap, jam, and false teeth.

Industry faced formidable handicaps, however. The local market was tiny. The British gave local products no real protection. There were no raw materials and little capital for investment. Some factories failed. The glassworks, the foundry, and the cement plant were bought out by Solel Boneh so that their workers could continue to be employed.

During World War II, industry got its first big break. Shipping restrictions in the Mediterranean suddenly created a sellers' market. The whole Middle East became an outlet for Palestinian goods. The British set up a Middle East supply center in Haifa and clamored for canned foods, clothing, pharmaceutical supplies, and war materiels. The Jews responded.

Manufacturers of cooking utensils worked round-the-clock producing mines and bazookas. Immigrants from Central Europe who had some capital and industrial techniques opened new factories. When the West's source of industrial diamonds was cut off with the Nazi occupation of Belgium and Holland, refugees from the Low Countries opened diamond-polishing plants in Netanya and started what was to become Israel's biggest dollar-earning industry after citrus.

The *kibbutzim* also industrialized for the war effort. They began setting up canneries to process their agricultural products and turned their communal workshops into factories.

The decision of the *kibbutzim,* where farm work had been an ideology, to contribute to the war effort followed an agonizing appraisal and created a problem they haven't solved to this day. Before the war, most collective farms had been unable to provide work for their entire memberships. There hadn't been much demand for the produce because Arab farmers had undersold them. Part of their manpower, accordingly, had been farmed out to work for private employers. *Kibbutz* treasurers collected their wages.

When the war broke out, their young men and women volunteered for the armed forces and the settlements therefore needed all their remaining members. Expansion of their economies would force them to bring hired labor into the communities. Should they commit that sacrilege or limit their war effort?

Many decided to expand. They salved their consciences by telling themselves it would be best for their movement in the end. They reasoned that they could exploit the opportunity to strengthen their economies. After the war, when the soldiers would come home and the immigrants from Europe would join them, the hired workers would be replaced by members.

They miscalculated. The immigrants who came after the war shunned the *kibbutzim*. The settlements were chronically short of hands and had to remain "exploiters" of hired labor to keep going.

When Israel became independent, the socialist-minded leaders of the new country hoped that their views would prevail. Mrs. Meir's first Cabinet post was Minister of Labor in 1949. At the first May Day rally in a Tel Aviv stadium that year, she made a play on the traditional Jewish chant "Next year in Jerusalem," which climaxes Yom Kippur and Passover Seder services.

"Next year," she exclaimed, "in a socialist state!"

Mr. Ben-Gurion was a little more patient. His slogan was "Socialism in our lifetime!" He was then in his sixties.

But slogans were slogans and realities were realities. The leaders of the country looked high and low for capitalists to invest in the new country. Capitalists were offered the Haifa refineries which the British owners, with their oil interests in Arab countries, had balked at operating. Investors could have had the copper mines, the phosphate fields, the potash works, and a great deal else.

But they wouldn't bite. Jewish millionaires who signed fat checks to the United Jewish Appeal and other charities were hardheaded when it came to business. Israel was a tiny country, boycotted by her neighbors and blockaded. Moreover, the intemperate socialistic rhetoric of Premier Ben-Gurion and his Minister of Labor hardly encouraged potential foreign investors.

Nor did the immigrants bring in capital. Before World War II, immigrants from Europe generally had more money, more skills, and more education than the older inhabitants. But the survivors of the European death camps and the refugees from Arab countries who began streaming in after independence were mostly penniless and unskilled. The rich Jews from Middle Eastern and North African countries didn't come to Israel.

So the capital available to Israel during its first chaotic years of mass immigration were mostly public funds. The U.J.A. contributions financed the transfer of immigrants and their settlement. The Jewish Agency and American Jewish welfare funds borrowed hundreds of millions of dollars from banks against future collections by the United Jewish Appeal. The government obtained loans from the Export-Import Bank and the World Bank as well as grants and other assistance from the United States government.

The State also used its new-found authority to print money. The first currency was issued by the Bank Leumi, a commercial bank that had been founded and is still controlled by the Zionist movement.

The bank president whose signature appeared on the first bills was

Cotton is harvested in Bror Hayil, a kibbutz *in the northern Negev.*

Dr. Aharon Barth. He was a religious man. As he signed the official papers at a festive session of the Provisional State Council, he recited an appropriate benediction: "Blessed art Thou, O Lord, King of the Universe, who has kept us in life and has preserved us to reach this season."

In the Orthodox fashion, before uttering the benediction he covered his head with a small black *yarmulke,* a skullcap.

"It's the only cover," he was heard to remark.

So objective conditions rather than ideology gave the government a near monopoly on the allocation of resources for investment. There had to be a controlled economy. With food, housing, clothing, and foreign currency so scarce, there had to be stringent rationing and government control of prices, imports, raw material allocations, rents, and practically everything else.

Food was the most pressing problem. It wasn't only a matter of filling the stomachs of a fast-growing population, but also of rehabilitating a war-ravaged agriculture. In the two years that the country had been a battlefield, agricultural output had dropped by 50 per cent. Much of the food had previously been supplied by other sources—Arab farmers and neighboring countries.

The shortage was so severe that whatever could be diluted was officially watered down to enable the supply to go further. A doctor's prescription was needed to buy a package of unadulterated butter or a jar of cream. Housewives got up at the crack of dawn to be early in line at the grocery or butcher shop. The most unlikely foods became delicacies. In the members' dining room of the Knesset, parliamentarians had the rare privilege of ordering boiled cow's udder.

The greatest part of the resources was therefore directed to agricultural development. Dire necessity happened to dovetail with ideology. Hundreds of new settlements—most of them smallholders' cooperatives—were established. They served a multiple purpose: they dispersed the population; they eased the food situation; they tied the newcomers to the land.

During the period of British rule, Jews had been practically confined to half a million acres by land sale restrictions. Victory in the 1948 war and the flight of the Arabs opened five million acres for Jewish settlement.

Some of the immigrants who settled in the wide open spaces were the most improbable human material. Many had never in their lives manipulated forks or knives, let alone tractors.

One clan of North Africans that for generations had lived in caves in the Sahara Uplands was settled near Hadera in the coastal plain. In line with standard practice, the immigrants were lodged in tents and were put to work building rectangular, two-room stone houses with tile roofs for themselves. Until their own farmsteads were ready, they also worked in farms in neighboring villages to get some agricultural experience.

When their own village was completed, a senior Jewish Agency official came to inspect. He found some of the new houses empty. Next to them were dugouts. Wooden posts held up the ceilings and metal chimneys protruded through them like vents in air raid shelters.

That's where the older people preferred to live. "It's better," a patriarch told the visiting official with deep conviction. "In Tripolitania even the Italians who lived in houses came down to our caves to cool off in the summer."

Old-time farmers helped make modern husbandmen out of the unseemly material. They sent them their sons and daughters born and raised in *moshavim*. The youths went to live for two-year periods in the bleakest immigrant villages as counselors, agricultural instructors, teachers, and in other capacities. The dedicated youths were a blessing, but a mixed one.

In their zeal to remold primitive patriarchal societies into shining replicas of their own *moshavim*, some of the young idealists committed psychological blunders. They were highhanded with the traditional leadership and sparked frictions. Some immigrants became dispirited and quit their farmsteads. They moved to slums in the peripheries of the cities.

Sociologists and anthropologists were called in to recover the fumbles. They laid down more tactful, patient, and flexible guidelines and taught the young volunteers to work through traditional leaders instead of fighting them. It worked. By using the old leaders as levers for development, they got through to the people more effectively.

The immigrant farmers were provided with up-to-date American equipment bought with the first 100-million-dollar Export-Import

Bank loan in 1949. What they did to the equipment was heartbreaking. Levi Eshkol, who was the Jewish Agency official in charge of land settlement, turned pale when he saw it.

"They made metal out of the machines quicker than the American factories made machines out of the metal," he moaned to an aide.

Gradually the immigrants mastered the modern machines and techniques. Not all of them could pronounce "superphosphates" or "potassium nitrate." They may have called one "sugar" and the other "salt." But they knew exactly how many fistfuls to apply and when. They learned to irrigate by the sprinkler system and mastered sophisticated methods of controlled cultivation under polyethylene sheets.

At first the immigrants' *moshavim* were organized along the pattern of the old ones, as mixed farms. Each smallholder had a few cows and chickens, raised his own fodder, and grew some vegetables. They also picked up the *moshav* principles of cooperation and mutual aid. However, for the immigrants they were not ideals; they were techniques.

Before long it became apparent that mixed farming was not expedient anymore. Under the British there had been a political or tactical reason for each settlement to strive for maximum self-sufficiency in food. In the sovereign Jewish State, there was absolutely no reason why each village should bake its own bread and bottle its own milk. On the contrary, it was ridiculously inefficient, raised food costs, and was a barrier to economic independence.

Zionists hadn't concerned themselves with trade balances and the stability of currency as long as Palestine had been under foreign rule. They let the Bank of England worry about it. Now it became their concern. So one of their first tasks was to raise the efficiency of food production.

They set up planning bodies. Experts studied climate and soil and water conditions to determine what could grow best and where. Farmers gradually cut back on crops that were less suitable for their regions and specialized in those that promised better yields. One distressing but unavoidable outcome of the shift from mixed to specialized farming was a departure from the *moshav* principle of self-labor. Work on the farms became highly seasonal and at times the smallholders had to hire workers; in turn they hired themselves out in periods when there was little for them to do on their own holdings.

On the other hand, specialization helped keep people in the country-side. It permitted the establishment of regional enterprises for packing and sorting, cold storage, fruit and vegetable dehydration, grain-meal production, and other industries. Those enterprises created liveli-hoods for surplus rural labor and helped obviate an exodus to the cities.

By the end of Israel's first decade, agriculture faced an extraordinary problem. There was a glut of vegetables, milk, and eggs. The govern-ment set production quotas for various commodities and tried to control them by rationing water, feed, seeds, and other supplies at subsidized prices. But efficiency grew too quickly. The quotas were always ex-ceeded.

So there had to be a cutback. Fodder, poultry, and vegetable production were reduced and industrial crops were encouraged. Be-fore independence, Turkish tobacco had been the country's only industrial crop. The Israelis introduced cotton, sugar beets, peanuts, and others.

Assorted United Nations and Point Four experts helped expand and modernize Israeli agriculture. The biggest individual contribution was made by Sam Hamburg of Los Banos, California, who set himself up as a private Point Four program and gave Israel her cotton in-dustry.

Mr. Hamburg first came to Israel in 1952 to visit relatives he hadn't seen in thirty years. He showed them pictures of his flourishing farm in the San Joaquin Valley and newspaper clippings describing how he had transformed California wasteland into the "most utilized, most mechanized, and most modern farm in the United States."

His relatives' mouths watered. The food situation in 1952 was at its worst. One cousin, Colonel Aharon Zeev, decided that the wonder worker must be hooked for Israel. He introduced Mr. Hamburg to Cabinet ministers and other prominent people. The Californian talked of the possibility of raising cotton in Israel, but he made no commit-ments. As the date for his return to the United States approached, Colonel Zeev became desperate and concluded that only one person-ality could kindle the flame—Premier David Ben-Gurion. He arranged a meeting between them.

Mr. Ben-Gurion waved his visitor to an armchair across his glass-topped desk and said:

"They tell me you're a great farmer. We have great farmers in this country.

"They say you're a man of great wealth. We have rich people too.

"I understand you're also a man of great vision. We also have some men of great vision.

"But you combine all three! That," he snapped, "is what we need here."

The Prime Minister, who was obsessed with the idea of bringing the Negev to life, told his visitor that he was traveling southward later in the week and invited him to come along. Mr. Hamburg said he was sorry but he had to leave the following morning to keep a lecture engagement at the University of Chicago.

Mr. Ben-Gurion sighed. "If you'd been an Israeli, I might have seen to it that you wouldn't leave tomorrow," he smiled. "But you're a subject of Truman. . . ."

Mr. Hamburg felt uncomfortable. He took out his pocket diary and offered to go another time. They made an appointment to meet in exactly one month at 8:30 A.M. at Mr. Ben-Gurion's home in Tel Aviv. The American turned up on the dot.

They traveled with army brass to inspect the highway then under construction between Beersheba and the Dead Sea. The American needed only one close look at the fine-textured loess of the deep Negev. He shook his head sadly.

He was gloomy as he rode back to Tel Aviv with the Chief of Staff, Lieutenant General Yigael Yadin. The general boosted his spirits.

"You want to grow cotton?" he asked. "Go ahead. You need land and water? I have plenty. You need workers? I'll send soldiers to work for you. All you need. Under orders."

At that time the military service law contained a provision—which could never really be implemented because of pressing security needs —requiring every conscript to spend nine months working on the land after his three months' basic military training.

Two days later army officers took Mr. Hamburg to the Beisan Valley on the west bank of the Jordan River. When the American saw the soil, he beamed. He lay on the ground, stroked the gray, chalky earth, smelled it, tasted it, and exclaimed: "We don't have such good soil in California!"

From that moment on there was no stopping him. He flew to California the following morning and returned in ten days with a water engineer. He shuttled back and forth, bringing different experts, seeds, tools, and insecticides. He ignored officials who counseled caution, scolded Cabinet ministers who disappointed him, hugged and kissed planters who did things as he wanted. When the next sowing season arrived in March, he laid down experimental crops in three areas. They all took. The yield from seventy-five acres was thirty tons of fiber.

Today Israeli cotton fields produce all the middle-length fiber that local spinneries can handle as well as surpluses for export. The exports earn nearly enough to cover the cost of short- and long-staple fibers that have to be imported.

The main producers of cotton are *kibbutzim*. Since the collectives' holdings are sizable, they tend to specialize in crops that permit large-scale mechanization. On the other hand, *moshav* farmers who pioneered in cotton tended to drop it when mechanization became necessary. The smallholders became the main suppliers of vegetables and dairy and poultry products. Private Jewish farmers remained predominant citrus growers and Arabs specialized in nonirrigated crops, including tobacco and grain.

In the early 1960's, Israel finally reached self-sufficiency in food. Farmers produced 70 to 80 per cent of its foodstuffs and exported citrus and other surpluses to earn enough foreign currency for all the food and agricultural input items that had to be bought abroad. Everything apart from rice, tea, and coffee was grown locally, although domestic grain, oil seeds, sugar, and beef production was inadequate and had to be supplemented by imports. A decade earlier the country had produced only 30 per cent of its food at a very, very low level of nutrition.

A reappraisal of agricultural production became necessary. It was obvious that if there was to be any further expansion, it would have to be mainly for export. Citrus then accounted for 70 per cent of the agricultural exports. It was profitable. The other 30 per cent was made up largely of eggs, bananas, and other surpluses that were actually losing propositions since they were subsidized by the government.

Accordingly, the government ordered studies into foreign markets and eating habits to see where Israel could fit in. After careful consideration, it was concluded that Israel's best bets were subtropical fruits, winter and early spring vegetables, and flowers for the affluent of Western Europe.

So mango, avocado, loquat, guava, and persimmon orchards were planted. The first to pass the 1-million-dollar-a-year mark in exports was the avocado crop.

To prod vegetables and flowers into sprouting at times when they can't grow in Europe, farmers planted them in polyethylene tunnels where temperature, humidity, nourishment, and other factors were regulated scientifically. Strawberries, tomatoes, lettuce, celery, artichokes, carrots, onions, peppers, cucumbers, roses, and gladioluses raised under plastic were transported by air or packed onto refrigerated vessels and shipped to Europe, where they found buyers.

The sophistication of agriculture has been helped considerably by Israeli scientific institutions, but much of it was initiated by the farmers themselves. The government has encouraged such initiative by contributing half the cost of the experiments. Farmers read the latest technical literature and they take quickly to innovations. Frequently, theories put forward in American scientific journals are tested in the field in Israel before they get around to it in the United States. Israeli agriculture is today in the front rank by any international standard.

That's particularly impressive when one takes into account that the pioneer husbandmen had been mostly bred in asphalted cities and that their farmland had been chosen less for the quality of the soil than for sentiment, politics, security, population dispersal, and other considerations extraneous to efficient production.

14

Industry Pulls Its Socks Up

"It was resolved never again to be so reliant on foreign suppliers."

...n-Gurion dedicates a training jet assembled in Israel,
...t. Above, a computer built at the Weizmann Institute.

Potash works at the Dead Sea

INDUSTRIAL DEVELOPMENT has lagged far behind agriculture. Manufacturing was hardly a prime concern of the country's leaders during the hectic first years of independence. Feeding and housing immigrants, building an army, and setting up government services occupied all their attention and resources. There was little time or money left for industrial development.

Not until 1953, when reparations shipments from West Germany began reaching Israel, did the government give manufacturing its first serious push. The Bonn government, as a token of atonement for the Nazi atrocities against Jews, had undertaken to send the Jewish State goods and services worth 714 million dollars over a period of twelve to fourteen years. (Those reparations were in addition to the hundreds of millions the Germans paid as restitution and indemnification to individual victims of Nazism, many of them Israelis.)

Quotas were fixed in the reparations pact providing that 38 per cent of the funds go for ships, machinery, and equipment; 30 per cent for fuel; 24 per cent for raw materials; and the rest for services connected with the purchases.

In allocating reparations goods to industrial entrepreneurs, Israeli officials were influenced not so much by the economic merits of the applicants' enterprises as by the immediate problems of absorbing and supplying the fast-growing population. Preference was given to promoters with projects calculated to supply consumer goods and to provide jobs for unskilled workers after short training periods.

German machinery, equipment, and raw materials were sold to the chosen enterprises in exchange for Israeli currency, often on credit. The proceeds went into the State's development budget. Those selected also received cash grants, tax concessions, and other incentives, particularly if they went to new towns that had no chance of surviving without industries.

There was no necessity for their operations to be efficient. Prices were fixed by the government on the basis of cost plus a reasonable percentage as profit. The higher the cost, the bigger the profits. There was no competition. Customs on competitive imports sometimes exceeded 100 per cent, and the government also restricted such imports by means of administrative regulations.

The factories that mushroomed in that hothouse atmosphere were mainly declining industries, the kind that Europe was passing on to the developing countries of Asia and Africa. Most of them produced textiles and wearing apparel, processed foods, or building materials. The heavy industries that were started were typical of those that new countries with inferiority complexes feel impelled to build for reasons of prestige, such as an automobile assembly plant and a steel mill. The resultant products were more expensive than foreign-made articles and often inferior to them in quality. There was no investment in research and development and little innovation.

A conspicuous exception to the general trend were the military industries. The armed forces, unlike the helpless consumer, wouldn't settle for less than the best and constantly demanded perfection. Some defense industry plants in due course branched out, making stainless-steel kitchenware, television sets, air conditioners, and electronic equipment. They were highly efficient and competitive.

One of the first successful defense enterprises was a plant near Lod Airport to maintain and overhaul aircraft. It was manned mainly by technicians who had come to Israel to fight as volunteers in the 1948 War of Independence and had stayed. Surplus American machinery was bought piece by piece and shipped over to start the enterprise. Later the plant acquired the most efficient and modern machinery.

The company serviced not only air force planes, but also international airliners that landed at Lod Airport. Later, manufacturing operations were begun. The plant produced parts for French Mysteres and other warplanes under subcontracts, and obtained a license from France to build Fouga Magister trainers. Innovations were incorporated into the design of the Israeli trainers to enable them to be used as close support planes in combat, a function they performed well during the 1967 war. Now the plant is manufacturing for export. A locally designed civil, commuter-type turboprop plane and an American-designed executive jet are being produced.

Another exciting export product developed in the early days was a submachine gun that became standard issue in the armed forces of several European, Asian, and Latin American countries.

It was invented by Uzi Gal, a gun fancier from Kibbutz Yagur, who had studied mechanical engineering by correspondence while he was behind British bars for gunrunning as a member of the Haganah. He was reprieved on the occasion of King George VI's birthday in 1946 and returned to his *kibbutz*, where he busily applied his correspondence-course knowledge to weaponry.

When the 1948 war broke out and the young gun fancier reported for duty, he brought along a homemade submachine gun. The standard submachine gun in the Israeli army was a locally assembled weapon copied from the British Sten gun. But the army was so short of guns that the recruit's superiors were delighted to allow him to use his private weapon. Mr. Gal thus tested his gun under real battle conditions and noted its weaknesses.

After the war, Mr. Gal was sent to officers' training school. He showed his invention to his superiors and asked them to pass it on to the high command. He acknowledged that his gun was too heavy and had other faults, but he had definite ideas as to how the deficiencies could be overcome.

The top army command had in fact been dissatisfied with the Sten gun, which had not been sufficiently safe or accurate. Accordingly, the Chief of Staff appointed a commission to examine other weapons and recommend a more suitable one.

By coincidence, young Mr. Gal's prototype was sent to headquarters the very day the commission was appointed. Army brass were impressed and workshop facilities were put at the inventor's disposal. He perfected his weapon, and in due course the gun was accepted for production. It gradually replaced the Sten gun as the standard Israeli weapon. When the Dutch army organized fire tests for various guns, the Israelis submitted Mr. Gal's. It took top honors and the Dutch armed forces adopted it. Then others bought it and the submachine gun, called Uzi after its inventor, has attained a worldwide reputation.

While the defense industries were expanding, some consumer goods industries developed. Locally made or assembled products—including textiles, automobiles, refrigerators, tires, and household goods—satisfied local needs and in some cases even found export markets. They were heavily subsidized, however, and in a way they were a drain on the economy.

Certainly the factories enabled immigrants to earn a living. But the bosses also made money—in some cases, millions. They had obtained government loans when the Israeli pound was officially worth three dollars and repaid the loans after the pound was devalued to one dollar or later to fifty-six cents. After the first devaluation, the government linked new loans to the dollar or the cost-of-living index, but it was an unhappy solution. If the government didn't show confidence in Israeli currency, who would?

Factories were overstaffed but it didn't hurt the bosses. Under the cost-plus-profit price system, the inefficiency was paid for by the consumer or by the government through subsidies.

That inefficiency was one element in a vicious circle that blocked economic viability. As prices and wages went up and up, the pound went down and down and the trade gap grew wider and wider.

The deficits were plugged by foreign aid and charity: United Jewish Appeal receipts that financed the transport and settlement of immigrants, American grants-in-aid, international loans, German reparations and restitution, and the sale of Israel government bonds abroad.

A reappraisal became imperative at the end of the 1950's. Some of the fiscal plugs were about to be lost. Reparations deliveries were drawing to a close. German restitution was tapering off. The United States no longer regarded Israel as a developing country meriting grants. Government bonds sold abroad in the early 1950's were about to fall due, and a substantial part of the revenue from new issues would be spent to redeem the earlier ones.

The establishment of the European Economic Community in 1958 further complicated the problem. The six founding members accounted for 30 per cent of Israel's export trade. Great Britain, which was seeking membership, took another 12 per cent. As the Common Market began abolishing customs duties among its members and raising them on outsiders, important outlets for Israeli goods were imperiled.

The government sought an associate status in the Common Market. Such an arrangement would enable Israel to share the privileges of membership, but it would also involve opening the Israeli market gradually to duty-free imports from highly industrialized European countries. Few native industries would be able to meet the competition.

In 1962 the government adopted a new economic policy. The pound was devalued to thirty-three cents, giving sound enterprises a better chance on foreign markets. At the same time, the inefficient manufacturers were served notice that they would either have to pull up their socks or go out of business. They would be coddled no longer. Administrative bans on imports would gradually be abolished. Customs duties would be lowered several percentage points at a time until they were more or less level with European rates. If manufacturers could adjust, well and good. If not, they could fold up.

It was obvious that industries utilizing imported raw materials and large numbers of semiskilled workers would have a tough struggle. Israel couldn't compete in primitive industries with developing countries. Factory hands earned $150 a month, four or five times the wages in some Asian and African countries. Israeli pay scales were low in comparison with the United States, but so was the output.

Israel could best be internationally competitive in sophisticated industries requiring brainpower and higher skills. All sorts of chemists, physicists, and engineers had been graduated from the universities and the Technion in the 1950's. Their capabilities had been several cuts above the level of Israel's bush-league industry, but ironically the talent hadn't been absorbed. Complacent Israeli manufacturers had felt no need to invest in research and development when things were going their way. There was a resultant brain drain, particularly to the United States.

Israelis reached responsible positions at Bell Laboratories, IBM, General Electric, and other big American companies. There was hardly a large corporation without an Israeli expatriate on its staff. Hundreds of Israelis were pursuing advance studies in the United States and receiving very tempting job offers.

The government took steps to lure them home and tap their accumulated experience. A bureau for Israeli professionals was set up on Park Avenue in New York City. It maintained contact with the men and women, fed them with information about developments in Israel, organized summer trips home, and arranged contacts with potential employers. The government also offered to help them go into business and bent over backward to encourage enterprises in the electronics, chemical, and other science-based fields.

Among those who came home was Ephraim Arazi, the son of a prominent Jerusalem civil engineer. Young Arazi had served in the Israeli air force in electronics maintenance. When he completed his military service in 1958, there was no electronics industry in Israel beyond the assembly of radio sets. The air force equipment was all foreign made.

The young man went to the United States, and on the strength of his electronics experience in the air force he was admitted to the

Massachusetts Institute of Technology in Cambridge. To pay his way through school, he got a job as a technician with the Raytheon Corporation in Boston, where he worked on the Hawk and Sparrow missiles. Before his freshman year ended, he was employed as an engineer. At the end of his sophomore year, he worked in the Harvard Observatory on a satellite project. Later he worked as a consultant to the Itek Corporation in Boston, an electronics company specializing in defense and space projects. He invented a stabilized bombsight that made telescopic pictures clear even when the instrument or the object it was focused on vibrated. The corporation invited him to join the staff and put his ideas into practice. Five patents were taken out. They brought the corporation millions of dollars worth of business.

The day Mr. Arazi completed his studies at M.I.T. in 1965, an executive of Itek called him over and asked: "Well, young man, what's next?"

"I'm going back to Israel," he replied.

The corporation wanted to continue its association with the inventor. "Look things over at home," he was told, "and see whether there are possibilities of doing things together."

Back home he found that during his seven years' absence the situation had changed considerably. There was the nucleus of an electronics industry, stimulated mainly by the military.

It had started hesitatingly. At first the defense forces had wanted proven and tested equipment. They obtained licenses to assemble foreign products in Israel under the supervision of imported experts. Then local components were introduced. As confidence in local talent increased, they advanced to locally designed products. Finally it was found that Israeli industry could answer the armed forces' needs for equipment with special peculiarities better and more cheaply than foreign manufacturers could.

From military supplies, the electronics industry branched into civilian goods, producing TV sets, two-way radios, and telephone systems. Other science-based industries also rose. They worked partly on defense contracts and partly for civilian needs.

A new radioisotope test for thyroid function—developed at the Hebrew University-Hadassah Medical School by Dr. Jack Gross— was produced in a plant in Jerusalem by the Ames Company of Elkhart, Indiana. Small computers, special testing equipment, and nuclear research instruments were manufactured in Haifa. Heavy-oxygen compounds and hundreds of chemicals were manufactured for export at the Weizmann Institute of Science in Rehovot.

Mr. Arazi decided to commercialize the technology he had developed while working on American defense and space projects. He set up a company, Scientific Technology Limited, in partnership with his former American employers and an Israeli investment corporation headed by his former commander in the air force. The Weizmann Institute rented the firm space on its Rehovot campus.

From a pool of Israeli scientists and engineers with American industrial experience, Mr. Arazi picked eight men. All but one were graduates of the Technion in Haifa. They had gone to the United States for advanced studies, and stayed on to fill key positions in various industries. The repatriates became the core of the new enterprise. Later they were joined by younger engineers and technicians fresh from the Technion or from military service.

Half the company's work is for the military, finding crazy solutions to crazy problems. Details are secret. The other half is for the world civilian market. The plant produces highly sophisticated items, such as an optical scanning device that makes it possible to knit or weave complicated textile designs by computer without manual key-punching.

Scientific Technology pays its engineers $8,000 a year, a high wage by Israeli standards. American enterprises would pay the same people at least $17,000 in salaries and fringe benefits. Mr. Arazi's payroll is also 20 per cent lower than it would be if he operated in Europe.

The basic advantage of science-based industries is thus obvious. Even the *kibbutzim* recognized it and sent young people to universities to learn sciences and techniques to enable them to set up enterprises.

Meanwhile the old-type industries weathered the first stages of the liberalized economic policy better than had been expected. The 1962 reforms were introduced during a boom. As long as there was full employment and a sellers' market, the inefficient industries survived. They made less money, but they muddled through and there were few bankruptcies.

But in the mid-1960's, an economic recession hit the country. It is

A textile plant in Israel

arguable whether or not the government planned it, but it certainly served the economic planners' purposes and they let it run.

It started with a real estate slump resulting from a drop in immigration to the level of the period of British restrictions. Public housing companies and contractors had ten thousand unsold apartments on their hands and fifteen thousand more under construction. They cut back on building. The cutback happened to coincide with the completion of some major construction projects, including the nuclear reactor near Dimona, the Jordan-Negev water carrier, and the main piers at the new port of Ashdod. Industries associated with construction, such as the cement works and haulage companies, naturally suffered too. Thousands of workers were laid off.

That in turn affected consumer goods industries, retail trade, and the service industries. The recession snowballed. Taxi drivers, night-club operators, theater managers, newspaper publishers, and practically everybody else complained that business was bad. So there were more dismissals.

Manufacturers accustomed to the old ways came to the Ministry of Trade and Industry demanding government help to keep their plants running and their workers employed. The government didn't panic. They reasoned that it would be more feasible to pay doles to the unemployed than to maintain unprofitable enterprises. They let the recession do its work and they were delighted with some of the consequences.

Labor discipline improved as workers shaken out of their complacency by the dismissals going on about them became more diligent. There was less absenteeism. Productivity improved markedly. Some workers even agreed to raise their normal output to make it possible for their employers to accept certain orders.

Wage earners unsure of holding their jobs began saving for a rainy day. The pressure for goods thus dropped and the race between wages and prices halted. Erstwhile free spenders began putting off purchases in the expectation that they would pay less if they waited. This was a sharp reversal of the trend during the years of galloping inflation. The people showed a new respect for Israeli money. The black market rate dropped.

Hebrew University professors made a dramatic contribution to the new climate. They announced that if the government would contribute toward restraining prices by cutting back some indirect taxes that had been raised and restoring certain food subsidies that had been cut, they on their part would waive part of their salaries. The government agreed. The action was followed by an incredible wave of patriotic wage renunciations. Artisans, teachers, journalists, factory workers, executives, government and municipal officials, and others volunteered to take pay cuts. The sums involved were token, but the wave contributed to a new mood of restraint and stability.

Stocks of consumer goods began piling up in factory warehouses.

Manufacturers who had been snooty about export orders during the fat years suddenly manifested an eagerness for foreign outlets. Apparel manufacturers began studying tastes in Europe and the United States and adapted their silhouettes, colors, and styles. Similar adjustments were made in other areas. Producers began cultivating foreign buyers they had previously snubbed.

Export industries had been understaffed during the boom years; other employers had paid salaries far in excess of trade union wages, and export enterprises had been unable to match them. Now, during the recession, exporters absorbed many of the displaced workers. The diamond-polishing industry, for example, had not worked to its full capacity during the prosperous years. They had had difficulty getting workers willing to serve apprenticeships at low wages while they learned the craft. Now they got all they needed. The trade gap narrowed.

Ministers cheerfully forecast that the recession would continue, and that it would finally end with a stronger and healthier economy.

That vision was shattered in May, 1967. When the defense forces began mobilizing reservists for what turned out to be the Six Day War, unemployment and the recession ended abruptly.

After the war, there was another boom. The main impetus was provided by a tremendous stream of defense orders. Under the impact of President de Gaulle's arms embargo, it was resolved never again to be so reliant on foreign suppliers. The army decided that every weapon, bullet, or part that could conceivably be made in Israel should be ordered locally, even if it cost more.

The metal-working industries had the know-how for the job. In some cases they also had the machinery. After the lesson of the recession, they were eager for orders and willing to retool and retrain their workers if necessary. A surprising discovery was that the local products often cost far less than what Israel had paid European or American suppliers.

Defense orders for a large variety of instruments gave a boost to the electronics industry.

Altogether there were some five thousand approved suppliers to the defense forces. Their output totaled some 300 million dollars a year, about one-fifth for export. Israeli-made arms and ammunition are

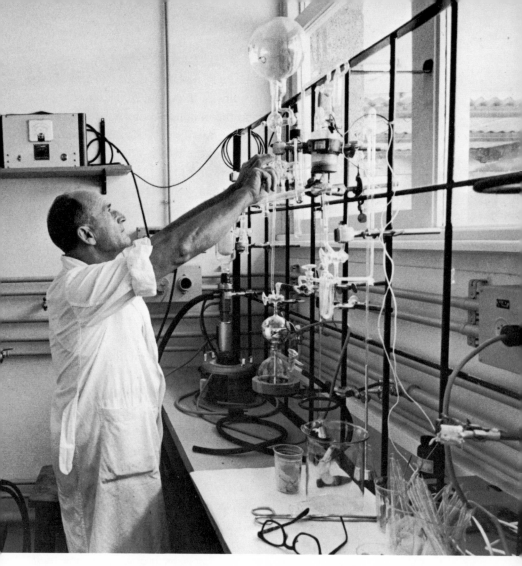

Science and industry collaborate at the Weizmann Institute of Science.

used by fifty countries.

There was also a building boom after the war, as Jews streamed to the country in growing numbers to live, to visit, to study, or to invest. Construction couldn't keep up with the demand, particularly in the reunited Jerusalem. The armed forces also spent hundreds of millions of dollars on construction, fortifying the new frontiers, building bases, roads, airfields, and other installations in the occupied areas.

Moreover, the Six Day War brought a million more consumers into Israel's orbit, even though the Arabs in the occupied areas were poor consumers. While they increased the population under Israeli rule by 40 per cent, they increased consumption by only 5 or 6 per cent. But that counted too, and it contributed to the boom.

There was overemployment again, and tens of thousands of Arabs from the occupied areas were brought across the former armistice lines to relieve the shortage of hands in factories, construction, and agriculture.

In the postwar boom, investment capital was plentiful but feasible projects were in short supply. This time the government followed a more selective and judicious policy. No one needed official permission to invest his private capital anywhere he liked, but the government tried to dissuade people from going into businesses not considered viable. Government incentives and aid were extended only to ventures that promised to be internationally competitive and likely to help the economy advance toward independence.

In the broad planning, the government was helped by some of the best Jewish business brains in the world. Powerful representatives of the worlds of finance, industry, technology, science, and merchandising assembled in Jerusalem, diagnosed Israel's economic problems, and offered suggestions. Some initiated ventures of their own. Some used personal contacts to get international corporations to start industries. Others used their business connections to get Israeli products into new markets abroad.

In the United States, owners and executives of merchandising chains, buyers, designers, salesmen, artisans, public relations men, and other specialists voluntarily pooled their expertise to help get Israeli goods into American stores. Organized through a society called Atid (American Trade and Industrial Development with Israel), they studied Israeli products like a team of doctors in a laboratory and advised the manufacturers how to gear them to the tastes of American consumers.

The country's economic growth was among the highest in the world, but economic independence, which had loomed on the horizon during the prewar recession, was further away. The dollar gap widened unprecedentedly. One obvious and unavoidable cause was the heavy defense expenditure. The Phantom jets and the Skyhawks bought in the United States alone set the Israelis back hundreds of millions of dollars.

Another obstacle to economic independence has been the rising standard of living, although some economists believe that serious industrial development would be impossible without rapidly growing domestic consumption.

Government statistics show that at the start of Israel's third decade 86 per cent of the households had electric refrigerators and gas ranges, compared to 35 per cent in 1958; 35 per cent had washing machines, compared to 9 per cent; and 13 per cent had private cars, compared to 4.1 per cent.

Incomes are generally between one-third and one-half of American levels and luxury items cost two or three times as much because of taxes. So an Israeli must pay more than $6,000 for a small European car that cost just over $2,000 c.i.f. Haifa. Refrigerators, washing machines, and other electrical appliances retail at double the American prices.

Visitors from the United States who have been conditioned by fund-raising propaganda to regard Israel as an institution and Israelis as beneficiaries have been astonished by the way Israelis live, dress, and eat. Sometimes they've found them living in nicer homes and dining off finer china than they themselves had.

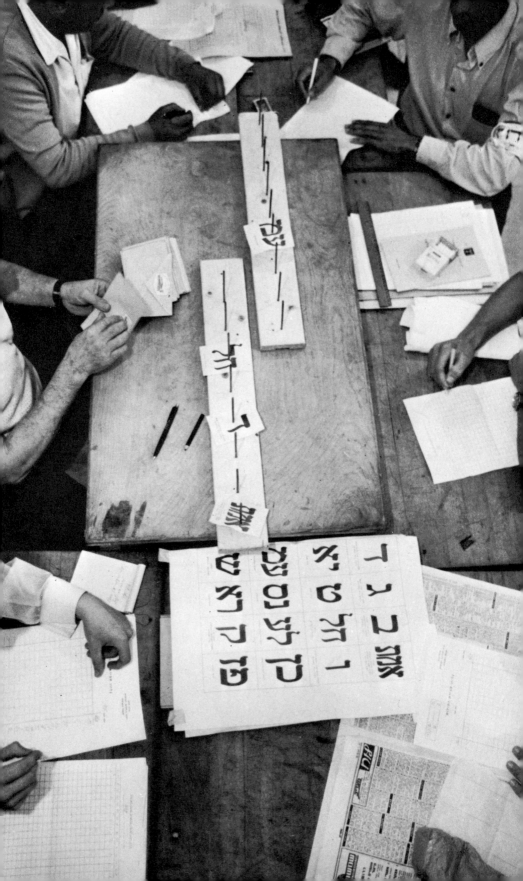

15

Readjustments

*"A Zionist is a Jew who takes money from a second Jew
to send a third Jew to Palestine."*

Left, votes are tallied on Israeli election day. The comfortable living room above is at Kibbutz Bror Hayil.

269

The swimming pool at Kibbutz *Yiftah, in northern Galilee, is sheltered by a plastic roof.*

THE RISE IN living standards has been most striking in the *kibbutzim*. Gone are the days when no one had more than a cot and a chair in his quarters and when collective mess halls, with their backless benches and long wooden tables, smacked of medieval orphanages. Settlements are now pretty plush.

Some old *kibbutz* puritans shake their heads sadly over the cozier life, as though it were a betrayal of cherished values. Others are more rational. They say the old asceticism had never really been part of their ideology. Their lives had been bleak and spartan because they simply hadn't been able to afford comforts. They had kidded themselves in glamorizing the drabness as part of their revolt against their middle class European backgrounds. Now that they have achieved middle class standards, they rather like it.

As the *kibbutzim* prospered, their members tended to revise their interpretation of egalitarianism although they clung to it in principle. When nobody had had anything, equality had been complete and rigid. Privacy and individuality had been taboo. If a member received a fountain pen or a radio from a relative, he turned it over to the commune to be shared. Clothing was pooled. Members turned their dirty garments into the collective laundry and drew clean ones from the pool.

The first breakthrough for privacy was scored by women who revolted against the common wardrobe. They wanted bloomers and blouses that fit. They insisted on marking their garments for the laundry so that they could get their own back after washing.

As economic conditions improved, another concession was made to female vanity. A small variety of clothing styles was introduced. Later, electric fans, radios, and other appliances were supplied to dormitories. Once members were allocated things for personal use, they became tolerant of private possessions. Small personal gifts were no longer turned over to the commune. Some members spent vacation allowances on things for their rooms: books, paintings, phonographs, and records.

One thing led to another. Originally, a member who had preferred privacy to the group experience had been considered a misfit. Eyebrows had been raised if someone took a glass of tea to his room instead of drinking it in the communal mess hall. But as quarters became more comfortable, members tended less and less to remain in the dining room after supper. Groups gathered in members' rooms to talk or listen to records. Eventually the shift in behavior was accorded formal recognition. The *kibbutzim* voted to issue electric kettles and coffee, tea, and biscuits for the dormitories.

Today even greater scope is allowed for individuality and privacy. Arrangements vary from one *kibbutz* network to another. The general idea has been to continue the distribution of standard supplies such as work clothes, bedding, and towels, but to allow for individual choice in dressy apparel, shoes, and furniture. Coupons are issued that are valid in shops in town where the *kibbutzim* have charge accounts. Some settlements run their own nonprofit shops, but permit members to make their purchases in town if they prefer.

271

Movies, concert artists, and shows are still brought to the villages, but in addition members receive coupons valid for a given number of shows a year in town. Those who want still more theater or entertainment in town can buy tickets out of their general cash allowances for personal needs.

The *kibbutzim* now also provide cosmetic service. The larger settlements sent members to be trained as cosmeticians, hairdressers, and pedicurists. Others have brought beauticians to their villages from time to time.

Better-groomed females is not the only change in the physical setting. Settlements have acquired landscaped lawns. Most have swimming pools. Some have laid out tennis courts. In torrid climates, communal dining halls and living quarters are air-conditioned. Formica-topped tables for four and comfortable chairs have replaced the long, crude wooden tables and the backless benches in the dining rooms.

Many settlements are still short of comfortable housing. The tradition has been to invest first in children's quarters and barns. Priority in allocating housing is based on seniority of arrival in the settlement. Veteran couples generally have comfortable apartments in two-family houses comprising a bedroom, a fairly large-sized living room, and a kitchenette. The rooms have carpets, curtains, *objets d'art,* and other fineries that would have evoked rude noises from the old callus-handed pioneers. All apartments have their own showers. That, of all things, represented a hurtful break with tradition. The communal showers used to be an important *kibbutz* institution, a gossip and social center. Old-timers still miss them.

Other changes have been wrought inevitably by biology. The founders of *kibbutzim* were men and women homogeneous in age as well as in social, political, and religious outlook. That's still the case with settlements founded recently. But older villages have evolved into communities with two or three generations. Some have more than a thousand members. More and more, important functions in the villages have been taken over by *sabras* who had not deliberately chosen the collective way of life.

The young people are socialists but not militant like their elders, who had been inspired by the drama of the Russian Revolution and the "ten days that shook the world." Having been born into a socialist society, the *sabras* are not rebels. They have not inherited their elders' prejudices against European middle class conventions.

The founders of the *kibbutz* movement, for example, had derided marriage as a silly bourgeois custom. When couples decided to pair off, they simply notified the *kibbutz* secretariat that they wanted family quarters. If they decided to separate, they simply returned to their bachelor quarters. Only when women became pregnant did couples slip away to the rabbinate to legalize their status. Weddings were smirking affairs.

The second generation tended to marry before pregnancy, although the date they moved into family quarters and the date of the wedding didn't necessarily coincide.

The new generation marries young, at eighteen or nineteen. Financial problems that may prevent city couples from marrying early are obviously not relevant in the *kibbutzim*. The weddings are generally fussy. The youngsters want all the trimmings and trappings.

Some far-out *kibbutzim* had unconventional notions about sex relationships among their children. They had a theory that boys and girls who sat on chamber pots together in communal nurseries would develop a relaxed comradeship if they continued to share dormitories through adolescence.

The experiment proved contrary to human nature, at least partly. Children reaching puberty balked at the mixed showers, although one matron raised in a *kibbutz* recalled recently: "It wasn't the boys I grew up with who embarrassed me. It was the stares of the new boys who came into the shower room with their glasses on."

Accordingly, boys and girls now get separate showers at the age of twelve. But they continue to sleep in the same rooms until they leave for military service when they are eighteen.

The experiment may have indeed contributed to a brother-sister relationship. The records show that *kibbutz* youths generally find their spouses in the army or in inter-*kibbutz* high schools or special courses rather than in the settlements where they were raised.

The unconventional attitudes toward marriage and sex have created legends that the *kibbutzim* have had a hard time living down. For some years it has been fashionable for young world travelers to spend a few months living and working in a *kibbutz*. Some had expected to find nests of free love; they were in for a surprise. They discovered that their hosts strongly disapproved of sexual promiscuity and were patently shocked by teen-aged American girls who had brought the Pill. Drug users were promptly sent packing lest they corrupt the *kibbutz* youth. Americans found *kibbutz* society "puritanical."

The features of modern life that have had the greatest impact on *kibbutz* ways have been automation and industrialization. They have forced the settlements to modify some of their ideology. One of the basic principles has been that members should carry out specific tasks for limited periods only. Among other considerations, the goal is to obviate the development of a managerial class. *Kibbutz* managers, euphemistically called secretaries, are elected by the entire membership at general meetings for one-year periods. At the end of their tenures, the secretaries are supposed to go back to their plows or lathes and let others take over the management.

In practice secretaryships have rotated among a select few with the aptitude for it. The principle has also been to shift workers from job to job in industry, agriculture, and the services. But as more and more machines were introduced in farms and kitchens and the settlements branched into manufacturing, guest facilities for tourists, haulage, and other fields, there was a growing need for specialization that made job rotation difficult and in some cases impossible.

Nevertheless, the settlements contrive to remain egalitarian societies. The brilliant chemist or engineer, who may be the key man in a million-dollar factory, has the same rights as the least-skilled member. If his job requires it, he gets the keys to a *kibbutz* car or business trips abroad. But as a consumer, he is like anyone else.

If he happens to be young and single and belongs to a settlement where there is a shortage of housing, he lives in an old-style, elongated structure with rooms leading out to a common porch while he waits his turn for modern housing on the basis of the standard *kibbutz* criteria. From time to time, his name appears on the work roster for a stint as a field hand or a waiter.

The same goes for *kibbutz* members who have become Cabinet ministers, university professors, senior government officials, or heads of Histadrut corporations. When they come home to their families for weekends or holidays, they are put to work—not necessarily be-

The executive committee of the Histadrut in session

cause their labor is needed, but to symbolize the equality of their society. Usually they are assigned to the dining room, where they are very visible symbols.

Once, at a meeting of the Knesset, an American tourist near me pointed toward the Cabinet table at Minister of Agriculture Aharon Zisling, who was from *kibbutz* Ein Harod. "Isn't that the waiter from Ein Harod?" she exclaimed.

Kibbutzim have always been represented in positions of power out of proportion to their numerical strength. They're the closest thing in Israel to an aristocracy. In the ruling Labor party, never having belonged to a *kibbutz* is something of a political handicap. Of Israel's first four prime ministers, Moshe Sharett, who headed the government during Mr. Ben-Gurion's temporary retirement in the 1950's, was the only one without any *kibbutz* background.

Not only the labor parties have returned *kibbutz* members to the Knesset. The National Religious Party, the Independent Liberals, and the ultra-Orthodox Agudat Yisrael have done so too. In relation to its size, the *kibbutz* movement merits four or five seats. In fact it has always had more than four times that number.

The movement has also provided an extraordinary amount of leadership in the armed forces. *Kibbutz* youths are conspicuous among officers in combat units and as air force pilots—and among the casualties in the most daring operations by naval commandos, paratroopers, and reconnaissance units. They are also prominent among soldiers who leave fortified positions under fire to rescue wounded comrades. There's obviously something in their grooming that makes them instinctive volunteers. One consideration that may restrain other soldiers doesn't apply to them. They don't need to worry about who will look after their families if they become casualties. The outstanding record of *kibbutz* youths in the armed forces has added a new dimension to the movement's aura of altruism and nobility.

As Cabinet ministers and senior government officials, *kibbutz* members are generally informal and easily accessible—particularly to members of their own movement. While working on this book, I went to see an official equivalent in rank to an American assistant secretary of state. I found him behind a big, glass-topped desk eating a bagel.

While we were talking, a man in rumpled work clothes walked into the office without even a knock on the door. The official walked around his desk to greet the caller. From their conversation, I gathered the visitor was a *kibbutz* member who needed some sort of certificate from another ministry. The official made arrangements over the telephone for his friend to be taken care of. He told his caller where to go and added: "If there's any problem, phone me and I'll be right over."

Then he returned to his desk, apologized for having kept me waiting, and proceeded with the interview.

The Israelis have a term for that sort of thing. It is *protektsia,* which is Yiddish for "pull." The Yiddish term goes back to the period before there was a State of Israel. The typical Jewish immigrant at that time had been quite helpless without political connections.

In the absence of a government they had faith in, the Jewish parties had engaged in various governmental functions ranging from education to the organization of self-defense. Their primary concern had been to promote constructive projects to help their adherents sink roots in the country. Thus they were more like action groups than conventional parties that seek to influence the policies of a government.

Parties or groups of parties organized in institutions such as the Histadrut promoted competing school systems, employment bureaus, and trade unions; health insurance schemes, housing and land settlement projects, consumer and producer associations, and sports and youth clubs that were frequently fronts for illegal self-defense units.

Accordingly, a Jew who wanted a smallholders' farm on Jewish national land or an apartment in a public housing project had to go through a political organization. Parties also helped members get jobs or loans to start businesses. In return for the bounties, the parties demanded constant manifestations of support.

They needed public support to claim a greater share of power. They needed power to claim a greater share of public funds. They needed the funds to promote more constructive projects to help integrate more of their supporters who would help them claim more power.

The main center of power was the Jewish Agency which, as the executive arm of the World Zionist Organization, controlled the millions mobilized through the United Jewish Appeal and fund-raising organizations throughout the world.

The Jewish Agency was democratically elected. It was chosen by Zionist Congresses whose delegates were elected by the movement's rank and file. A Jew anywhere in the world who subscribed to the Zionist program and paid a few cents for a certificate called a *shekel* could vote. The ballots of Palestinian Jews counted double.

The Jewish Agency had offices in London, New York, and Jerusalem. The Jerusalem section was sort of a shadow cabinet of the nascent Jewish State. When the State surfaced in 1948, the key Palestinian members of the Agency Executive became the core of the provisional government. The transition came naturally.

Mr. Ben-Gurion had been chairman of the Executive and head of the Security department; he became Prime Minister and Minister of Defense. Mr. Sharett had been head of the Political department dealing with international relations; he became Minister of Foreign Affairs. Eliezer Kaplan had been Treasurer; he became Minister of Finance. Peretz Bernstein had been head of the Trade and Industry department; he became Minister of Trade and Industry. And so on, down the line. A few outsiders, including nominees of the extremely Orthodox, anti-Zionist Agudat Yisrael party and Jews of Oriental stock, were given seats to make the government more representative.

Some felt that once the Zionist goal of creating a Jewish State had been achieved and the Jewish Agency's functions had been taken over by the government of Israel, the World Zionist Organization had become an anachronism. Cynics used to define a Zionist in the dispersion as "a Jew who takes money from a second Jew to send a third Jew to Palestine." With the emergence of Israel, the difference between Zionists and non-Zionists became blurred. Many of the Jewish State's most assiduous fund raisers and biggest contributors were non-Zionists in that they had never paid fifty cents for a *shekel* or enrolled in any Zionist club. Practically every Jewish non-Zionist organization gave the State of Israel unstinting support. Accordingly, the usefulness of preserving a separate Zionist Organization was questioned.

Mr. Ben-Gurion was among those who advocated its dissolution. He had been disappointed because hardly any top leaders of the Zionist movement in the dispersion had moved to Israel after the Jewish national homeland was restored.

But the view that prevailed was that the Zionist Organization was needed. The executive was indeed stripped of its political and other functions, but it was recognized by the government as competent in matters including immigration, the preliminary integration of new arrivals, and land settlement. Since these activities were financed by world Jewish philanthropy, it was only fair that a world Jewish organization should have a say over them.

Moreover, it was expedient. If United Jewish Appeal funds were spent in Israel by a government agency instead of by a philanthropic society, they would be taxable in the United States.

The spheres of activities of Israeli political parties were also trimmed by the new regime. Obviously there was no longer any need for them to operate underground units, school systems, or employment bureaus in the Jewish State.

Mr. Ben-Gurion first ordered the dissolution of some crack formations of the Israeli defense forces that had evolved from underground groups associated with political parties. Notwithstanding huffy resignations by some military heroes of the War of Independence and pained protests by the parties, the Prime Minister disbanded the formations and dispersed the soldiers in other units.

Later the parties' school networks were unified into a state system, but with separate secular and religious trends. Only the ultra-Orthodox Agudat Yisrael Party insisted on maintaining its own network of Yeshiva-type schools. Labor exchanges were nationalized to eliminate political *protektsia* in job distribution. Public-housing and land-settlement projects made it possible for Israelis to get flats or smallholders' farms without showing any party membership cards.

Civil service examinations were made the almost exclusive avenue to government employment. When government departments had first been organized, ministers had packed their offices with political supporters. One could usually tell by walking into an office what party the minister in charge belonged to. If the Minister of Immigration was Orthodox, *yarmulkes* were omnipresent. If the Minister of Labor was from Mapam, the ministry was staffed largely by *kibbutz* members and there wasn't a necktie in sight. When there were Cabinet shuffles, incoming ministers created new jobs for party members. Now the civil service regulations permit a minister to engage only three members of his staff without a public tender: his bureau director, a secretary, and a chauffeur.

In setting up their regime, the Israelis married British methods of administration and procedure with an election system they had carried over from Zionist Congresses. The match was not so good. Voters don't choose between candidates but between entire slates of them. The whole country is one constituency and seats are divided among the slates in proportion to the votes each receives. The system has encouraged splinter parties. It has enabled small groups to gain parliamentary representation, although they never could have done so under

An intense conversation during a courtroom recess

the American or British system of constituency elections.

Since the government derives its authority from the parliament in accordance with the British system of administration, the fragmentation in the Knesset has affected stability. The dominant party has always been the moderate socialist group—originally called Mapai, but after a series of splits and reunions transformed in 1968 into the Israel Labor party.

In national elections, the party has always come out stronger than the next two, three, or four parties combined. Under the British or American election systems, it would have been firmly in the saddle. But because of the proportional representation, it has never been able to win a clear parliamentary majority.

To assure the government a reliable parliamentary majority, the dominant party has had to form coalitions with smaller groups. That means a Prime Minister has not been able to pick his own Cabinet but has had to accept some ministers designated by coalition partners. The ruling party also has had to make concessions to junior partners in government programs. Generally, the terms of the National Religious Party have been easiest to meet, and they have nearly always been in the government. Sometimes coalitions have embraced parties to the right, sometimes parties to the left, and sometimes both.

There is no constitution, no high court veto, and no presidential veto to challenge the supremacy of the Knesset. The presidency, like the British monarchy, is a ceremonial and decorative office. Its first incumbent was Dr. Chaim Weizmann, who had for many years been the towering figure of the Zionist movement and its revered president.

Dr. Weizmann, who had been a chemist of international repute as well as a Zionist leader, exalted the presidency rather than having the office exalt him. He had been in his declining years when his dream of a Jewish State materialized, and the presidency was created more to provide a pedestal for him than to fill any real administrative need. When Dr. Weizmann died in 1952, in the middle of his second term, the problem of a worthy successor arose. Premier Ben-Gurion sounded out Professor Albert Einstein, who had been a longtime supporter of the Zionist cause. The thought had been that the presidency should go to the greatest Jew in the world, not necessarily an Israeli. But Professor Einstein declined. The succeeding presidents were Yitzhak Ben Zvi and Zalman Shazar, veterans of the Labor Zionist movement.

One of the president's ceremonial functions is naming the judiciary —civil court judges, rabbinical court judges, and Moslem Sharia court judges. The appointments are made for life to guarantee the judiciary's maximum independence. Nominees for the civil court are selected by a commission in which the politicians—Cabinet ministers and Knesset members—are outnumbered by jurists representing the Supreme Court and the Bar Association. Rabbinical and Sharia court judges are nominated by the respective religious authorities.

The Jewish community had not run its own civil law courts, police force, or prison service during the period of British rule, so they had to be set up from scratch. The law books, however, were taken over from the British. Minutes after the independence of Israel was proclaimed, the Provisional State Council extended the validity of all legislation with two specific exceptions—the laws restricting Jewish

A military trial of suspected Arab terrorists

immigration and land purchases.

The inherited jurisprudence was a hodgepodge. It included not only British laws, but also French and Ottoman legislation carried over from the pre-World War I regime. The French laws incorporated were commercial and maritime measures that had been forced on weak sultans by European powers in the nineteenth century. Turkish laws included the Mejele, an antiquated civil code that the Turks themselves had discarded after World War I but which the British conquerors of Palestine had retained in the statute books. In matters of personal status, the prevailing laws were those of the Torah, the Koran, and the various Christian churches, depending on the religious affiliations of the citizens concerned.

The Knesset amended or annulled hundreds of old laws and initiated hundreds of new ones to modernize the legal code. Of course, the House could not touch religious laws, but it corrected some outlandish situations of personal status through new social laws. For example, the Women's Equal Rights law of 1951 made unilateral divorce a criminal offense. So while Moslem law permits a husband to divorce his wife merely by repeating three times before witnesses the words "I divorce you," the husband can be sent to an Israeli jail for invoking that right. Polygamous marriages that had been practiced by Moslems and to a lesser extent by Oriental Jews were also prohibited.

When those measures were introduced in the Knesset, someone asked, "What about Islam?" The reply was that the reforms did not infringe on freedom of religion. Islam did not require the faithful to marry four women or to make room for additional wives by divorcing old ones.

Laws enacted by the British during the period of the Mandate were for the most part found worth retaining. Amendments that were made altered penalties rather than principles of law. Punishment by flogging was done away with; hanging, except for war crimes and treason during wartime, was abolished; penalties for infiltration and harboring infiltrators were stiffened, as were bribery laws.

Laws carried over from the era of Turkish rule were mostly archaic and had to be replaced. The process has been slow and painstaking and, at the start of the 1970's, some quaint items of jurisprudence were still valid. The law, for example, still required anyone climbing a fruit tree to cry out a warning so that womenfolk on his neighbor's property should have a chance to cover their faces.

In preparing new laws, Israeli draftsmen have studied European and American codes for up-to-date ideas. However, they first tried to base legislation on principles of justice laid down in the Bible, elaborated in the Talmud, codified in Maimonides' works and other sources of traditional Jewish law. They borrowed models only when Jewish law was considered unsuited to modern conditions.

16

Who Gave the Order?

"The issue clouded Israeli political life for a decade."

*The Knesset (parliament) can be seen from the Israel
Museum in Jerusalem, left. Above, Ben-Gurion at home.*

Moshe Dayan relaxes with his family and friends.

In THE SALAD DAYS of the Knesset, I once approached a Communist deputy in the members' dining room. His speech in the House a short while earlier had been partly drowned out by hecklers and I wanted to check on what he had said. Later, as I walked away from him, I heard someone at an adjacent table mutter: "Couldn't you find better company?"

The chider was the parliamentary reporter of a Labor daily and the chiding reflected the intolerance, bitterness, and intensity of political conflict during Israel's infancy. Party loyalists behaved like warriors in a struggle between righteousness and evil. They really hated their opponents.

But as the State matured, the pitch of political life mellowed. Today it is relatively sophisticated. There are still hot exchanges across the Knesset floor, but animosities are not so deep. People no longer ostracize one another socially because of political differences.

The fierce political animosity of the early days brought the country to the brink of a civil war. It happened a month after the establishment of Israel. The Irgun Zvai Leumi, the Jewish terrorist organization just risen from the underground, was then in the process of being integrated into the Israeli national army, but old sores still festered.

During the period of the British Mandate, it will be recalled, the Irgun had spurned the authority of the official Zionist leadership. While Mr. Ben-Gurion and the Jewish Agency cooperated with the British government, the Irgun's thinking had been expressed in its emblem. It showed a map of Palestine in its historic boundaries. Superimposed was a hand gripping a gun. The inscription read: "Only Thus!"

Irgun members had considered Jewish Agency leaders to be quislings who drank tea with the British occupation forces whom young patriots were risking their necks to oust. The Agency leaders, on their part, had felt that the irresponsible terrorist activities of the dissident underground group had been undermining their political work. They went so far as to send Haganah squads to abduct Irgun members and turn them over to the British, who jailed or deported them.

While the Zionist Establishment had accepted the United Nations partition plan of 1947, the Irgun had rejected it, demanding all of Palestine as a Jewish State. The following year, however, when Mr. Ben-Gurion proclaimed the State of Israel in a part of Palestine, the dissidents recognized the provisional government. They signed an agreement for the integration of Irgun battalions under their own officers into the national army. Only in Jerusalem did the Irgun retain its independence. Since the provisional government had not then claimed sovereignty over Jerusalem in deference to the United Nations resolution calling for the internationalization of the city, the Irgun reserved its right to remain independent there.

Some of the Irgun's warmest admirers at the time were in high positions in Paris. The French had been smarting over Great Britain's role in evicting them from the Middle East after World War II and relished the way the Jewish terrorists were twisting the lion's tail. During the 1948 War of Independence, Paris secretly supplied Irgun agents with a substantial arsenal, including 5,000 Lee-Enfield rifles, 250 machine guns and 5 million bullets.

The Irgun planned to issue the precious equipment partly to their independent units in Jerusalem and partly to their battalions that were being absorbed into the national army. They loaded the weapons at Marseilles on a World War II surplus LST they called the *Altalena,* took one thousand Jewish refugees on board also, and set sail.

While they were at sea, the United Nations proclaimed a truce in the Arab-Israeli fighting. The terms of the truce, which Israel had accepted, included a prohibition of arms imports into the area of hostilities. Accordingly, Israel's ports were being watched by United Nations observers.

Irgun representatives in Tel Aviv consulted officials of the provisional government and it was agreed to bring the ship clandestinely to Kfar Vitkin, an agricultural village on the Mediterranean coast north of Netanya. Kfar Vitkin was a stronghold of Mr. Ben-Gurion's Mapai party. The Irgun negotiators left the meeting with the impression that they could expect help to unload the cargo and that they would come to terms on the distribution of the weapons. Mr. Ben-Gurion said later there had never been any such understanding.

When the LST beached at Kfar Vitkin, Menahem Begin, the Irgun commander, and other officers of the organization were on hand. They were surprised that no government help had arrived. However, news of the landing had reached Irgun battalions in the national army and some men broke camp and drove to Kfar Vitkin to help land the immigrants and the weapons. During the operation, two Israeli corvettes appeared from the sea and government troops began taking up positions on the beach in a wide circle. An officer approached Mr. Begin and handed him a note. It threatened force unless the ship and the arms were surrendered unconditionally within ten minutes.

The Irgun leaders were stunned. They held a hasty conference on the beach and agreed that Mr. Begin should board the *Altalena* and sail with her to Tel Aviv, away from the Mapai stronghold. As he sailed in a motor launch to the LST, shots rang out from the corvettes and from government positions on the beach.

The *Altalena,* with Mr. Begin on board, sailed southward. She was shadowed by a corvette. When the ship reached Tel Aviv, she veered full speed for the beach and ran ashore off Frishman Street. Soldiers of the Irgun battalions also raced to Tel Aviv. The crew tried to unload some weapons, but national forces on the beach opened fire.

Shots were exchanged and there were casualties on both sides.

It was the blackest day in Israel's history. It ended when a shell from a big gun somewhere on the coast hit the *Altalena* and started a fire. There was a series of explosions in the cargo hold and the vessel had to be abandoned. The precious cargo was lost. The death toll was sixteen Irgun members and two soldiers. Many more on both sides were injured.

Someone later told me that he had walked into a room in the Defense Ministry headquarters in Ramat Gan that day and found Mr. Ben-Gurion there, alone and red-eyed. If true, it was a contradiction of his tough public stance. When the affair was debated in the provisional state council, he showed no remorse at all. "Blessed be the cannon that blew up the ship," he exclaimed. "It would have been better if the ship had been given to us intact but it wasn't; the best thing to have done was to sink it."

To some Israelis, Mr. Ben-Gurion's handling of the affair was the biggest stain on his historic record. Seventeen years after the event, Shmuel Katz, an Irgun leader, alleged that the Prime Minister's motive had been to liquidate a political rival. In his biographical *Days of Fire,* Mr. Katz reasoned that Mr. Begin had been extremely popular as he emerged from the underground and that Mr. Ben-Gurion had feared the consequences in the forthcoming national elections. Accordingly, Mr. Katz wrote with deep conviction, the Prime Minister had deliberately consented to the Irgun's plan to bring in the arms ship in order to maneuver Mr. Begin into a position where he might be treated as a rebel and killed.

At the other extreme there are people who argue that Mr. Ben-Gurion's order to destroy the *Altalena* brought out the true greatness of the statesman. They believe he averted a civil war—not necessarily because the Irgun leaders had really intended using the *Altalena* arsenal for a putsch at the time, but because a collision in the future would have been inevitable if the State had allowed private or partisan armies to equip themselves.

The Prime Minister's mind was one of the few that had grasped what a transformation in Jewish mentality was required to turn the wilderness generation into a sovereign people. The whole attitude toward authority had to be revised. When the Jewish national institutions had had no power to enforce decisions, there had been endless negotiations and bargaining to try to reach decisions by persuasion, compromise, or consensus. Accommodations had had to be made toward dissident views. That mentality had led Mr. Begin to believe he could bring an arms ship to the shores and then bargain with the authorities on how many of the weapons the Irgun could keep. Certainly that could not be tolerated in a country of law and order. The pity was that the lesson had to be learned so tragically.

Eight months after the *Altalena* tragedy, Mr. Ben-Gurion and Mr. Begin were brought under the same roof for the first time in their lives. Both were elected to the first Knesset, Mr. Ben-Gurion as head of the ruling Mapai party and Mr. Begin as leader of Herut, a new party made up mainly of former Irgun terrorists. Communists, Arabs, anti-Zionist rabbis, and the former leader of the terrorist Stern Group were also in the fascinating motley that made up the parliament.

At first political opponents didn't fraternize. Press photographers hung around the members' dining room to catch pictures of former Irgun and Haganah leaders together. But before long the photos stopped being newsworthy. The ice broke and it became commonplace for political rivals to sit down together for a meal or a cup of coffee. Gradually the intensity of political strife softened, particularly after the affable and warm-hearted Levi Eshkol succeeded Mr. Ben-Gurion as Prime Minister in 1963. Opponents learned they could disagree with one another and yet work together. The ultimate in political rapprochement was reached on the eve of the Six Day War when Mr. Eshkol formed a government of national unity embracing every substantial party in the Knesset, including, for the first time, Herut. Granted, it took the threat of genocide to bring them all together, but there had been grave crises earlier, and such a coalition had been unthinkable.

The broad coalition held together when the war ended, and Premier Golda Meir reconstituted it after the 1969 elections. The various parties were still sharply divided on fundamental issues, such as peace terms with the Arabs. Mr. Begin and his supporters, who had never acquiesced to the partition of Palestine, regarded the territories captured in the war as "liberated" and were not willing to part with any of them. The left-wing Mapam was ready to give up practically everything for a genuine peace treaty. The rest of the coalition took intermediate positions. However, as long as the Arabs were talking of battle lines for the next war and not of peace borders, the divergencies were academic. So the parties agreed to disagree and continued to cooperate in government.

Tolerance has also increased in the economic sphere as mentalities adjusted to realities. Socialists no longer consider making money shameful and unpatriotic. Even the Marxist *kibbutzim* send their bright young men to college to study business administration. Some have established business partnerships with capitalist entrepreneurs. The government, rather than nationalizing private ventures, has been divesting itself of its profitable holdings and selling them to private investors.

Not many years ago a prominent lawyer who was a Mapai member of the Knesset accepted shares in an oil-prospecting company in lieu of a fee for his legal work. The company struck oil. The press splashed stories of the lawyer's coup and his colleagues in the Knesset wrinkled their noses. They said it was unseemly that a socialist member of the House should acquire sudden wealth. Under the pressure of that criticism, the lawyer gave up his Knesset seat in midterm.

That wouldn't happen today. In fact, the lawyer, Yaakov Shimshon Shapiro, later returned to political life as Minister of Justice, representing the Labor party.

In international relations, too, the Israelis had to face up to realities. They had cherished an illusion that they could remain noncommitted between East and West. They had thought it would be prudent to stay out of the Cold War, considering the vulnerability of the Jews behind the Iron Curtain.

Traditionally, Communism has been anti-Zionist. The Russian Revolution broke out five days after the Balfour Declaration was issued in 1917. Since the Balfour Declaration was British and Great Britain had then been the leader of world capitalism, it followed that Communism had to regard Zionism as a tool of British imperialism. The Soviets outlawed the movement, banished its adherents to Siberia, and banned the study of Hebrew.

The Kremlin somersaulted in 1947 and voted together with the United States in the United Nations to establish a Jewish State in partitioned Palestine. It was a sensational turnabout. Soviet spokesmen in the General Assembly spoke of sympathy for the Jewish people after the World War II holocaust, but their motives were really less compassionate.

They were seeking a foothold in the Middle East. At the time, Arab nationalists had refused to have anything to do with Communists. Many had in fact been Nazi sympathizers. So the Russians saw the Jews of Palestine as an instrument to push the British out of that country and hoped to use the Jewish State as a shoehorn to intrude themselves into the region.

They had hopes of alienating the Jewish State from the United States. During the 1948 war, when Washington maintained an arms embargo in the region, the Kremlin arranged for warplanes and other weapons to reach Israel from Czechoslovakia. Without them the Jewish State might well have been knocked out.

Less than a month after the truce that halted the Arab-Israeli fighting, the first Soviet ambassador arrived. He beat the first American diplomatic representative by forty-eight hours. The embassy opened by the Russians in downtown Tel Aviv was the Soviet Union's first in the region.

Moscow received overt encouragement not only from the tiny Communist party but also from Mapam, which had considered Communism and Zionism compatible. They were a sizable element. In the first national elections, Mapam polled 14.7 per cent of the Israeli vote; the Communists polled 3.5 per cent.

The Russians tried to organize a fifth column. Soviet agents uncovered by the Israelis included a senior aide to Mr. Ben-Gurion in the Defense Ministry. In most cases, the courts found the agents had not been mercenaries but had acted out of a sincere conviction that they had been serving Israel's interests.

However, while Soviet diplomats in Tel Aviv were glibly trying to cultivate the Israelis, communication between the Russian and Israeli peoples was prohibited. An Israeli who posted a letter to a relative in the Soviet Union exposed his kin to grave peril. News from Moscow spoke of Stalin's killing off the Jewish intellectual elite. So most Israelis couldn't return the Soviet diplomats' smiles.

With the United States it was the other way round. Communication between the peoples left nothing to be desired, but American government policy was disturbing. Washington had then been intent on coaxing Arab countries into a regional anti-Soviet treaty organization and sometimes seemed embarrassed by friendship with Israel. The United States was generous with financial and technical assistance but reserved in political support, and it balked at selling armaments the Israelis felt they needed. Israeli sympathizers in the United States who had shipped weapons clandestinely were jailed.

One time when the U.S. State Department was being particularly infuriating and the Kremlin particularly ingratiating, Foreign Minister Moshe Sharett put Israel's position in perspective. "There's night and there's day," he said. "Sometimes the nights are starry and moonlit and the days are hazy and overcast. But it's still a difference of day and night."

So the Kremlin's expectations from the Jewish State were not fulfilled. Moscow was further disconcerted by the unexpected emotional impact on Soviet Jews of the revival of Jewish sovereignty. Israel's first ambassador to Moscow was Mrs. Meir. When she went to the local synagogue on the first Rosh Hashanah after her arrival, forty thousand Jews jammed the area. Normally the services attracted two thousand. Ecstatic Jews engulfed her, tried to touch her. It was incredible, especially since Jewish consciousness had been relentlessly suppressed for thirty years! It further soured the Kremlin on Israel. Russia somersaulted back to her traditional hostility.

The reversion came into the open in 1952 when Mordecai Oren, a prominent member of Mapam, was arrested in Prague as an Israeli spy. He was summoned as a witness in the treason trial of Rudolf Slansky and other Czechoslovakian Communist leaders, nearly all of them Jews. Among the fantastic charges attributed to the prisoners was that they had plotted with Ehud Avriel, a former Israeli ambassador, to subjugate the Czechoslovakian economy to American imperialism. After Mr. Slansky and eleven others were executed, Mr. Oren himself was sentenced to fifteen years' imprisonment.

Then Prague ejected Dr. Aryeh Kubovy, who had succeeded Mr. Avriel as ambassador. He was charged with having encouraged the emigration of Zionists. Mr. Kubovy had also been accredited to Poland, and Warsaw declared him *persona non grata*. Russia closed her embassy in Tel Aviv, but after Stalin died it was reopened.

At the same time the Russians gradually cemented ties with the Arabs. Colonel Gamal Abdel Nasser, who had seized power in Egypt, was dissatisfied with the amount of money and arms the Western powers had been giving him. The Russians stepped in. They financed the Aswan Dam electric power project and gave Egypt planes and tanks far superior to those the Israelis had. In the United Nations, the Communist bloc began backing the Arabs down the line. Starting in 1954, they supported every resolution favored by the Arabs. In the Security Council, the Russians vetoed anything they disliked.

At that time Israel had developed a close alliance with France. President Nasser had then been backing the Algerian struggle for independence, so he was France's sworn enemy as well as Israel's. Having a close political ally was an unaccustomed and comfortable feeling for Israelis. France sold them armaments the United States had balked at providing, including modern jets that were qualitatively a match for the Migs Egypt had acquired from Russia.

In 1956 the French government colluded with Israel and with Great Britain in an unsuccessful plot to bring President Nasser to his knees by an Israeli thrust into Sinai and an Anglo-French landing in the Suez Canal Zone. For another decade close relations with France prevailed until President De Gaulle, having made his peace with the Algerians, sought to re-establish French political and commercial positions in the Arab world. His alliance with Israel was an encumbrance and he abandoned it with a thud, imposing an arms embargo in June, 1967, precisely when Arab armies were massed on Israel's borders and threatened to throttle the Jewish State. Fortunately, the Six Day War was over before the embargo had any serious effect.

In contrast to the turmoil and vicissitudes of her international relations, Israel's regime has been remarkably stable. Considering how the country changed demographically, the stability has been incredible: 80 or 90 per cent of the voters in the 1969 parliamentary elections had been unborn, too young to vote, or citizens of other countries twenty years earlier, when the first national elections had been held. Yet the results hardly changed over the years. It was almost as though immigrants and children had been admitted to society in quotas based on party loyalty.

The main changes in the political picture have been inside the parties. The trend has been toward consolidation into major blocs. For example, in 1949 there had been three parties (apart from religious groups) to the right of Mapai: Herut, the General Zionists, and the Progressives. First the latter two merged to form the Liberals. Then the Liberals formed a bloc with Herut called Gahal, which became the second largest party in the country. Gahal has not seriously threatened Labor hegemony in national affairs, but has won control of some local administrations.

The series of mergers did not end the political fragmentation. Liberals who had opposed joining forces with Herut formed the Independent Liberals. Disaffected elements in Herut formed the Free Centre. Due to the proportional representation system of elections, they were each able to win a few seats in the Knesset. But neither was a serious factor in the power struggle.

On Mapai's left, there had been Mapam and the Communists. They had tended to blame the Ben-Gurion government's Western orientation for the alienation of Russia. They had argued that if Israel had been more evenhanded, she would have gotten a fairer deal from Moscow. However, they too eventually faced realities. Their disillusionment came in stages.

At the time of the Slansky trial, Mapam officially maintained that its own Mordecai Oren was of course innocent, but for the rest they expressed full confidence in "socialist justice." Nearly half their members quit in disgust and formed the Ahdut Haavodah party. Ahdut Haavodah functioned independently for a few years and later merged with Mapai.

In 1953, when nine doctors were arrested in Moscow and charged with a Jewish nationalist conspiracy to kill Soviet leaders by medical means, it was too much for the rump of Mapam. They denounced the calumny. A tiny fringe that stood by the Kremlin was expelled. They joined the Communists.

Later even the Communists couldn't stomach it. They were shaken by the massive flow of Soviet arms to Arab states committed to destroy Israel and sickened by foul-mouthed Kremlin propagandists who likened Israeli soldiers to Nazis. One brokenhearted Israeli Communist flagellated himself in an open letter to a dead Israeli soldier,

Demonstrators in Tel Aviv demand that the Soviet Union allow its Jews to emigrate to Israel.

Yossi Kilman, who had been born in the Bergen Belsen concentration camp.

"I have come to ask your forgiveness. . . ," he wrote. "The injury to you, Yossi, a child of Bergen Belsen, has wounded the very heart of my Movement, the Communist Movement. . . .

"Among us there are hundreds of thousands who have come out of the camps of Bergen Belsen, Treblinka, and Matthausen. For we are the people of Auschwitz. . . . And it is our feet that are being put into hobnailed Nazi boots in cheap caricatures, our Magen David is juxtaposed with the swastika and the shape of our noses is being copied from the defamatory press of the Nazis.

"Dear Yossi, I am ashamed. . . ."

The Communist party split. One wing, predominantly Arab, formed the New Communist party, which supported the Moscow line. The Jewish wing kept the name Israel Communists and continued to attack the Soviet Union's Middle East policies.

The most dramatic change took place in the ruling party. Mr. Ben-Gurion, for decades Mapai's undisputed leader, became its most implacable opponent. Curiously, his break with the party stemmed from a chain of events that began in 1954 when he was temporarily out of office, shearing sheep in his Negev *kibbutz*. He had retired from the government to meditate in the desert, leaving the premiership in the hands of Moshe Sharett and the defense portfolio with Pinhas Lavon.

That summer the Israeli press carried reports of bombings in United States libraries in Cairo and Alexandria and in Egyptian movie theaters playing American or British pictures. Israelis didn't give the matter much notice, but ears perked up when it was reported that Israeli agents had been arrested in connection with the incidents.

Premier Sharett asked his Defense Minister what it meant. Mr. Lavon shrugged. General Moshe Dayan, then Chief of Staff, was abroad. His deputy knew nothing. Finally Mr. Lavon told the Premier he had learned the answer to the puzzle. A major on reserve duty in the intelligence corps had ordered the operation in accordance with instructions from Colonel Binyamin Gibli, chief of military intelligence.

The operation had been naively conceived. The bombings had been calculated to get the United States and Great Britain angry at the

Egyptians and thus, perhaps, to torpedo negotiations that seemed to be leading to an Egyptian takeover of British military installations in the Suez Canal Zone. The operation was clumsily executed and ended in tragedy. One member of the ring committed suicide in jail, two were later executed, and six went to prison for long terms.

When General Dayan came home, he questioned Colonel Gibli. The intelligence chief said he had ordered the operation on instructions from the Defense Minister himself. He claimed that after a meeting in Mr. Lavon's home, the Defense Minister had taken him aside and told him to go ahead with the plan. Mr. Lavon denied this indignantly.

Thus was born an issue that clouded Israeli political life for a decade, brought down a government, split a party, made bitter enemies out of bosom friends, and tarnished the image of Mr. Ben-Gurion, who at the time had been away from the seat of power. Did Colonel Gibli or Mr. Lavon initiate the order?

The first to seek the answer was a secret commission appointed by Premier Sharett. More competent adjudicators were impossible to find: Chief Justice Yitzhak Olshan and General Yaakov Dory, a former Chief of Staff. They heard witnesses, studied documents, and finally had to acknowledge that they were stumped.

Their inconclusive finding left Mr. Lavon in an untenable position. He resigned from the Cabinet.

Mr. Ben-Gurion was then persuaded to leave his *kibbutz* and return to the Cabinet as Defense Minister under Premier Sharett. The scandal had shaken morale in the armed forces and it was felt a man of Mr. Ben-Gurion's stature was needed to restore it.

Mr. Ben-Gurion transferred the compromised intelligence chief to London as military attaché and Mr. Lavon was elected secretary general of the Histadrut. But Mr. Lavon was not willing to call it quits; he had been aggrieved and wanted rehabilitation.

His break came in 1960. One of Colonel Gibli's former cloak-and-dagger men, who had operated in Cairo under the name of Paul Franck, was brought before the district court of Jerusalem on security offenses that had nothing at all to do with the 1954 snafu. At his secret trial, he turned against his former boss. He confessed that evidence he had given on Colonel Gibli's behalf before the Olshan-Dori commission had been untrue. The reservist major, with the tacit approval of Colonel Gibli, had encouraged him to lie, he said.

Mr. Ben-Gurion, who was by then back in the premiership, appointed a commission to investigate. This commission came to a definite decision; the reservist major with the knowledge of Colonel Gibli, had suborned the witness. The statute of limitations saved the officers from prosecution, but Colonel Gibli was discharged from the armed forces.

The finding was a triumph for Mr. Lavon. True, the commission had not specifically established who had issued the order. But Mr. Lavon felt the implication was obvious. He went to Mr. Ben-Gurion and demanded official exoneration. The Premier said "no."

Exonerating Mr. Lavon, he reasoned, would implicitly proclaim that Colonel Gibli had initiated the order. That was beyond the competence of the executive, he said. If Mr. Lavon wanted a decision, his only avenue was a judicial investigation.

Mr. Lavon was vehement. He said he had suffered enough and there was no reason to prolong his ordeal. In his frustration, he turned to the parliamentary foreign affairs and security committee, where there were opposition deputies who were only too eager to hear his grievances.

Before the committee, Mr. Lavon lashed out like a wounded animal. He alleged that not only Colonel Gibli, but a whole clique in the security establishment had conspired to oust him as Defense Minister. He insinuated that Mr. Ben-Gurion himself had somehow been involved, since he had turned up in the Defense Ministry in Tel Aviv precisely on Sundays when Mr. Lavon was in Jerusalem attending Cabinet meetings.

The former Defense Minister said the Cairo snafu had not been the only example of the security establishment's incompetence. He told Knesset members that the son of one of their colleagues had been killed in a phone-tapping operation in Syria that had been "folly from beginning to end."

Such allegations roiled Mr. Ben-Gurion. One thing he could never tolerate was anyone besmirching the Israeli armed forces. He regarded Mr. Lavon as a scoundrel. The feud became personal.

But in Mr. Ben-Gurion's Cabinet, developments were working in Mr. Lavon's favor. As a device to cut off discussions in the parliamentary committee, the Cabinet set up a committee of seven ministers to consider how the affair should be handled. The ministers went beyond their terms of reference. They dealt with the dispute itself and solicited testimony.

Sensational new evidence reached the ministerial committee. It included a statement by a typist who had worked for Colonel Gibli in 1954. She had typed a letter from her boss to General Dayan about the Cairo operation. Shown a copy of the letter that had been introduced as evidence before the Olshan-Dori commission, the typist said it included a phrase that had not been in the original: "according to Lavon's instructions." The committee concluded there had been a fabrication of evidence and deduced that the 1954 operation had been ordered without Mr. Lavon's knowledge.

Mr. Ben-Gurion fumed. He denounced the finding as a "miscarriage of justice" and "one-sided." He gave the impression he was furious over the exoneration of his mortal enemy, but he maintained that his outrage was over a moral issue—the fact that the government had dared adjudicate at all.

As he described it, a group of politicians had set themselves up as judges in a dispute between their powerful colleague and an army officer. Without hearing the officer, they decided in favor of their colleague. They thus implicitly condemned the officer. That was an unpardonable intrusion by the executive into the sphere of the judiciary.

In fighting it, Mr. Ben-Gurion fancied himself an Émile Zola crusading against an injustice to Captain Dreyfus. But he had difficulty persuading the public he would be fighting for the moral principle so assiduously if the commission had decided against Mr. Lavon. The suspicion that he was engaged in a personal vendetta was strengthened when Mr. Ben-Gurion set out to liquidate Mr. Lavon politically.

He demanded that Mapai oust Mr. Lavon as secretary general of the Histadrut. The grounds? Anyone who had besmirched the armed forces as Mr. Lavon had done could not represent the party in any forum. Mr. Ben-Gurion put the screws on the party by resigning the premiership, automatically bringing down the government. He refused to accept the party's mandate to form a new government as long as Mr. Lavon represented the party in any public office.

Mr. Ben-Gurion got his way. He was still very much the party boss.

By a vote of 159–96, the central committee ousted Mr. Lavon from his Histadrut post. Taking into account that Mr. Ben-Gurion had staked his political future on the outcome, the close vote was a Pyrrhic victory.

Mr. Ben-Gurion resumed the premiership but he never regained his old esteem. His one-time worshipers spoke of him as a sore loser, vengeful and undemocratic, and accused him of hurting the image of the State. When, at the age of seventy-seven in 1963, he resigned from the government finally, even his loyal supporters felt it was a good thing. But before leaving, Mr. Ben-Gurion rattled the skeleton in the closet once more.

He hired a newspaper reporter, swore him in as a temporary employee of the Defense Ministry to give him access to confidential files, and instructed him to prepare a dossier on the Lavon Affair. The aging leader seemed determined to vindicate himself before he died.

Mr. Ben-Gurion was already a private citizen when the reporter finished his job. Among other things, his dossier purported to show that Mr. Lavon had trapped Colonel Gibli, abusing his trust to trick him into writing memos that later incriminated him.

The former Premier submitted the bulky report to the government of Levi Eshkol. He asked Attorney General Moshe Ben Zeev to consider his proposal for a judicial inquiry. The Attorney General studied the data and concluded it warranted reopening the case. Justice Minister Dov Joseph concurred. Neither had been in office in 1960 when the Cabinet had cleared Mr. Lavon.

But Premier Eshkol, who had been a key member in the controversial ministerial inquiry commission, insisted there was nothing in the report to justify re-examining the case. A Cabinet majority backed Mr. Eshkol.

That raised the curtain on the third act of the drama. Mr. Lavon became the forgotten man of the Lavon Affair as Mr. Ben-Gurion transferred the full blast of his wrath to Mr. Eshkol, whom he had personally chosen to succeed him in the premiership. Mr. Ben-Gurion accused Mr. Eshkol and his government of suppressing truth and justice and undermining the moral foundation of the State for the sake of partisan expediency.

He took the issue to the Mapai central committee, where he tried to unseat Mr. Eshkol. But he no longer overawed that body as he used to and he was defeated. He appealed to the party's national convention. He was defeated again. He walked out of the party.

In refusing to yield to the majority, Mr. Ben-Gurion invoked the image of Moses smashing the Tablets. He quoted the biblical account describing how Moses had descended Mount Sinai carrying the two Tablets of stone written with the finger of God and found the majority of the people of Israel dancing around the golden calf. "Moses' anger waxed hot," the Bible relates, "and he cast the Tablets out of his hands and broke them beneath the mount."

Would anyone, Mr. Ben-Gurion asked, dare suggest that Moses should have democratically yielded to the will of the majority?

So he formed the Rafi party, together with his favorite disciples, Moshe Dayan and Shimon Peres, who had followed him out of Mapai. He carried the issue to the electorate. He was defeated again. Mr. Eshkol's slate polled nearly five times more votes than Mr. Ben-Gurion's. The old fighter took his place in the Opposition benches of the Knesset and continued to heap scorn on his former protégé until Mr. Eshkol's death in 1969.

But the public was bored with his crusade, which it regarded as a useless exercise in self-flagellation. Even his dyed-in-the wool Rafi supporters had dropped the issue. In 1967, after the Six Day War, they voted to merge Rafi with Mapai and Ahdut Haavodah to form the new Israel Labor party. Mr. Ben-Gurion refused to go along with the decision. He remained a solitary figure in the Opposition. But his charisma and messianic aura were still great; in 1969, when he was eighty-three, he attracted enough votes to sweep him and three others on his slate into the Knesset. But he was no longer a political power, and the following year he resigned his Knesset seat in midsession.

17

The *Sabras* Take Over

"The newcomers learned quickly that in Israel Jews stood up for their rights."

Above, the old and the new: an immigrant and his sabra *grandchild. Left, Independence Day fireworks in Tel Aviv.*

Mrs. Meir chats with a group of young Israelis.

As Mr. Ben-Gurion and his contemporaries faded into history, the complexion and temperament of the political leadership changed. The East European element, which had been the driving force leading to the founding of the State, remained predominant, but its monopoly of power was diluted.

Jews from countries of Islam had taken over from old-guard types as local political bosses and mayors in some towns, while on the national level *sabra* ministers held some of the key portfolios and were leading contenders for succession to the premiership.

At the start of the 1970's fifteen of the twenty-four ministers in Mrs. Golda Meir's government were still immigrants from Russia or Poland. However, two of them had come as children and were *sabras* in spirit. And there were four genuine *sabras* in the government. Three of them —Yigal Allon, Moshe Dayan, and Ezer Weizman—were former generals. Moreover, most men mooted as Cabinet timber for the 1970's were *sabra* generals or former generals. That is not fortuitous.

306

When the generation now ripening for top leadership was in its teens, the elite had not gone to college but to the underground. They had fought the British and the Arabs and had bucked British naval blockades with illegal shiploads of Jewish refugees from Europe. Naturally, after independence these men were commissioned officers in the armed forces.

In a small and informal army such as Israel's, where the distance between officers and men was small, those who caught the eye were the natural leaders—quick-witted, charismatic men who were eloquent in an impish *sabra* way. Theirs were the most attractive personalities in the country. Political parties wanted them, sometimes for window dressing.

Since the defense forces' policy has been to retire officers in their forties at the latest, these men had to think of new careers at middle age. Some have become prominent in archaeology and business, scholarship and public service. A number have found new vistas in politics.

Ideologically there is no generation gap between them and the old Establishment. The *sabra* generals run the gamut from Marxist *kibbutz* members to rugged individualists. They have blended into established parties.

The differences are rather in style and in tone. Accustomed to brisk and efficient general staff meetings, the new leaders have little patience for oratorical flourishes and ideological dogmatism. They have brought a refreshing frankness into the realm of public discussion. They like to lay facts on the table and discuss them openly and realistically.

Sabra slang for "hot air" is *"Tsionut,"* which means Zionism. Old leaders groomed in Zionist politics were indeed accustomed to marathon meetings where speeches were notoriously long-winded and not always realistic. They were full of references to generalized ideology. The straightforward *sabra* approach upset some of the old-timers. They called the *sabras* technocrats and unidealistic. But it isn't so. Idealism burns in the *sabras*, but they consider it poor form to shoot off sparks.

Like Jews everywhere, *sabras* were deeply affected by the World War II Holocaust. But they were affected in a uniquely *sabra* way. It wasn't so much what the Nazis had done that they couldn't shake off; it was the vision of an endless file of Jews shuffling with sheeplike docility to their doom. *Sabras* couldn't understand why the victims had not lashed out and gone down fighting. The uprisings in Warsaw and in other ghettos only slightly relieved their sense of national humiliation.

The helplessness of the civilized world to prevent the slaughter also left an indelible mark on the *sabras*. It warned them that in a crunch they could rely only on themselves.

Such memories motivated the Israelis in 1948, when the Arab League proclaimed a "momentous war of extermination which would be spoken of in history like the Mongolian massacre and the Crusades." The specter of the Holocaust also haunted them in 1967, when one Arab country after another announced that it was joining the war to erase the Jewish State once and for all. No one was going to accuse this generation of Jews of docility!

Israel's plucky stand against overwhelming odds won international applause, but the spectacular victories created public relations complexities. Much of the compassion that the civilized world had been ready to shower on the Israelis when they had been threatened with extinction shifted after the victories to the frustrated Arabs, particularly the unfortunate refugees who fled to Arab countries during the fighting and were prevented by the Israelis from returning to their homes.

When a year passed after the Six Day War and then another and another, and the Star of David still flew from the Suez Canal to within thirty miles of Damascus, Israel acquired an imperialistic image. Erstwhile sympathizers seemed to have forgotten why the Israelis had dislodged the Arabs in the first place. There was a ground swell of resentment around the world over Israel's intransigence in refusing to restore any of the conquered territory to Egypt, Jordan, or Syria before the Arabs signed a genuine peace treaty.

To the Israeli mind, those critics completely miss the point. Territory isn't the issue at all. The Arabs don't acknowledge Israel's right to exist in any part of the world they consider theirs. It wouldn't matter if the Jewish State consisted only of Tel Aviv and its suburbs. On the contrary, the smaller and weaker the Jewish State, the more the Arabs would be encouraged to try to eliminate it.

As for security, the borders after the 1967 war were the most comfortable the Israelis had ever had. A *sabra* general once impishly described the Suez Canal as the "best man-made tank trap in the world." Egyptian air bases that had been only four minutes flying time away from Tel Aviv became a safer twenty-five to thirty minutes away. For the first time since 1948, Jordanian guns were not able to fire across the narrow waist of Israel and hit Tel Aviv. Arab armies no longer pressed against Jerusalem and other major centers of population. The Syrian heights of Golan, towering over Jewish settlements in the Jordan Valley, were in Jewish hands.

So, the reasoning goes, it would be the height of folly to surrender the tactical advantages as long as the Arabs intend to use the territory as a springboard for another go at Israel.

Israelis are certain that the only thing that deters the Arabs from starting another war is the knowledge that they would be beaten. The continued occupation of Arab territory is thus seen as a deterrent. No amount of Arab harassment could conceivably persuade the Israelis to retreat from the cease-fire lines and permit the Arabs to pursue their attacks from more advantageous positions closer to sensitive Israeli areas.

Apart from unwonted elbowroom for defense, the Israelis acquired levers for a political settlement through their conquests of 1967. For the first time they had something with which to bargain; they had territory they could cede in peace negotiations. The million Arabs brought under Israeli rule gave them another lever for peace.

General Dayan's policies in the occupied areas were influenced considerably by impressions he had gathered in Vietnam, where he served as a war correspondent for an Israeli newspaper not long before he became minister of defense.

"A war of liberation will fail," he observed, "if the regime is difficult to undermine or easy to live under. Certainly," he added, "it will fail if both factors are combined."

Accordingly the military government came down hard on guerrillas and their accomplices. They were hunted down assiduously. Military courts imposed severe sentences—but not death, so as not to make martyrs out of the terrorists. In cases where the security services balked at revealing sources of information, suspects were not brought to court but were detained for long periods under administrative orders. Agitators were banished to Bedouin encampments in Sinai, to Hussein's kingdom across the Jordan bridges, and to various other regions.

With typical *sabra* realism, General Dayan recognized that the sympathy of the Arab population must be with the terrorists and that fear of Israeli retribution was the only consideration that would deter them from harboring gunmen. The military government instilled fear into the Arabs. Any house where a suspected terrorist was known to have eaten, slept, or drunk was blown up summarily.

But if an innocent neighbor's window was cracked by the blast, the military governor sent a glazier to replace it. That was the other side of the coin. The occupation forces were under orders that Arabs who took no part in the unrest should be treated liberally.

In contrast to Vietnam, where it was inconceivable for the Americans to retain a Vietcong hospital director or schoolteacher in a captured town, the Israelis kept enemy mayors in office and encouraged policemen, judges, teachers, health and education inspectors, and other Arab officials to remain at their posts. The Israelis could afford to do so because theirs was not a war over ideologies. They wanted the inhabitants of the occupied areas to remain good Arabs. They encouraged them to maintain their ties across the cease-fire lines and to trade and visit across the Jordan bridges.

Israeli experts were assigned to the occupied territories to teach Arab farmers to grow high-value crops under plastic. Modern methods of packing, marketing, irrigation, fertilizing, and pest control were introduced. Israeli manufacturers subcontracted in the occupied areas, and tens of thousands of Arab workers were brought across the former armistice lines daily to work in factories, farms, or buildings at Israeli trade-union wages.

It wasn't altruism. The liberal policy was calculated to create a schism between the population and the guerrillas by giving the people something they would lose in case of civil rebellion or unrest. It paid off. A substantial number of Arabs had a vested interest in law and order. Some indeed tipped off the Israelis about terrorist hideouts and arms caches, and a number of cells were broken up before they could launch their first actions.

Israelis draw no false illusions from the situation. At a meeting of

Arab mayors, chamber of commerce officials, and other notables in occupied Ramallah, near Jerusalem, General Dayan turned to his hosts and remarked: "If you think I don't know that at least seven times a day you say 'to hell with Israel' and 'to hell with Dayan'. . . ."

"You're wrong," one of the mayors corrected him. "Seventy-seven times." The Israeli officers and the Arabs joined in the hearty laughter.

It is precisely such encounters that offer a glimmer of hope for the future. Israeli realists don't expect the Arabs to like them, no matter how decently they are treated or how generously benefits are heaped on them. The Israelis acknowledge that their occupation must be offensive to Arabs.

The most they hope for is to demonstrate that it is possible to live with Jews without loving them. The hope is that once the idea sinks in among the Arabs in the occupied areas, the seed will be carried across the open bridges of the Jordan to the neighboring Arab states. It may take time. This generation of Arab rulers may not be capable of accepting the idea, but perhaps the next one or the one after will be. In the meantime the Israelis are trying to impress the Arabs with their invincibility.

So one day, it is hoped, sensible Arab rulers will recognize the futility of their dream of erasing Israel and the feasibility of living side by side. To the Israeli mind, a withdrawal from the occupied areas and the repatriation of refugees will then become negotiable. Only then, and not earlier.

That inflexibility has alienated friends and cost the Jewish State much sympathy. Israelis are sorry. But their experience has taught them that they'd be a lot sorrier if they staked their fortunes on world sympathy instead of on themselves.

Special Interest Guide

THE FOLLOWING SECTION is addressed to readers who want precise information about fields that are of particular interest to them. It is intended for businessmen and specialists who wish to establish professional or social ties with Israeli colleagues; for radio hams, stamp collectors, and other hobbyists who would like to communicate with Israelis of similar enthusiasms; and for travelers who may find their visits to Israel enriched if they are able to penetrate more deeply into the areas of their special interests.

The directory is not, of course, all-inclusive, nor does it answer all questions that might arise. But it does cast a wide net. Under appropriate headings it informs an oceanographer or an orthodondist, for instance, how to contact colleagues, and an amateur pugilist how to find a sparring partner in Israel.

In some respects the directory reflects Israeli interests. Israel is a country where a golfer hacking his way out of a sand trap, a bather on a beach, and a worker excavating the foundation of a new building all keep their eyes open for archaeological finds. Archaeology is a national pastime, and the guide accordingly devotes considerable space to that field.

On the other hand, rotary clubs are certainly not characteristic of Israel. Bowling, badminton, and golf are by no means popular sports. But some travelers may be glad to know that they will be able to drop in on a luncheon of their club or enjoy a round of their favorite sport, so the guide does list that information.

The directory sometimes includes information that can be found in conventional guidebooks, but the approach is different. Instead of listing museums and describing what they contain, this guide focuses on the various fields of art, natural history, archaeology, and so forth, and lists under those headings exhibits or information relating to each field.

Some of the specialized societies listed have small memberships. Often they have no fixed headquarters. The directory supplies the addresses of current officers who will be glad to arrange contacts with colleagues from other countries. There can be no guarantee that the persons listed will remain in office indefinitely or that they will not themselves attend international conventions in other countries periodically. It is therefore recommended that travelers write to the societies well in advance of their planned visits.

The same recommendation applies to those who wish to visit private collections of hobbyists or special museums that are not open at regular times. The collectors listed have expressed readiness to welcome travelers genuinely interested in their respective fields, but they would like to be given advance notice.

When Viscount Samuel assumed office as the first British High Commissioner for Palestine, he was asked to sign the following receipt: "Received from Major General Sir Louis J. Bols, K.C.B., One Palestine, complete."

He signed the paper and added the initials "E. & O.E.," which often appear on British commercial documents.

We give you the Special Interest Guide with the same reservation. The initials stand for "Errors and Omissions Excepted."

Agriculture

The Ministry of Agriculture and its regional offices provide information and arrange visits to its facilities. The Ministry may be contacted by addressing:

Ministry Spokesman, 8 Rehov Daled, Hakirya, Tel Aviv or Scientific Advisor to the Minister, 10 Rehov Daled, Tel Aviv. Regional Offices are located near the following cities: Acre, Safed, Nazareth, Hadera, Raanana, Afula, Rehovot, Beersheba, East Jerusalem, Gaza

INSTITUTIONS OF HIGHER LEARNING

HEBREW UNIVERSITY, FACULTY OF AGRICULTURE

Rehovot

The activities of the faculty are coordinated with the Volcani Institute (see Agricultural Research, below). Emphasis is on both teaching and research.

TECHNION-ISRAEL INSTITUTE OF TECHNOLOGY, FACULTY OF AGRICULTURAL ENGINEERING

Technion City, Haifa

ASSOCIATIONS

FARMERS' FEDERATION OF ISRAEL

Beth Haikar, 8 Rehov Kaplan, P.O.B. 209, Tel Aviv

Central association of private farmers.

AGRONOMISTS ASSOCIATION IN ISRAEL

P.O.B. 468, Tel Aviv

Aims to advance all branches of agriculture in Israel, disseminate agricultural information, protect professional interests of members, and support research work.

ISRAEL SOCIETY FOR AGRICULTURAL ENGINEERING

Faculty of Agricultural Engineering, Technion, P.O.B. 4910, Technion City, Haifa

Advances scientific and applied agricultural research, encourages cooperation with those in related fields, and improves training methods and fosters professional advancement of members. Affiliation: International Commission of Agricultural Engineering.

ISRAEL SOCIETY OF SOIL SCIENCE

Faculty of Agriculture, Hebrew University, P.O.B. 12, Rehovot

Advances soil science in Israel. Affiliations: Association for the Advancement of Science in Israel; International Association of Soil Science.

AGRICULTURAL RESEARCH

VOLCANI INSTITUTE OF AGRICULTURAL RESEARCH

P.O.B. 6, Beth Dagan

Responsible for the planning and execution of agricultural research in Israel. Has departments and divisions dealing with all aspects of agriculture: Soils and Water, Agronomy, Horticulture, Plant Protection, Livestock, Food Storage and Technology, Forestry, Statistics and Experimental Design, and Scientific Publication.

THE AGRICULTURAL ENGINEERING INSTITUTE

P.O.B. 6, Beth Dagan

Conducts research in four main fields: 1. Theoretical aspects and principles of agricultural engineering; 2. Systems analysis and improvement of agricultural methods from the point of view of production and marketing; 3. Development of prototypes of new machinery and modifications of existing machinery; 4. Testing of locally produced machinery and of the suitability of imported machines to local conditions.

KIMRON VETERINARY INSTITUTE

P.O.B. 12, Beth Dagan

Engages in research in animal pathology, diagnosis of livestock diseases, animal produce hygiene, production of vaccines, and clinical medicine.

SEA FISHERIES RESEARCH STATION

P.O.B. 699, Haifa

Carries out research relevant to Mediterranean and Red Sea fisheries.

FISH CULTURE RESEARCH STATION

Dor, Hof Hacarmel Mobile Post

Among other related subjects, conducts research activity in pond fertilization; fish population dynamics; physiology of spawning, feeding, nutrition, and biology of pond fish; and acclimitization of new species.

LABORATORY FOR RESEARCH OF FISH DISEASES

Nir David, Gilboa Mobile Post

Does basic and applied research into fish diseases and their identification and control. Gives advisory service to breeders.

SOIL EROSION RESEARCH STATION

Ruppin Institute of Agriculture, Emek Hefer

Determines the hydrologic balance of typical small catchments in Israel, conducts research on differences in soil moisture consumption of different vegetation types and its effect on the water balance in the Carmel region, measures soil erosion under field conditions, studies fertilization of range land and the development of mechanical methods for sowing and planting protective vegetation on heavy slopes and canals.

IRRIGATION AND SOIL FIELD SERVICE

Ruppin Institute of Agriculture, Emek Hefer

Conducts soil, water, and plant tests to direct irrigation practices, recommends fertilizer programs, surveys soil for plant use, and seeks to improve quality of soil and water.

STORED PRODUCTS RESEARCH LABORATORY
RODENT RESEARCH LABORATORY
LOCUST RESEARCH LABORATORY
LABORATORY OF PESTICIDE RESIDUES

6 Rehov Dror, Jaffa

All are research laboratories of the Ministry of Agriculture, Plant Protection Department.

BIOLOGICAL CONTROL INSTITUTE

27 Rehov Keren Kayemet, Rehovot

Carries out research on citrus pests, aiming to control them by the dissemination of useful insects in citrus orchards rather than by pesticides.

Archaeology

Permits from the government Department of Antiquities are required for archaeological excavations and they are granted only to scientific expeditions. Any person discovering an antiquity is required by law to take reasonable measures to protect it and to report the find to the Department of Antiquities and Museums, Rockefeller Museum, P.O.B. 586, Jerusalem, or to the nearest District Office. Exporting and trading antiquities also require licenses.

Amateurs wishing to participate in digs may communicate with the Assistant Director of Antiquities, P.O.B. 586, Jerusalem.

THE ARCHAEOLOGICAL PERIODS ARE AS FOLLOWS:

Lower Paleolithic Period:
 1,000,000–70,000
Middle Paleolithic Period:
 70,000–35,000
Upper Paleolithic Period:
 35,000–10,000
Mesolithic (Natufian) Period:
 10,000–7500
Neolithic Period: 7500–4000
Chalcolithic Period: 4000–3200
 Ghassulian Period: 3700–3300
Early Bronze Age
 I: c. 3200–2900
 II: c. 2900–2600
 III–IV: c. 2600–2200
Middle Bronze Age
 (Age of the Patriarchs)
 I: c. 2200–2000
 IIA: c. 2000–1750
 IIB: (Hyksos): c. 1750–1550
Late Bronze Age (Canaanite Period)
 I: c. 1550–1400
 IIA: c. 1400–1300
 IIB: c. 1300–1200

Iron Age (Israelite Period)
 I: c. 1200–930
 II: c. 930–586
Persian Period: 586–332
Hellenistic Period: 332–37
Roman Period: 37 B.C.–A.D. 324
Byzantine Period: A.D. 324–A.D. 640
Early Arab, Crusader, Mameluke, and
 Turkish periods: A.D. 640–A.D. 1700

ARCHAEOLOGICAL SITES

AKKO (ACRE)—The earliest city of Akko was located on Tell el-Fukhar, east of the modern city, and remains there date from the Early Bronze Age to the Hellenistic Period. In the Hellenistic Period, settlement moved from the tell closer to the sea, and this site has been occupied up to the present day. The present-day Old City was the most important port of the Crusaders, and the remains of the harbor, jetty, lighthouse, towers, churches, and fortifications can still be seen. A large vaulted hall in an early Gothic style, known as the Crypt of the Knights of St. John, was found under the later Turkish citadel. It is now believed to have been the refectory of a twelfth-century Crusader hostel built by the Order of St. John. Another Crusader vault was found beneath the large patio of the mosque of Al-Jazzar; it is presumed to be part of the Crusader Church of St. John. The mosque of Jami er-Ramel is also on the site of a Crusader church, which was probably erected late in the twelfth century. Three inns in Acre have Crusader foundations: Khan el-Faranj, which adjoins one corner of a Franciscan convent; Khan el-'Umdan, originally a Dominican monastery; and Khan esh-Shawarda, which perhaps stands on the site of the convent of the Franciscan sisters.

ARAD—The earliest remains on the site date from the Chalcolithic Period. In the Early Bronze Age II a large fortified city with a thick stone wall and semicircular towers was built. Private and public buildings and streets have been revealed in the excavations. The site was abandoned until the Iron Age I, when a citadel was built on the northeastern ridge of the early town. A series of citadels followed, one upon the other, until early in the Arab Period. A temple first built in the tenth century was rebuilt in the succeeding periods. The general plan of the temple resembles that of the Temple in Jerusalem. It consisted of a court with an altar, a porch, a sanctuary, and a holy of holies. An archive of the seventh-century Israelite citadel, containing ostraca in Hebrew script, has been found. Many Aramaic ostraca of the Persian Period have also been discovered.

ASHKELON—The port city was first established in the Middle Bronze Age II and is situated today in the national park of Ashkelon. The site was occupied until the end of the Crusader Period, with a break

The excavations at Hazor

in occupation between the Late Bronze Age and early in the Iron Age. It was a very large and important port city from the Hellenistic to the Crusader periods. The remains of walls that surround the present-day national park were built by the Crusaders. A collection of Roman and Greek statues, columns, and marble reliefs is on view in the park. Granite pillars, remains of the ancient harbor, can be seen. Close to the beach at Ashkelon a third-century A.D. Roman tomb with colorful decorations painted on the vaulted ceiling and plastered walls has been excavated.

AVDAT—Located some forty miles south of Beersheba, the site was first inhabited by the Nabataeans in the third century B.C. It flourished as a Nabataean city until A.D. 106. Remains from this period include private houses, a potter's workshop, rock-cut graves, and a unique system of irrigation consisting of dams, cisterns, and water channels. At the end of the second century A.D. a Roman fort was built. Remains of the fort, of a colonnaded terrace, and of private houses have been uncovered. The Byzantines built a citadel there. Two churches and a monastery, and the remains of houses and a bath, date from the Byzantine Period.

BELVOIR (KOHAV HAYARDEN) —This citadel overlooking the Jordan Valley was built by the Hospitalers in A.D. 1168 and was destroyed in 1219. The fortress had a symmetrical plan and it was defended by a moat, an outer wall, and an inner citadel. The outer wall was built in the shape of a pentagon, with towers at each corner. The inner citadel was rectangular in shape, with a tower at each corner, and was built around a central court. The second story was used for living quarters and a church. Two gates have been found in the eastern face of the outer defenses and one in the western face.

BETHLEHEM—In the fourth century a basilica known as the Church of the Nativity was built over the cave where Jesus was believed to have been born. The church was destroyed and rebuilt by Justinian in the sixth century, and was restored in the twelfth century by the Crusaders. Within the church is the Grotto of the Nativity. The Milk Grotto of the Franciscans is nearby.

BETH-SHAN (BEISAN)—The site was first inhabited in the fourth millennium, and settlement continued until the Arab Period. A series of temples dating from the Late Bronze Age to the Iron Age I have been revealed through excavations. Also of the Late Bronze Age are Egyptian steles, a statue of Ramses III, and an orthostat showing a fight between a dog and a lion. Meager remains of walls from the Iron Age were also found, along with a Hellenistic temple and a well-preserved Roman theater built about A.D. 200 with a seating capacity of eight thousand. Nearby are the remains of a Samaritan synagogue constructed late in the fourth or early in the fifth century A.D., with a mosaic floor depicting plants and geometric designs. A monastery of the sixth century with mosaic floors was also revealed.

BETH SHEARIM (SHEIKH ABREIK)—The site was first occupied in the eighth or seventh century B.C. and continued to be inhabited in later periods. Only from the Roman Period, however, have extensive remains been uncovered. A large synagogue, public buildings, and workshops have been excavated on the site. The importance of the city increased when the Patriarch Rabbi Yehuda (Judah) Hanasi made it his residence and the seat of the Sanhedrin at the end of the second and beginning of the third centuries A.D. He was reportedly buried in the nearby necropolis consisting of rock-cut catacombs in the slopes of the hill. Some of these catacombs were family vaults and others were public burial quarters. Jews from as far away as Antioch, Babylon, Sidon, and South Arabia were buried there. Most of the catacombs consisted of steps leading down to a large central hall with many side chambers on both sides. Some comprised several stories. Sarcophagi with carved or sculptured decoration, ossuaries, wall paintings, engravings, and reliefs have been found in the catacombs. The epitaphs were usually written in Greek, but some were in Hebrew or Aramaic. The largest catacomb so far exposed held about two hundred sarcophagi. The city was destroyed in the middle of the fourth century A.D. and continued to be inhabited on a small scale until early in the Arab Period.

CAESAREA—The city was founded by the Phoenicians in the fourth century B.C. as a maritime colony called Strato's

Tower. In 22 B.C. King Herod rebuilt and fortified the city, naming it in honor of the Roman Emperor Caesar Augustus. He constructed a deep sea harbor, a temple to Augustus, an amphitheater, a hippodrome seating twenty thousand, and an aqueduct. A Roman theater dating from the second century A.D. has been excavated and restored. A synagogue dating from the second to the fourth centuries A.D. has also been uncovered, along with fragments of mosaics and marble capitals, two decorated with candelabra (menorahs). From the Byzantine occupation are the ruins of a church with a mosaic floor, and streets paved with crude mosaics and marble. In one building of the Byzantine Period two Roman statues were found, one dating from the second century A.D. and the other from the third century. The Crusaders rebuilt the city with large fortifications and excavated a moat surrounding the entire area of thirty-five acres. The harbor was also rebuilt at that time, and a large cathedral was erected.

EN-GEDI—Several sites near the spring of En-gedi on the shore of the Dead Sea were occupied in various periods. The earliest building remains belong to a Chalcolithic temple built on a cliff above the spring. The temple consisted of an enclosure with two gatehouses surrounding a sanctuary and the house of the priest. The later occupation on Tel Goren began late in the Iron Age II and consisted of a citadel. In one building installations for the manufacture of perfume, perhaps from balsam, have been found. Occupation on the site continued until the Byzantine Period. A public bath, dating from the revolt of Bar Kochba (Roman Period) has been uncovered near the tell.

EMMAUS (NICOPOLIS)—On this site north of Latrun the Templars built a castle called Les Toron des Chevaliers. Nearby are the remains of another Crusader church, built upon the remains from the Hellenistic, Roman, and Byzantine periods.

HAZOR (near Kibbutz Ayelet Hashahar) —The first settlement at Hazor dates from the Early Bronze Age. In the Middle Bronze Age IIB the city was enlarged and consisted of an acropolis of thirty acres and a lower city of about two hundred acres. The lower city was fortified with a large rampart and was surrounded by a

moat. Four successive layers of occupation dating from the Middle Bronze Age IIB to the end of the Late Bronze Age were uncovered in the lower city. A temple built at the end of the Middle Bronze Age was rebuilt three times. It consisted of a court, a shrine, and a holy of holies. A small sanctuary that contained various cult objects was constructed on the rampart in the Late Bronze Age II. Two city gates in the rampart, first constructed in the Middle Bronze Age II, were reused until the end of the Late Bronze Age. On the acropolis remains from the Early Bronze Age through the Hellenistic Period have been uncovered. They include a Middle Bronze Age II palace and sanctuary and a fortified Solomonic (tenth century) enclosure and gate like those found at Gezer and Megiddo. In the ninth century King Ahab constructed a new city wall that enclosed a large citadel and the largest water system yet discovered in Israel.

HERODION—A citadel built by Herod is situated on the top of a hill about six miles south of Jerusalem. The circular citadel is symmetrical in plan, with four towers and an inner and outer wall. After the outer wall was completed it was strengthened on the outer face by beaten earth from top to bottom like a glacis. In the area within the citadel were a colonnaded court, a bath, and storerooms. The Zealots used this citadel in the time of the First Jewish War, and remains of the occupation have been found in the towers. The last occupation of the site dates from the Byzantine Period.

JERICHO—The earliest fortified city so far uncovered in the Near East (7000 B.C.) has been excavated here. Remains of the earliest prepottery Neolithic settlement include circular or oval brick houses and fortifications consisting of a large circular stone tower with a hidden stairway built inside the stone city wall. In the following period the city was fortified with a new stone wall. The square or rectangular brick houses were plastered inside, painted in red or yellow, and burnished with pebbles. Several small sanctuaries in private houses have been uncovered, as has a temple consisting of a portico, a wide antechamber, and a large inner room with two columns. Burial sites have been found under the floors of the houses, and several plastered human skulls and skulls shaped from plaster have been revealed. Few remains of the following Neolithic phases have been found, but pottery first appears at this time. After a break in occupation, the site was resettled in the Early Bronze Age and a succession of fortified cities was built. The Early Bronze Age I city contained a sanctuary. With the destruction of the latest Early Bronze Age city, nomadic peoples of the Middle Bronze Age I settled on the site. Strong defenses consisting of a moat, a glacis, and a wall were built in the Middle Bronze Age IIB. Settlement on the site continued up to the Late Bronze Age II, and there is evidence of settlement in the Iron Age. Graves from almost all the periods of occupation have been found on the site.

JERUSALEM—The first settlement on the site of Jerusalem dates from the end of the fourth millennium B.C. Tombs found on the western slope of the Mount of Olives indicate that the city was inhabited throughout the Bronze Ages. Part of a wall and a tower that have been excavated date from the Middle Bronze Age IIA. Scant remains were found of the cities of David and Solomon (tenth century B.C.). In the time of Solomon the city included the area of the City of David, the hill of Ophel, and the Temple Mount. Remains of a city wall and towers and of a rock-cut water tunnel constructed by Hezekiah date from the eighth century B.C. The city was destroyed by the Babylonians in 586 B.C. and was rebuilt by Nehemiah in the Persian Period. Part of the walls of the latter period have been discovered on the hill of Ophel. In the Hellenistic Period, especially in the time of the Hasmonaeans, the city was enlarged, and the western hill known as the Upper City was built, as indicated by the discovery of the remains of the city wall and towers. The Upper City and the Temple Mount were connected by a bridge, known today as Wilson's Arch. In the time of Herod (37 B.C.–A.D. 4) the city plan was completely changed. Herod rebuilt the Temple and enlarged and fortified the Temple Mount. His fortifications include Antonia's Tower and thick revetment walls surrounding the Temple Mount. Remains of this revetment, including the Western Wall, can be seen today. Herod also built a palace in the

northwestern corner of the Upper City and defended it with three towers, of which only the foundation of one is preserved and serves today as the base of the so-called David's Tower. Recent excavations have revealed a paved Herodian plaza south of the Temple Mount. Agrippa I enlarged the city by building the Third Wall north of the modern city wall. The city was destroyed by Titus in A.D. 70, and evidence of this destruction has recently been found in the Upper City. The city was rebuilt by the Emperor Hadrian.

The Kidron Valley, east of Jerusalem, supplied the city with water. In the bed of the valley is the spring of Gihon. King Hezekiah (eighth century B.C.) diverted the waters of the spring into the city via a subterranean tunnel. The tunnel can still be seen running from Gihon to the pool of Siloam. On the eastern slope of the Kidron Valley were the cemeteries of Jerusalem, dating from the Bronze Ages onward. Several Iron Age rock-cut tombs, such as the Tomb of Pharaoh's Daughter, have been found. Rock-cut tombs of the second to the first centuries B.C. include Absalom's Tomb, the Tomb of the Sons of Hezir, and the Tomb of Zechariah. The cemeteries of Jerusalem also continued to the north and northwest of the city. The rock-cut Tomb of the Kings is believed to be the tomb of Queen Helena of Adiabene and the members of her family who converted to Judaism in the first century A.D. Next to the King David Hotel is Herod's Family Tomb. The rolling-stone that formed the door can be seen at the entrance. In the northern part of Jerusalem are the rock-cut tombs attributed to the Sanhedrin, the supreme court of Israel in the days of the Second Temple. The tomb is a three-storied cave with many burial chambers. Jason's Tomb in Rehov Alfasi dates from the Hasmonaean Period (second to first centuries B.C.).

The earliest and the most important church in Jerusalem is the Church of the Holy Sepulcher, built in 326 on the hill of Calvary. In the sixth century it was reconstructed by the Emperor Justinian. The church was destroyed and reconstructed several times before the Crusaders rebuilt it in 1149. The street along which Christ went to his death is still called the Via Dolorosa. The Chapel of Calvary inside the church marks the last stages of Christ's Passion. One of the best-preserved Cru-

Archaeologists at work in Tel-Gezer

sader buildings in Jerusalem is St. Anne's Church, near St. Stephen's Gate. In the New City of Jerusalem is the Monastery of the Cross, originally built by Georgian monks in the eleventh century.

Mount Zion is a site venerated by both Jews and Christians. A fourth-century A.D. synagogue is now part of the traditional Tomb of David. The rock-cut chamber in which the sepulcher is placed is reached through the court and hall of a twelfth-century Crusader basilica, which was built above a fifth-century basilica. The second story of this building contains the Coenaculum, where the Last Supper presumably took place. The present-day refectory was rebuilt in the fourteenth century by Franciscan monks. Adjoining the building is the Dormition Abbey. Mary is said to have ascended to heaven from this site.

Jerusalem is also a holy city for the Moslems, and on the Temple Mount (in Arabic, the Haram esh-Sherif) in the Old City stand two mosques: the Dome of the Rock, built in A.D. 691 and the Al-Aksa Mosque, built in 693. Both have been restored numerous times.

KURNUB—This city near Dimona is usually identified with Mampsis and is the only known fortified city in the Negev. The first settlement was built by the Nabataeans and dates from the first half of the first century B.C. This city was destroyed by the Arabs in the second half of the first century A.D. After 106 the city was rebuilt by the Nabataeans. (Remains of large fortified houses, usually of two stories, have been found there.) At that time Nahal Mamshit was dammed to supply water to the city. Of the same period are a Roman and Nabataean cemetery. Early in the third century A.D. the city was fortified, but no changes were made in the plan. In one of the houses, frescoes of mythological figures and a hoard of 10,500 silver coins were found. In the Byzantine Period two mosaic-paved churches were erected, and at the same time the city plan was somewhat changed. The city was destroyed at the time of the Arab conquest.

MASADA—According to Josephus, this isolated rock-fortress by the Dead Sea was first fortified in the second century B.C. by Alexander Jannaeus, who erected a fortress on the upper terrace. The fortress built by King Herod has been excavated. The fortifications consisted of a casemate wall with thirty-seven towers that surrounded the entire area. He also constructed storehouses, barracks, arsenals, and granaries. Two aqueducts channeled water from two nearby wadis to

320

cisterns within the fortress. Herod built two palaces, one on the edge of the northern precipice. It was divided into three terraces. The residential quarters on the upper terrace were decorated with wall paintings and black and white mosaics and adjoined a semicircular terrace. The middle terrace consisted of a circular pavilion. On the lower terrace was a double colonnade surrounding a large patio. It was decorated with frescoes in green, red, and black, and some panels were painted to resemble marble. The various levels of the palace were connected by rock-cut stairways. South of the northern palace was a large complex of storerooms. Near the storerooms was a large public bath containing rooms with frescoes and mosaic-paved floors. In the western part of the plateau was the main palace, with a throne room. Here two mosaic floors have been found. In the northwestern part is a synagogue, the earliest known structure of its kind, that dates from the occupation of the Zealots who made a last stand against the Romans at Masada in A.D. 66–73. Other remains from the time of the Zealots are their living quarters, built inside the casemate wall, and their ritual bath (*mikve*). At the foot of Masada are the remains of the Roman camps, a siege wall, and the ramp for their battering ram. Among the many finds on Masada are scrolls including five chapters of the Book of Psalms and parts of the lost Hebrew original of Ecclesiasticus. On the summit are the remains of a sixth-century Byzantine church.

MEGIDDO—Occupation on this site dates from the fourth millennium. The large Early Bronze Age city was fortified by a thick stone wall. A series of Early Bronze Age temples and an altar have been uncovered. In the Middle Bronze Age II the city was fortified with a glacis, and one of the Early Bronze Age temples was rebuilt. A palace, built near the gate, was in use from the end of the Middle Bronze Age to early in the Iron Age. In the Late Bronze Age three successive fortified temples were constructed on the spot of the earlier temples. A hoard of ivories, jewelry, and gold vessels dating from the Late Bronze Age and the early Iron Age have been discovered in the palace. Remains of a city wall and gate date from the reign of King Solomon (tenth century)

and an extensive stable complex from the reign of King Ahab (ninth century). A water system, consisting of a rock-cut cistern and tunnel, probably dates from the Iron Age. The site was occupied until the Persian Period.

MONTFORT, MAHALIYA, AND JIDDIN—Three Crusader castles were built in the region of Acre, and their remains can be seen today. They were originally erected by the Templars but later passed into the hands of the Teutonic Order. Montfort and Mahaliya were never rebuilt, and parts of the fortifications, chapels, cisterns, ceremonial halls, and living quarters still stand. Jiddin was rebuilt by the Turks in the eighteenth century, but parts of the original Crusader castle can still be distinguished.

NAZARETH—Many Christian shrines were erected here. The oldest one is the church on the site of the Annunciation. In a small cell near a cave in the Annunciation compound is a grotto where a sixth-century Greek mosaic inscription was found. Excavations have revealed the foundations of the ancient village and the walls of medieval churches.

Ancient catacombs at Beth Shearim

QUMRAN—In a number of caves overlooking the Dead Sea several jars containing parchment scrolls wrapped in linen were found. They were placed there by a religious sect, perhaps the Essenes, in the time of the Second Temple. Known as the Dead Sea Scrolls, they contained the texts of several books of the Bible and special documents of the sect that deposited them. Also found in the caves were fragments of phylacteries (tephillin) and torn linen. Remains of the building where this sect lived were found a short distance from the caves; this structure had been erected on the foundations of an earlier Iron Age building. In the later building, three phases of occupation can be distinguished: c. 135–103 B.C.; c. 103–31 B.C.; 4 B.C.–June, A.D. 68. This building contained a kitchen, communal rooms, writing rooms with tables and small clay inkpots, water reservoirs, and several ritual baths. The finds include a complete head tephillin of the Second Temple Period and hundreds of coins. The building was destroyed by the Romans, who partially rebuilt it. This was the last occupation of the site.

RAMAT RAHEL—Located just south of Jerusalem, Ramat Rahel is identified with the biblical Beth Hakerem. It was first occupied in about the ninth century B.C. The earliest structure to be found, a royal palace, was erected in the last part of the eighth century, but was completely destroyed by the erection of a fortified palace on the same spot at the end of the seventh century B.C. This palace consisted of a large court surrounded by walls of ashlar masonry, all of which was fortified by a casemate wall. In the Persian Period a citadel was constructed; it was destroyed and then reoccupied in the Roman Period. From the latter occupation there are remains of a stately building with a court and columns and a bath. In the fifth century A.D. the Byzantines erected a monastery and a church.

SAMARIA (BIBLICAL SHOMRON)—This city, located northwest of Nablus, was first built and fortified in the ninth century B.C. by King Omri, who established it as the capital of the Kingdom of Israel. Building remains include the fortified palaces of kings Omri and Ahab, and the city wall and gate. Numerous carved ivories, presumably the remains of the

Ivory Palace built by King Ahab, have been found in the palace, as well as ostraca dating from the eighth century. The city was destroyed in 722–720 B.C. by Shalmaneser V and Sargon II. Fortifications of the Hellenistic Period consisted of a city wall, several round towers, and a gate. Herod rebuilt the city (first century B.C.) and constructed a colonnaded road, a temple to Zeus Augustus on the acropolis, an agora, and a hippodrome. A theater dates from the Roman Period. The Cathedral of St. John the Baptist, just outside the limits of the ancient city, is a twelfth-century Crusader monument built on the ruins of an earlier Byzantine cathedral. A mosque was built within the church in later times.

SHECHEM—Scant remains were found at Shechem of a late fourth millennium B.C. occupation. The city was fortified with a series of city walls in the Middle Bronze Age II. A Middle Bronze Age IIB city gate with three pairs of pilasters and two guardrooms was found in the western wall. At the end of the Middle Bronze Age a fortified, multistoried temple with an altar in front was built near the city gate. The temple was destroyed and rebuilt at the beginning of the Late Bronze Age and remained sacred until the Iron Age. Fortifications of the Late Bronze Age have also been revealed. Occupation continued from the Iron Age to the Hellenistic Period, with a short gap after the fifth century. The Hellenistic city was important and large and was destroyed in 107 B.C. by John Hyrcanus. In the Roman Period, occupation moved from the tell to the site of the modern city.

SHIVTA—Situated about thirty miles southwest of Beersheba, Shivta was founded by the Nabataeans in the third or second century B.C. The city was occupied throughout Roman and Byzantine times until the twelfth century A.D. Remains of private houses, streets, and water reservoirs can still be seen. Three triapsidal churches and a large paved square with shops dating from late in the Byzantine Period have been uncovered. A mosque was erected in the ninth century.

WADI EL-MUGHARA—On Mount Carmel, along Wadi el-Mughara, a series of cave sites dating from the Middle Paleolithic to the Mesolithic periods has been

322

MEDITERRANEAN SEA

■ Montfort ■ Hazor

■ Acre

SEA
OF
GALILEE

Beth Shearim
■ ■ Nazareth
Wadi el-Mughara ■ Belvoir
■ Megiddo

■ Caesarea

■ Samaria
■ Shechem

JORDAN RIVER

Jericho ■
Jerusalem
Ramat Rahel ■ Qumran ■
Bethlehem ■
■ Ashkelon ■ Herodion

En-gedi ■

DEAD SEA

Masada ■
Arad ■

■ Kurnub

■ Shivta

■ Avdat ■ Archaeological Sites

found. The Mesolithic deposits—known as Natufian after Wadi en-Natuf, where the culture was first uncovered—included graves with skeletal remains. These people were mainly hunters, although they perhaps practiced incipient agriculture, as attested by numerous sickles found there. They frequently adorned their dead with bone and shell necklaces and crowns. Two sickle hafts found there were carved in the shape of animals.

ARCHAEOLOGICAL COURSES

Courses in the archaeology of the Holy Land are given at the following institutions:

Jerusalem

The Hebrew University,
Givat Ram

American School of Oriental Research,
Rehov Salah e-Din

British School of Archaeology,
Bab el-Zahara

Ecole Biblique et Archéologique Française, St. Etienne Monastery,
Derech Shechem

German Evangelical Institute for Archaeology of the Holy Land,
Sheikh Jarah

Hebrew Union College Biblical and Archaeological School,
13 Rehov Hamelech David

Tel Aviv

Tel Aviv University,
Ramat Aviv

ARCHAEOLOGICAL MUSEUMS

Akko (Acre)

MUNICIPAL MUSEUM

Old City

Objects from the Early Canaanite Period to the Turkish Period found in Akko and vicinity, including pottery, glass, coins, statues, and weapons.

Ayelet Hashahar

HAZOR MUSEUM

Exhibition of the Hazor finds: Middle Canaanite pottery and scarabs; Late

Canaanite pottery, steles, figurines, and a reconstruction of the temple; Israelite Hebrew-inscribed shards of pottery; decorated bone and ivory vessels and figurines, and pottery from the Persian and Greek periods.

Beersheba

NEGEV MUSEUM

Old Mosque of Beersheba

Chalcolithic pottery and stone vessels found in the area; tomb finds from Israelite period; Astarte figurines; Byzantine church mosaic; Roman and Byzantine glass vessels.

Elath

MARITIME MUSEUM

Amphorae from Roman, Byzantine, and Crusader periods found by divers.

Kibbutz Hazorea

BETH WILFRID ISRAEL

Includes Late Stone Age to Bronze Age finds found in the area.

Haifa

DAGON COLLECTION, ARCHAEOLOGICAL MUSEUM OF GRAIN HANDLING

Dagon Building, Plumer Square

Exhibits showing the cultivation, handling, storing, and distribution of grain from prehistoric t mes to the Byzantine Period, including grains of wheat over four thousand years old, clay fertility statuettes, flint grain sickles, and other objects.

MARITIME MUSEUM

2 Rehov Hanamal

Models of ancient boats; nautical maps, navigational instruments, archaeological finds illustrating five thousand years of seafaring in the Near East, Mediterranean Sea, Red Sea, and Indian Ocean; and undersea archaeology finds. On exhibit are three Egyptian "burial vessels" of the second millennium B.C.

MUNICIPAL MUSEUM OF ANCIENT ART

City Hall, 4 Rehov Bialik

Exhibition of ancient Mediterranean art; stone and bronze statuettes and figurines from Egypt, Israel, Greece, and Italy; mosaic floors; glass and clay lamps of Hellenistic, Roman, and Byzantine periods; also Jewish, Hellenistic, and Roman coins and a large collection of Coptic textiles.

MUSEUM OF PREHISTORY

Gan Ha'em (Ha'em Park),
124 Rehov Hatishbi

Exhibition illustrating prehistoric cultures from the Carmel range and northern Israel; dioramas from Paleolithic hunting scenes; Mesolithic and Neolithic cave dwellings; beginnings of agriculture and village life; and implements from various prehistoric periods, including reconstruction of evolutionary stages of the human body.

Jerusalem
ISRAEL MUSEUM

The Samuel Bronfman Biblical and Archaeological Museum. The most important exhibits, arranged chronologically, include the following:

The Lower Paleolithic to Neolithic periods are represented by stone implements, stone artifacts and vessels, fossilized human and animal bones found in the Jordan Valley; elephant tusk (Lower Paleolithic Period) found in Holon; a skull with characteristics of the Neanderthal and Homo sapien man from Nahal 'Amud; ornaments and Natufian harvesting implements found in Nahal Oren and 'Einan; and Neolithic fertility goddesses, stone figurines, farming implements, and pottery.

The Chalcolithic Age is represented by finds from Beersheba region, including Beersheba Ivories, amulets, beads, earrings, a bronze scepter, stone and pottery ossuaries, and storage jars.

A treasure found in a cave in Nahal Mishmar (Judean Desert) comprising more than four hundred bronze, copper, and ivory objects, matting, and fabrics.

The Early Bronze Age is represented by finds from tells and tombs; these include red and black burnished "Khirbet Kerak" ware and objects from the Ai excavations.

The Middle Bronze Age is represented by miniature offerings from a Hyksos temple found at Naharia; a stone mold for the casting of the horned Canaanite goddess; figurines of animals and birds

and a seven-cup pottery offering bowl; also cuneiform inscriptions and cylinder seals.

The Late Bronze Age is represented by finds from Hazor: basalt steles, and a basalt gate lion from the "orthostat" temple; biochrome pottery from Tell Nagila; weapons and alabaster vessels.

The Iron Age is represented by Phoenician pottery from Achzib; ivories from Hazor; monumental proto-Ionic capitals from Ramat Rahel and a restored city gate from Hazor; a restored sanctuary with two altars from the temple of Arad; materials and pottery vessels for the making of perfume from Arad and En-gedi; figurines and altar vessels; weights and seals.

The Persian, Hellenistic, and Early Roman periods and the finds from Masada are represented by a hoard of shekels, including the bronze jar in which they were found; stone sarcophagi from Jerusalem, bronze figurines, and Nabataean inscriptions from Avdat; and objects from the Bar Kochba Caves.

The Roman and Byzantine periods (period of the Mishnah and the Talmud) are represented by objects illustrating daily life—glass vessels, jewelry, pottery, and Greco-Roman statues.

A section is devoted to objects from churches and monasteries in Beisan, Tantura, and the Negev: a lead sarcophagus from Jerusalem, lamps and bowls with Christian inscriptions, and amulets.

The Shrine of the Book. Displays the Dead Sea Scrolls from the Qumran Caves; the Bar Kochba Letters, and papyruses found in Nahal Hever.

THE ROCKEFELLER MUSEUM

East Jerusalem

Some of the most important exhibits, arranged chronologically are as follows:

The Lower Paleolithic to Neolithic periods are represented by a skeleton of Mount Carmel Man (Paleoanthropus Palestinensis); a skeleton from Wadi el-Mughara in contracted position, with beads encircling the skull; jewelry and animal carvings of the Natufians; a skull plastered over into the likeness of human features, with inserts of shells for eyes and a plastic marl statue (also with shell eyes) from pre-pottery phase of Neolithic Jericho.

The Bronze Age is represented by exhibits including a copper axe for cutting trees from the Adonis River region; a chess game from Beth Shemesh; cylinder seals and scarabs; gold jewelry from Lachish, Megiddo, and Tel el'-Ajjul; a bronze dagger from Lachish, with incised signs presumably connected with the proto-Semitic alphabet; tablets with the earliest writing from Canaan, proto-Sinaitic and proto-Canaanite; Ivories from Megiddo and Lachish (of particular interest is the ivory perfume bottle in the form of a woman).

The Iron Age is represented by two Philistine anthropoid pottery coffins; incense altars from various sites; the Samaria Ivories from the palace of King Ahab; and the "Lachish Letters," written in ink on potsherds.

The Hellenistic Period is represented by finds including a terra cotta statuette of Aphrodite from Mount Carmel.

The Roman Period is represented by exhibits including a statue of Mercury in white marble from Ashkelon and the "Amazon sarcophagus" from Tell Barak.

The Moslem Period is represented by finds including the Omayyad sculptures from the palace of Caliph Hisham ibn 'Abd al-Malik in Khirbet el-Mafjar (near Jericho), and the carved wooden beams and panels from the Al-Aksa Mosque.

HERBERT E. CLARK COLLECTION, Y.M.C.A. BUILDING

26 Rehov Hamelech David

Finds from prehistoric to Moslem periods.

MUSEUM OF THE PONTIFICAL BIBLICAL INSTITUTE

3 Rehov Paul E. Botta

Chalcolithic finds from the Teleilat el-Ghassul excavations: wall paintings, flints, pottery, bone, and stone vessels; Mesopotamian cylinder seals; a mummy and statues from ancient Egypt.

Sdot Yam (Caesarea)
CAESAREA ANTIQUITIES MUSEUM

Finds from the Hellenistic to Turkish periods: pottery, glass vessels, seals, jewelry, statues, game dice, and others.

Tel Aviv-Yafo
MUSEUM OF ANTIQUITIES OF TEL AVIV-YAFO

Rehov Mifrats Shlomo, Yafo (Jaffa)

Excavated objects from thirty sites in the area arranged chronologically: The Neolithic to the Chalcolithic periods are represented by parts of Chalcolithic pottery ossuaries. The Canaanite Period is represented by pottery and weapons from Hyksos burial grounds; portions from city gate dating from Ramses II (1292–1225 B.C.). The Israelite Period is represented by objects from the Tell Qasile excavations; colored glass amphorae, glass objects, and lamps. The Roman and Byzantine periods are represented by pottery and glass vessels.

HA'ARETZ MUSEUM

Ramat Aviv

Excavated finds of Tell Qasile from the Early Israelite (1200 B.C.) to Arab periods.

Architecture and Town Planning

SCHOOL

TECHNION-ISRAEL INSTITUTE OF TECHNOLOGY

Technion City, Haifa

The Faculty of Architecture and Town planning is the only degree-granting architectural program in Israel.

ASSOCIATIONS

ASSOCIATION OF ENGINEERS AND
ARCHITECTS IN ISRAEL

Beth Hamehandess,
200 Rehov Dizengoff,
P.O.B. 3082, Tel Aviv

*Advances architecture and engineering
in Israel and aims to raise the professional standards of members. Affiliation (architecture): International Union
of Architects.*

SOCIETY OF ARCHITECTS

200 Rehov Dizengoff,
P.O.B. 3082, Tel Aviv

*Promotes the status of architects and
architecture. Affiliation: Association of
Engineers and Architects.*

ARCHITECTS CIRCLE

P.O.B. 17195, Tel Aviv

*Open only to graduate architects, the
circle is an autonomous group that
studies architectural problems.*

ISRAEL ASSOCIATION OF
ENVIRONMENTAL PLANNING

P.O.B. 26235, Tel Aviv

*Open to members of all disciplines rel-
evant to environmental planning.*

TOWN PLANNING

Israel's new cities, built since the
founding of the State in 1948,
offer an opportunity to see examples of implemented plans
and associated dwelling units
designed to conform to environmental and social conditions.
Design and implementation is the
responsibility of the Town Planning Department, Ministry of
Housing, Hakirya, Tel Aviv.

*Beersheba provides the contrast of
different neighborhood plans built
over the past twenty years to conform to
varying objectives. European architects
initially attempted to create a garden
city in the desert. Today the "model"
neighborhood stresses an enclosed unit*

*utilizing pedestrian arcades, semiroofed
so that light comes through, to provide
protection from an intense sun and wind.
Ram Karmi of Karmi and Associates
was responsible for the design.*

Nazareth Illit *contains different types
of dwelling units representing experimental planning since the early 1950's.
The aim was to create housing suitable
to the environmental conditions indigenous to the hilly northern region
of Israel.*

Arad, *one of Israel's new desert cities,
is being built according to a plan adopt-
ing a "linear center" design. Construction in Arad makes use of pre-
fabricated elements.*

Carmiel, *a development town in the
lower hills of Galilee, is also constructed
according to the "linear center" system,
but it has units suited to the different
climatic conditions.*

*The design and building units of Arab
towns are of interest, not because they
conform to a predetermined system, but
because they have influenced architecture and town planning. The inspiration
for the ultramodern Habitat of architect
Moshe Safdie was the Arab town. Two
such towns easily accessible are* **Abu
Gosh** *and* **Lifta,** *near Jerusalem. The*
Old City *of Jerusalem is another example.*

ARCHITECTURE

Jerusalem contains buildings
that reflect the Arab architectural
tradition as well as buildings of
modern design. All Jerusalem
buildings, with the exception of
emergency immigrant housing,
make use of Jerusalem stone
facing.

Rehavia and Talbieh. *Two well-estab-
lished residential areas in Jerusalem
that have many examples of traditional
and modern dwellings.*

Yad Eshkol. *A new residential quarter
that crosses the old armistice line and
demonstrates the incorporation of
traditional patterns of Arab style into
modern apartment design.*

327

The Dome of the Rock

Yemin Moshe. *One of the first Jewish settlements outside the walls of the Old City. The design and grillwork of these duplex row houses is reminiscent of dwellings in New Orleans.*
Gonen "Tet." *A new residential quarter in the modern style designed by M. Nadler, S. Nadler, and S. Bixon.*
Hadassah Hospital, *Mount Scopus. Designed by E. Mendelsohn.*
Bank Leumi, *21 Rehov Yafo. Designed by E. Mendelsohn.*
Hebrew Union College, *Rehov Hamelech David. Designed by H. Rau.*
Synagogue, *Hebrew University, Givat Ram Campus. Designed by H. Rau and D. Reznik.*
Hebrew University Campus, *Givat Ram. Diverse buildings of architectural interest designed by several leading Israeli architects.*
Israel Museum. *A group of buildings combined into a unit housing several museums, a library, and an auditorium. Designed by A. Mansfeld and D. Gad.*
The Sculpture Garden. *Designed by Isamu Naguchi.*
The Shrine of the Book. *Designed by A. Bartos and F. Kiesler.*
Restoration of the **Jewish Quarter of the Old City.** *The first completed project is the* **Yeshivat Hakotel,** *executed by the team Y. and O. Yaar, E. Frankle, and S. Mandle.*
A model of **Jerusalem at the time of the Second Temple** *has been built on a quarter of an acre at the Garden of Holyland Hotel, Bayit Vegan. It was constructed under the supervision of*

Professor Michael Avi-Yonah on a scale of 1 to 50.

Tel Aviv, a coastal city with a milder climate than Jerusalem and no prior tradition to uphold, has a varied architectural past. The more revolutionary changes, which are transforming Tel Aviv from a typical Mediterranean city to one containing high-rise buildings, have been the work of younger Israeli architects.

Sephardic Synagogue. *Designed by Z. Berlin in the 1920's.*
Heichal Hatarbut *(Frederic R. Mann Auditorium). Designed by Z. Rechter and D. Karmi.*
Tel Aviv Hilton Hotel. *Designed by Y. Rechter and M. Zarhy.*
El Al Building. *Easily recognized by its outside spiral staircase. Designed by D. Karmi, R. Karmi, and S. Meltzer.*
Hadar Dafna Building, *Sderot Shaul Hamelech. Designed by R. Karmi.*
Law Courts, *Sderot Shaul Hamelech. Designed by Y. Rechter.*
Tel Aviv Museum, *Sderot Shaul Hamelech. Designed by I. Yashar and D. Eitan.*
Tel Aviv University, *Ramat Aviv. Diverse buildings of architectural interest.*

Restoration of the **Old City of Jaffa,** *now the Artists' Colony. Executed by the team Y. and O. Yaar, E. Frankle, and S. Mandle.*

Haifa Area

Technion Campus. *Technion City contains some controversial buildings.*
Rest Home, *Zichron Yaacov. Designed by Y. Rechter and M. Zarhy.*

Bat Yam

Municipality Building. *Ultramodern design illustrates the "space-packing" theory of A. Neumann. Designed by Z. Hecker.*

Yad Mordechai

Museum. *Designed by A. Sharon, B. Idelson, and E. Sharon.*

Art and Sculpture

MUSEUMS

Jerusalem
ISRAEL MUSEUM

The Bezalel National Art Museum: *Contains paintings from the fifteenth through the twentieth centuries, including works by Rubens, Picasso, Van Gogh, Cezanne, and Chagall; graphic arts (prints and drawings) from the fifteenth century to modern times. There are collections of ancient European, pre-Columbian, African, East Asian, and Oceanian art. The museum is increasing its collection of art from neighboring countries, and a section is devoted to ancient Iranian art (fourth millennium B.C. to the eighteenth century A.D.). Also displayed is a complete eighteenth-century French salon. Temporary exhibits of works by Israeli and foreign artists are held. The museum has a Youth Wing where didactic exhibitions are held. The library contains 50,000 volumes.*

The Billy Rose Art Garden: *The Sculpture Garden and Pavilion, designed by Isamu Noguchi, contain works by Rodin, Daumier, Epstein, Arp, Moore, Lipchitz, Danziger, and others.*

Bat Yam
RYBACK MUSEUM

Rehov Hadady,
Ramat Yosef

A collection of fifty-nine paintings by Issachar Ber Ryback.

Ein Harod
MUSEUM OF ART
(MISHKAN LE'OMANUT)

Exhibits paintings and sculptures by Jewish artists of the nineteenth and twentieth centuries from all over the world. Special sections devoted to Jewish milieu (life in the nineteenth-century East European ghetto); paintings by artists who perished in the Holocaust.

Haifa
MUSEUM OF MODERN ART

4 Rehov Bialik

Contemporary art exhibits by Israeli painters; graphic art exhibits by Israeli and foreign artists.

MUSEUM OF JAPANESE ART

89 Sderot Hanasi,
Mount Carmel

Exhibits Japanese art from the twelfth century to the present. Main collection features Ukiyoe prints, paintings, drawings, ceramics, lacquer, old books, and swords.

Kibbutz Hazorea
BETH WILFRID ISRAEL

Exhibits Far Eastern sculpture and paintings and ancient Mediterranean arts and crafts.

Safed
GLICENSTEIN MUNICIPAL MUSEUM

Rehov Hativat Yiftah

Paintings, engravings, sculptures, and drawings executed by Jewish artists of the nineteenth and twentieth centuries.

Tel Aviv
TEL AVIV MUSEUM

16 Sderot Rothschild
(until spring, 1971)
Sderot Shaul Hamelech
(after spring, 1971)

A collection of paintings, sculptures, drawings, and prints. Western Europe represented by Dutch, Flemish, French, and Italian artists from sixteenth to eighteenth centuries; Britain by eighteenth-century artists; European Jewry by artists from the nineteenth and twentieth centuries; and Israel by twentieth-century artists. The museum holds temporary exhibitions by foreign and Israeli artists.

Helena Rubinstein Pavilion: *Guest exhibitions by foreign and Israeli artists. 6 Sderot Tarsat.*

ARTISTS' ORGANIZATION

PAINTERS' AND SCULPTORS'
ASSOCIATION

The Helena Rubinstein Pavilion of the Tel Aviv Museum

Haifa: *Marc Chagall Artists' House (Beth Haomanim al Shem Marc Chagall). Permanent gallery of works by artists from north Israel; also special exhibitions. 24 Sderot Um.*

Jerusalem: *Exhibition Hall and Club Room. For local and foreign artists. Lectures and films on art. 12 Rehov Shmuel Hanagid.*

Tel Aviv: *Exhibition Hall. 9 Rehov Alharizi.*

ARTISTS' VILLAGES

Ein Hod (east of Atlit)
Silversmiths, ceramicists, sculptors, painters, and tapestry weavers reside and work in the village. Studios are not open to visitors, but there is a permanent exhibition in a central gallery. International symposiums are held to discuss new techniques. Art classes are held throughout the year.

Jaffa, Old City
Exhibitions of works by resident painters, ceramicists, goldsmiths, silversmiths, jewelers, and sculptors in galleries and studios.

Jerusalem
THE JERUSALEM HOUSE OF QUALITY
(BETH OT HAMUTZAR)

12 Derech Hevron

A center for production, exhibition, and marketing of handicrafts, silk and hand prints, batik, weaving, silver and gold smithery, enamel, ceramics, metal and mosaic work, glass blowing, religious and ceremonial articles.

Safed
ARTISTS' COLONY
(KIRYAT HA'OMANIM)

Studios are open to visitors, and works are displayed in a special gallery.

ART EDUCATION

THE HEBREW UNIVERSITY
OF JERUSALEM

Givat Ram, Jerusalem

Has a Department of History of Art (B.A. degree).

THE HEBREW UNIVERSITY
OF JERUSALEM-HAIFA
UNIVERSITY COLLEGE

Mount Carmel, Haifa

Has a Department of Art (B.A. degree).

BEZALEL SCHOOL OF ARTS AND CRAFTS

10 Rehov Shmuel Hanagid,
Jerusalem

Academy of Arts and Design. Courses in Fine Arts; Industrial, Interior, and Graphic Design; Ceramics; Metal and

330

Silversmithing; Photography; Printing; Typography; Packaging and Silkscreen Printing.

MANUSCRIPTS and PRINTING ART

Jerusalem
THE ISRAEL MUSEUM

The Bezalel National Art Museum: *Has a section devoted to illuminated manuscripts, including a fourteenth-century Ashkenazi Haggada; a fifteenth-century Rothschild manuscript from Italy, illuminated marriage contracts, and copies of the Koran and Persian folios.*

SCHOCKEN INSTITUTE FOR
JEWISH RESEARCH

6 Rehov Balfour

Rare old books including fifty incunabula; early printed Bibles and Haggadot. Library of 60,000 volumes.

WOLFSON MUSEUM

Heichal Shlomo,
58 Rehov Hamelech George

Collection includes old manuscripts, scrolls, illuminated marriage contracts, and prayer books.

Haifa
MARITIME MUSEUM

2 Rehov Hanamal

Has a section devoted to cartography (fifteenth century onward) and naval prints.

Sculpture by Ygal Tomarkin

Tel Aviv
ALPHABET MUSEUM

26 Rehov Bialik

Documentary exhibits on the origin, history, and development of writing.

The art section of the famed Israel Museum, Jerusalem

Clubs and Lodges

Netanya—22 Rehov Yerushalayim
Petah Tikva—Rehov Gad Machness
Ramat Gan—59 Rehov Herzl
Rehovot—47 Rehov Gordon
Rishon le Zion—13 Rehov Rothschild
Safed—35 Rehov Yerushalayim
Tel Aviv—5 Sderot Weizmann
Tiberias—Hadar Hotel Building,
Kiryat Shmuel

B'NAI B'RITH

District Grand Lodge No. 14,
Beth B'nai B'rith,
10 Rehov Kaplan,
Tel Aviv

Lodges

Haifa—11 Rehov Pevzner
Har Hacarmel—2 Sderot Wedgewood
Jerusalem—3/5 Rehov Keren Hayesod
Netanya—10 Rehov Hanoteah
Petah Tikva—Beth B'nai B'rith,
Rehov Jabotinsky, corner Rehov Karol
Ramat Gan—27 Rehov Arlosoroff,
4 Rehov Yahalom
Rehovot—183 Rehov Herzl
Tel Aviv—7 Rehov Esther Hamalka,
220 Rehov Ben Yehuda
Tiberias—Beth David, Kiryat Shmuel

LIONS INTERNATIONAL

District No. 356,
P.O.B. 5170, Tel Aviv

Meeting Locations

Haifa—Zion Hotel
Jerusalem—President Hotel
Netanya—Four Seasons Hotel
Safed—Mizpor Hotel
Tel Aviv—Hilton, Ramat Aviv, and
Sheraton hotels

MASONIC LODGES

Temples

Acre—Old City 12/41
Beersheba—Desert Inn Hotel
Elath—Health Department Offices
Hadera—17 Sderot Rothschild
Haifa—119 Sderot Hanasi,
Mount Carmel
Herzlia—Tiran Hotel
Jerusalem—13 Rehov Ezrat Yisrael
Naharia—8 Rehov Bialik

ROTARY CLUBS

District No. 199,
5 Rehov Professor Schor, Tel Aviv
Acre—Hof Hatmarim Café.
Thursdays at 8:30 P.M.
Afula—San Remo Café, 4 Kikar
Haatzmaut. Tuesdays at 8:15 P.M.
Ashdod—Wizo Club, Rehov Yair.
Tuesdays at 8:30 P.M.
Ashkelon—Dagon Hotel, Afridar Beach.
Thursdays at 8:30 P.M.
Bat Yam—Beth Hanoar, Rehov Kurzak.
Thursdays at 8:30 P.M.
Beersheba—Desert Inn Hotel.
Mondays at 8:30 P.M.
Beisan—Public Library.
Wednesdays at 8:30 P.M.
Dimona—Wizo Club. Mondays, 8:30 P.M.
Elath—Elath Hotel.
Sundays at 9:00 P.M.
Givatayim—Kalaii School. Sundays at
8:30 P.M.
Hadera—Wizo Center, 57 Rehov
Hagiborim. Wednesdays at 8:00 P.M.
Haifa—Appinger Pension, 28 Sderot
Hacarmel, Wednesdays at 1:00 P.M.
Communal Center, Neveh Shaanan,
Carmel, Mondays at 8:15 P.M.
Herzlia—Sharon Hotel. Wednesdays
at 8:00 P.M.
Holon—Beth Tarbut Lenoar. Rehov
Hatzerim, Neot Rahel. Wednesdays
at 8:15 P.M.
Jerusalem—President Hotel. Mondays at
7:00 P.M. Y.M.C.A., Rehov David
Hamelech. Wednesdays at 1:00 P.M.
Kfar Saba—Beth Wizo. Sundays at
8:30 P.M.
Kiryat Gat—Magen David Adom Build-
ing. Thursdays at 8:30 P.M.
Kiryat Malachi—Gil Hall. Tuesdays at
8:30 P.M.
Kiryat Motzkin—Beth Hatarbut. Mondays
at 1:30 P.M.
Kiryat Shmona—Danziger School. Mon-
days at 9:00 P.M.

Kiryat Tivon—Naveh Pension. Mondays at 8:30 P.M.
Naharia—Laufer Pension. Sundays at 8:30 P.M.
Netanya—Yahalom Hotel. Mondays at 7:45 P.M.
Nazareth—Y.M.C.A. Wednesdays at 7:00 P.M.
Nes Ziona—Beth Hatarbut. Thursdays at 8:30 P.M.
Petah Tikva—Chen Hall, 14 Rehov Pinsker. Mondays at 1:30 P.M.
Raanana—Beth Fisher. Sundays, 8:30
Ramat Gan—Atzmaut Café (October to June), Tuesdays at 1:30 P.M. Hadar Hall (July to September), Tuesdays at 1:30 P.M.
Ramle-Lod—Miftan School, Ramle. Sundays at 8:00 P.M.
Rehovot—Beth Haikar. Mondays at 8:30 P.M.
Rishon le Zion—Wizo Center. Tuesdays at 8:30 P.M.
Safed—Yair Hotel. Mondays at 8:45 P.M.
Savyon—Youth Center Ganei Yehuda. Tuesdays at 8:00 P.M.
Tayiba—Histadrut Hall. Fridays, 7:00 P.M.
Tel Aviv—Ramat Aviv Hotel, Sundays at 1:30 P.M. Sheraton Hotel, Thursdays at 8:30 P.M. Z.O.A. House, Thursdays at 1:15 P.M.
Tiberias—Ganei Hamat Hotel. Mondays at 9:00 P.M.
Zichron Yaakov—Gavniel Pension. Mondays at 8:00 P.M.

NATIONAL UNION OF SOROPTIMIST

President—Dr. Dahlia Greidinger, 98 Rehov Hatishbi, Haifa

Club Presidents

Ashkelon—Rachel Cohen, Shikun Shimshon
Beersheba—Varda Gershfeld, 15 Rehov Barak
Hadera—Betta Shnitzer, Rehov Nordau
Haifa—Mary Hayam, 18 Rehov Shimshon
Herzlia—Esther Leket, 12 Rehov Habrosh, Nof Yam
Hofit—Dr. Judith Gassner, Beth Harari, Kfar Vitkin
Jerusalem—Dr. Anita Pardo, 13 Rehov Keren Hayesod
Jerusalem (west)—Dr. Renata Cohen, 14 Rehov Hakeshet

Kiryat Tivon—Nelly Almosnino, 34 Rehov Shoshanim
Naharia—Chana Rotmann, 3 Rehov Jabotinsky
Netanya—Roni Zamir. 6 Rehov Remez
Pardes Hanna-Karkur—Esther Breitbart, Talme Elazar
Ramat Gan—Hanni Krispin, 3 Rehov Frug
Rehovot—Zipora Tov, 49 Rehov Levin Epstein
Tel Aviv—Ruth Hirsch, 21 Sderot Smuts

Commerce and Industry

MANUFACTURERS' ASSOCIATION OF ISRAEL

13 Rehov Montefiore,
Tel Aviv

Represents private enterprises in all branches of industry.

HEVRAT OVDIM LTD.

93 Rehov Arlosoroff,
Tel Aviv

A holding company of the Histadrut (General Federation of Labor) engaged in various branches of industry.

KIBBUTZ INDUSTRIES ASSOCIATION

13 Rehov Tiomkin,
Tel Aviv

CRAFTSMEN AND SMALL INDUSTRIES ASSOCIATION

16 Rehov Merkaz Baalei Melacha,
Tel Aviv

INVESTMENT AUTHORITY

Shalom Mayer Tower,
9 Rehov Ahad Haam,
Tel Aviv

A department of the Ministry of Finance. Aids the potential investor in all phases, from making appointments to providing information regarding regulations and financing.

ISRAEL EXPORT INSTITUTE

Shalom Mayer Tower,
9 Rehov Ahad Haam,
Tel Aviv

Represents all approved exporters, many small companies, and export agents, and provides guidance, including the arrangement of business appointments, for visiting buyers and trade delegations. Arranges annual fashion week and a shoe fair.

ISRAEL DIAMOND EXCHANGE

3 Rehov Jabotinsky,
Ramat Gan

Represents the diamond industry in Israel.

BANK OF ISRAEL

Beth Mizpah, Rehov Yafo,
Jerusalem

Similar to the Federal Reserve Bank of the United States. It does not handle commercial transactions, but it acts as a banker's bank for commercial banks and as the fiscal agent of the State of Israel.

TEL AVIV STOCK EXCHANGE

113 Rehov Allenby,
Tel Aviv

CHAMBERS OF COMMERCE

Tel Aviv: 84 Rehov Hahashmonaim
Jerusalem: 10 Rehov Hillel
Haifa: 53 Rehov Haatzmaut

TRADE FAIR

An International Trade Fair sponsored by the Tel Aviv Municipality is held every two years at the Exhibition Grounds, north of Tel Aviv.

ASSOCIATION OF BANKS IN ISRAEL

5 Rehov Barzilai,
Tel Aviv

Advances professional interests of banking institutions and coordinates their activities.

ISRAEL INSURANCE ASSOCIATION

113 Rehov Allenby,
Tel Aviv

Represents the interests of Israeli and foreign insurance institutions operating in Israel. All branches of the industry are represented except life insurance.

ASSOCIATION OF CERTIFIED PUBLIC ACCOUNTANTS

1 Rehov Montefiore,
P.O.B. 2281, Tel Aviv

Advances the skill, proficiency, and professional ethics and status of members and watches legislation of interest to the profession.

ISRAEL INSTITUTE OF PRODUCTIVITY

4 Rehov Henrietta Szold, Tel Aviv

Concerns itself with improving the efficiency of management and of administrative and productive systems. Conducts surveys and carries out research in the various branches of industry. Carries out pilot projects, advises enterprises on methods of increasing productivity, and provides training courses for all levels of management.

ISRAEL MANAGEMENT CENTER

4 Rehov Henrietta Szold,
P.O.B. 14138, Tel Aviv

Develops and improves the art and practice of management, initiates and fosters research in management and administration, and provides means for the professional advancement of managers.

ISRAEL CONSUMERS ASSOCIATION

35 Rehov Hamelech George, Tel Aviv

Protects consumers' rights and represents them to government, industrial, commercial, and other bodies. Aims to improve the standard of Israeli production and services and to raise hygienic conditions in production and services. Affiliation: International Office of Consumer Unions.

INDUSTRIAL RESEARCH

BRAVERMAN CITRUS PRODUCTS RESEARCH LABORATORY

P.O.B. 501, Rehovot

Conducts research into the technology of citrus products and preserves.

CENTER FOR INDUSTRIAL RESEARCH, NCRD, LTD.

Technion City, Haifa

Applies basic research results as a means of accelerating industrial de-

velopment. *Emphasis is on areas that are potential export industries, such as food science, plastics, textiles, fibers, minerals, and industrial chemistry.*

FERMENTATION UNIT

Hebrew University-
Hadassah Medical School,
Ein Karem, Jerusalem

Carries out research into fermentation processes and provides facilities to scientific and industrial organizations concerned with research, development, and teaching of fermentation technology.

FOOD INDUSTRIES ADVISORY SERVICE

1 Rehov Peretz,
Tel Aviv

Aids local food industry in technology and in product development. Gathers information and channels it to the interested parties.

INSTITUTE FOR FIBERS AND
FOREST PRODUCTS RESEARCH

P.O.B. 8001, Jerusalem

Advances the textile, timber, pulp, paper, and leather industries and prepares ground for new industries based on proprietary techniques by applied and basic research and new process and product development. Implements and demonstrates industrial processes and research and development services for industry.

INSTITUTE FOR SAFETY AND HYGIENE

P.O.B. 1122, Tel Aviv

Seeks to improve safety and hygiene conditions through inspections and recommendations.

ISRAEL CENTER OF WATERWORKS
APPLIANCES

Standards Institution of Israel,
Rehov Bnei Yisrael,
Ramat Aviv, Tel Aviv

Conducts research on waterworks appliances and defines suitability for conditions prevailing in Israel.

ISRAEL CERAMIC AND
SILICATE INSTITUTE

Technion City, Haifa

Conducts research in refractories, cement, glass and enamels, new uses of inorganic and nonmetallic materials, high-temperature technology, physical chemistry, and microstructures, with emphasis on the exploitation of local raw materials.

ISRAEL INSTITUTE OF METALS AND
MECHANICAL TESTING LABORATORY

Technion City, Haifa

Coordinates research, testing, instruction, and dissemination of knowledge in the fields of metals and mechanical testing.

ISRAEL INSTITUTE OF PACKAGING
AND INDUSTRIAL DESIGN

2 Rehov Carlebach, Tel Aviv

Seeks to raise Israel's standards of packaging and design for industrial products.

ISRAEL MINING INDUSTRIES (IMI),
INSTITUTE FOR RESEARCH AND
DEVELOPMENT

P.O.B. 313, Haifa

Conducts applied research and process development in the fields of physical, inorganic, and organic chemistry and chemical engineering.

ISRAEL WINE INSTITUTE, LTD.

P.O.B. 529, Rehovot

Aims to improve the country's wines and further their export. Studies wine and brandy technology, especially aging problems, carries out quality control, conducts market research, and participates in international exhibitions.

NATIONAL PHYSICAL LABORATORY

Hebrew University Campus,
Jerusalem

A part of the National Council for Research and Development, the laboratory maintains basic physical standards for precision measurement and calibration and executes research and development in the physical sciences, directed toward advancing the industry of the country.

PAINT RESEARCH ASSOCIATION, LTD.

Technion City, Haifa

Aims to raise the quality of local raw materials for the paint industry and to improve and standardize the final product.

RUBBER RESEARCH ASSOCIATION, LTD.

Technion City, Haifa

Maintains a laboratory to carry out research, experiments, and tests on rubber, plastics, and related materials.

STANDARDS INSTITUTION OF ISRAEL

Rehov Bnei Yisrael,
Ramat Aviv,
Tel Aviv

Publishes and prepares standards, specifications, and testing methods and tests the compliance of commodities with Israeli and foreign standards.

Data Processing

INFORMATION PROCESSING ASSOCIATION

4 Rehov Lampronti,
P.O.B. 13009, Jerusalem

Aims to promote knowledge and increase efficiency of data processing methods and equipment among computer users.

ILTAM CORPORATION FOR PLANNING AND RESEARCH, LTD.

27 Rehov Keren Hayesod,
P.O.B. 7170, Jerusalem

Promotes the export of Israeli knowledge in computer sciences in all its forms. Offers general and specific information on Israel's software industry, including employment opportunities.

Dentistry

DENTAL SCHOOL

HEBREW UNIVERSITY-HADASSAH SCHOOL OF DENTAL MEDICINE

Ein Karem, Jerusalem

Has six departments in the faculty and a research and postgraduate center with five laboratories.

ASSOCIATIONS

DENTAL ASSOCIATION OF ISRAEL

49 Rehov Bar Kochba, Tel Aviv

Advances professional and scientific interests of dental surgeons in Israel. Affiliation: International Dental Federation.

ISRAEL ORTHODONTIC SOCIETY

Dr. J. Berg, Kiryat Rivlin, Herzlia

Promotes the art and science of orthodontics, contributes to dental health services, and protects the professional interests of its members. Affiliation: Dental Association of Israel.

Drama

REPERTORY COMPANIES

HABIMAH NATIONAL THEATER

Sderot Tarsat, Tel Aviv

Performs Hebrew adaptations of foreign-language plays and original Israeli works in large hall; stages experimental plays in small hall. Also tours country.

CHAMBER (CAMERI) THEATER

Dizengoff Passage,
101 Rehov Dizengoff, Tel Aviv

Performs Hebrew adaptations and original Israeli plays. Also tours.

HAIFA MUNICIPAL THEATER

50–52 Rehov Pevzner, Haifa

THEATER CLUBS

THE KHAN CENTER

2 Kikar David Remez, Jerusalem

Modern culture center for performances of plays, chamber music, dance, and poetry readings.

THEATER PRODUCERS

BIMOT, LTD.

3 Rehov Dov Hos, Tel Aviv

Produces plays and musicals in Hebrew in various theaters.

336

A popular Tel Aviv show, "Once There Was a Chassid"

GIORA GODIK PRODUCTIONS, LTD.

10 Rehov Glickson,
Tel Aviv

Produces Hebrew adaptations and original Israeli musical plays nightly (except Fridays) in the Alhambra Theater, Sderot Yerushalaim, Jaffa.

SCHOOLS

TEL AVIV UNIVERSITY

Ramat Aviv, Tel Aviv

Department in Theater Arts and courses leading to a B.A. degree.

BETH ZVI SCHOOL OF DRAMA

Rehov Gurei Yehuda,
Ramat Gan

A workshop school with three-year courses.

STUDIO OF ACTING

26 Rehov Dov Hos, Tel Aviv

A school for actors. Special courses for stage managers, instructors, and designers. Three-year course given daily in the afternoons and evenings. Limited to fifteen new students a year. Basic knowledge of the Hebrew language is essential.

Economics

Appointments with the following Israeli institutions should be prearranged by visitors.

BANK OF ISRAEL ECONOMIC RESEARCH DEPARTMENT

Beth Mizpah,
Rehov Yafo,
Jerusalem

MINISTRY OF COMMERCE AND INDUSTRY ECONOMIC PLANNING UNIT

Palace Building,
Rehov Agron,
Jerusalem

MINISTRY OF FINANCE ECONOMIC PLANNING AUTHORITY

Building 1,
Hakirya,
Jerusalem

GENERAL FEDERATION OF LABOR (HISTADRUT) ECONOMIC AND SOCIAL RESEARCH UNIT

93 Rehov Arlosoroff,
Tel Aviv

MAURICE FALK INSTITUTE FOR
ECONOMIC RESEARCH

17 Rehov Keren Hayesod, Jerusalem

Concerned with fostering macro-economic research in Israel and providing Israeli scholars with experience in empirical research. Carries out studies in the fields of national accounting, labor force, foreign trade, banking, agriculture, and industry.

SCHOOLS

HEBREW UNIVERSITY, DEPARTMENT OF
ECONOMICS AND GRADUATE SCHOOL
OF BUSINESS ADMINISTRATION

Givat Ram Campus,
Jerusalem

TEL AVIV UNIVERSITY, DEPARTMENT
OF ECONOMICS AND GRADUATE
SCHOOL OF BUSINESS
ADMINISTRATION

Ramat Aviv,
Tel Aviv

BAR ILAN UNIVERSITY, DEPARTMENT
OF ECONOMICS AND POLITICAL
STUDIES

University Campus,
Ramat Gan

The Israeli-built Golem Computer at the Weizmann Institute of Science.

Education

UNIVERSITIES

WEIZMANN INSTITUTE OF SCIENCE

Rehovot

A center for research and graduate training in the Natural Sciences. The institute, through its Feinberg Graduate School, grants M.S. and Ph.D. degrees. The Institute has the latest scientific facilities, equipment, and laboratories. Libraries contain 87,500 books and bound journals and subscribe to some 1,600 scientific periodicals. Research Units: *Applied Mathematics, Biochemistry, Biodynamics, Biological Ultrastructure, Biophysics, Cell Biology, Chemical Immunology, Chemical Physics, Chemistry, Experimental Biology, Genetics, Electronics, Isotope*

Research, Nuclear Physics, Plant Genetics, Polymer Research, and Science Teaching.

THE HEBREW UNIVERSITY
OF JERUSALEM

Givat Ram, Jerusalem

Has modern, well-equipped laboratories. The Jewish National and University Library contains over 1,750,000 volumes. Faculties have their own departmental libraries. Current periodicals received exceed 20,000.
Faculties: *Humanities (Ph.D. degree), Social Sciences (Ph.D.), Law (Dr. Jur.), Science (Ph.D.), Agriculture (Ph.D.), Medicine (M.D.), and Dental Medicine (D.M.D.).*
Schools: *Pharmacy (Ph.D.), Education (Ph.D.), Social Work (B.S.W.), Graduate Library (Diploma), and Home Economics (Diploma).*
Campuses at *Givat Ram, Mount Scopus, and Ein Karem in Jerusalem and Rehovot.*

338

THE HEBREW UNIVERSITY OF JERUSALEM-HAIFA UNIVERSITY COLLEGE

Mount Carmel, Haifa

The Hebrew University of Jerusalem assumes academic responsibility for the college. Bachelor of Arts degrees in the Humanities or Social Sciences are awarded after completion of three years study. Graduates may then be admitted to the Hebrew University of Jerusalem for postgraduate courses. Departments: Biblical Studies, Hebrew Language and Literature, History of the Jewish People, Arabic Language and Literature, History of the Islamic Peoples, Philosophy, History, English Language and Literature, French Language and Literature, Geography, Education, Teacher Training, Psychology, Sociology, Political Science, Economics, Statistics and the School of Social Work (B.S.W. degree).

TECHNION-ISRAEL INSTITUTE OF TECHNOLOGY

Technion City, Mount Carmel, Haifa

Faculties cover disciplines of engineering and the exact sciences. Leading center of basic and applied research in chemistry and all aspects of engineering, mathematics, and physics. Has the largest scientific and technological library in Israel, with over 150,000 volumes. Subscribes to more than 5,000 journals. In addition each faculty has its own departmental library. Facilities include the most modern laboratories and equipment for instruction and for research.

Faculties: Aeronautical Engineering, Agricultural Engineering, Architecture and Town Planning, Chemical Engineering, Civil Engineering, Electrical Engineering, Industrial and Management Engineering, Materials Engineering, Mechanical Engineering (D.Sc. degrees).

Departments: Chemistry, Food and Biotechnology, Mathematics, Mechanics, Nuclear Science, Physics, Biometrical Engineering, Mineral and Petroleum, Food and Biotechnology (D.Sc. degree), Computer Science, and Science teaching (M.S. degree).

A psychology class at Hebrew University, Jerusalem

339

TEL AVIV UNIVERSITY

Ramat Aviv, Tel Aviv

Possesses modern scientific equipment. Library contains 225,000 volumes and periodicals. Also has a library of Exact Sciences, which contains over 25,000 volumes.
Faculties: Humanities (Ph.D. degree), Social Sciences (M.A.), Natural Sciences (M.S. The university grants a Ph.D. degree in Physics), Law (LL.B.), Continuing Medical Education (including postgraduate courses in Dentistry and in Veterinary Medicine (Diploma).
Schools and Departments: School of Medicine (upper year registration— fourth year) (M.D.), School for Communication Disorders (speech and hearing) (B.A.), Graduate School of Business Administration (M.B.A.), Academy of Music (Teaching or Artist Diploma), Technological and Engineering Sciences Center (M.S.), School for Social Work (B.S.W.) and Technical College.

BAR ILAN UNIVERSITY

Ramat Gan

Primary goal of the university is the integration of modern education with Jewish spiritual traditions. Because the school has an absolute charter from the New York Board of Regents, its degrees are recognized in the United States. The university is equipped with modern scientific instruments and equipment. The library contains some 200,000 books and 435 current periodicals.
Faculties: Judaic Studies (Ph.D. degree), Languages and Literature (Ph.D.), Humanities (Ph.D.), Social Sciences (M.A.), Natural Sciences, and Mathematics (Ph.D.).
Schools: Education (M.A.), Social Work (B.S.W.), and Institute of Criminology (B.A.)

UNIVERSITY OF THE NEGEV

Hias House, Beersheba

Studies are under the academic supervision of the Hebrew University, the Weizmann Institute of Science, and the Technion-Israel Institute of Technology. The university has a library of 50,000 volumes and 400 scientific

periodicals, and laboratories.
Faculties: Humanities and Social Sciences (B.A. degree jointly with the Hebrew University), Engineering (B.Sc. degree jointly with the Technion), Natural Sciences (Biology: B.Sc. degree jointly with the Hebrew University), Postgraduate Studies (Engineering, Physics, Industrial Engineering, Nuclear, Physical Chemistry, and Biology: M.S. degree jointly with Technion or Weizmann Institute).

HOLON UNIVERSITY OF TECHNOLOGY

52 Rehov Golomb, Holon

Founded in 1969. Departments in Mechanical, Electrical, and Production Engineering.

HEBREW UNION COLLEGE BIBLICAL AND ARCHAEOLOGICAL SCHOOL

13 Rehov Hamelech David, Jerusalem

A postdoctoral research center serving American and other universities, seminaries, and museums as a base for advanced biblical and related studies and archaeological investigation in Israel. It provides the resources for scholarly exchange and communication in the fields of Bible study, biblical and post-biblical archaeology, and cognate fields.

ADULT EDUCATION

ULPAN SYSTEM OF THE JEWISH AGENCY

More than a hundred Ulpanim (Hebrew Language Study Centers) provide new immigrants with intensive instruction in basic Hebrew. Some provide room and board for a fee. Some are in kibbutzim, where students work half days and study half days and there is no fee. Applications through Jewish Agency offices in major cities in Israel and all over the world.

ULPAN AKIVA

Netanya

An independent center for adults for the study of Hebrew, including an extracurricular program of Bible, literature, art, folk dancing, and singing. The basic full course is eighteen weeks, five hours a morning and two more twice a week in the afternoons. There is also an eight-week course.

ENGLISH LANGUAGE HIGH SCHOOLS

ALONEI YITZHAK SECONDARY SCHOOL

Youth Aliyah Village, near Binyamina

An American-Israel boarding school program for students entering sophomore or junior year. The General Studies program is based on the curriculum of the New York City school system. Courses in Judaica taught partly in Hebrew. Under supervision of the Israel Ministry of Education, in cooperation with the Jewish Agency for Israel. Dietary laws are observed.

THE AMERICAN INTERNATIONAL SCHOOL IN ISRAEL

Kfar Shmaryahu

A kindergarten through grade twelve program for English-speaking students. Basic curriculum and teaching methods are American. There are no boarding facilities.

ENGLISH LANGUAGE SENIOR HIGH SCHOOL

Sdeh Boker

Junior and senior high school classes for children of temporary residents or immigrants. Prepares the students for Israeli matriculation exams. Apart from general subjects, which are taught in English, there are compulsory courses in Hebrew (Bible and Hebrew Language and Literature in a special simplified program). Graduates are qualified for acceptance at all universities. Only students who intend to stay in the country at least two years are accepted. They must also have someone in Israel who is responsible for them.

KFAR BLUM SECONDARY SCHOOL

Upper Galilee

American-Israel boarding school offers sophomore-year classes in accordance with curriculum of the New York City school system. Judaica taught largely in Hebrew. Sponsored by the American Habonim Association, in cooperation

with the Jewish Agency for Israel and under the supervision of the Israel Ministry of Education. Students are "adopted" by the kibbutz families and live with the kibbutz children.

THE MOLLIE GOODMAN ACADEMIC HIGH SCHOOL

Kfar Silver, near Ashkelon

An American boarding school for pre-college education, conforming with the curricula of United States high schools. While at the beginning most subjects are taught in English, the use of Hebrew is progressively increased from freshman to senior year. In the senior year there are separate programs for those wishing to enter universities in Israel or colleges or universities in the United States. Founded and directed by the Zionist Organization of America. Dietary laws observed.

Engineering

SCHOOL

TECHNION-ISRAEL INSTITUTE OF TECHNOLOGY

Technion City,
Haifa

Technion has undergraduate and graduate programs in the following engineering faculties: Aeronautical Engineering, Agricultural Engineering, Chemical Engineering, Civil Engineering, Electrical Engineering, Industrial and Management Engineering, Materials Engineering, and Mechanical Engineering.

ASSOCIATIONS

ASSOCIATION OF ENGINEERS AND ARCHITECTS IN ISRAEL

Beth Hamehandess,
200 Rehov Dizengoff,
P.O.B. 3082,
Tel Aviv

Advances architecture and engineering in Israel and aims to raise professional standards of members. Affiliations (engineering): International Association for Bridge and Structural Engineering;

International Commission on Irrigation and Drainage; International Commission on Illumination; International Confederation of Consulting Engineers; International Conference on Large Electrical Systems; International Council for Building Research Studies and Documentation; International Federation for Housing and Planning; International Federation for Municipal Engineers; International Society of Soil Mechanics and Foundation Engineering; International Union of Building Centers; International Water Supply Association; Permanent International Association of Navigation Congresses: World Power Congress.

INSTITUTE OF ELECTRICAL AND
   ELECTRONICS ENGINEERS (IEEE).
   ISRAEL SECTION
200 Rehov Dizengoff,
P.O.B. 3082,
Tel Aviv
   Advances knowledge in fields of electronics, radio, and allied branches and watches over professional standards among members, Affiliation: IEEE.

ISRAEL ASTRONAUTICAL SOCIETY
Faculty of Aeronautical Engineering,
P.O.B. 4910, Technion,
Technion City, Haifa
   Fosters interest in and advances knowledge of astronautics through scientific work, lectures, meetings of professional groups, and annual conferences. Affiliation: International Astronautical Federation.

ISRAEL INSTITUTE OF
   CHEMICAL ENGINEERS
Department of Chemical Engineering,
P.O.B. 4910, Technion,
Technion City, Haifa
   Advances theory and practice of chemical engineering in Israel and watches over professional standards among members. Affiliation: European Federation of Chemical Engineering.

ISRAEL SOCIETY OF AERONAUTICAL
   SCIENCES
14 Rehov Liesin,
P.O.B. 2596, Tel Aviv,
or Faculty of Aeronautical Engineering,
P.O.B. 4910, Technion,
Technion City, Haifa

Advances and disseminates knowledge of aeronautical sciences and technology. Affiliations: Association for the Advancement of Science in Israel; International Council of the Aeronautical Sciences.

ISRAEL SOCIETY OF NAVAL ARCHITECTS
   AND MARINE ENGINEERS
200 Rehov Dizengoff,
P.O.B. 3082,
Tel Aviv

   Advances art of naval architecture, shipbuilding, and marine engineering. Represents the profession in Israel, advises public organizations on technical matters, and watches over the ethical and professional standards of its members.

ISRAEL SOCIETY FOR THEORETICAL
   AND APPLIED MECHANICS
Division of Mechanics,
Department of Aeronautical Engineering,
P.O.B. 4910 Technion,
Technion City,
Haifa

   Advances study of mechanics in Israel. Affiliations: Association for the Advancement of Science in Israel; International Union of Theoretical and Applied Mechanics.

Hobbies

BELLS

DR. MICHAIL BAKSCHT
41 Rehov Bar-Ilan,
Netanya
   Member, American Bell Association. Has a large collection of bells from various countries. Will show his collection only to visitors with a special interest in campanology.

BIBLES

TELLEY MUNICIPAL LIBRARY
Rehov Homa Umigdal,
Corner Rehov Shenkar,
Holon
   Four hundred translations of the Bible.

BIRDS

IZHAK FISHER

10 Rehov Hashoftim,
Tel Aviv

> *Has seventy canaries. Specializes in breeding those with the most beautiful voices and training them to sing according to his instructions.*

ISRAEL PIGEON ASSOCIATION

c/o Yosef Vinocour,
4 Rehov Mane,
Tel Aviv

> *150 members in Israel.*

**FIELD STUDY CENTER,
KIBBUTZ MA'AGAN MICHAEL**

Mobile P.O.,
Menashe

> *Will assist serious bird watchers and Friends of Nature.*

BRIDGE

ISRAEL BRIDGE FEDERATION

c/o Isaac Elenberg,
18 Rehov Ben Yehuda, Tel Aviv

> *Israel competes in all international festivals, world and European championship games. An International Bridge Festival with leading players is held annually in February/March. In addition to weekly tournaments there is a national tournament once a month in the cities. Master points are awarded. There are about twelve hundred registered members. Affiliations: European Bridge League; World Bridge Federation.*
>
> *Games usually start at 8:00 P.M. at the following branches:*

Beersheba: Desert Inn, on Mondays
Jerusalem: Sports Club, 30 Rehov Hatzefira, German Colony, on Wednesdays
Haifa: Beth Hagefen, 33 Sderot Um
Netanya: Wizo Hall, on Thursdays
Rehovot: 15 Rehov Weizmann, on Tuesdays
Savyon: Savyon Country Club, on Sundays during the summer months; at the Avia Hotel from October to March
Tel Aviv: Dukes Club, 76 Rehov Ibn Gvirol, on Wednesdays and Thursdays

BUTTERFLIES

REICH COLLECTION

Esther Melamed,
c/o Kibbutz Gelil Yam
(near Tel Aviv)

> *The collection of fifteen thousand butterflies from all over the world belonging to the late Dr. Reich. Begun in 1894. Now housed in Kibbutz Gelil Yam. Open to serious viewers.*

CAMPING

> *There are some sixty camping sites in one hundred thousand acres of forest throughout the country. The following have facilities that include drinking water, cooking stoves, and toilets. Those that also have playgrounds are marked with an asterisk.*

Northern District

Achzib (near Achzib Bridge)
Banias (in an olive grove near the source of the Banias River)
Biriya (near Safed)
Hahof (opposite Moshav Liman on Naharia–Sulam Zor highway)
Hameyasdim (near Yesod Hamaala Village)
Hurshat Tal (near Kibbutz Hagoshrim)*
Mashtelat Kabri (500 yards east of Kabri crossroads)
Meron (near Gush Halav, on the way to Safed)*

Central District

Ben Shemen (east of Ben Shemen Village)*
Derech Burma (Jerusalem–Tel Aviv highway. Turn from Shaar Hagai to Har Tuv)
Eshtaol (entrance to Eshtaol plant nursery)
Har'el (Kilometer 31 of the old Jerusalem–Tel Aviv highway)
Kesalon (Kesalon–Har Tuv highway)
Mitzpeh Eshtaol (near Har Tuv road junction)
Mitzpeh Har'el (on Kilometer 31 of the old Jerusalem–Tel Aviv highway, near Mekorot Water Pumps)*
Tivon (east of Kiryat Tivon)*
Ya'ar Hanasi (on Kilometer 30 of the old Jerusalem–Tel Aviv highway, east of Moshav Tarom)*

Southern District

Ashkelon (near the Antiquities)*
Sharsheret (Beersheba–Gaza highway)
Neve Zohar
Ya'ar Ha'aluf Simhoni ($1\frac{1}{4}$ miles from Sa'ad-Beersheba crossroads, in the direction of Gaza)
Ya'ar Hamalahim (Shahria) (Kiryat Gat–Beth Govrin highway)
Yotvata (south of Yotvata)

CANDLESTICKS

PROF. ERWIN RABAU

21 Rehov Levi Yitzhak, Tel Aviv

Has a collection of over two hundred copper candlesticks from Late Gothic to nineteenth century.

CHESS

THE ISRAEL CHESS FEDERATION

6 Rehov Daniel Frisch,
P.O.B. 21143, Tel Aviv

Member, The International Chess Federation. Has three thousand registered players and one hundred fifty clubs throughout the country. There are three International Masters and thirty-one National Masters. At the end of May and beginning of June the federation is host to the annual International Tournament, held in Netanya. Visiting chess players may play at the chess clubs for nominal fees. Some of the larger clubs are:

Ashdod: Beth Lazarus, Rehov Hamaapilim, on Mondays and Wednesdays from 7:00 to 9:30 P.M.
Elath: c/o Samuel Taggar, Keren Tarbut, P.O.B. 18
Hadera: Merkaz Hanoar, Rehov Hagiborim, daily between 4:00 and 7:00 P.M. and on Saturdays from 11:00 A.M. to 1:00 P.M. and 4:00 to 7:00 P.M.
Jerusalem: Beth Haam, Rehov Bezalel (Room 5), daily except Fridays from 5:00 to 10:00 P.M.
Haifa: Lasker Club, 13 Rehov Nordau, Sundays to Thursdays from 1:00 to 11:00 P.M., Fridays from 1:00 to 10:00 P.M., and Saturdays from 9:00 A.M. to 10:00 P.M.
Netanya: "Ohel Shem," Rehov Raziel,

on Sundays and Wednesdays from 6:30 to 11:00 P.M.
Ramat Gan: Beth Hahistadrut, on Sundays, Wednesdays, and Thursdays from 7:00 to 11:30 P.M
Rishon le Zion: Beth Hahistadrut, Rehov Jabotinsky, every evening
Tel Aviv: Lasker Club, 54 Rehov Hayarkon, daily from 10:00 A.M. to 11:00 P.M.
The Central Youth Club (ages fourteen to eighteen), 18 Rehov Sprinzak, Tel Aviv

---

COINS

THE ISRAEL NUMISMATIC SOCIETY

c/o Kadman Numismatic Museum, Haaretz Museum, P.O.B. 17056, Ramat Aviv, Tel Aviv

Affiliation: The International Numismatic Committee. Holds seminars on second Monday of every month and lectures on last Thursday of every month, from October to June at 8:30 P.M. at the Kadman Numismatic Museum. The society's branches are:

Haifa: c/o N. Shahaf, 19 Rehov Pua
Jerusalem: c/o Dr. A. Eran, 56 Rehov Hehalutz
Tel Aviv: c/o Dr. Josef Meyshan, 39 Rehov Balfour

KADMAN NUMISMATIC MUSEUM

Director: Arie Kindler, Haaretz Museum Center, Ramat Aviv, Tel Aviv

Has a permanent exhibition illustrating the history of money from its beginnings to the present day, and the history of Israel as reflected in its coins. The largest collection of Jewish coins in the world. More than fifty thousand items.

Exhibitions

Jerusalem: Israel Museum, Hakirya
East Jerusalem: Rockefeller Museum
Haifa: Museum of Ancient Art, Rehov Bialik

COOKING

CHAINE DES ROTISSEURS

c/o M. Benin,
10 Rehov Huberman, Tel Aviv

Has more than two hundred members.

ISRAEL FOOD PARADE BUREAU

P.O.B. 2160, Jerusalem

Organizes the Israel Chef Competition for professionals, held every even numbered year in July, and the Queen of the Kitchen contests for amateurs held every odd-numbered year in January.

FLOWERS

INTERNATIONAL FLOWER SHOW

Haifa Municipality,
14 Rehov Hassan Shukri, Haifa

Held annually during Passover Week in Gan Ha'em, Mount Carmel, Haifa. Arranged by the Sport and Youth Department.

FLYING

AERO CLUB OF ISRAEL

67 Rehov Hayarkon,
Tel Aviv

Amateur pilots wishing to fly must produce, apart from an International Flying License, a permit from the Air Crew Registration Unit, Operation Department, Civil Aviation Administration, Lod Airport; and references from well-known citizens of Israel.
Applications require approval from the Ministry of Defense's security officer and may take between two weeks and ten weeks for clearance.

Planes may be rented from:

Chimavir Ltd.,
Aeroplane Garage,
Kfar Shmaryahu Airfield
Tel Aviv office: 79 Sderot Rothschild
Ya'af, Ltd.,
Office and Aircraft Hangar,
Airport Herzlia

The airplane companies will rent planes (Cherokee or Piper) after an initial flight with a company pilot.

HIKING

HAHEVRA LEHAGANATH HATEVA
(NATURE PRESERVATION SOCIETY)

4 Rehov Hashfella,
Tel Aviv

Arranges walking tours to archaeological sites and areas of interest to Friends of Nature. Long-distance tours are arranged by bus or truck. Overnight in youth hostels, occasionally in the open. Language used usually Hebrew.

PHOTOGRAPHY

ASSOCIATION OF PHOTOGRAPHY CLUBS

P.O.B. 25029, Tel Aviv

Meetings held at:

Haifa: Beth Hagefen, 2 Rehov Hagefen, Thursdays at 8 P.M.
Ramat Gan: Beth Zvi Youth Cultural Center, 3 Rehov Gurei Yehuda, Tuesdays at 8 P.M.
Tel Aviv: Z.O.A. House (Beth Zionei America), 1 Rehov Daniel Frisch, Tuesdays at 8 P.M.

PIPES

SOLOMON FRADIS

14 Rehov Prague, Tel Aviv

A large collection of rare pipes. Will show his collection only to serious collectors.

RADIO HAMS

ISRAEL AMATEUR RADIO CLUB

4X4—4Z4 ISRAEL
ASIA—ZONE 20
Cards may be sent via I A R C,
P.O.B. 4099, Tel Aviv
Affiliation: International   Amateur Radio Union.

There are approximately five hundred registered radio hams. Some of the most active are the following:

Beersheba: 4x4GV—Imanuel Shalmon, 4 Rehov Yad Vashem
Haifa: 4x4UF—Israel Lavee, 20 Rehov Hayarok
Herzlia: 4x41x—Abe I. Nagel, Beth Charsina, Rehov Hakeshet
Jerusalem: 4x4CY—Reuven Gross, 21 Rehov Shahal, Givat Mordechai
4x4WP—Itzchak Staffel, 68 Rehov Borochov
Kiryat Motzkin: 4x4KT—Zvi Pomeranz, 2 Shvil Modiin
Petah Tikva: 4x4JU—Malik Webman, 2 Rehov Harav Kook
Rehovot: 4x4AS—Shlomo Menuchin, 19a, Rehov Weizmann

Tel Aviv: 4x4GT—Tuvia Gringroz,
55 Rehov Tchernihovsky
4x4AH—Jacob Izhaki, 16 Rehov
Hapardess

SHELLS

DAVID BAHRAL

8 Rehov Ibn Gvirol,
Tel Aviv

Has a large collection of shells, especially the specie cowry and cones. Will show his collection only to visitors with a special interest in shells.

VITAL TREVES

44 Sderot Haatzmaut,
Bat Yam

Has a very large collection of shells from all over the world.

SPOONS

HALINA BEN-MOSHE

53 Rehov Katzenelson,
Rishon le Zion

Has a collection of over seven hundred crested souvenir spoons.

MIRIAM BANIEL

42 Rehov Herzog, Tel Ganim,
Givatayim

Has a collection of 270 crested souvenir spoons.

STAMPS

Currency regulations permit the dispatch of stamps abroad by the Philatelic Services only against payment in foreign currency. Dispatches are made by surface mail unless otherwise requested by the purchaser. A minimum payment for opening an account is $10.

DIRECTOR OF THE GOVERNMENT ISRAEL
PHILATELIC SERVICES:
MOSHE COHEN

12 Sderot Yerushalayim,
Jaffa

The postal authorities maintain special philatelic counters at the following addresses:

Beersheba: Main Post Office
Haifa: Haneviim Post Office Branch,
22a Rehov Haneviim
Jerusalem: Main Post Office, Rehov Yafo
Lod Airport
Netanya: Main Post Office
Tel Aviv: 2 Rehov Pinsker
3 Rehov Mendele
Tiberias: Main Post Office

Dealers can send stamps abroad only under export licenses obtainable from the Ministry of Posts.
A collector is permitted to send stamps up to a maximum value of 30 Israeli pounds per month without a license.

FEDERATION OF ISRAEL PHILATELIC
SOCIETIES

16 Rehov Hess,
P.O.B. 2896,
Tel Aviv

Affiliation: International Federation of Philately, Geneva.
Meetings for buying, selling, and exchanging are held at the Societies offices as follows:

Haifa: 24 Rehov Herzlia, on Sundays
at 7 P.M.
Jerusalem: (no fixed address) P.O.B.
1361, on Tuesdays at 7 P.M.
Netanya: 9 Rehov Solomon, on Sundays
at 7 P.M.
Tel Aviv: 16 Rehov Hess (P.O.B. 782),
on both Mondays and Thursdays at
7 P.M.

Lectures are given once a fortnight in most of the Societies.

TOBY JUGS

ZIPORA KENNER

9 Rehov Mishmeret,
Afeka,
Tel Aviv area

Has an almost complete collection of Toby jugs.

YESHAYAHU ROSENBERG

9 Rehov Haemek,
Haifa

Has a collection of eight hundred toy soldiers representing the historical development of various armies from the Middle Ages to the present.

WEAPONS

HAIM KRAVI

43 Rehov Haalonim,
Kiryat Tivon

Has a large collection of antique weapons. Consists of muzzle loaders, pistols, and guns, oriental powder horns and flasks, swords, and some African weapons including bows and arrows and spears.

SHMUEL BARKAI

10 Rehov Hess, Tel Aviv

Has a large collection of antique weapons.

FELIX BURIAN

17 Rehov Bnei-Moshe, Ramat Gan

ERICH FRIEDMANN

54 Rehov Bialik, Ramat Gan

Each has a large collection of prehistoric weapons (Mesolithic and Neolithic eras), which they collected together from about forty sites in Israel. The collections include three thousand flint stone arrowheads from the Stone Age.

Law

The Israeli judiciary comprises civil courts administered by an independent unit within the Ministry of Justice as well as religious courts run by the respective religious communities. The Rabbinical, Sharia (Moslem), and Druse courts are subsidized by the Ministry for Religious Affairs, but Christian courts are self-supporting. The police force is governed by a separate ministry.

The civil courts administer Israeli law, which consists of enactments by the Knesset as well as some legislation inherited from the former British and Turkish regimes. Religious courts adjudicate in matters of personal status according to the respective laws of each major community.

The civil courts system comprises a Supreme Court, which sits in Jerusalem as a High Court of Justice and a Court of Appeal; district courts in Jerusalem, Tel Aviv, Haifa, Beersheba, and Nazareth; and magistrates courts in twenty-six localities. Judges or magistrates sit in traffic, admiralty, and juvenile courts. Sessions of the juvenile courts are closed to the public except by special permission.

Judges are appointed by the president of Israel on recommendations of independent nominations committees. Appointments are by tenure, guaranteeing independence of the judiciary. There is no jury system.

A tribal court comprising three sheikhs sits in Beersheba at no fixed address and hears cases referred to it by the District Court of Beersheba. The judges are appointed by the Ministry of Justice on the recommendation of the government's district representative. Their decisions based on tribal law are binding provided that they are not contrary to natural justice or morality.

There are also municipal courts comprising magistrates or laymen appointed by the Minister of Justice to deal with infringements of local bylaws. Labor courts appointed by the president comprise laymen nominated by the Ministers of Justice and Labor. Rent Tribunals are appointed by the president.

MINISTRY OF JUSTICE

21 Rehov Yafo, Jerusalem

ATTORNEY GENERAL'S OFFICE

21 Rehov Yafo, Jerusalem

DISTRICT ATTORNEY'S OFFICES

Afula: 6 Rehov Rimon
Beersheba: Rassco Building, Derech Hanesiim
Haifa: Government House, Rehov Hassan Shukri
Jerusalem: 8 Rehov Koresh
Tel Aviv: 1 Rehov Weizmann

LEGAL AID BUREAUS

Haifa: 3 Rehov Shmaryahu Levin
Jerusalem: Migrash Harusim
Tel Aviv: 7 Derech Petah Tikva

CIVIL COURTS

SUPREME COURT

6 Rehov Hessin, Jerusalem

DISTRICT COURTS

Beersheba: Derech Hanesiim
Haifa: 12 Rehov Hassan Shukri
Jerusalem: 6 Rehov Hessin
Nazareth: 6 Rehov Rimon
Tel Aviv: 1 Rehov Weizmann

MAGISTRATES COURTS

Acre: 2 Rehov Ben Ami
Afula: Givat Hamoreh, Ezor Mischari, Rassco
Ashdod: Rehov Nordau

Ashkelon: Merkaz Nafati Shimshon
Beersheba: Derech Hanesiim
Beisan
Beth Shemesh
Dimona: Rehov Malchei Yisrael
Elath: Solel Boneh Building
Hadera: 7 Rehov Hillel Yaffe
Haifa: 12 Rehov Hassan Shukri
Jerusalem: Migrash Harusim
Kfar Saba: Rehov Tchernichovsky
Kiryat Gat: Binyan Hamoatza, Merkaz Mischari
Kiryat Shmona: Rehov Hayarden
Naharia: Rehov Sokolov
Nazareth: Binyan Harusim
Netanya: 30 Rehov Herzl
Or Yehuda
Petah Tikva: 20 Rehov Hess
Ramat Gan: 40 Rehov Bialik
Ramla: 80 Rehov Herzl
Rehovot: 9 Rehov Rojansky
Safed: Binyan Hamishtara (Police Station), Canaan
Tel Aviv: 1 Rehov Weizmann
Tiberias: Rehov Nazareth

TRAFFIC COURTS

Haifa: Rehov Hassan Shukri
Jerusalem: 1 Rehov Hessin
Rehovot: 9 Rehov Rojansky
Tel Aviv: 1 Rehov Weizmann

JUVENILE COURTS

Haifa: Rehov Hassan Shukri (two sittings a week)
Jerusalem: Migrash Harusim (one sitting a week)
Tel Aviv: 39 Rehov Nahlat Binyamin (four sittings a week)

MILITARY COURTS

No fixed schedule. Some courts are inside military areas where entry permits are required. Trials of Arab terrorists are as a rule held in open court. Internal military tribunals generally sit *in camera*. For information about time and place of trials, contact Public Relations Officer, Israel Defense Forces, 9 Rehov Ittamar Ben Avi, Tel Aviv.

RELIGIOUS COURTS

Sessions of religious courts are closed to the public except by special permission.

RABBINICAL SUPREME COURT

Near Western Wall, Jerusalem

DISTRICT RABBINICAL COURTS

Ashdod: 21 Rehov Beeri
Beersheba: Rehov Haatzmaut
Haifa: 29 Sderot Um
Jerusalem: 40 Rehov Yafo
Petah Tikva: 9 Rehov Montefiore
Rehovot: 41 Rehov Yaakov
Tel Aviv: 33 Sderot Hamelech David
Tiberias: 51 Rehov Herzl

MOSLEM (SHARIA) COURTS

Acre: Rehov Salah el Din
Haifa: Derech Haatzmaut
Jaffa: 82 Sderot Yerushalayim
Nazareth: Rehov 604/19

DRUSE COURT

6 Rehov Hassan Shukri, Haifa

CHRISTIAN COURTS

Armenian Catholic: Armenian Catholic
 Bishopric, Old City, Jerusalem
Armenian Gregorian: Armenian
 Patriarchate, Old City, Jerusalem
Chaldean Uniate (Catholic): Chaldean
 Uniate Community, Old City,
 Jerusalem
*Evangelical-Episcopal Community (Arab
 Anglicans):* St. George's Cathedral,
 Old City, Jerusalem
Greek Catholic: Greek Catholic
 Bishopric, 33 Rehov Hagefen,
 Haifa;
 c/o Greek Catholic Church,
 Bab el Khalil, Old City,
 Jerusalem;
 c/o Greek Catholic Seminary,
 Nazareth
Greek Orthodox: Greek Orthodox
 Patriarchate, Old City, Jerusalem;
 Greek Orthodox Convent,
 Rehov Shimon Habursaki,
 Tel Aviv-Yafo;
 c/o Greek Orthodox Metropolite,
 Nazareth
Latin: Latin Patriarchate, Old City,
 Jerusalem;
 c/o The Bishop, Patriarchal
 Vicariate, Rehov 315/11, Nazareth
Maronite: Maronite Church, 5 Simtat
 Rubin, Haifa
Syrian Catholic: Syrian Catholic

Bishopric, Old City, Jerusalem
Syrian Orthodox: Syrian Orthodox
 Patriarchate, Old City, Jerusalem

LAWYERS

THE ISRAEL BAR

*A statutory body in charge of all legal
professional matters.*

Haifa: 21 Rehov Herzl
Jerusalem: 2 Rehov Hasoreg
Tel Aviv: 10 Rehov Daniel Frisch

INTERNATIONAL LAW ASSOCIATION

P.O.B. 7267, Jerusalem

*Advances international private and
public law and studies comparative law.*

ISRAEL SOCIETY OF THE INTERNATIONAL COMMISSION OF JURISTS

4 Rehov Yehuda Halevi, Tel Aviv

*Affiliation: International Commission of
Jurists. Advances the rule of law and
the independence of the judiciary.*

LAW FACULTIES

Hebrew University,
Mount Scopus, Jerusalem

Tel Aviv University,
Ramat Aviv, Tel Aviv

Harry Fischel Institute for Research in
Jewish Law and Seminary for Rabbis
and Rabbinical Judges, 14 Rehov
Habucharim, P.O.B. 5199, Jerusalem

POLICE

MINISTRY OF POLICE

Beth Agron, 37 Rehov Hillel, Jerusalem
Branch: 8 Rehov Het, Hakirya, Tel Aviv

NATIONAL POLICE HEADQUARTERS

Sheikh Jarah, Jerusalem

DISTRICT POLICE HEADQUARTERS

Northern District: Kvish Zipory,
 Nazareth
Tel Aviv District: 14 Rehov Harakevet,
 Tel Aviv
Southern District: Ras el Amud,
 Jerusalem

INTERNATIONAL POLICE ASSOCIATION

P.O.B. 4013, Tel Aviv

ISRAEL SOCIETY OF CRIMINOLOGY

P.O.B. 1260, Jerusalem

Affiliation: International Society for Criminology. Studies delinquency in all its aspects.

INSTITUTES OF CRIMINOLOGY

The Bar Ilan University, Ramat Gan

The Hebrew University, Givat Ram, Jerusalem

PRISONS SERVICE

Beth Agron,
37 Rehov Hillel,
Jerusalem

THE LEAGUE OF SOCIETIES FOR THE REHABILITATION OF OFFENDERS IN ISRAEL.

83 Rehov Allenby, Tel Aviv

Medicine

MEDICAL SCHOOLS

HEBREW UNIVERSITY-
HADASSAH MEDICAL SCHOOL

Ein Karem, Jerusalem

The medical school is under the joint direction of the Hebrew University and the Hadassah Medical Organization. It has over thirty basic medical sciences departments. Most staff members are engaged in research, in addition to their teaching and clinical duties at the adjoining Hadassah Hospital.

TEL AVIV UNIVERSITY
MEDICAL SCHOOL

Ramat Aviv, Tel Aviv

The medical school is comprised of medical and biomedical faculties from institutes and units belonging to the major hospitals in the greater Tel Aviv region.

MEDICAL RESEARCH

Extensive research programs are carried out at the Hebrew University Medical School and at the institutions affiliated with the Tel Aviv University Medical School.

ISRAEL INSTITUTE FOR BIOLOGICAL RESEARCH

P.O.B. 19, Nes Ziona

Conducts basic and applied research into problems connected with preventive medicine, especially in the fields of epidemiology, bacterial and viral infections, air pollution, insecticides, and the development of new drugs.

INSTITUTES AT TEL HASHOMER HOSPITAL

Ramat Gan

Baruk Institute for Radioclinical Research, Heart Institute, Heller Institute of Clinical Research, Institute of Cardiology and Cardiac Rehabilitation, Institute of Endocrinology, Institute of Hematology, Institute of Human Genetics, Institute of Patho-Radiological Research.

INSTITUTES AT BEILINSON HOSPITAL

Petah Tikva

Institute of Nephrology, Isotope Institute, Rogoff-Wellcome Medical Research Institute.

INSTITUTE AT DONOLO GOVERNMENT HOSPITAL

P.O.B. 93, Jaffa

Donolo Institute of Physiological Hygiene

ASSOCIATIONS

ISRAEL MEDICAL ASSOCIATION

49 Rehov Ibn Gvirol, Tel Aviv

Works for professional advancement and welfare of doctors and for higher scientific and ethical standards of the medical community in Israel. Conducts research in all fields relating to medicine in general, to pathology of the Jewish people in Israel and abroad, and to medical problems peculiar to Israel.

INDUSTRIAL MEDICAL SOCIETY

Dr. K. Dror,
22 Rehov Gideon, Ramat Gan

Advances knowledge and ensures adequate services in all aspects of industrial health. Affiliations: Israel Medical Association; Israel Association of Public Health Physicians.

ISRAEL ASSOCIATION OF
CHEST PHYSICIANS

Dr. F. Krotowsky,
22 Sderot Nordau,
Tel Aviv

Informs members of the latest scientific information, methods, and techniques for the treatment of chest diseases. Affiliation: Israel Medical Association.

ISRAEL ASSOCIATION OF
GENERAL PRACTITIONERS

Dr. E. Arditi,
76 Rehov Habanim,
Nes Ziona

Aims to raise general medicine to equal rank with other branches of the medical profession, to assure high professional standards of members, and to promote postgraduate training, research, and good relations among general practitioners, other medical specialists, and hospitals. Affiliations: Israel Medical Association; College of General Practitioners, London.

ISRAEL ASSOCIATION FOR PHYSICAL
MEDICINE AND RHEUMATOLOGY

Dr. H. I. Weiser,
15 Rehov Pinsker,
Tel Aviv

Sets standards whereby physicians are recognized as specialists in physical medicine and rheumatology. Affiliations: Israel Medical Association; International Society for Physical Medicine and Rehabilitation; European League Against Rheumatism.

ISRAEL ASSOCIATION OF
PLASTIC SURGEONS

Dr. N. Ben-Hur,
Hadassah Hospital,
Jerusalem

Advances science and art of plastic surgery and maintains high professional standards. Affiliations: Israel Surgical Society; Israel Medical Association; International Confederation for Plastic Surgery.

ISRAEL ASSOCIATION OF PUBLIC
HEALTH PHYSICIANS

Dr. A. Atsmon,
12 Rehov Avner,
Zahala, Tel Aviv

Organizes members of the Israel

Medical Association recognized as specialists in public health in order to create a platform for discussion on public health problems and to raise the standard of the profession. Affiliation: Israel Medical Association.

ISRAEL CARDIOLOGY SOCIETY

Prof. H. Neufeld,
25 Rehov Dubnov, Tel Aviv

Fosters knowledge of cardiovascular diseases. Affiliations: Israel Medical Association; International Society of Cardiology; Asian-Pacific Cardiac Society.

ISRAEL CHRONIC AND GERIATRIC
DISEASES ASSOCIATION

Dr. E. Geltner,
65 Sderot Chen,
Rehovot

Organizes physicians interested in chronic and geriatric diseases from sociomedical and clinical aspects. Affiliation: Israel Medical Association.

ISRAEL ENDOCRINOLOGICAL SOCIETY

Prof. I. Gross,
Hebrew University-
Hadassah Medical School,
P.O.B. 1172, Jerusalem

Organizes recognized specialists in endocrinology and other physicians interested in the study of the secretion of internal organs for academic research and for clinical practice. Affiliations: Israel Medical Association; International Endocrine Society.

ISRAEL NEUROPSYCHIATRIC SOCIETY

Dr. S. Flugelman,
90 Sderot Hanasi, Haifa

Advances the study of psychiatry, neurosurgery, and neurology among recognized specialists in these fields. Affiliations: Israel Medical Association; World Association of Psychiatry.

ISRAEL OPHTHALMOLOGICAL SOCIETY

Dr. A. Laviel,
3 Rehov Disraeli,
Ahuza, Haifa

Concerned with the advancement of ophthalmology in Israel. Affiliations: Israel Medical Association; International Federation of Ophthalmological Societies.

ISRAEL PEDIATRIC SOCIETY

Dr. A. Brand-Aurban,
Jerusalem Academy of Medicine,
72 Rehov Haneviim,
Jerusalem

Advances study of pediatrics and protects child health standards in Israel. Affiliations: Israel Medical Association; International Pediatric Association.

ISRAEL RADIOLOGICAL SOCIETY

Beth Harofe,
2 Rehov Wingate,
Haifa

Advances science of radiology, maintains high standards of professional ethics, and protects professional interests of members. Affiliations: Israel Medical Association; International Society of Radiology.

ISRAEL SOCIETY OF ALLERGY

Dr. J. Glaser,
89 Rehov Bograshov,
Tel Aviv

Increases interest and advances research in allergy and allied subjects. Affiliations: Israel Medical Association; Association for the Advancement of Science in Israel; International Association of Allergy.

ISRAEL SOCIETY OF ANESTHESIOLOGISTS

Dr. I. T. Davidson,
6 Rehov Brachyahu,
Beth Hakerem, Jerusalem

Improves standing of anesthesiology and position of anesthesiologists in Israel. Affiliations: Israel Medical Association; World Federation of Societies of Anesthesiologists.

ISRAEL SOCIETY OF CLINICAL PATHOLOGY

Prof. A. Laufer,
3 Rehov Bialik, Jerusalem

Maintains high professional standards, serves professional interests of members, and coordinates scientific and technical methods in clinical pathology. Affiliations: Israel Medical Association; International Society of Clinical Pathology; Association for the Advancement of Science in Israel.

ISRAEL SOCIETY OF DERMATOLOGY AND VENEREOLOGY

Prof. I. Katzenellenbogen
6 Rehov Ben Ami, Tel Aviv

Advances study of dermatology. Affiliations: Israel Medical Association; International Society of Dermatology and Venereology.

ISRAEL SOCIETY FOR GASTROENTEROLOGY

Prof. D. Birnbaum,
37 Derech Aza,
Jerusalem

Advances knowledge of gastroenterology. Affiliations: Israel Medical Association; World Organization of Gastroenterology.

ISRAEL SOCIETY FOR HEMATOLOGY AND BLOOD TRANSFUSION

Prof. G. Izak,
15 Rehov Jabotinsky,
Jerusalem

Encourages research in clinical and theoretical hematology. Affiliations: Israel Medical Association; International Society of Hematology; European Society of Hematology; Asian and Pacific Society of Hematology.

ISRAEL SOCIETY OF INTERNAL MEDICINE

Dr. A. Gidron,
Rothschild Hospital, Haifa

Advances study and practice of internal medicine. Affiliations: Israel Medical Association; International Society of Internal Medicine.

ISRAEL SOCIETY FOR OBSTETRICS AND GYNECOLOGY.

Dr. N. Soferman,
13 Rehov Feivel,
Tel Aviv

Advances study of obstetrics and gynecology. Affiliations: Israel Medical Association; International Federation of Gynecology and Obstetrics.

ISRAEL SOCIETY OF ORTHOPEDIC SURGEONS

Dr. G. Torok,
15 Rehov Shlomo Hamelech,
Beersheba

Provides scientific and professional representation of orthopedic surgeons in Israel. Affiliations: Israel Medical Association; Israel Surgical Society.

ISRAEL SOCIETY FOR THE STUDY
OF FERTILITY

Prof. I. Halbrecht,
Hasharon Hospital,
Petah Tikva

Advances the study of human reproduction. Membership is open to basic scientists as well as gynecologists. Affiliations: Israel Medical Association; International Federation of Fertility Societies.

ISRAEL SURGICAL SOCIETY

Prof. H. Milwidsky,
57 Rehov Hehalutz,
Jerusalem

Advances surgery, fosters research, and protects standards of professional training. Affiliations: Israel Medical Association; International Federation of Surgical Colleges.

JERUSALEM ACADEMY OF MEDICINE

72 Rehov Haneviim, Jerusalem

Promotes medical science, provides facilities for postgraduate studies and research, and serves as center for the advancement of medical practice and public health.

OTOLARYNGOLOGICAL SOCIETY
OF ISRAEL

Dr. H. Sacher,
12 Rehov Hameasfim,
Tel Aviv

Furthers knowledge and professional objectives of otolaryngologists. Affiliation: Israel Medical Association.

UROLOGICAL SOCIETY OF ISRAEL

Prof. M. Cane,
2 Rehov Hovevi Zion,
Jerusalem

Advances knowledge of urology in Israel. Affiliations: Israel Surgical Society; Israel Medical Association.

ISRAEL SOCIETY OF NEPHROLOGY

Dr. I. Rosenfeld,
29 Rehov Remez,
Tel Aviv

Advances science of and research in nephrology. Affiliations: Israel Medical Association; International Society of Nephrology.

MEDICAL CLUBHOUSES

Beth Harofe (Doctor's House), 1 Rehov Heftman, Tel Aviv

Beth Harofe, 2 Rehov Wingate, Haifa

VETERINARY MEDICINE

ISRAEL VETERINARY MEDICAL
ASSOCIATION

P.O.B. 1871,
Tel Aviv

Maintains high professional and ethical standards and protects the interests of veterinarians in Israel. Affiliation: World Veterinary Association.

Museums

In addition to the institutions listed under Art and Sculpture, Archaeology, and other headings, the following museums are of interest:

HISTORICAL MUSEUMS

Acre (Akko)
MUSEUM HAGVURA

Akko Citadel

Collection of documents, photographs, maps, personal effects, and models illustrating trial, imprisonment, and execution of the Jewish underground fighters during the period of British rule.

Jerusalem
HERZL MUSEUM

Mount Herzl

Near the tomb of Dr. Theodor Herzl, first president of the World Zionist Organization. Contains reconstruction of his study, including photographs, books, and personal effects.

YAD VASHEM

Har Hazikaron

Monument and exhibitions relating to the Nazi Holocaust.

Kibbutz Lohamei Hagetaot

GHETTO FIGHTERS' HOUSE

Exhibits from the ghettos and Nazi extermination camps, including photographs, documents, films, letters, and models of the camps.

Rehovot

EXHIBITION HALL, WEIZMANN INSTITUTE

Yad Weizmann

The Weizmann Archives—documents, photographs, and personal effects of Dr. Chaim Weizmann, the first president of Israel.

Tel Aviv

HAGANAH MUSEUM, BETH ELIAHU GOLOMB

23 Sderot Rothschild

History of the Haganah, including the weapons, photographs, and documents of the Jewish underground during the period of the British rule.

JABOTINSKY INSTITUTE MUSEUM

38 Rehov Hamelech George

Archives and personal effects of Zeev Jabotinsky and of the Revisionist Movement, which he headed.

CEREMONIAL ART, ETHNOGRAPHY, AND FOLKLORE

Jerusalem

THE ISRAEL MUSEUM

The Bezalel National Art Museum. *Has a major collection of Jewish ceremonial art from the eleventh century to the present day. Includes the interior of a seventeenth-century Italian Baroque synagogue, eighteenth-century painted wooden synagogue from Horb, a pair of Saracenic doors from an old Cairo synagogue, ornamented Oriental Torah scrolls, brocade Torah mantles and Torah crowns, Hanukkah lamps, and ritual vessels for festivals.*

Collection includes traditional costumes from Yemen, Afghanistan, Kurdistan, Bukhara, Persia, Algeria, Tunisia, and Morocco.

HEICHAL SHLOMO

Wolfson Museum. *Collection includes an eighteenth-century Holy Ark from Mantua, Italy, Torah scrolls, Holy Ark curtains, Hanukkah lamps, cabalistic amulets, ritual vessels, coins, medals, and seals.*

Heichal Shlomo Synagogue. *In the synagogue are doors from a seventeenth-century Holy Ark from Cracow, Poland, and an eighteenth-century Holy Ark and pulpit from Padua, Italy. 58 Rehov Hamelech George.*

ITALIAN SYNAGOGUE
(KFI MINHAG BNEI ROMI)

27 Rehov Hillel

Has Holy Arks of the sixteenth to nineteenth centuries from Mantua, San Daniele del Friuli, Siena, and Pisa synagogues. An eighteenth-century Holy Ark and general outlay of the Conegliano Veneto Synagogue is also in this synagogue.

Acre (Akko)

MUNICIPAL MUSEUM

Old City

Has dioramas on the daily life of the Arabs and Druse communities, including work implements, jewelry, fabrics, and embroidery.

Bnei Brak

PONIVEZ YESHIVA SYNAGOGUE

Has a seventeenth-century Holy Ark from Mantua, Italy.

BENDHAM YESHIVA SYNAGOGUE

Has a nineteenth-century Holy Ark from Moncalvo, Italy.

Ein Harod

MUSEUM OF ART (MISHKAN L'OMANUT)

Has a section devoted to the display of objects of religious and secular folk art from the fifteenth to twentieth centuries.

Haifa

CENTRAL SYNAGOGUE

Kiryat Shmuel

Has an eighteenth-century marble Holy Ark and pulpit from Reggio nell'Emilia, Italy.

ETHNOLOGICAL MUSEUM AND FOLKLORE ARCHIVES

19 Rehov Arlosoroff

Has a large collection of African

masks, sculpture, and other tribal arts, Far Eastern applied art and ethnographical material from all over the world. The Folklore Archives have collected more than nine thousand folk tales from Jews, Samaritans, Arabs, Druses, and Circassians and have published some of them. The library specializes in Jewish art, ethnology, folklore, and Far Eastern art.

HAIFA MUSIC MUSEUM AND
AMLI LIBRARY

Herman Struck House,
23 Rehov Arlosoroff

Exhibits eight hundred rare musical folk instruments from Africa, Asia, Europe, and North and South America, and coins and medals on musical themes. A section is devoted to ethnomusicology.

Tel Aviv
HA'ARETZ MUSEUM

Ramat Aviv

Museum of Ethnography and Folklore. Has a collection of religious and secular Jewish art and ethnic costumes, a section devoted to ceremonial objects arranged according to festivals, and scenes from daily life of Jewish ethnic communities, including traditional costumes, jewelry, and household utensils.

MUSEUM ADAM VA'AMALO
(MAN AND HIS WORKS)

14 Rehov Beeri

Devoted to the history of tools and crafts in the region.

BETH YESHAYAHU SYNAGOGUE

18 Rehov Tchlenov

Has an eighteenth-century Holy Ark from Mantua, Italy.

CENTRAL SYNAGOGUE

Sderot Smuts, Shechunat Rassco

Has an eighteenth-century marble Holy Ark from Trieste, Italy.

CENTRAL SYNAGOGUE OF YAD ELIAHU

Rehov Margolin,
Yad Eliahu

Has a seventeenth-century marble Holy Ark, wooden carved pulpit and table from Padua, Italy.

MISCELLANEOUS COLLECTIONS

Glass
HA'ARETZ MUSEUM
Ramat Aviv, Tel Aviv

A costume display at the Bezalel Ethnological Museum

Has a major collection of ancient glass from beginning of glass making (fifteenth century B.C.) to the fifteenth century A.D. *Library.*

Ceramics

HA'ARETZ MUSEUM

Ramat Aviv, Tel Aviv

Exhibits diverse aspects of ancient ceramics—historical, functional, and artistic. Full-size replica of an Israelite Period house (1200–587 B.C.) demonstrating the use of pottery in daily life.

Coins

HA'ARETZ MUSEUM

Ramat Aviv, Tel Aviv

Kadman Numismatic Museum. *Illustrates the history of money with special emphasis on Jewish history as reflected in coins.*

The Israel Museum in Jerusalem

Music

ORCHESTRAS

THE ISRAEL PHILHARMONIC ORCHESTRA

Permanent home and office:
Frederic R. Mann Auditorium,
Rehov Huberman, Tel Aviv

Music Director: Zubin Mehta. Permanent Conductor: none. Basic strength: 106 musicians. Performs five or six concerts weekly between October and June/July under guest conductors. Orchestra has thirty-five thousand subscribers in Tel Aviv, Jerusalem, and Haifa. Most performances are in subscription series, but the ensemble also gives frequent special concerts, mainly in Tel Aviv.

THE ISRAEL BROADCASTING SYMPHONY ORCHESTRA

Israel Broadcasting Authority,
9 Rehov Helena Hamalka, Jerusalem

Director: Shalom Ronly-Riklis. Chief Conductor: Mendi Rodan. Basic strength: sixty musicians. Broadcasts live concerts on Tuesdays between September and June, usually at the

Y.M.C.A. Auditorium, Rehov David Hamelech, Jerusalem, and elsewhere in the country.

HAIFA SYMPHONY ORCHESTRA

50 Rehov Pevzner,
Har Hacarmel, Haifa

Director: Shraga Hornung. Permanent Conductor: Avi Ostrowsky, Basic strength: forty-one musicians. Performs subscription and youth concerts between September and June, usually in the Haifa Municipal Theater, and summer concerts during July and August in Gan Ha'em, Har Hacarmel.

THE ORIENTAL ORCHESTRA OF THE ISRAEL BROADCASTING HOUSE

Israel Broadcasting Authority,
9 Rehov Helena Hamalka, Jerusalem

Director: Isaac Aviezer. Basic strength: eleven musicians with five to ten guest performers. Broadcasts over the State radio and gives concerts throughout the country without a set schedule.

GADNA NATIONAL YOUTH ORCHESTRA

Army Post Office Box 2119

Music Director and Conductor: Shalom Ronly-Riklis. A symphony orchestra of young people between fourteen and eighteen years old in the Gadna, the youth battalions sponsored by the Israel Defense Forces.

THE ISRAEL CHAMBER ENSEMBLE

103 Rehov Ibn Gvirol,
Tel Aviv

Comprises The Israel Chamber Orchestra and The Israel Chamber Opera. Music Director: Gary Bertini. Basic strength: twenty-eight musicians and five solo singers. Gives a series of subscription concerts in Beth Hehayal, 60 Rehov Weizmann, Tel Aviv, Givat Haim, and Ein Hashofet from October to June. Also performs in Jerusalem, Haifa, Beersheba, Elath, and kibbutzim throughout the country. Six chamber concerts given in Tel Aviv Museum, 16 Sderot Rothschild, Tel Aviv, during the year, and repeated in Jerusalem.

THE HAIFA CHAMBER ORCHESTRA

P.O.B. 7191, Haifa

Music Director and Conductor: Dalia Atlas. Basic Strength: twenty-five musicians. Gives subscription concerts in Beth Abba Khoushi, 71 Rehov Abba Hillel Silver, Haifa, from November to May, and regular concerts throughout the country.

HOLON CHAMBER ORCHESTRA

Yad Labanim Cultural Center,
11 Sderot Kugel,
Holon

Basic strength: nineteen string instruments, occasionally augmented by wind instruments. Performs throughout the country.

ISRAEL CHAMBER ORCHESTRA

P.O.B. 138, Ramat Gan

Basic strength: twelve string instruments. Performs twice weekly in kibbutzim and outlying villages.

THE NEW ISRAELI QUARTET

Yacov Mense,
13 Rehov Weizmann,
Tel Aviv

First violinist, Alexander Tal; second violinist, Raphael Markus; violist, Zeev Steinberg; violincellist, Yacov Mense. Performs throughout the country.

THE TEL AVIV STRING QUARTET

Uzi Wiesel,
14 Sderot Motzkin,
Tel Aviv

First violinist, Chaim Taub; second violinist, Menachem Breuer; violist, Daniel Benyamini; cellist, Uzi Wiesel. Performs throughout the country.

THE ISRAEL WOODWIND QUINTET

8 Rehov Berliner,
Ramat Aviv, Tel Aviv

Flute, Uri Shoham; oboe, Eliahu Thorner; clarinet, Richard Lesser; horn, Morris Secon; bassoon; Mordechai Rechtman. Performs all over the country.

CHORAL GROUPS

THE ISRAEL BROADCASTING CHOIR, LTD.

c/o The Israel Broadcasting Authority,
9 Rehov Helena Hamalka,
Jerusalem

Conductor: Avner Itai.

THE ISRAEL BROADCASTING YOUTH CHOIR

c/o The Israel Broadcasting Authority,
9 Rehov Helena Hamalka,
Jerusalem

Conductor: Zvi Ben-Porath.

THE ISRAEL PHILHARMONIC CHOIR

c/o Ruth Zohar-Cohen,
32 Rehov Hameyasdim,
Ramat Hasharon, Herzlia

Music Director: Joe Friedland.

RINAT ISRAEL CHAMBER CHOIR

6 Sderot Chen,
Tel Aviv

Music Director: Gary Bertini.

ZADIKOW CHOIR

c/o Music Department, Cultural and Educational Department of the Histadrut,
93 Rehov Arlosoroff,
P.O.B. 303, Tel Aviv

Conductor: Laslo Roth.

THE ISRAEL BACH SOCIETY

6 Rehov Shatz, Jerusalem
or c/o Daniel Amarilio,
1 Rehov Balfour,
Tel Aviv

Director: Eli Freud. Performs such seldom-heard music as cantatas by Bach and other composers on Saturdays from September to June. Has concerts in churches during the summer and in rented halls during the winter.

OPERA

THE ISRAEL NATIONAL OPERA

1 Rehov Allenby,
Tel Aviv

Producer and Director: Edis de-Philippe. Performs throughout the year. Conductors: George Singer, Alexander Tarsky, Shalom Ronly-Riklis, Franklin Choset.

DANCE

BAT-DOR DANCE COMPANY

9 Sderot Hahaskala,
Tel Aviv

Producer: Batsheva de Rothschild. Combines classical and modern dance techniques. Performs in various parts of the country.

BATSHEVA DANCE COMPANY

9 Sderot Hahaskala,
Tel Aviv

Artistic Director: Jane Dudley. Artistic Advisor: Martha Graham. Founder:

Batsheva de Rothschild. Performs modern dance only. Performances take place in various parts of the country.

INBAL DANCE THEATER

74 Rehov Arlosoroff,
Tel Aviv

Founder and Artistic Director: Sara Levi-Tanai. Musical Director: Ovadia Tuvia. Repertoire includes a wide variety of dances and songs with biblical, traditional, folk, Oriental, and modern Israeli themes.

EDUCATION

RUBIN ACADEMY OF MUSIC

7 Rehov Peretz Smolenskin,
Jerusalem

General Director: Yocheved Dostrovsky-Kopernik. Awards teacher's and artist's diplomas. Library of 25,000 books and scores and 2,000 records.

SAMUEL RUBIN ISRAEL ACADEMY OF MUSIC

Tel Aviv University,
Ramat Aviv, Tel Aviv

Director: Prof. Oedoen Partos. Awards teacher's and artist's diplomas.

The Israel Broadcasting Service's orchestra during a recording session

358

THE SAMUEL RUBIN CONSERVATORY
of Music

9 Rehov Haparsim,
Haifa

Music Director: Zvi Rothenberg. Includes department of Oriental Music and does practical work in music therapy for children classified as disturbed.

THE HEBREW UNIVERSITY OF
JERUSALEM

Givat Ram,
Jerusalem

Head of Musicology Department: Joseph Tal. Offers courses leading to B.A. degree; also has departments for Near Eastern, Arabic, and Judeo-Arabic music and electronic music. The Jewish Music Research Center, directed by Dr. Amnon Shiloah, collects and studies documents relating to past and present musical life and to traditions of Jewish communities and fosters publication and development of recorded documentation of Jewish and Eastern music for the National Sound Archives. Also compiles inventory of Jewish musical sources.

SEMINARY FOR RELIGIOUS MUSIC
TEACHERS

Mosad Aliyah,
Petah Tikva

Music Director: Haim Kirsch.

THE STATE MUSIC TEACHERS
TRAINING COLLEGE

8 Rehov Ben Saruk,
Tel Aviv

Director: Ovadia Tuvia.

BAT-DOR STUDIOS OF DANCE

30 Rehov Ibn Gvirol,
Tel Aviv

Conducts daily classes in Classical ballet and modern dance (based on the Martha Graham technique). Has guest teachers from abroad periodically. Also offers courses in jazz, music, and dance composition.

ORGANIZATIONS

ACUM, LTD.

118 Sderot Rothschild,
Tel Aviv

Société d'Auteurs, Compositeurs, et Éditeurs de Musique en Israel. (Society of Authors, Composers, and Music Publishers in Israel.) Member of the CISAC. General Manager: Menahem Avidom

LEAGUE OF COMPOSERS IN ISRAEL

73 Sderot Nordau,
P.O.B. 11180,
Tel Aviv

Israel section of the International Society for Contemporary Music (ISCM). President: Menahem Avidom. General Secretary: Benjamin Bar-Am.

CANTORS ASSOCIATION OF ISRAEL

c/o Benjamin Ungar,
14 Rehov Nathan Hehacham,
Tel Aviv

CENTER FOR ISRAELI MUSIC

6 Sderot Chen,
Tel Aviv

Embraces a large collection of scores and recorded music, enabling visitors (professional and amateur musicians) to listen to the work and peruse the score. Director: William Elias.

ISRAEL MUSIC INSTITUTE

6 Sderot Chen,
Tel Aviv

Publishes and promotes in Israel and abroad outstanding music by Israeli composers. William Elias is the institute's director.

ISRAEL MUSICOLOGICAL SOCIETY

c/o Dr. J. Cohen,
34 Rehov Balfour,
Tel Aviv

Does research in Israeli and Jewish music. Chairman: Dr. Herzl Shmueli.

THE CULTURAL AND EDUCATIONAL
DEPARTMENT OF THE HISTADRUT

93 Rehov Arlosoroff,
P.O.B. 303, Tel Aviv

Music Director: Shlomo Kaplan. Organizes orchestras and choral and dance groups in both towns and kibbutzim.

HANOAR HAMUSICALI B'ISRAEL
(MUSICAL YOUTH OF ISRAEL)

Frederic R. Mann Auditorium,
Rehov Huberman, Tel Aviv

Affiliated with Les Jeunesses Musicales, Belgium. Chairman: Emanuel Amiran. Director-general: Moshe Hoch. Arranges concerts and lectures on music for youth. Has 25,000 members, between the ages of thirteen and thirty, all over the country.

LIBRARIES AND MUSEUMS

A.M.L.I. CENTRAL MUSIC LIBRARY IN ISRAEL

1 Rehov Huberman,
Tel Aviv

Director: Zvi Avni. 37,000 books and scores. 12,000 recordings.

HAIFA MUSIC MUSEUM AND AMLI LIBRARY

Herman Struck House,
23 Rehov Arlosoroff,
Haifa

Director: Moshe Gorali. Eight hundred rare musical instruments from many ethnic groups all over the world. Sections devoted to Ethnomusicology and coins and medals on musical themes. Library of 4,000 books, 7,000 scores, 1,500 records, and forty musical periodicals in five languages and archives.

THE MUSEUM OF MUSICAL INSTRUMENTS

c/o Rubin Academy of Music
7 Rehov Peretz Smolenskin,
Jerusalem

Director: Claude Abravanel. 370 musical instruments.

MUSIC LIBRARY OF THE HEBREW UNIVERSITY OF JERUSALEM

Givat Ram,
Jerusalem

Director: Dr. Bathja Bayer. Contains 33,000 scores, 11,000 books, 5,500 records, 2,100 tapes, microfilms, and photostats.

FESTIVALS

EIN-GEV MUSIC FESTIVAL, ESCO MUSIC CENTER

Kibbutz Ein-Gev

Held annually during Passover week (April).

THE ISRAEL FESTIVAL

c/o A. Z. Propes,
The Ministry of Tourism,
9 Rehov Ahad Ha'am,
P.O.B. 2839,
Tel Aviv

An international festival with Israeli character. Classic and contemporary music, opera, ballet, drama, and folklore. Held annually from the end of July until the end of August in Caesarea, Jerusalem, and other parts of the country.

MUSIC FESTIVAL ABU GOSH-KIRYAT YEARIM

8 Rehov Hamaapil,
P.O.B. 825,
Ramat Gan

Oratorios, masses, cantatas, and passions during May in Abu Gosh by an ensemble of fifty singers, twenty-five musicians and four vocal soloists. Conductor and manager: Sigi Stadermann.

INTERNATIONAL HARP CONTEST

c/o A. Z. Propes,
The Ministry of Tourism,
9 Rehov Ahad Ha'am,
P.O.B. 2839,
Tel Aviv

Held every three years.

ZIMRIYA, HAZAMIR WORLD ASSEMBLY OF CHOIRS

c/o A. Z. Propes,
The Ministry of Tourism,
9 Rehov Ahad Ha'am,
P.O.B. 2839, Tel Aviv

Held every three years.

Natural History

Kibbutz Degania 'A'
BETH GORDON

Displays fauna, flora, minerals, fossils, and soils of Israel with special emphasis on the Jordan Valley. Library of 50,000 books, laboratory and astronomical observatory, and meteorological station.

Kibbutz Dan
BETH USSISHKIN

Exhibits stuffed animals and preserved plants from the Hula Valley, especially aquatic animals of the drained Hula marshes. Also has a section on geology.

Haifa
BETH PINHAS

Exhibits flora and fauna of Israel.

Jerusalem
MUSEUM OF NATURE AND SCIENCE

6 Rehov Mohilever,
Moshava Germanit

Presents exhibitions on the biology of the human body. Shows many types of fauna as dioramas in their natural habitat or as individual preserved specimens. Also has a geological exhibition of minerals and fossils.

Midreshet Ruppin
EMEK HEFER REGIONAL MUSEUM

Exhibits the habitation, fauna, and flora of Emek Hefer.

Elath
MARITIME MUSEUM

Has aquariums containing aquatic animals of the Red Sea—coral fishes, sea anemones, sea horses, sea urchins, starfishes, pipefishes, sunfishes, surgeonfishes, triggerfishes and sea shells, conches and snails, and various corals; fossils, dried sharks, and other sea life.

Kfar Blum
BETH HATEVA
(HOUSE OF NATURE STUDY)

Exhibits flora and fauna of the Hula before and after drainage of the swamps.

Pets

Cats and dogs must be inoculated against rabies thirty days before entering Israel and must have a Certificate of Health from a veterinarian, including a record of inoculations and injections received. In addition, the animals must be inoculated again by an Israeli veterinarian within forty-eight hours of arrival. Anyone bringing more than two pets requires an import license from the Ministry of Agriculture.

Import licenses from the Ministry of Agriculture are also required to bring monkeys or birds into the country.

CATS

ISRAEL CAT LOVERS' SOCIETY

c/o M. Rohatyn,
3 Rehov Einstein, Haifa

The society will answer requests for information. Kindly attach international postage coupons.

DOGS

ISRAEL KENNEL CLUB

P.O.B. 33055, Tel Aviv

Holds dog show once a year in spring or autumn. Any purebred dog registered in a studbook recognized by the F.C.I., Brussels, may enter. Entries must be filed at least one month before the show. Dogs must be of required age at the time of the show. Youngest: 9 to 15 months. Adults: 15 months to 6 years. Veterans: 6 years and over. Secretary in charge of Israel studbook: P. Schiller. 37 Rehov Shalom Aleichem, Tel Aviv.

DOG LOVERS' ASSOCIATIONS

Hasharon: Chairman: Gabriel Zalel,
8 Rehov Rashi, Raanana
Haifa: Chairman: Erika Zeevi, 5 Rehov
Nordau, P.O.B. 8083
Jerusalem: Chairman: Róni Markovits,
P.O.B. 2637
Kiryat Tivon: Chairman: Dr. A. Frank,
P.O.B. 110, Kiryat Amal
Netanya: Chairman: Richard Walker,
11 Rehov Usshishkin

Tel Aviv area: Chairman: Joseph Lavok,
9 Rehov Hahashmonaim, P.O.B.
17188, Bat Yam

CANAAN DOGS

*Prof. Rudolfina Menzel has bred
Canaan dogs for thirty years. 57 Rehov
Barak, Kiryat Motzkin, Haifa.*

ISRAEL PULI CLUB

c/o Pharmacy Tivon,
Kikar Haherut,
Kiryat Tivon

*Breeder and Chairman: Elisabeth
Csengery. Brought the original Pulis
from Hungary and breeds them.*

SCHNAUZER CLUB

Aluf Mishne,
5 Rehov Hadar,
Neve Magen, Ramat Hasharon

Chairman: A. D. Sela.

INSTITUTE FOR THE TRAINING OF
GUIDE DOGS FOR THE BLIND

c/o Prof. Rudolfina Menzel,
57 Rehov Barak,
Kiryat Motzkin,
Haifa

S.P.C.A. (SOCIETY FOR THE PREVENTION
OF CRUELTY TO ANIMALS)

30 Derech Shalma, Tel Aviv

Chairman: Dr. E. D. Ralbag.

Pharmacy

HEBREW UNIVERSITY SCHOOL
OF PHARMACY

Ein Karem, Jerusalem

*Has four departments and two research
units and offers courses leading to degrees of Phar.B., M.S. (Pharm.) and
Ph.D. The School of Pharmacy maintains an active research program.*

PHARMACEUTICAL ASSOCIATION OF
ISRAEL

6 Sderot Rothschild, Tel Aviv

*Promotes scientific and professional
advancement of pharmacy in Israel.
Affiliation: International Pharmaceutical Federation.*

Science

Government-sponsored scientific
research is coordinated by the
National Council for Research
and Development in the Prime
Minister's Office, Jerusalem.
Each university has its own authority, which oversees research
on its campus.

NATIONAL COUNCIL FOR RESEARCH
AND DEVELOPMENT

Prime Minister's Office,
Building 3,
Hakirya, Jerusalem

WEIZMANN INSTITUTE OF SCIENCE

Rehovot

TECHNION-ISRAEL INSTITUTE OF
TECHNOLOGY RESEARCH AND
DEVELOPMENT FOUNDATION, LTD.

Technion City, Haifa

HEBREW UNIVERSITY AUTHORITY
FOR RESEARCH AND DEVELOPMENT

4 Rehov Emile Botta,
Jerusalem

TEL AVIV UNIVERSITY RESEARCH
AUTHORITY

Ramat Aviv, Tel Aviv

BAR ILAN UNIVERSITY (FACULTY OF
NATURAL SCIENCES AND
MATHEMATICS)

University Campus, Ramat Gan

ASSOCIATIONS AND INSTITUTES

ISRAEL ACADEMY OF SCIENCE AND
HUMANITIES

43 Rehov Jabotinsky,
P.O.B. 4040, Jerusalem

*Comprises eminent local scholars and
promotes scientific work. Advises the
government on national research policy
and planning and represents Israel on
national and international bodies.*

ASSOCIATION FOR THE ADVANCEMENT OF SCIENCE IN ISRAEL

Weizmann Institute of Science,
P.O.B. 26, Rehovot

Aims to strengthen cooperation among the various sciences and to stress the importance of science, technology, and higher education among youth.

BIOLOGY AND APPLIED DISCIPLINES

ISRAEL BIOCHEMICAL SOCIETY

Weizmann Institute of Science,
P.O.B. 26, Rehovot

Advances biochemical research and study. Affiliations: Israel Chemical Society; Association for the Advancement of Science in Israel; International Union of Biochemistry; Federation of European Biochemical Societies.

ISRAEL PHYSIOLOGICAL AND PHARMACOLOGICAL SOCIETY

Department of Physiology,
Hebrew University-
Hadassah Medical School,
P.O.B. 1172, Jerusalem

Promotes research and development in all branches of physiology and pharmacology. Affiliations: Association for the Advancement of Science in Israel; International Union of Physiological Sciences.

MICROBIOLOGICAL SOCIETY OF ISRAEL

Hebrew University-
Hadassah Medical School, P.O.B. 1172,
Ein Karem, Jerusalem

Aims to achieve high scientific standards in microbiology and to deal with professional problems of members. Affiliations: Association for the Advancement of Science in Israel; International Association of Microbiological Societies.

ZOOLOGICAL SOCIETY OF ISRAEL

Department of Zoology,
Tel Aviv University,
Ramat Aviv, Tel Aviv

Advances and disseminates knowledge of zoology and acts for protection of nature in Israel. Affiliation: Association for the Advancement of Science in Israel.

CHEMISTRY

ISRAEL CHEMICAL SOCIETY

P.O.B. 517, Jerusalem

Promotes research in chemical science and industry. Advances scientific standards and protects the professional interests of members. Affiliations: Association for the Advancement of Science in Israel; Israel Academy of Science and Humanities; International Union of Pure and Applied Chemistry.

ENVIRONMENTAL RESEARCH

THE NEGEV INSTITUTE FOR ARID ZONE RESEARCH

P.O.B. 1025, Beersheba

Studies environmental stresses and their effect on human, animal, and plant life in arid and semiarid zones; exploits natural resources in these zones; desalinizes water; investigates the chemical and mechanical properties of desert soils and other materials.

OCEANOGRAPHIC AND LIMNOLOGICAL RESEARCH COMPANY, NCRD, LTD.

120 Rehov Haatzmaut, Haifa

Initiates and develops oceanographic and limnological research in order to explore natural resources in the Mediterranean and Red seas; explores fishing areas in neighboring and distant seas; develops the pond culture of sea fish and initiates sea farming; develops techniques of marine research and human endurance at great depths.

DESALINATION PLANTS, LTD.

P.O.B. 18041, Tel Aviv

Carries out research in water desalination by the freezing method.

HYDROLOGICAL SERVICE

P.O.B. 667, Jerusalem

Investigates the influence of natural factors and water management procedures on water resources.

CENTRAL LABORATORY FOR PREVENTION OF AIR POLLUTION AND RADIATION HAZARDS

27 Rehov Prof. Schor, Tel Aviv

Conducts surveys and research on air pollution and radiation hazards.

THE ISRAEL METEOROLOGICAL SERVICE
P.O.B. 25, Beth Dagan

Carries out meteorological research.

GEOLOGY

ISRAEL GEOLOGICAL SOCIETY
P.O.B. 1239, Jerusalem

Advances geological research and facilitates exchanges of information among institutions and individuals engaged in this field.

GEOLOGICAL SURVEY OF ISRAEL
30 Rehov Malchei Yisrael, Jerusalem

Apart from its major task of geological mapping, the survey engages in research and exploration in the fields of mineral deposits, hydrogeology, petroleum, geology, and marine geology.

INSTITUTE FOR PETROLEUM RESEARCH AND GEOPHYSICS
P.O.B. 120, Azor

Conducts long-term geophysical, geological, geochemical, and engineering research projects to provide the background and knowledge required for efficient oil exploration.

MATHEMATICS AND OPERATIONS RESEARCH

ISRAEL MATHEMATICS UNION
Department of Applied Mathematics,
Tel Aviv University,
Ramat Aviv, Tel Aviv

Advances teaching of mathematics and mathematics research. Affiliations: Association for the Advancement of Science in Israel; International Mathematics Union.

OPERATIONS RESEARCH SOCIETY OF ISRAEL (ORSIS)
Faculty of Industrial and Management Engineering, Technion City, Haifa

Represents societies, institutions, and individuals working in operations research, systems analysis, and the quantitative management sciences. ORSIS sponsors an annual conference in Israel at which original papers are presented. Affiliation: International Federation of Operations Research Societies.

NUCLEAR SCIENCE

Basic research is carried out at the Weizmann Institute in Rehovot, at Technion in Haifa, and at the Hebrew University in Jerusalem. Governmental research is supervised by the Atomic Energy Commission of the Prime Minister's Office. The actual research and development activities are conducted at two centers: Nahal Sorek Nuclear Research Center, which is open to visitors, and Negev Nuclear Research Center at Dimona.

PHYSICS

PHYSICAL SOCIETY OF ISRAEL
Physics Department,
Technion, Technion City, Haifa

Affiliations: Association for the Advancement of Science in Israel; International Union of Pure and Applied Physics.

NATIONAL PHYSICAL LABORATORY
Hebrew University Campus, Jerusalem

Part of the National Council of Research and Development, its dual functions are the maintenance of basic physical standards for precision measurement and calibration and the execution of research and development in the physical sciences.

Sports

BADMINTON

Rackets and shuttlecocks obtainable. Games usually held in the evenings between October and May.

Ashdod: Maccabi Ashdod Badminton
  Club. Samuel Bloom, Givat Hanamal
Haifa: Games held once a week in
  Maccabi Sport Club, 3 Rehov Shabtai
  Levi; Samuel Shellim, 17 Rehov
  Tchernihovsky
Herzlia: M. Karmon,
  4 Rehov Hahavatzelet, Neve Magen
Naharia: Phil Minster,
  45 Rehov Herzl, B entrance

BASKETBALL

BASKETBALL ASSOCIATION OF ISRAEL

10 Rehov Marmorek, Tel Aviv

National league events take place from September to June.

BOWLING

Haifa: Carmel Haifa Bowling,
124 Sderot Hanassi,
Merkaz Hacarmel (16 lanes)
Tel Aviv: Oren Bowling,
130 Rehov Ibn Gvirol (22 lanes)

BOWLING ON THE GREEN

Savyon: Savyon Country Club. Open April to mid-October daily except Mondays. From mid-October to March 31 open Tuesdays, Fridays, and Saturdays.

BOXING

Amateurs (registered in home countries) wishing to train may obtain facilities. National championships in April.

Tel Aviv: Betar Sport Center,
38 Rehov Hamelech George
Maccabi Sports Association,
4 Rehov Hamaccabi

CRICKET

Cricket is played according to rules and regulations laid down by the M.C.C., England. Games held Saturdays in Ashdod, Amiad, Beersheba, Dimona, Haifa, Jerusalem, Kfar Shmaryahu, Kiryat Shmona, Lydda, Ofakim, and Yeruham. Affiliation: Israel Cricket Association, P.O.B. 1854, Haifa.

Beersheba: Ben Zion Abrams.
67/2 Shikun Hey
Haifa: Maxim Kahan, Deputy Commander of Police, Derech Dalia,
Hod Hacarmel
Jack Lieff, 53 Derech Zorfat,
Ramat Shaul
Herzlia: David Golding, 45 Rehov Sirkin
Jerusalem: Alec Meyer, 31 Rehov Bait Vegan
Alex Woolf, c/o Intercontinental Hotel

CYCLING

Visiting cyclists should contact the Cycling Committee of the Israel Sports Federation, c/o Arye Doron, 39 Rehov Ahad Bemai, Holon

FENCING

Visiting fencers may obtain facilities for practicing in any of the fencing clubs by contacting the Fencing Committee of the Israel Sports Federation, c/o Judge Amnon Carmi, Rehov Hapalmach, P.O.B. 66, Safed. Largest fencing clubs are as follows:

Beersheba: Sport Department,
Municipality
Haifa: Hapoel, Beth Hapoel, 9 Rehov Alexander Zaid
Jerusalem: A.S.A., Hebrew University,
Givat Ram
Ramat Gan: Maccabi, Binyan Maccabi
Safed: Moadon Hanoar Darom

GOLF

Caesarea: Caesarea Golf and Country Club. Open daily except Mondays from 8 A.M. to sunset. Eighteen-hole course, 6,600 yards. Special greens fee for non-members. Clubs may be rented. Club professional on duty every day except Mondays and Wednesdays.

HORSEMANSHIP

THE ISRAEL HORSE SOCIETY

c/o Dr. Rolbag, P.O.B. 14111,
7 Rehov Kaplan, Tel Aviv

Affiliation: Federation Equestré Internationale (F.E.I.)

Caesarea: Riding School of Caesarea,
Caesarea Hotel, c/o Siegfried Ramaut.
Horses rented only to experienced riders.
Galilee: Vered Hagalil, Ltd., c/o
Yehuda Avni, Korazim. Horses obtainable with guide only.
Haifa: Galilee Riding Club, c/o Yigal Nir, 9 Rehov Gedalyahu
Savyon: Riding Center of Israel,
c/o Anthony Heller, 18 Rehov Hagderot. Specialized instruction in all branches of horsemanship.

The annual race around Mount Tabor

Tel Aviv: Gordon Sport Farm (Riding and Sport Club), Sderot Rokach, Ramat Aviv. Horses obtainable with guide only. Open Sundays through Thursdays

Yearly event: Sussiyada (gymkhana) in Afula during Succoth week (September/October). Sponsored by local council.

Chairman of event: Moshe Ben Dov, 11 Rehov Aviv, Afula

JUDO, JU-JITSU, KARATE, AND IKADO

ISRAEL JUDO FEDERATION

P.O.B. 26195, Tel Aviv

Affiliation: European Judo Union, part of the International Judo Federation. Visiting sportsmen may train at the following clubs:

Beersheba: Moadon Noar Irony (Municipal Youth Club), Beersheba Daled

Haifa: Beth Hapoel, Har Hacarmel
Beth Rothschild, Har Hacarmel

Jerusalem: Y.M.C.A., 26 Rehov Hamelech David

Kibbutz Gonen: under the supervision of Amos Gilead

Netanya: Dojo "Imi" (under the supervision of Imi Lichtenfeld), 2 Rehov Sheshet Hayamim

Tel Aviv: Dojo "Gadi" (under the supervision of Gad Skornik), 9 Rehov Hess

Dojo "Imi," (under the supervision of Imi Lichtenfeld), 27 Rehov Pinsker

In all branches of the Academic Sport Association (A.S.A.), 12 Rehov Bar Giora, Tel Aviv

---

MARCHING

In the spring: Four-Day March to Jerusalem arranged by the Israel Defense Forces for civilians and soldiers. Open to civilians and tourists of all ages. Registration forms must be submitted two months in advance. They are obtainable at all Israel Tourist Offices abroad or in Israel, or from the Israel Defense Forces spokeman's offices, 9 Rehov Ittamar Ben Avi, Tel Aviv, or at any post office. Those between eighteen and forty walk twenty-five miles a day. Those under eighteen and over forty walk two days, nineteen miles a day. The route of the march passes over both paved and unpaved roads.

ROWING

Visiting oarsmen should contact the Rowing Committee of the Israel Sports Federation. c/o Jonah Szabo, 12 Rehov Bialik, Ramat Gan.

Rowing Clubs

Haifa: Haifa Rowing Club, Kishon Harbor. Open Saturdays.
Hapoel Rowing Club, Kishon Harbor. Open Saturdays.
Tel Aviv: Tel Aviv Rowing Club, Rehov Ussishkin, at the Yarkon River. Open Monday, Tuesday, Wednesday, and Friday afternoons and Saturday mornings.
Tiberias: Tiberias Rowing Club at the sea front. Open Saturday mornings.
Annual event: Kinneret Regatta during Passover week (April/May). Rowboats rentable on the Yarkon River and in Elath.

SAILING

Sailing events are held throughout the year, mostly on Saturdays, at Bat Yam, Elath, Haifa, Naharia, Netanya, Sea of Galilee, Sdot Yam, and Tel Aviv. Types of boats used: Caravel, Dragon, Flying Dutchman, 420 Dinghy, Minisail, Snipe, X Plus, and Whaleboat.

Main Events

April: Passover Week

April/May: Independence Day
May/June: Shavuot week
September/October: Succoth Week

Main Branches of Sailing Centers

HAPOEL
8 Rehov Ha'arbaah,
Tel Aviv

ZEBULUN SEAFARING SOCIETY OF ISRAEL
Rehov Ussishkin (behind Pe'er Cinema), on the bank of the Yarkon River, Tel Aviv

ZOFEI HAYAM (SEA SCOUTS)
52 Rehov Lohamei Hagetoat,
Tel Aviv

Sailing amateurs wishing to participate in ten-to-fourteen-day study trips to Rhodes, Cyprus, and Turkey (in Whaleboats) with the Zebulun Municipal Navy High School graduating class may contact Joseph Dolgin, chairman of the Zebulun Seafaring Society of Israel, 4 Rehov Druyanov, Tel Aviv. 420 Dinghies are available for rental in Elath by experienced sailing amateurs only.

SCUBA DIVING

At Elath, Caesarea (ancient port)

SHOOTING

The Four-Day March to Jerusalem

367

Trapshooting (Rifle and Pistol Sections)

Two complete, up-to-date, international-style trapshooting Olympic Shooting Ranges complete with electronically released "phono-pull" apparatus are available. Practice shoots Friday afternoons from 2 P.M. to sundown throughout the year.

Olympic Skeet Ranges (three-second delay-timer and others) are superimposed on the trap ranges. Practice shoots Saturday mornings (9 A.M. to lunchtime) during the closed hunting season (February 1 to September 1).

Both trap and skeet are conducted according to rules and regulations of the International Shooting Union, Europe. Guns and ammunition available at the following ranges:

Isfiya (on Mount Carmel): The Partridge Club, Chairman: Maxim Kahan, Deputy Commander of Police, 132 Derech Dalia, P.O.B. 1504, Hod Hacarmel, Haifa.

Michmoret (near Hadera): Israel Hunters' Association, Chairman: Dr. Leo Osheroff, 30 Rehov Hagivah, Savyon.

Hunting

Visiting hunters wishing to go on a "safari" must be accompanied by an official guide or a member of one of the hunting clubs. Applications for hunting licenses should be made in advance of arrival. Information available through hunting clubs. Game available: wild boar, dove, duck, hare, partridge, pigeon, porcupine, and quail. Firearms and ammunition may be obtained for reasonable fees at the following clubs:

Isfiya (on Mount Carmel): The Partridge Club, Chairman: Maxim Kahan, Deputy Commander of Police, 132 Derech Dalia, P.O.B. 1504, Hod Hacarmel, Haifa.

Tel Aviv: Israel Hunters' Association, Chairman: Dr. Leo Osheroff, 34 Rehov Hagivah, Savyon (in Tel Aviv: c/o ARTA, 81 Rehov Allenby). Affiliations: International Shooting Union; Asian Shooting Union; National Rifle Association (U.S.A.).

Air Rifle and Air Pistol Ranges

Givat Nesher (Haifa area): Beth Landau
Jerusalem: Binyan Histadrut, Kiryat Menachem
Kiryat Ono: Beth Hapoel
Petah Tikva: Beth Hapoel, Rehov Wolfson
Tel Aviv: 3 Rehov Ussishkin

Small Bore Rifle and Pistol (0.22 caliber) Ranges

Ramat Gan: Municipality's Shooting Range, near Stadium, Derech Abba Hillel

---

SOCCER

ISRAEL FOOTBALL ASSOCIATION
12 Rehov Carlebach,
Tel Aviv

Israelis play British-style football, called soccer. National league games are from September to June, and cup finals take place in May and June. League games are held mostly on Saturdays.

SQUASH

Y.M.C.A.
26 Rehov Hamelech David,
Jerusalem

Reservations must be made in advance.

SWIMMING

Tourists are advised to swim only at beaches supervised by lifeguards. Undercurrents are strong in many parts of the sea front, and rocks abound. The swimming season begins at the end of May and ends September 30. The water at Elath beach and the Dead Sea is warm throughout the year. Swimmers are advised that sharks have been found in the deep Elath waters. The salt water of the Dead Sea must be washed off the body immediately after leaving the sea. Extreme care must be taken not to get the salt water into the eyes or mouth. Competitions are held from August until October. National championships are held at the end of September and the beginning of October. Sponsored by the Israel Sport Federation, 10 Rehov Marmorek, P.O.B. 4575, Tel Aviv.

The yearly crossing of the Lake of Kinneret

The most popular annual event is the noncompetitive 2.8-mile Kinneret (Sea of Galilee) swim in September, with some ten thousand swimmers. Registration accepted by the government tourist offices all over the world or by the Hapoel Sports Organization, 8 Rehov Ha'arbaah, Tel Aviv. Medical certificate of health is required.

Other Popular Events

August: Off Ashkelon. Various distances.
September: Off Hof Hefer (near Kfar Vitkin). Various distances.
September/October: Across Haifa Bay. 2.4 to 3 miles.
October: Elath Bay. 600 yards to 1.8 miles.
Jonah Race. From Jaffa Port to Sheraton Hotel, Tel Aviv.
Rosh Hanikrah Race. 600 yards to 2.4 miles.
Shavei Zion to Naharia. 3 miles. Competitive and popular.

Registration for all the above at Hapoel Sports Organization, 8 Rehov Ha'arbaah, Tel Aviv.

Swimming events arranged by the Committee for Popular Sport, Maccabi Sport Organization, 12 Rehov Ahad Haam (P.O.B. 315), Petah Tikva, are:

May: Red Sea Swim off Sharm el Sheikh. 2 miles. For fourteen-year-olds and above. Wooden clogs or rubber-soled sandals are obligatory for beach use.
December: Dead Sea Swim from south of Ein Bokek to Ein Bokek. 1¼ miles for seventeen-year-olds and above. 600 yards for under seventeen and elderly.

Diving glasses must be worn in the water, and rubber-soled sandals or wooden clogs on the beach.

Pools in Hotels

Ashkelon:
Semadar
Dagon
Beersheba:
Desert Inn
Caesarea:
Caesarea (operated by Club Mediterranee), for club members only
Straton (café & restaurant).
Semadar Villa Hotel
Kayit veShayit (Kibbutz Sdot Yam). Also childrens' pool.
Elath:
Queen of Sheba
Red Rock
Haifa:
Dan Carmel (Mount Carmel)
Ben Yehuda (Mount Carmel)
Sanatorium Yaarot Hacarmel

Herzlia:
 Accadia
 Sharon (heated)
 Validor
Jerusalem:
 Holyland
 Ivy Juda Youth Recreation Center
  (Jerusalem Forest)
 Judea Gardens
 King David
 President
 St. George
 Y.M.C.A. (Nablus Road)
 Y.M.C.A. (26 Rehov Hamelech
  David). (heated)
 Y.M.-Y.W.H.A.
Kiryat Tivon:
 Seidler
Michmoret:
 Miramar (Hadera Beach)
Naharia:
 Carlton
Netanya:
 Four Seasons (heated)
 Green Beach Resort Village (heated)
 Hadar Chavazeleth Hasharon (near
  Netanya)
Shuafat:
 Mount Royal (on road to Ramallah)
Tel Aviv:
 Hilton
 Sheraton (heated)
 Avia (near Lod Airport)
 Ramat Aviv
 Kfar Hamaccabia (Ramat Gan)
Shavei Zion:
 Dolphin House
Tiberias:
 Chen

Pools in Clubs
Savyon: Savyon Country Club
Tel Aviv: Tel Aviv Country Club

Pools at Guest Houses in Kibbutzim and Agricultural Settlements
Ayelet Hashahar (upper Galilee)
Beth Oren (Haifa area)
Beth Yesha (Givat Brenner)
Beth Zayit (Judean Hills)
Hanita (western Galilee)
Hagoshrim (upper Galilee)
Kfar Blum (upper Galilee)
Kfar Giladi (upper Galilee)
Kiryat Anavim (Judean Hills)
Maale Hachamisha (Judean Hills)
Moshav Shoresh (Judean Hills)

Public Swimming Pools
Haifa:
 Maccabi Swimming Pool, Rehov
  Bikurim, Har Hacarmel
 Bat Galim
 Hapoel, Rehov Alexander Zaid
 Galei Hadar, 7 Rehov Hapoel
Jerusalem:
 Beth Taylor, Kiryat Hayovel
 Beth Zayit, Yaar Yerushalayim
 German Colony, Rehov Emek Refaim
Kiryat Bialik (near Haifa)
Kiryat Tivon:
 Rehov Hannah Szenesh
Tel Aviv area:
 Galit, Rehov Wingate, Yad Eliahu
 Givat Rambam, Rehov Elath,
  Givatayim
 Hanitzachon, Rehov Halochamim,
  Holon
 Kiryat Ono, Rehov Keren Kayemet,
  Kiryat Ono
 Tel Aviv Swimming Pool, Rehov
  Hayarkon, corner Rehov Gordon
  (on sea front)

Small Lakes
Gan Hashlosha (also called Sachne or
Breichat Amal), near Beisan
Hurshat Tal, near Hagoshrim

Pond
Maayan Harod, Ein Harod

TABLE TENNIS
---

*League games between October and
May. Annual championships in May
and June.*

Main Clubs
Haifa: Hapoel, 41 Rehov Hachalutz
  Maccabi, 3 Rehov Shabtai Levi
Tel Aviv: A.S.A., 12 Rehov Bar Giora
  Elizur, 22 Rehov Zeitlin
  Hapoel, 3 Rehov Ussishkin
  Maccabi Zafon, 7 Rehov Mapu

TENNIS

ISRAEL LAWN TENNIS ASSOCIATION

79 Rehov Maze,
P.O.B. 4423, Tel Aviv

*Championship and open tournaments
are held in April/May (during Passover
week) and September/October (Succoth
week). Most courts require players to
wear white tennis attire. Most public*

courts are available free of charge for tourists. Courts are usually open from 6 A.M. to 10 P.M. Affiliation: The International Lawn Tennis Federation.

Hotels with Tennis Courts

Beersheba:
Desert Inn
Caesarea:
Caesarea (operated by Club Mediterranee), for Club members only
Semadar Villa
Elath:
Queen of Sheba
Michmoret:
Miramar (Hadera Beach)
Haifa:
Windsor
Herzlia:
Accadia
Sharon
Validor
Jerusalem:
Holyland
Ivy Judah Youth Recreation Center
King David
Y.M.C.A., Rehov David Hamelech
Y.M.C.A., Nablus Road
Y.M.-Y.W.H.A.
Naharia:
Carlton
Netanya:
Four Seasons
Hadar Chavazeleth Hasharon
Reuven
Tel Aviv:
Avia (near Lod Airport)
Hilton
Kfar Hamaccabia
Ramat Aviv
Tiberias:
Ganei Chamat

Courts at Guest Houses in Kibbutzim and Agricultural Settlements

Hagoshrim (upper Galilee)
Kfar Blum (upper Galilee
Kfar Giladi (upper Galilee)
Kayit ve Shayit (Sdot Yam Kibbutz, Caesarea)
Neve Yam (Carmel beach)

Courts in Holiday Villages and Motels

Caesarea: Straton (Café)
Netanya: Blue Bay
Green Beach

Public Courts

Tel Aviv:
Hapoel Sports Organization, Sderot Rokach
Maccabi Tennis Club, 10 Rehov Tchernichovsky
Maccabi Hazafon Tennis Club, Sderot Rokach
Tel Aviv Country Club, Derech Haifa
Beersheba:
Beersheba Tennis Club
Haifa:
Carmel Country Club
Netanya:
Maccabi Tennis Club
Ramat Gan:
Ramat Gan Tennis Club
Savyon:
Savyon Country Club

WALKING

Noncompetitive popular events for all ages and both sexes are held throughout the year, usually on Saturdays. Open to tourists. A small fee is usually charged. Contact sports organizations for dates and registration. Events organized by Hapoel Sports Organization, 8 Rehov Ha'arbaah, Tel Aviv, are as follows:

February: Carmel Navigation Race. On the Carmel Mountain range. 31 miles.

March: Tel Kazir Races (in Galilee). From 880 yards to 6 miles.

Hasharon Races (in Hod Hasharon area). From 880 yards to 6 miles.

Ashkelon Hike. 14 miles.

Negev March (Beersheba area). Various distances up to 18 miles.

Yehiam Races (western Galilee–Naharia area). Various distances.

Hagilboa March (between Beisan and Emek Yizrael). 6 to 18 miles.

Gaza Strip Races (near Kibbutz Erez). 880 yards to 6 miles.

Nazareth Navigation Race (Galilee). 4 to 22 miles (walk and run with compasses).

Mount Tabor Races. 880 yards to 6½ miles.

Hagalil March (Galilee). 12 to 30 miles.

April: Menashe Forest March (near Megiddo). 6 miles to 14 miles.

Kinneret March (around the whole Sea of Galilee). 10 to 15 miles.

May: Sovu Zion Vehakifuha. March around Mount Zion Walls, Jerusalem.

Citrus Races (Rehovot area). 880 yards to 6 miles.

September: Shomron March (near Hadera). 1¾ miles to 6 miles.

December: Sinai Race (in Kiryat Tivon). In memory of Kiryat Tivon's Sinai War fallen.

Events arranged by the Committee for Popular Sport, Maccabi Sport Organization, 12 Rehov Ahad Haam, (P.O.B. 315), Petah Tikva, are as follows:

January: From Arad to Masada. 12½ miles.

Ya'ar Herzl Race (Lydda area). Various distances up to 3 miles.

February: From Mount Carmel to Kohav Hayarden (Belvoir Forest-Beisan Valley). 45½ miles.

March: From Lydda to Jaffa. 12½ miles.

Dead Sea March. From En-gedi to Ein Fash'ha. 19¾ miles.

Red Sea March. A four-day excursion from Elath to Sharmel-Sheikh. 150 miles, partly by truck, and approximately 15 miles per day on foot.

April (Passover week): The Benjaminite Marathon. 26 miles. 385 yards. Open to athletes of all countries. Medical fitness certificates must accompany entry form, and a physical examination must be made before the race by a doctor appointed by the organizers. The race is held according to the International Amateur Athletic Federation Rules. Deadline for entries is fourteen days before the race. The race covers the route taken by the Hebrew runner from the tribe of Benjamin, who in the year 1080 B.C., ran from Even Haezer to Shiloh in one day.

May: Kadesh Barnea to Jabel Hal'el (one of the areas believed to be Mount Sinai). Two-day excursion. From 12 to 15 miles covered on foot per day.

October: Mount Carmel Race. Various distances. For fourteen-year-olds to elderly.

November: Navigation March from Tel Aviv along the banks of the Yarkon River to the Fortress of Antipartis. 15 miles.

December: Modi'in March. From Modi'in to Bar Ilan University, Ramat Gan. 25 miles.

Mount Hermon Climb. 12½ miles.

WATER POLO

League games held in July and August. Visiting water poloists may train with the following clubs:

Brit-Maccabim-Atid, 68 Rehov Ibn Gvirol, Tel Aviv
Train at Givat Rambam Swimming Pool, Givatayim.

Hapoel Tel Aviv, 3 Rehov Ussishkin, Tel Aviv
Train at Galit Swimming Pool, Rehov Wingate, Yad Eliahu, Tel Aviv

Hapoel Haifa, Rehov Alexander Zaid, Haifa
Train at Galei Hadar Swimming Pool, 7 Rehov Hapoel, Haifa

Hapoel Kibbutz Givat Haim, Kibbutz Givat Haim

Hapoel Kiryat Tivon, Kiryat Tivon

WATER SKIING

On Lake Kinneret and Elath Beach.

WEIGHTLIFTING

Amateurs wishing to train can obtain facilities at the following clubs:

Acre: Hapoel, c/o Dov Kimchi, Moetzet Poalei Akko, Merkaz Akko
Haifa: Hapoel, Rehov Hapoel, Hadar Hacarmel
Jerusalem: Hapoel, Beth Strauss, Rehov Strauss
Kiryat Haim: Hapoel, near Stadium, Kiryat Eliezer
Ramat Gan: Hapoel, Rehov Maalat Hazofim
Tel Aviv: Hapoel, 3 Rehov Ussishkin; Maccabi, 4 Rehov Hamaccabi

---

WRESTLING

Amateurs wishing to train can obtain facilities at the following clubs:

Ashkelon: Hapoel, Beth Hanoar Usport, Afridar
Haifa: Hapoel, Rehov Hapoel, Hadar Hacarmel
Jerusalem: Hapoel, Beth Strauss, Rehov Strauss
Tel Aviv: Hapoel, 3 Rehov Ussishkin; Maccabi, 5 Rehov Hamaccabi

SPORT FOR THE HANDICAPPED

ILAN'S SPORT CENTER
(SPEWACK SPORT CLUB)

123 Rehov Rokach, Ramat Gan

Director: Gershon Huberman. Facilities for handicapped sportsmen from ten years old to elderly. Open from 3 to 10 P.M.
Facilities for archery, basketball, billiards, bowls, fencing, javelin, swimming, snooker (pool), table tennis, track and field, and weightlifting.
Competitions: Basketball finals, May and June. Track and Field, April (Passover week). Swimming championship, last week in August. Table tennis, usually in December (Hanukkah week). All activities take place throughout the year except July and August, when the emphasis is on swimming.

HELEN KELLER HOME
FOR THE DEAF AND MUTE

13 Sderot Yad Labanim,
Yad Eliahu, Tel Aviv

Open for fourteen-year-olds and up. Facilities for basketball, soccer, swimming, table tennis, track and field, chess, and dance.

SPORTS MEDICINE

ISRAEL ASSOCIATION OF SPORTS
MEDICINE

c/o Dr. Herbert Rotter,
13 Derech Hayam, Haifa

Affiliations: Israel Medical Association; International Federation of Sportive Medicine. Encourages research in sport medicine, sets standards for medical tests for athletes, and holds courses and lectures.

ISRAEL INSTITUTE FOR SPORTS
MEDICINE

8 Rehov Ha'arbaah,
P.O.B. 88, Tel Aviv

Sponsored by Israel Football Association. Gives medical treatment, physical fitness tests, and physiotherapy.

SPORT EDUCATION

WINGATE INSTITUTE FOR PHYSICAL
EDUCATION

Kilometer 24 on Tel Aviv–Netanya road

National center for the training of teachers and instructors in physical education.
Departments: The Physical Education Teachers' College, School for Physiotherapy, School for Sports Coaches, School for Army Physical Training Instructors, Department for workshops and short-term courses, Training camps for national teams and outstanding athletes, Research Institute, Committee for the Publication of Sport Literature, Center for Sports Medicine. The Institute has an archives of Israel sport and physical education, and a library of 15,000 volumes.

THE STATE TEACHERS' COLLEGE
OF PHYSICAL EDUCATION

31 Rehov Bezalel,
P.O.B. 378,
Beersheba

GOVERNMENT RELIGIOUS TEACHERS'
COLLEGE GIVATH WASHINGTON
(BETH RABAN)

Mobile Post Evtah (near Gedera)

Department for Physical Training Teachers.

STATE TEACHERS TRAINING COLLEGE
(OF THE KIBBUTZ MOVEMENT)

1 Rehov Bnei Ephraim,
Tel Aviv

Department for Physical Education Teachers' training.

BIRANIT FENCING SCHOOL

Biranit (near Lebanese border)

Trains fencing instructors.

MAJOR SPORTS ORGANIZATIONS

Maccabi Sport Organization,
68 Rehov Ibn Gvirol,
P.O.B. 1526, Tel Aviv

Hapoel Sport Association,
8 Rehov Ha'arbaah,
P.O.B. 7170, Tel Aviv

Elizur Religious Sporting Association,
166 Rehov Ibn Gvirol,
P.O.B. 431, Tel Aviv

Betar Sport Center,

38 Rehov Hamelech George, Tel Aviv

A.S.A. Academic Sports Association,
12 Rehov Bar Giora, Tel Aviv

INDEX TO MAIN TEXT

374

375